THE CULTURE OF THE HORSE

EARLY MODERN CULTURAL STUDIES

Ivo Kamps, Series Editor

PUBLISHED BY PALGRAVE MACMILLAN

Idols of the Marketplace: Idolatry and Commodity Fetishism in English Literature, 1580–1680
by David Hawkes

Shakespeare among the Animals: Nature and Society in the Drama of Early Modern England
by Bruce Boehrer

Maps and Memory in Early Modern England: A Sense of Place
by Rhonda Lemke Sanford

Debating Gender in Early Modern England, 1500–1700
edited by Cristina Malcolmson and Mihoko Suzuki

Manhood and the Duel: Masculinity in Early Modern Drama and Culture
by Jennifer A. Low

Burning Women: Widows, Witches, and Early Modern European Travelers in India
by Pompa Banerjee

England's Internal Colonies: Class, Capital, and the Literature of Early Modern English Colonialism
by Mark Netzloff

Turning Turk: English Theater and the Multicultural Mediterranean
by Daniel Vitkus

Money and the Age of Shakespeare: Essays in New Economic Criticism
edited by Linda Woodbridge

Arts of Calculation: Quantifying Thought in Early Modern Europe
edited by David Glimp and Michelle R. Warren

The Culture of the Horse: Status, Discipline, and Identity in the Early Modern World
edited by Karen Raber and Treva J. Tucker

The Figure of the Crowd in Early Modern London: The City and Its Double
by Ian Munro

THE CULTURE OF THE HORSE
STATUS, DISCIPLINE, AND IDENTITY IN THE EARLY MODERN WORLD

Edited by

Karen Raber
and
Treva J. Tucker

THE CULTURE OF THE HORSE
© Karen Raber and Treva J. Tucker, 2005.

First published in 2005 by
PALGRAVE MACMILLAN™
175 Fifth Avenue, New York, N.Y. 10010 and
Houndmills, Basingstoke, Hampshire, England RG21 6XS
Companies and representatives throughout the world

PALGRAVE MACMILLAN is the global academic imprint of the Palgrave Macmillan division of St. Martin's Press, LLC and of Palgrave Macmillan Ltd. Macmillan® is a registered trademark in the United States, United Kingdom and other countries. Palgrave is a registered trademark in the European Union and other countries.

ISBN 1–4039–6621–4 hardback

Library of Congress Cataloging-in-Publication Data

The culture of the horse : status, discipline, and identity in the early modern world / edited by Karen Raber and Treva Tucker.
    p.cm.—(Early modern cultural studies)
    Includes bibliographical references (p.).
    ISBN 1–4039–6621–4
    1. Horses—History—16th century. 2. Horsemanship—History—16th century. 3. Horses—History—17th century. 4. Horsemanship—History—17th century. 5. Horses in literature. I. Raber, Karen, 1951– II. Tucker, Treva. III. Series.

SF283.C85 2005
636.1'09—dc22   2004050854

A catalogue record for this book is available from the British Library.

Design by Newgen Imaging Systems (P) Ltd., Chennai, India.

First edition: January 2005

10 9 8 7 6 5 4 3 2 1

Printed in the United States of America.

CONTENTS

List of Illustrations

ABOUT THE CONTRIBUTORS

BRUCE BOEHRER is Professor of English at Florida State University. He is the author of *Shakespeare among the Animals: Nature and Society in the Drama of Early Modern England* (Palgrave, 2000), *Monarchy and Incest: Literature, Culture, Kinship, and Kingship* (University of Pennsylvania Press, 1992), and *The Fury of Men's Gullets: Ben Jonson and the Digestive Canal* (University of Pennsylvania Press, 1997). He is also the founding editor of *The Journal for Early Modern Cultural Studies.*

PIA F. CUNEO is Associate Professor of Art History at the University of Arizona. Her books include *Art and Politics in Early Modern Germany: Jörg Breu the Elder and the Fashioning of Political Identity* (Brill, 1998), and she is editor of *Artful Armies, Beautiful Battles: Art and Warfare in Early Modern Europe* (Brill, 2000).

KEVIN DE ORNELLAS holds a doctorate from Queen's University, Belfast, where he now teaches English Renaissance literature. His book, "Bridled, Curbed, Tamed: The Horse in Early Modern Culture," will be published by Associated University Presses in late 2005. He reviews animal-related books for *The Times Literary Supplement* and is now pursuing an ecocritical project on Shakespeare's birds.

ANN M. KLEIMOLA is Professor of History at the University of Nebraska. She is the author of *Justice in Medieval Russia* (American Philosophical Society, 1975) and co-editor and translator of *Russian Private Law in the XIV–XVII Centuries* (with H. W. Dewey; University of Michigan, 1973) and *Culture and Identity in Muscovy, 1359–1584* (with G. D. Lenhoff; ITZ-Garant, 1997).

DONNA LANDRY is Professor of English at Wayne State University and an Honorary Research Fellow at the University of Exeter, UK. Her most recent book is *The Invention of the Countryside: Hunting, Walking and Ecology in English Literature, 1671–1831* (Palgrave, 2001); she is also the author of *The Muses of Resistance: Laboring-Class*

Women's Poetry in Britain, 1739–1796 (Cambridge University Press, 1990) and co-editor of *The Country and the City Revisited: England and the Politics of Culture, 1550–1850* (with G. MacLean and J. Ward; Cambridge University Press, 1999).

ELISABETH LEGUIN is Associate Professor of Musicology at the University of California, Los Angeles, and performs on the cello and baroque cello. Her publications include "Boccherini's Body: An Essay in Carnal Musicology" (University of California Press, forthcoming 2005).

RICHARD NASH is Associate Professor of English at Indiana University, Bloomington. His book *Wild Enlightenment: The Borders of Human Identity in the Eighteenth Century* is forthcoming from the University of Virginia Press; he is also the author of *John Craige's Mathematical Principles of Christian Theology* (Southern Illinois University Press, 1991) and is currently at work on a book about the invention of the Thoroughbred.

KAREN RABER is Associate Professor of English at the University of Mississippi. She is author of *Dramatic Difference: Gender, Class and Genre in the Early Modern Closet Drama* (University of Delaware Press, 2002) and co-editor of *Measure for Measure: Texts and Contexts* (with I. Kamps; Bedford/St. Martin's, 2004). Her previous work on horsemanship treatises has appeared in P. Fumerton and S. Hunt (eds.), *Renaissance Culture and the Everyday* (University of Pennsylvania Press, 1999).

SANDRA SWART, who received her doctorate in History at the University of Oxford is Lecturer at Stellenbosch University in South Africa. Her field is environmental history and her essays on animals, the environment, guns, horses, and the impact of all of these on South Africa have appeared in the *South African Journal of History, Agenda, Scientia Militaria*, and the *Journal of Southern African Studies.*

ELIZABETH TOBEY is completing a dissertation in Art History at the University of Maryland, specializing in Italian Renaissance art.

TREVA J. TUCKER is completing a doctorate in History at the University of Southern California. Her dissertation is entitled "From *Destrier* to *Danseur*: The Role of the Horse in Early Modern French Noble Identity." Her article "Eminence over Efficacy: Social Status and Cavalry Service in Sixteenth-Century France" appeared in the *Sixteenth Century Journal* in 2001. Before pursuing her doctorate,

Tucker taught, trained, and competed in the disciplines of dressage and eventing for many years.

KATE VAN ORDEN is Associate Professor of Musicology at the University of California, Berkeley. She is the editor of *Music and the Cultures of Print* (Garland, 2000) and author of *Music, Discipline, and Arms in Early Modern France* (University of Chicago Press, 2005). In 2000 and 2002, she directed performances of Plunivel's 1612 equestrian ballet. She also performs and records on historical bassoons.

Acknowledgments

This collection grew out of a panel organized by Treva J. Tucker for the 2002 meeting of the Renaissance Society of America. Along the way we have had the assistance of a number of organizations and individuals: the English Department of the University of Mississippi gave generous support for aspects of the volume's production, for which we sincerely thank Joseph Urgo, Chair and Professor; Erica Fudge offered astute criticism and helpful comments that improved both individual chapters and the collection's overall shape; the Huntington Library, Beinecke Library of Yale University, Houghton Library of Harvard University, Palazzo Te, Cleveland Museum of Art, National Gallery of Ireland, and August Herzog Bibliothek have all helped in providing art and images. Permission to reprint Elisabeth Le Guin's essay "Man and Horse in Harmony," which first appeared in Robert Mitchell and Phillip Thurtle (eds.), *Data Made Flesh* (2003), was granted by Routledge.

SERIES EDITOR'S FOREWORD

The editors of *The Culture of the Horse*, Karen Raber and Treva J. Tucker, aim to reintroduce scholars to "the significance of the horse in the early modern period," and thereby to fill a void in the current state of scholarship. The horse, they claim, was not only ubiquitous in early modern life, and a literal vehicle in labor markets, food production, warfare, and geographical exploration, but also a metaphorical vehicle that helped place and define human beings in the social structure. This broad reexamination of the horse is an ambitious project in that it ranges over several centuries, from the late medieval period well into the eighteenth century, and crosses the boundaries of gender, class, ethnicity, and region, as well as those of nation. Twenty or thirty years ago it would have been impossible to write a study of this kind, but the rise of cultural studies in general, and the important work of Donna Haraway and Harriet Ritvo, as well as more recent studies by Erica Fudge, Nigel Rothfels, Garry Marvin, Donna Landry, Steve Baker, and Bruce Boehrer, have paved the way for a literary study of the horse in the early modern period.

Setting aside various differences among these scholars, it appears that they draw on a Foucault-inspired critique of the unified, autonomous, and naturalized human subject to situate animals in relation to human beings, and vice versa. Specifically, their work in animal studies has continued the process of exposing "the human" as a construct, manufactured through processes that involve setting "the human" alongside or against equally constructed categories such as "the animal" (the beast, the noble creature, nature, the wild thing, the irrational). *The Culture of the Horse* also insists that, if we are going to understand human social, political, historical, religious, economic, and other developments in the early modern period, we must do so by reconstructing the changing interfaces between "human" and "animal" that underwrote those developments. What distinguishes *The Culture of the Horse* from the work of earlier critics is that it addresses a specific area of human/animal studies that is not generally available through "normal" historical or literary scholarship, precisely because horses, although utterly ubiquitous (and so perhaps even more important than other animals in the process of constructing the "human") in the early modern period, are almost entirely alien to most ordinary readers and thinkers today—more so even than other animals of more exotic origins in many cases.

The critical shift manifest in *The Culture of the Horse* both stimulates and addresses the kinds of questions we have wanted to ask but that went unanswered by earlier scholarship. Reading Shakespeare's *Henry V* in graduate school, for instance, I once had occasion to want to know more about Renaissance horses. My interest arose from the lengthy exchange between the French nobles in Act 3, scene 7, in which the Dauphin boldly proclaims to prefer his horse to his mistress because the horse "bears" well, has his own hair, and is composed of "pure air and fire." The Dauphin even confirms a rumor that once he composed a sonnet in praise of his mount. This loaded representation of the horse, it seems, is as crucial as the horse itself, and it tells us about the place of the horse in the culture of the play and about its owner, the crown prince of England's enemy, who is here associated with homoeroticism and bestiality.

To learn more about horses in early modern culture, one of my professors referred me to a chapter in the monumental two-volume set *Shakespeare's England* (1916). The chapter entitled "Horsemanship" in *Shakespeare's England*, however, tendered only the thinnest description of horse culture. It imparted a cluster of "facts" devoid of any worthwhile analysis, and offered little help, despite a paragraph dedicated entirely to the Dauphin's horse. In fact, the entire discussion of horses—what kinds there were, what training they received, what bits they wore, what ailments they acquired, and so forth—remained disturbingly *passive*, despite the presence of numerous dense and provocative quotations such as the one in which Shakespeare applies horse terminology to a woman in *Pericles* and writes, "My lord, she's not paced yet; you must take some pains to work her to your manage." What was lacking was the type of "thick description" that many of us think ought to accompany what Doug Bruster has recently called "thin description."

But where *Shakespeare's England* was consistently silent about what horses meant in early modern culture—how people *felt* about them and what their magnitude was in people's daily lives—*The Culture of the Horse* succeeds precisely in making the *significance* of the horse and its representations in literature and art resonate in our understanding of early modern culture. *The Culture of the Horse* allows us to see the horse for what it was to early modern people, not merely a tool that loses vital presence in the context of its utility—a journey completed, a load of merchandise delivered to market, a magnificent prop to support a king in a painting—but a living beast that from Russia to Italy and from Germany to South Africa helped to enrich and define the lives of individuals, social groups, and relations, as well as whole nations.

Ivo Kamps
Series editor

Introduction

Karen Raber and Treva J. Tucker

When Shakespeare's Richard III wanders the field at Bosworth crying, "A horse! A horse! My kingdom for a horse!,"[1] his position on foot presages the failure of his campaign to save his kingdom from Richmond's efforts to end the division between the houses of York and Lancaster, and it represents just punishment for his illicit machinations and murders. Indeed, Richard's horselessness signals his profound unfitness for rule—hunched of back and afoot, he is made common, literally pedestrian, worthy of nothing better than a traitor's death. Richard's words have become a familiar and now nearly comic example of the importance of practical things to great enterprises: kingdoms, empires—whole worlds, both material and immaterial— were built on the backs of horses. But scholars as a rule must approach early modern culture with only a limited, usually secondhand understanding of the horse's role in defining and delimiting that culture. Thus they are, not entirely unlike the pedestrian Richard, trying to succeed while lacking a basic and profoundly necessary tool. This volume reintroduces scholars, in depth and on many fronts, to the significance of the horse in creating the early modern world we now study.

Historians long have agreed that early modern life was saturated with horses and horse culture. The animals themselves were the literal and figurative vehicles for the transmission of goods, people, and ideas, the bodies upon which empires were advanced, and the bodies on which the ideals and values of empires were inscribed. They functioned both as a kind of technology in and of themselves, in such spheres as agriculture and the military, and as objects of some important technological developments, in areas extending from bits to breeding. Horses served man at all levels of society: they pulled both carts and carriages; they carried farmers to market and noblemen into battle; they plodded across poor fields and pranced in equestrian ballets. Images and literary representations of horses and riders promoted and defined what it meant to be human, to be an individual, to be of a certain class, to have a certain national identity, to hold a certain set of values.

Perhaps especially in their role as servants of the elite, horses performed a wide variety of functions. Both in the flesh and in artistic representations, they served as evidence of wealth and leisure, even of power and glory. At the highest level, horses advanced, both literally and figuratively, the political agendas of those in positions of power. Such agendas most obviously went forward on horses in combat, but political ambitions also could be furthered through the judicious exchange of horses between one power and another. The establishment of trade relations of this nature in some cases created opportunities for cultural exchange that otherwise might not have occurred. Political intentions also could be manifested in iconographically loaded artwork and public spectacles of various kinds. Certain types of horsemanship—both actual and portrayed—could serve as a metaphor for the proper relationship between a subject (the horse) and his ruler (the rider). Elite-specific mounted activities also could foster a sense of group superiority to and differentiation from those of less exalted status, who did not participate in or even have access to such activities.

Finally, the ubiquitous presence of horses throughout early modern society created a market for all sorts of horse-related labor, not only for those directly involved in the care of the animals themselves but also for those employed in more tangential industries: manufacturers of horse-related equipment of various kinds (bits and spurs, tack and harness, carts and carriages, riding boots, grooming tools, and so on), growers of hay and grain, builders of stables, breeders, trainers, local merchants, importers and exporters, jockeys, coachmen, farriers.[2] The list could be continued, but the point, we hope, is clear.

Unfortunately, although scholars of the period have been successful in recuperating the everyday importance of a host of objects and practices, the recuperation of early modern horse culture in all its infinite variety and consequence has eluded most.[3] There is a simple reason for this: whereas in the early modern world horses were truly everywhere, known in some or all aspects to literally everyone, in our postmodern world the horse and its attendant bodies of knowledge are an oddity, uncommon in the extreme.[4] To write anything intelligent on the subject of the horse, it is often necessary to combine training in the academic professions with training in, or at least substantial exposure to, the arts and nuances of horsemanship; yet few people now ride, given the expense and cultural marginalization of riding, and even fewer of those are also academically trained scholars.

It is entirely possible for any of us to instantly understand why artworks, or architecture, or textiles, or educational practices, or violent crime, or cartography, or race (to name just a few topics of recent and important scholarly books) are important to our achieving a comprehensive picture of the early modern world, because we still in some part of our lives interact with versions of all of these. It is, however, much, much more difficult for us to instantly see why *horses* are so central to various domains of early modern culture and, more importantly, what they meant to that culture. The simple, most appropriate analogy by which to viscerally comprehend this divide is to imagine a future population to which car culture is utterly defunct. How would one communicate the ubiquity of these machines to a world that reserves them for the elite few, a world in which there are no longer gas stations on every corner, where not everyone knows what rack and pinion steering is, or where the oil gauge is, or what a speedometer is for? How would one explain why a Mercedes is better than a Ford and what it means to others if you drive one, or why everyone laughs at Yugos or Gremlins (or for that matter, what on earth these names refer to)? How would one convey the importance of the automobile to a world in which no one knows or cares who Mario Andretti and Dale Earnhardt are, what the difference between a beautiful car and an ugly one is, what constitutes good handling or why that could possibly matter? And so on.

The car analogy is a useful and even common one. Walter Liedtke laments that "the automobile has inevitably clouded our view of how important the horse once was."[5] It is simply impossible to imagine anyone in the United States, the United Kingdom, Europe, or many other parts of the world right now who would not have at least some clue what most car-culture references are about. But correlative gaps in our general knowledge of horse culture might be expressed through some simple questions, questions that most people living in European or European-influenced societies ca. 1450–1800 could have answered, or on which they would at least have had an opinion: What part of the bit is the shank? What is a *capriole*? What is the difference between a courser and a genet? Why is a Spanish horse preferable to any other? Why is a "forward seat" useful—for that matter, what is it? To whom would you turn for medical treatment for a horse? How do you make a reluctant horse go forward? What skills of horsemanship are truly useful on the battlefield? How is a well-made horse recognized? For the general reader and general scholar of today, answering even one of these questions would prove difficult. Anthony Dent lists a selection of commonplaces using horses as references in the work of the English historian William Camden (1551–1623) to illustrate the way horses saturated the metaphoric and proverbial layers of early modern English. Today, only one or two are still familiar: "Look not a given horse in the mouth," and "When the steed is stolen shut the stable door."[6] It is a fair guess that even the first of these would stump most scholars attempting a complete explanation.

This volume is thus an attempt to fill, at least in part, a unique and vastly significant gap in the analysis of early modern history and culture by offering discussions that, taken collectively, outline the scope of the importance of horse culture in the early modern world. Each chapter also provides a snapshot of how horse culture and the broader culture—that tapestry of images, objects, structures, sounds, gestures, texts, ideas, and so on—articulate. Knowing more about horses gives scholars a stronger and more complete sense of many aspects of early modern culture: the relationship between political power and diplomacy on the one hand and trade and gift-giving on the other; where and why the idealization of restraint and discipline emerged, whom it targeted, and how it was articulated across arenas as varied as the social, the political, and the self; how group and national identity and self-definition were created and enforced, and how these distinctions interfaced with ideas about social, cultural, and even racial differentiation; how Western cultures responded to foreign or "exotic" cultures, and how they constructed and deployed notions of Other-ness, both national and racial. Again, this volume seeks to demonstrate that, without knowledge of how the horse figured in all these aspects, no version of political, material, or intellectual culture in the period can be entirely accurate.

We have taken as our period parameters a relatively loose definition of "early modern" in the interests of indicating both the pre-history of horse culture during this period and its later transformations and repercussions. We thus include material ranging from the late Middle Ages through the end of the eighteenth century, and even beyond in chapters that deal with cultures that did not move into the modern era until the nineteenth century. Our coverage reaches geographically around England and Europe to Russia and Africa, precisely because the horse itself traveled these distances, in many cases extending European concepts and ideas into non-European cultures. In each chapter, however, the role of the horse in shaping cultural trends is foregrounded. We intend this volume to be of interest not just to specialists but to all those working in the disciplines here represented, and we hope that it will help redress the lack from which the present state of knowledge on the subject suffers.

The one thing we cannot and do not claim is complete coverage of this vast and largely unexplored topic. In part this is because a comprehensive treatment of horse culture in the early modern world would be an encyclopedia, not a volume of critical essays; to a far greater extent, however, it is because so little critical attention has been paid, for example, to horse culture in the Americas, North Africa, the Middle East, India, China, or Japan—all regions in which the horse played an important role during the period we consider. A number of important topics, such as the military role of the horse, the role of the horse in everyday agriculture, and the association of gender with horses and horsemanship, have by no means been fully exhausted. Our hope is that this volume will stimulate further scholarly interest in the crucial role of the horse in human culture and that, perhaps in a future collection, these other areas will receive the attention they deserve.

One final issue regarding coverage that bears mentioning is the apparent preference given here to scholars working on British horse culture. This is not necessarily the product of any bias on the part of the editors but rather the random result of the essays submitted for consideration. One might speculate that this imbalance in the scholarship is related to the relative centrality of horses and horsemanship to British identity, something a few chapters seem to support. As Karen Raber, Donna Landry, and Richard Nash all point out, horse culture had a profound impact on the formation of national identity in early modern England. In contrast, the chapters by Treva Tucker and Sandra Swart, for example, describe a similar impact on the formation of the identity only of a specific group, not an entire nation: the ancestral nobility of France and the Dutch colonists of South Africa. It is possible, then, to suggest that horse culture had a wider and more generalized importance for the English during the early modern period than it may have done elsewhere, an importance that may well survive to the present day. Landry's references to the response of modern British citizens to the successes and failures of British equestrians in international competitions make it clear that horses remain a compelling aspect of British national identity to this day, at least to a greater extent than in many other modern cultures. It is perhaps for both these reasons that research on equestrian topics is more current and active among scholars of early modern England, who—regardless of their own nationality—inevitably are impacted by the dominant cultural beliefs (both current and historical) of those they study. However, it is equally possible that this apparent connection is either entirely false—purely an artifact of a limited call for essays—or merely the byproduct of how trends in scholarship form, shifting into and out of one national literature after another. Here again, we hope that these chapters will stimulate further interest in equestrian topics and that as a result future scholarship will encompass a broader range than that covered by this volume.

The twelve chapters in this volume have been divided into three sections: Power and Status, Discipline and Control, and Identity and Self-definition. As is almost inevitably the case when this type of categorization is imposed after the fact, many of the chapters cross-refer into a category or categories beyond the one in which they have been situated. In the introductory material that follows, we have attempted to identify for the reader where such "cross-pollination" occurs.

POWER AND STATUS

Horses and horsemanship have long been associated with those at the upper end of the socioeconomic scale: the wealthy, the elite, the powerful. During the early modern period, owning a horse—from the lowliest pack animal to the priciest parade mount—was an expensive proposition. A large part of the reason why horse ownership was so costly was because so many of the expenses were ongoing. There were one-time costs, of course, such as the initial purchase price of the beast, the cost of building something (be it a simple fenced enclosure or an elaborate stable) in which to keep it, and the cost of the land on which the structure was built. The amounts involved here varied widely, based on the type of horse purchased and the size and nature of the structure built, but these one-time costs, no matter how exorbitant, represented only a tiny portion of the long-term total expense involved.

For the early modern horse owner, routine daily maintenance was both expensive and inescapable. Even the apparently least costly alternative, that of keeping the horse outdoors in a pasture, involved or had the potential to involve numerous hidden costs. Pastures could fail due to seasonal factors, thus requiring the purchase and transport of supplemental feed; horses kept outdoors always required substantial amounts of additional time and labor every time the horse was used;[7] and horses were more likely to injure themselves in a pasture than in a stable, so the increased potential for loss of use and the cost of medical attention had to be considered. Keeping the horse stabled would eliminate these disadvantages to a great extent, but stabling entailed all sorts of additional expenses: the transport of water, feed, and bedding, the cost of feed and bedding, daily waste removal ("mucking out"), and labor costs for those who chose to hire someone else to handle all these routine tasks of equine maintenance. Whether pastured or stabled, the vast majority of horses needed shoes; even those that did not almost invariably still needed to have their feet trimmed on a regular basis. In either case, the horse required regular attention from a skilled farrier, whose services did not come cheap. Any horse whose daily workload outstripped the number of calories supplied by hay or grass alone required a grain feed of some kind, which then entailed the purchase of costly grain.[8] Some horses needed more exercise than they received from routine use, in which case the owner needed to have either the leisure time necessary to do it himself or the financial capacity to hire someone else to do it for him.[9] Before a horse could be used, it needed to be groomed and tacked up; after it had been used, it needed to be untacked and hand-walked until it was cool and dry.[10] Finally, in addition to all the routine costs of daily maintenance, there were all the virtually unavoidable, albeit intermittent, special costs of horse ownership: repairing damage to stabling and fencing, providing special care for an ill or injured horse, replacing worn or broken equipment, cleaning and oiling all the leather goods, and so forth.[11]

All things taken into consideration, it is clear that ownership of any type of horse in the early modern period was limited to a very great extent to the wealthy—that is, to those who could afford not only the initial costs but also all the ongoing expenses of maintenance. Ownership of horses at the very high end of the spectrum, on the other hand, required not only a substantial amount of surplus wealth but also, in many cases, a substantial amount of surplus time. Pleasure riding was a purely leisure activity in which only those who had spare time on their hands could afford to indulge. Hunting on horseback, while it might net something edible, often was pursued solely for the sport and offered no other return on the time invested. Mastering the complex and difficult mounted skills required for successful performance in battle, in a tournament, or in the manège[12] (not to mention training one's horse for any of these activities) required an enormous amount of time. These high-end mounted activities thus required both wealth and leisure time, so horse owners who could afford to indulge in them tended to be in the upper echelons not only of the economic spectrum but also of the social spectrum: the elite, the noble, the royal.

The activity that probably has the longest history of association with both horses and the elite is cavalry service. The horse itself has been venerated for its noble spirit, gallant heart, innate courage, and other anthropomorphized qualities associated with warfare since at least biblical times. One of the most oft-cited passages on the horse in fact comes from the Book of Job, where God makes reference to its naturally martial qualities:

> Do you give the horse his might? Do you clothe his neck with strength? Do you make him leap like the locust? His majestic snorting is terrible. He paws in the valley, and exults in his strength; he goes out to meet the weapons. He laughs at fear, and is not dismayed; he does not turn back from the sword. Upon him rattle the quiver, the flashing spear and the javelin. With fierceness and rage he swallows the ground; he cannot stand still at the sound of the trumpet. When the trumpet sounds, he says "Aha!" He smells the battle from afar, the thunder of the captains, and the shouting.[13]

In classical Greece and Rome, the horse continued to serve as an instrument of war and hence continued to be an appurtenance of the elite. As Bruce Boehrer reminds us in his chapter in this volume, the fourth-century B.C.E. Greek cavalry commander Xenophon already speaks of that "conjunction of martial heroism, horsemanship, and social privilege" that would continue to exist throughout the centuries of classical Rome and then on into the medieval and early modern periods.

While the supposed fierceness and noble nature of horses thus are thoroughly ancient, the horse's connection to particular codes of aristocratic behavior and merit was secured during the medieval period by its power on the battlefield in the hands of the nobleman–knight. Through the medium of cavalry service, the association between elite social status and the horse itself thus was firmly established long before the beginning of the period covered by this volume. Ultimately, the simple fact of being mounted came to have connotations for the status of the rider. In his thirteenth-century treatise on horse management and medicine, *De medicine equorum*, Jordanus Ruffus neatly summarizes these notions linking horses and elite social status: "No animal is more noble than the horse, since it is by horses that princes, magnates and knights are separated from lesser people, and because a lord cannot fittingly be seen among private citizens except through the mediation of a horse."[14] In his *Boke of the Ordre of Chyvalrye and Knygthode* (1484), William Caxton reminds us that medieval chivalry affirmed both the status of the horse itself and the status garnered by its rider through the proper use of the horse as a knightly weapon: "The horse was the most noble and convenable to serve man; after the horse, which is called Chyval in French is that man named Chyvaller . . . then to the most noble man was given the most noble beast."[15] Edmund Spenser puts Braggadocchio, the cowardly hypocrite of his *Faerie Queene* (1590), on horseback to illustrate as quickly and efficiently as possible that character's baseness: "So to his steed he got, and gan to ride / As one unfit therefore, that all might see / He had not trained been in chevalree." The braggart's noble steed, stolen from the noble elf Guyon, "who well could ménage and subdew his pride," despises to carry his low-born rider.[16]

Spenser's reference to Guyon's ability to "ménage" his horse brings us to another form of horsemanship that was associated almost exclusively with the elite during the early modern period.[17] The Italian rediscovery of Xenophon's *Art of Horsemanship* (through its first printing in Greek in 1516 and its translation into Latin in 1539) and the publication of Federico Grisone's *Gli ordini di cavalcare* (1550) ushered in a renaissance in horsemanship in sixteenth-century Italy. Grisone founded one of the first schools for horsemanship in Naples in the 1530s, and others soon appeared throughout the Italian peninsula. These schools were dedicated to teaching riders and training horses in the complex movements of what we now call dressage, and noblemen from throughout Europe traveled to Italy to learn the new riding style. A number of Italian riding masters followed Grisone's example and wrote important treatises on the art of riding during the second half of the sixteenth century.[18] Other European nations developed riding schools in the manner of the Italians, and still more benefited from a general renewal of riding skills, breeding practices, or riding technologies inspired by the Italian example. By the end of the century, however, the French were attempting to claim to be at the forefront of this new movement in horsemanship.[19] Antoine de Pluvinel established the first noble riding academy in Paris in 1594, and his 1623 text, *Le Maneige royal*, was one of several French contributions to the growing literature on the style of riding that eventually came to be known as the *haute école* (literally, "high school").[20] England joined the literary fray with the *New Method and Extraordinary Invention of Dressing Horses* (1666/67) by William Cavendish, Duke of Newcastle.[21] The vast majority of these writers were noblemen, and the art of riding that their texts describe clearly was something that could be attractive only to those with time and money on their hands.

Owning certain types of horses and participating in certain types of horsemanship clearly were testimony both to one's wealth and to one's high social status. Owning a large number and wide variety of horses sent that message even more emphatically. During the sixteenth century, a noble heavy cavalryman, for example, routinely took at least three and often five horses on campaign: a packhorse or two to carry his arms and equipment, a riding-horse to spare his warhorse while traveling to the battlefield, at least one warhorse to carry him into battle, and often a second combat mount to allow for the (not unlikely) possibility that the first one was killed, injured, or exhausted in battle. A nobleman who competed in the various types of mounted sports common during the early modern period—jousting, running at the ring or quintain, fencing on horseback—needed a string of horses, each selected and trained for optimum performance in its sport. From the late sixteenth century on, nobles who wished to indulge in the full range of the *haute école* almost always needed more than one mount, as it was rare to find a horse equally gifted for the discipline of the balletic lower "airs" and for the power and thrust of the dramatic "airs above the ground." From the seventeenth century on, the advent of the coach and carriage as the preferred conveyances of the elite could necessitate ownership of multiple teams of horses, each selected not only for its suitability to the vehicle it would pull but also on the basis of matching coat and way of going.

The stables of a wealthy early modern aristocrat thus could contain both a large quantity and a wide variety of horses: a selection of riding-horses, including some specifically for the ladies of the house; depending on the period, the location, and the interests of the individual nobleman, horses for hunting, for war, for mounted games, for the *haute école*, for coach and carriage, even for the racetrack; and of course the working types needed by any sizeable estate. The initial cost of any of these horses increased according to its "quality" (what today would be called its breeding) and to how well trained it was for its intended function at the time of purchase.[22] Well-trained horses of the breeds preferred for the *haute école*, for example, were prohibitively expensive, but even an untrained horse of good quality was not cheap. It also is worth reiterating that the purchase price of an individual horse was only the first drop in what was, for those who maintained a stable full, an almost bottomless bucket of expenses. The costs involved in keeping a large number of stabled horses fed, watered, mucked out, bedded, shod, groomed, tacked up, exercised, untacked, and cooled out must not be underestimated.[23]

The stable itself could cost as much as or more than a grand country house, and the architecture of noble stables became a separate art and science during the seventeenth century. England's Prince Henry built a riding house at St. James's Palace between 1607 and 1609, some details of which were copied by his friend William Cavendish, Duke of Newcastle (1593?–1676), for his riding house at Bolsover Castle. During his exile in Antwerp in the 1650s, Cavendish also added a riding gallery to Rubens's home, which he rented. Lucy Worsley and Tom Addyman note that in the course of his many riding house projects (including one at Welbeck Abbey in addition to those at Bolsover and the Rubens house), Cavendish's designs consistently moved the stables and riding court from the outdoors in, integrating them more closely into the domestic space of the rest of his homes. Riding houses belong "with the other constructions for hospitality and display such as banqueting houses, or even the playful pavilions and temporary sets built for entertainments or masques."[24]

Because horses were woven into the culture of the noble and the wealthy, they also were associated by extension with the culture of rule. Horses and horsemanship not only signified social superiority but also had various implications for political, military, and even economic power. Nations won and lost political power and territory in military conflicts carried out on the backs of horses throughout the early modern world. Whether a nation sought to expand or simply to defend itself on the battlefield, it relied largely on the horse to carry the day. In his 1603 introduction to Carlo Ruini's treatise on equine anatomy, *Anatomia & medicina equorum*, Peter Offenbach observed that "in order to sustain political societies, and in order to preserve and protect the people who make up these societies, you cannot do without the horse."[25] In his 1541 Bill regarding the breeding of great horses, England's Henry VIII acknowledged that "the generation and breed of good and strong horses . . . extendeth . . . to a great help and defense" of the nation.[26] Many rulers eagerly sought breeding stock from abroad to enhance the domestic pool of horses suitable for military service, often resulting in the creation or expansion of national breeding programs.

A nation's participation in the circulation of horses could play a surprisingly significant role in its place in global politics and economics in the early modern world. The preoccupation of the elite with an increasing range of equestrian activities required an ever-expanding trade in the equine types deemed most suitable for those activities, and the variety of horses on the market proliferated accordingly. As interaction between Western and non-Western cultures increased, Europeans were exposed to and rapidly became particularly intrigued with unusual or exotic breeds rarely or never before seen in Europe. Turks, Barbs, and Arabians represented the royalty of the early modern horse world, at least in terms of rarity and price. Lisa Jardine and Jerry Brotton remind us that today "familiarity [with such breeds] has de-exoticised them, and we can no longer retrieve their highly specific 'orientalism.' "[27] At the time, however, obtaining some of these exotic foreign breeds was notoriously difficult. The export of many of these horses was closely monitored or even forbidden, requiring the development of close relationships at the highest political level if trade were to commence. The Gonzaga family of Mantua, for example, negotiated extensively with the Ottoman Sultan during the late fifteenth and early sixteenth centuries, enduring long and expensive trips in order to bring home prized animals.[28] Exotic breeds in the hands of European princes also could be a significant tool of foreign policy: at the Field of the Cloth of Gold encounter in 1520, for example, England's Henry VIII used the gift of horses to demonstrate his friendship toward France's François I, and Henry eventually received invaluable breeding stock in return.[29]

Horses could have implications for various types of power at a more local level as well. The esteem in which a prominent family was held by its peers could be enhanced, for example, if that family were known as a breeder of fine horses, or even as the owner of a single particularly fine horse. A family or region that had a reputation for producing good quality stock might even find itself in a position to play for much higher stakes. The demand for truly good horses almost always far outstripped the supply, so those who enjoyed a position on the supply side often could negotiate highly beneficial political and economic favors from the rich and powerful, by selling or even giving them the horses they so desired. At least in part as a result of their involvement in the horse trade, some seemingly rather minor players in early modern Europe were able to reach a level of power and prominence that they otherwise might not have been able to achieve.

Not surprisingly, because horses were associated so closely with those who laid claim to elite status and to power of various kinds, the horse also became a symbolic vehicle for criticism of those who possessed—but misused—power and status: the nobility, royalty, and government. All these groups and institutions were linked in their own way with horses, and all therefore had the potential to be mocked or attacked through the use of equine imagery. An abused and neglected horse, for example, could serve as a metaphor for the political, economic, and social discontent of those who lacked power and status. Such a horse became what might be called an antisymbol of the elite and as such could be used to represent those who suffered from the tyrannies of the rich and well-born. Because of the horse's associations with the attributes considered appropriate to those who possessed power and status, equine imagery also could be deployed to criticize the elite when they failed to uphold and adhere to those attributes in the proper fashion. Here as well the horse became a sort of antisymbol, used to mock rather than to celebrate the qualities of the elite and the powerful. In such a context, horses and horsemanship ultimately could become part of a much larger and more pervasive concern about the future of traditional social structures and mechanisms of rule.

The four chapters in this section illustrate all the many ways outlined above in which horses and horsemanship could represent—or criticize—power and status. Ann Kleimola's chapter takes us to early modern Russia and illustrates how horses and horsemanship inter-acted with elite status in a non-Western culture. As Russia adopted European riding and coaching styles and developed breeding programs aimed at producing horses suited to those styles, it also picked up European associations between horses and elite social status. Muscovite horse culture thus contributed to the convergence between Russian and Western European elite culture and also reflected its progress.

Elizabeth Tobey's chapter on the horse in Italian *palio* racing touches on a range of issues related to power and status. Both in the flesh and in artistic images, these racehorses served as symbols of Italian power, glory, and superiority. They did so both at the local level, in the context of competition between prominent families, and at the international level, in the context of gifts and exports deployed to cement trade and political ties. In this latter context, Tobey docu-ments an engagement between East and West similar to that described by Karen Raber and Donna Landry in their chapters in "Identity and Self-definition" below.

The chapters by Bruce Boehrer and Kevin De Ornellas both illustrate the use of the horse as an antisymbol of power and status. Boehrer's chapter explores the ways in which Shakespeare used equine imagery to criticize the nobility. He contrasts the old nobility, a useful martial order for which horses were a business instrument, to the new nobility, a frivolous leisure class for which horses are only instruments of pleasure. He juxtaposes English military horseman-ship, which was practical, strong, and manly, to foreign manège horsemanship, which was frivolous, weak, and effeminate. Finally, he compares horses themselves, which are symbols of business, military service, and masculine control, to women, who represent pleasure, sex, and loss of control. Kevin De Ornellas's chapter illustrates how the horse "character" in the anonymous late sixteenth-century play *Woodstock* is the vehicle for an attack on royal neglect. Equine hunger and theft become a metaphor for societal discontent caused by inap-propriate state expenditure on warfare and ostentatious display and by bad harvests and falling wages. The horse becomes a symbol of the lower classes, who themselves are reduced to hunger and theft during a period of dearth, misrule, and corrupt political organization.

DISCIPLINE AND CONTROL

Over the centuries covered by this volume, changes in horsemanship and in the artistic portrayal of horses reflect parallel changes in ideas about control and discipline. The relationship between the two—horsemanship and equestrian art on the one hand, and notions about discipline and control on the other—is a many-faceted one. These apparently disparate issues intersect in areas as diverse as the nature of political power and command, the mastery of nature by science and technology, and the shift toward increasingly civilized norms of behavior.

The way in which the relationship between the horse and its trainer was viewed shifted slowly but fairly dramatically during the early modern period. In sixteenth-century manuals of horsemanship, training the horse in the movements of the manège is achieved by the trainer's forceful domination of the horse. Recommended techniques for overcoming resistance or subduing rebellion often are quite brutal, and there is little talk of the horse as anything other than an irrational obstacle in the trainer's quest to produce a correct performance. In seventeenth-century manuals, more refined and sympathetic methods begin to emerge. The rider's goal is still to master his horse's willful nature, to control its excesses, and to achieve its complete obedience and submission to his dictates. What has changed is the suggested means for reaching that goal. Rather than advocating bludgeoning or terrorizing the horse into submission, the manuals now emphasize the importance of understanding *why* a horse might resist or rebel when asked to perform certain movements. There is much discussion of the nature of the horse—its moods, its feelings, even its thinking—and of how that nature may frustrate the trainer's goals and what he might do about it all. By the eighteenth century, the battle between the rider's essentially rational wishes and the horse's essentially irrational nature has resolved itself into something more closely resembling a cooperative partnership between two reasonable creatures. Their thinking processes may differ, but they nonetheless are capable of reaching a negotiated compromise. As a result, there is a shift toward a more "natural" form of training the horse, which builds on a sympathetic connection between horse and rider and which diminishes the importance of the rider's control of and dominance over his mount.[30]

Toward the end of the period covered by this volume, another and more general shift in attitudes toward horses and horsemanship also was taking place. First in England and then spreading from there, we see the development of a style of riding which is a complete departure from the inherent restraint and containment of the *haute école*. Rather than the long stirrups and upright posture of manège riding, the new style involved shorter stirrups and a more forward posture: a position that allowed the horse to gallop freely forward and to jump obstacles and that therefore leant itself, for example, to racing and hunting across country. To this day, this style of riding is called "hunt seat" in Western nations, and, more broadly, usually is what is meant by the phrase "to ride English" often used to distinguish it from riding in the American cowboy style or the European dressage style. In the case of this later development, we thus see a broader shift from the control and discipline of the dressage seat and manège riding to the fluidity and freedom of the forward seat and hunting and racing.[31]

All of these changes are apparent in equestrian art, a venue in which the horse already had a long and proud history by the beginning of the early modern period.[32] The horse's noble beauty has captured human artistic imagination from at least the time of cave paintings. Once domestication occurred, the relationship between horses and elite social status discussed in the previous section gradually began to appear in the iconography. Representations of horses in the classical and medieval periods in Europe often reflect this relationship, but symbolic connections between horses and elite status seem to be particularly present in the equestrian art of the early modern period. The popularity of the horse in the paintings, drawings, and statues of the time certainly owes something to its role in defining nobility in human culture, since wealthy elite patrons often controlled artists' production and content. But there is also something intrinsically seductive in the image of this massive and powerful animal, capable simultaneously of such athletic feats and of such unmatched obedience and service to its rider.

Throughout much of the period covered by this volume, most art depicts the horse under the serenely regal control of its (usually noble) rider. These images are particularly prevalent in the sixteenth and seventeenth centuries, when the dominant view toward horses and their training still revolved around the concept of the discipline and control of the irrational (the horse) by the rational (the rider). Most seventeenth-century depictions of monarchs and high-ranking nobles on horseback, for example, emphasize the rational control of what is bestial. Roy Strong analyzes a ca. 1638 equestrian portrait of Charles I of England by Anthony Van Dyck (1599–1641) as part of a general salute to Charles's rational rule. The king's head, in this case, is nearly as large as the horse's unusually diminutive noggin (a physical impossibility), indicating the triumph of the royal intellect over bestial power.[33] The equestrian portraits of various members and high-ranking noble servants of the Spanish royal family painted by Diego Rodríguez de Silva y Velázquez (1599–1660) in the 1620s and 1630s all emphasize the effortless control of the elite riders over their powerful but obedient mounts. Even the wonderfully mobile animals of Peter Paul Rubens (1577–1640), whose flowing brush strokes convey such vigorous action, are subject to the rational direction and authority of their noble or royal riders.

In art as in literature, however, the horse is multivalent, capable of representing far more than one ideological perspective. Just as the literary images of horses evoked in the preceding section either could symbolize the elite and the powerful in a positive fashion or could serve as a vehicle for their criticism, so artistic images of horses could represent either domination and restraint or cooperation and freedom. In the eighteenth century, many representations of the horse thus focus not on the control, authority, and dominion of man over animal—wild and bestial in potential if not in fact—but rather on the horse as man's partner or even on the horse alone, worthy of appreciation purely for its own sake.[34] As Leidtke notes, although images of monarchs on horseback tended to reiterate the older symbolic message, "new forms and a new life were given to the tradition by portraits of aristocratic and bourgeois figures that . . . represent the sitters resting with their horses in a picturesque landscape, or riding out from their country house, or at the hunt."[35] The horse in this type of image still represents wealth and status, but it also reflects a new nostalgia for the recreative pleasures of nature and the countryside, which were associated with the horse in so many ways. Well-known artists who contributed to this new type of equestrian portrait include Sir Joshua Reynolds (1723–92) and George Stubbs (1724–1806). Reynolds often portrayed the rider dismounted, using the horse more for iconographic and characterological significance, and Stubbs's horses were clearly the stars of his paintings, albeit in the interests of depicting the gentility of country life. At around the same time, a Romantic version of the horse in art also began to emerge, in which the horse often is riderless—that is, at liberty or in a truly "free" state. These images "finally attribute the action of the horse to the power and, one might add, the nobility of the animal, not of his master."[36] This latter tendency was becoming ever more prevalent toward the

end of the period covered by this volume and is perhaps best represented by the paintings of nineteenth-century artists such as Théodore
Géricault (1791–1824) and Rosa Bonheur (1822–99).[37]

The depiction of horses in art over the centuries of the early
modern period thus closely echoes the shifting view of the horse and
its relationship with its rider revealed in contemporary manuals of
horsemanship. In both cases, we move from an irrational horse that
must be restrained and contained by the rational (and, if necessary,
forceful) control of its rider, to a rational horse that must be persuaded
by its rational rider to form a cooperative, yet still highly disciplined,
partnership. Ultimately, we end with a horse that apparently has
become so "rational" that it has moved beyond a necessary relationship with its rider: a horse that gallops freely across country under a
rider who positions himself so as to interfere as little as possible, or the
image of a horse portrayed totally at liberty, without any rider at all. In
literature, too, we see a similar evolution. Horses up through the seventeenth century are usually portrayed correctly subjected to human
dominance, no matter how abstract their uses in a literary text. Ken
Keffer has suggested that for the French essayist Michel de Montaigne
(1533–92), well-trained and well-ridden horses represent rational,
directed discourse: writing that is under the thorough control of its
author just as a horse should be under the thorough control of its
rider. When Montaigne's horse throws and nearly kills him, he can rely
on the reader to understand that the event functions as a kind of ret-
ribution for his (discursively) wandering ways.[38] From horses ideally
under strict human control, representations of horses and reason shift
toward the ideal of horses that are *more* rational, *more* enlightened
than humans can ever be: Jonathan Swift's eighteenth-century race of
horses, the Houyhnhnms, never stray from the straight and narrow,
and they model a degree of reason that is absent from human affairs.
Gulliver's Travels (1726) offers the reader bestial, irrational humans,
and sensible, orderly, self-governing horses, leaving the reader to
puzzle out where and how the balance has gone awry.

All the shifts in horse culture discussed above mirror a similar
evolution in ideas about relationships between "trainer" and
"trained" in the larger cultural context. Numerous scholars of early
modern Europe have noted, for example, changes over time in what
has been referred to variously as civility, manners, courtesy, *politesse*,
and so forth. Whatever the terminology, this change in European
behavioral norms involved increased "policing" of the self by the
self—a control and discipline voluntarily imposed from within rather
than from without. The natural instincts, impulses, and passions of

man increasingly were viewed as irrational behaviors that needed to
be disciplined and controlled by human reason. The body and its
nature needed to be "trained," the trainer in this case being the
rational mind of the body's inhabitant. There are clear parallels
between these evolving ideas about control and discipline as they per-
tained to notions of the self and what was happening in both riding
practice and equestrian art. This is perhaps most apparent in the *haute
école* of the sixteenth and seventeenth centuries, where the triumph of
the rational over the irrational is articulated both in the manuals
describing how to teach the manège movements and in paintings and
sculptures depicting these movements.

Liedtke notes that much incorrect analysis has been written of the
horse's appearance in early modern art due to incomplete understanding of the nuances of the *haute école*. Contrary to what many art
historians have assumed, formal statues and paintings of noble and
royal figures on horseback rarely depict the horse standing on its hind
legs or rearing, something a horse will do when it is excited, frightened,
or angry. Instead, such images tend to feature horses posed in the
levade, a highly controlled rise on the haunches at a much lower angle
to the ground than a full rear.[39] The portrayal of a monarch or a
nobleman on a horse in *levade* suggested not only the rider's control
of his mount but also the rider's control of his Self. Anyone who
hoped to manage the natural instincts of so huge and powerful an
animal first had to be able to contain and restrain his own impulses.
The gradual increase in self-discipline and self-control among members
of the elite thus facilitated a similar increase in their control over their
horses: as one trained oneself, so one was able to train one's horse.[40]

Even in artwork that does not specifically portray horses engaged
in the *haute école*, there is a symbolic iconography of the rational
versus the irrational, of reason versus passion, of control versus
impulse. An unbridled or unrestrained horse often represents the
human passions run amok. The bridle, when present, then represents
the restraint imposed by human reason, triumphing over and subduing
those passions. In such images, the bridle also can represent another
popular—and not dissimilar—early modern motif, the triumph of
(rational) science and technology over (irrational) Nature. During the
period covered by this volume, bits became highly sophisticated and
technically complex pieces of equipment; entire books were devoted
to their action and design, and a specialized industry grew up around
their production. Many horsemen believed that choosing the correct
bit could mean the difference between success and failure when
training a horse. When these beliefs and technical developments were

transferred to an artistic context, the symbolism is familiar: the bit and
bridle represent the science and technology side of the equation,
which, when manipulated by rational Man, inevitably triumphs over
irrational Nature as represented by the horse.

One of the most fascinating parallels between early modern horse
culture and larger ideas about relationships between trainer and
trained lies in the realm of political culture—that is, in the relationship between ruler and ruled. In this context, horsemanship and
equestrian art reflect evolving ideas, not only about control and
discipline of self and others in a more individual sense, but also about
command and power as those ideas were manifested in the interaction
between a ruler and his subjects. Some scholars have argued, for
example, that the gradual increase in self-discipline and self-control
among members of the elite facilitated a similar increase in political
control over the elite by their rulers. According to this argument,
social pressure toward more "civil" behavior eventually produced an
elite that was less likely to rebel and more likely either to acquiesce or,
at worst, to negotiate.[41] On the other hand, however much a ruler's
control over his more exalted subjects may have increased as a result
of civility, most scholars now agree that no early modern European
ruler ever enjoyed anything approaching the "absolute" power once
attributed to the likes of Louis XIV of France. Political power and the
ability to command one's subjects was far more equivocal than that
paradigm would suggest. Even Louis, that supposedly most absolute
of absolute monarchs, was forced to negotiate with his nobles in
order to achieve his goals, granting and withdrawing favor(s) in a
constantly fluctuating pattern that often was entirely dependent on
the circumstances of the moment.

These changing relations between a monarch and his subjects
mirror in several ways the similarly and contemporaneously changing
relations between a horse trainer and his "subjects." The shift among
elite members of society described above—from a control and discipline
that to a great extent were imposed by external sources to a more
internally and voluntarily imposed self-control and self-discipline—
indeed may have helped the monarch to control his subjects.
Powerful nobles who had been unruly and who had required
externally imposed royal discipline now were becoming well (and,
better yet, self-) disciplined. They were, in other words, better
"trained." All of this facilitated an increase in political control over
the elite by their rulers in precisely the same way that the shift in the
way horses and training were viewed facilitated an increase in control
over horses by their trainers. During the sixteenth century, training

manuals advocated forceful domination of the horse: horses, like nobles, were viewed as unruly subjects requiring externally imposed discipline. In the seventeenth century, in contrast, these manuals advocated a far more refined or "civilized" control and discipline of the horse. Horses increasingly were perceived, if not as entirely rational beings capable of self-discipline and self-control, then at least as beings capable of choosing to allow themselves to be disciplined or controlled by their riders.

The shift among elites toward increased civility thus led over time to a decrease in unruly or rebellious behavior and to an increase in willingness, if not to submit to the ruler's demands altogether, then at least to negotiate a compromise with him. In similar fashion, the shifting view of the horse and its innate capacity for rational partici-pation in the training process led from an initial belief that the horse simply could (and should) be forced to obey, to an interim belief that the horse had the capacity to choose whether or not to obey and thus had at least some rights as a partner in the relationship with its rider, to the ultimate belief that the horse was a full partner who had to choose freely to obey, as otherwise nothing worth having would or could be achieved. Monarchs might have preferred that their relationship with their more powerful subjects remain at the initial or interim stages, but ultimately rulers, like horse trainers, found that they could achieve the most favorable results through negotiation rather than through force. In politics as in horsemanship, power and the ability to command were equivocal in nature: the ruler/trainer could get more out of the ruled/trained through persuasion and cooperation than through domination and coercion.

One of the few areas in which a monarch could exercise, at least symbolically, the type of control he might wish he had over his subjects was the artistic one. On canvas or in statuary, a ruler could articulate what he considered to be the proper relationship between himself and his subjects. Equestrian art leant itself particularly well to this end, and much early modern sculpture and painting celebrated the imposing authority conveyed by the prince on horseback. The roster of monarchs who chose to have themselves portrayed in this guise includes Holy Roman Emperor Charles V, Philip II, III, and IV of Spain, Charles I of England, and almost every French king who reigned during the sixteenth through eighteenth centuries: François I, Henri II and IV, and Louis XIII, XIV, and XV.[42] Whatever one's national heritage, then, to be seen controlling a horse indicated one's fitness to control or rule others. The image of the mounted monarch thus became a metaphor for the proper relationship between ruler (rider) and subject (horse) . . . or at least for what the monarch wished was the relationship between ruler and subject.[43]

Yet even in the narrow realm of the artistic depictions of mounted rulers, we see signs of that same evolution away from enforced control and toward a more cooperative partnership that was occurring both in horsemanship and in politics. Liedtke contrasts the equestrian monument of Philip IV of Spain (1621–65), executed by Pietro Tacca between 1636 and 1640 and portraying the king on a horse in *levade*, with two statues of Louis XV of France (1715–74): a lost equestrian monument executed by Jean-Baptiste Lemoyne between 1731 and 1741 and an equestrian statuette by Edme Bouchardon of ca. 1760, both depicting the king on a trotting horse. Liedtke comments:

> One is tempted to suggest, as did contemporary authors, that riding style was a reflection of behavior in society. In contrast to the strict discipline imposed upon his horse by Philip IV, Louis XV's style of riding seems more like an art of persuasion, a system of subtle suggestions and thoughtful rewards.[44]

The three chapters in this section analyze and discuss various ways in which horsemanship and equestrian art mirrored, and even contributed to, changing ideas about control and discipline during the early modern period. Pia Cuneo's chapter examines sixteenth-century German bit-books and argues that changes in ideas about horsemanship are a reflection of larger changes in ideas about control. She uses bits as a lens onto not only the history of riding but also the histories of technology, art, and Renaissance culture, illuminating a number of the themes evoked above. Through technology (bits), rational man triumphs over irrational nature (horses); in art, reason (bit and bridle) opposes the passions (the horse); culturally, control shifts from the purely external (bits) to the more internal (mutual understanding between horse and rider).

Elisabeth LeGuin's chapter assesses the role of horsemanship in the shift toward a more internalized control of self, arguing that horsemanship contributes to the history of discipline in terms of the relationship between trainer and trained. She compares horsemanship to music, both processes in which cooperation or listening—a term that applies to riding as well as to music—is far better than force, which never produces harmony, either mounted or musical. When both parties listen to each other, it is unclear who is obeying whom, and horsemanship ultimately becomes a metaphor for the equivocal nature of command.

Kate van Orden's chapter focuses on horsemanship as part of the civilizing process in seventeenth-century France. Manège riding was one site of social pressure toward increased civility, which encouraged greater social discipline through attention to manners and personal discipline. Horsemanship also can be seen as a metaphor for the proper relationship between a monarch and his nobles. Just as manège training transformed the horse from rebellious to cooperative, so attendance at a royal riding academy helped "train" French nobles by educating them in the benefits of consonant relations with those in power. Van Orden's discussion of this transformation resonates with some of the issues addressed in Treva Tucker's chapter in the "Identity and Self-definition" section below.

IDENTITY AND SELF-DEFINITION

Numerous references already have been made to the association between horses and elite status during the early modern period. In many cases, however, that association had a deeper meaning than the relatively simplistic links between, say, wealth and horse ownership or leisure time and certain types of riding. Horses and horsemanship were not just signs or signifiers of elite status; in certain contexts, they could contribute to or even help to create elite identity and self-definition. In this role as shapers of group identity, horses were able to move beyond the confines of their longstanding association with the elite to help define the identity of groups that were not necessarily elite in the traditional sense, that were distinguished by gender as much as by social status, or that transcended the distinctions of social status altogether and encompassed an entire nation.

Even in the case of the elite, horsemanship was a crucial element of masculine identity as well as status identity. Specific types of horsemanship were associated with both high social rank and the male gender. In the Middle Ages, for example, heavy cavalry service and tourneying were mounted activities limited almost exclusively to noble men. In the early modern period, those activities were first supplemented and then ultimately displaced by the *haute école*, which also was limited (in theory if not in fact) to males of noble extraction. All these types of horsemanship were viewed as ways for noblemen to display those personal qualities and characteristics that were believed to be both quintessential to and innate in the true nobleman. By embodying so many of the ways in which noblemen defined themselves, horsemanship thus helped to create a sense not just of group identity but also of group superiority. Those who fell outside the "right" categories (noble and male) were not merely forbidden access to certain types of horsemanship. In circular fashion, outsiders also were deemed incapable of performing these mounted activities, or at least of performing them properly if somehow they managed to obtain access to them, because they lacked what accompanied noble manhood. Only those who came to the table (or in this case to the saddle) equipped with the correct rank and gender, and thus with the qualities and characteristics that accompanied that rank and gender, could hope to master the intricacies of military, tournament, or manège equitation.

This sociocultural aspect of horsemanship became particularly important when various military, political, economic, and social changes in the early modern world threatened to overturn longstanding social hierarchies and cultural beliefs. Throughout Europe in the centuries covered in this volume, aristocracies faced a wide range of changes that threatened both their status, or the way in which they were viewed by others, and their identity, or the way in which they viewed themselves. For example, for several centuries before the early modern period, heavy cavalry service had been associated with noble status. By the end of the Middle Ages, it had become one of the primary attributes by which true nobility supposedly could be recognized. For both tactical and economic reasons, however, traditional heavy cavalry—that is, the fully armored warrior riding an armored horse and fighting primarily with lance and sword—was in decline throughout the sixteenth century and had become virtually obsolete by the seventeenth. In addition, as armies became increasingly professionalized throughout the early modern period, they also became increasingly open to non-noble combatants. As a result, military service in general and heavy cavalry service in particular gradually began to lose their central importance as attributes of nobility.

In part as a corollary to military change, political power during this period gradually was shifting toward more centralized monarchies. As nobles slowly began to lose their relative autonomy, they struggled to redefine their service to king and country, while recent arrivistes looked for the means to secure a place in this brave new order. This latter group posed a particular threat to the noble status quo, as they represented a social category that called into question one of the other central attributes that supposedly defined true nobility, that of birth. Noble birth was not simply a question of parentage; it was the means through which all the personal qualities supposedly attached to noble status traveled from one generation to the next. Perhaps most importantly, birth also was the means through which those not of noble birth were denied access to those qualities and thus, by extension, to nobility itself. During the period covered by this volume, however, we witness the rise throughout Europe of well-educated and economically advantaged men whose success was based on personal skill and effort in arenas other than the battlefield, rather than on a combination of privileged birth and martial prowess. The growth of this segment of society helped spark a debate regarding the meaning of "virtue," or merit. Was merit innate, something with which one had to be born, as the nobles argued; or was merit something that could be acquired, through appropriate education and personal effort, as the non-nobles argued? Aspects of this debate are reflected in the increased popularity during this period of courtly literature and courtesy books, genres that offered suggestions to readers, both noble and not, on how to function more smoothly and effectively in the upper echelons of society. Baldessare Castiglione's 1528 *Book of the Courtier* famously offered something to both groups. Nobles could find in it a new outline for the political and sociocultural work they might be expected to do, while Johnny-come-latelies might find a lesson plan for success at court, an environment that became ever more complex for all participants as monarchs continued to consolidate their power.

Horses and horsemanship served as familiar and comforting touchstones to which the nobility could turn as it struggled to cope with these various threats. Horsemanship in general allowed nobles to retain some connection to heavy cavalry service, simply by virtue of the fact that it involved being mounted. Certain types of mounted activities—for example, mounted martial games and the more dramatic movements of the *haute école*—allowed nobles to display many of the personal qualities associated with military service. On the other hand, some of the newer additions to elite equestrian activities—horse ballets and *carrousels*, carriage culture—allowed nobles to display various nonmilitary qualities that were becoming increasingly important components of nobility as noble culture gradually shifted from predominantly martial to something far more courtly. All these forms of horsemanship allowed nobles to differentiate themselves from the detested parvenus who had achieved their status in society through means other than martial ones and who lacked the innate personal qualities that permitted those of noble birth to excel at equestrian activities. Ultimately, many nobles were able to use their relationship with horses to help them to refashion their identity and self-definition in ways that allowed them to meet the demands of their changing circumstances.

One of the most fascinating types of group definition to which early modern horse culture seems to have made a striking contribution is that of national identity. Styles of riding, the rider's position on horse-back, the type of horse being ridden: any or all of these can be trans-formed into a discourse about national character and values. If you wanted to illustrate what is most American about America, the cow-boy on his stocky cowpony surely would appear in your repertoire of images, his relaxed seat and one-handed hold on the reins indicating freedom from the constraints of "proper" riding, readiness with rope or weapon, and adaptation to long hours in the saddle as he traverses the wide open spaces of the American West. When we imagine foxhunting, we naturally conjure up neat green fields, transected by hedges and stone walls, a crowd of elegant red- and black-coated riders on long-legged hunters streaming across the landscape behind a pack of hounds—we're in England, of course, where else? We may not real-ize it, but the forward tilt of the riders and the freely flowing gaits of their horses also speak volumes about English liberty—an investment in freedom surprisingly not unlike the cowboy's. But in England, lib-erty is best displayed by the aristocracy; in America, it is the property of the common man (if not woman).

As some of the chapters in this section will show, England was deeply invested in manipulating horses and horsemanship as part of its national rhetoric during the early modern period. In the late sixteenth and early seventeenth centuries, the English had something of an inferiority complex about their homegrown breeds and riders. In 1566, Thomas Blundeville writes:

> But now to give the Countreyman his desire, which seeketh to breed horses for draught, or burthen, where should I wysh him to provyde himself of Mares and Stallions, better than here in Englande, whereas he may easily finde a number of strong Jades more mete for that purpose than for the Saddle, and all for lack of good order of breeding, which if it might be once observed thys Realme I believe there woulde be so good & so fayre Horses bred here as in any place in Christendome.[45]

Blundeville's concern is over a perceived decline in the breeding of good quality English horses in comparison with other countries (most prominently Spain and Italy) where more regularized practices had created purer and more refined animals. From the time of Henry VIII onward, prominent English aristocrats sought to acquire the types of horses that could remedy the situation Blundeville decries. In the case of some of the more exotic foreign breeds, these animals often were coveted as much for the mythology surrounding them as for their physical or other characteristics. Arabian horses, for example, were known for the purity of their jealously guarded bloodlines, some dating back thousands of years, and so could seem to nations of more recent lineage to represent a touchstone of ancient integrity. Their handling often resulted in a higher degree of bonding with their grooms and riders than Western horses might display, leading to stories about their fidelity and near-human behaviors. And the sheer fineness of many of the exotic "Oriental" breeds could make native horses seem ugly and common in comparison, with attendant consequences for the way one's horses spoke about national identity. English treatises on horsemanship are also full of self-criticism for the lack of national dedication to the art of riding, often bolstered with references to the Italian, Spanish, and French masters whose schools had no corollary in early modern England. The question was, however, how to incorporate both exotic breeds and the riding styles of one's near neighbors and competitors without losing a sense of coherent national character.

In the seventeenth century, the second part of this question was at least partially answered by the development of a specifically English form of *haute école*. The English approach was juxtaposed to the continental one in ways that made it clear that the English method was not merely different from but also far better than that practiced by the (detested) French and those who followed their ideas. This specifically English manège thus can be seen as one expression of a burgeoning national identity, in which horsemanship served to create a sense of both cultural differentiation and cultural superiority. Of course, at this stage in the development of English national identity, manège riding was still a distinctly elite pursuit, so the concepts of differentiation and superiority also applied, just as they did in other elite cultures, to those who stood outside the group defined by social status (and, let us not forget, by male gender), even if those outsiders also technically happened to be English.

By the late seventeenth century, however, the English had begun to develop a heightened interest in horseracing and other forms of riding across country at speed and often over obstacles.[46] These mounted activities differed dramatically from the *haute école* so beloved by the continental peers of the English. Riding at high speeds or over obstacles required an entirely new position or seat in the saddle and, ultimately, generated the development of an entirely new breed of horse: the Thoroughbred. This horse was suited, both conformationally and temperamentally, to galloping freely forward over a distance, rather than to the disciplined collection of the *haute école*. The breeding stock used to create this new horse, therefore, was not that used to create a horse suited to the manège but was instead those exotic Oriental breeds—the Barb, the Turk, and the Arabian—that the English had for so long admired. By manipulating these foreign horses to create a new and specifically English breed, the English thus were able to answer the first part of the question suggested above—how to incorporate exotic breeds without losing a sense of coherent national character. And by developing new sports and a new type of seat to go along with the new breed, they were able to put paid entirely to the second part of that question, as the adaptation of foreign riding styles had been supplanted by a specifically English style.

The new seat, the new breed, and the sports that they facilitated all came to be so closely associated with the English that they quite literally helped to create the national identity of this people. In this instance, we no longer are dealing with a horse culture that was essentially identical to that practiced by members of other nations (or, more specifically, by members of the elites of other nations) but that had been tweaked somehow to give it a specifically English flavor, as in the case of the "Englishing" of the manège. Instead, we are dealing with a horse culture that truly was unique to the English and that thus served to separate them clearly and distinctly from members of other nations. This newly clear-cut difference also allowed the English to argue more convincingly than ever before that their style of riding, their breed of horse, and their types of mounted sport were better than those of everyone else. The concepts of differentiation and superiority now contributed to a far more general sense of us versus them—that is, the English as a whole as against everyone else as a whole, rather than merely the English elite as against other elites or as against the non-elite, both foreign and domestic. Although the new horse culture still might have been socially restrictive, as a metaphor and interpretive device it became an inclusive definition of Englishness.

The timing of this major shift in English horse culture is well worth noting for what it tells us about larger changes in English culture more generally. The rise of horseracing, the appearance of the forward seat, and the development of the Thoroughbred all coincide with a parallel shift in perceived characteristics of English national identity, particularly in comparison with contemporary notions of identity and selfhood on the continent. Those nations that continued to privilege the *haute école* also continued to privilege the notions of control and discipline that went with it, whereas the English could claim to have broken through to the new and far better characteristics of freedom and liberty as manifested in, among other things, the nature of English horse culture. Horse culture in this case both shaped and reflected a larger discourse about national character and values, in which the freedom and liberty represented by fast riding echoed a sense of national identity in which those qualities became a key part of what it meant to be English.[47]

Of course, the English were not the only ones to develop a type of horsemanship or a breed of horse that reflected specifically "national" needs and characteristics. It was precisely during the centuries covered by this volume that many of the nations of Western Europe began to imagine themselves *as* nations, with a coherent communal identity that rendered them distinct from their neighbors. It was also during this period that equine breeds in the modern sense of the term began to emerge, and in at least some cases it can be argued that these breeds reflected the burgeoning sense of group identity of the state that developed them.[48] It may be no accident that many such breeds were created by aspiring, rather than dominant, national entities, since having a specialized breed could help to distinguish a small, emerging, or otherwise marginal state. The United States provides one example of this dynamic at work even today: home-grown breeds such as the Tennessee Walking Horse or the Morgan, while ostensibly bred for circumstances and environments peculiar to the country, also have become a rich source of self-congratulation and national pride and are now the material for a vast and profitable national show industry.

During the period covered by this volume, a local breed of horse could be an important player in the development of an emotional and sometimes practical attachment to a region, a state, or even a royal house. While this may not be precisely the same as attachment to a nation per se, this sense of connection to a given *locus* must precede and therefore is part of what eventually would be molded into nationalism in the modern sense of the term. By the late nineteenth and early twentieth centuries, these initial glimmerings of distinction and pride of place had developed into what we now would recognize as nationalist sentiments and ideas. While there may as yet be no concrete evidence that the development of certain breeds of horse was linked to the formation of nation-states, the timing in many cases is highly suggestive, and future research may well reveal such connections. Just a few examples will serve to indicate the proliferation of early modern breeds that potentially could have played a nationally defined and/or defining role.

One of the earliest and best known examples of a breed developed during the early modern period is the Lipizzan. In 1580, Archduke Charles II of Austria, brother of the Holy Roman Emperor,

Maximilian II (1564–76), founded a stud at Lipizza. He then imported Spanish and Barb horses to breed with the native Karst stock, ultimately resulting in the remarkable Lipizzan breed, still renowned today for its *haute école* performances at the Spanish Riding School in Vienna. The school itself, so called after the original stock from which the Lipizzan was developed, was built in 1735 to replace the original structure, the Winter Riding Hall, built in 1572. A lesser known contemporary cousin of the Lipizzan also was developed by the Austrian Hapsburgs. Around 1562, Maximilian II founded a court stud at Kladrub (then part of Austria, now in the Czech Republic), and he and his son, Holy Roman Emperor Rudolf II (1576–1612), imported Spanish and Italian horses that served as the root stock for the Kladruby, a heavier version of the Lipizzan. The Lipizzan was intended for riding and light carriage use, while the Kladruby was bred for heavier carriage and coach use.

In the seventeenth and eighteenth centuries, the German territories spawned several new breeds. Johann XVI of Oldenburg (1573–1603) established several studs in that tiny kingdom, which at the time was in the center of the kingdom of Hanover (now in Lower Saxony in northern Germany). Johann began crossing imported Barb, Turkish, Danish, and especially Neapolitan and Spanish stock with native Friesian horses from nearby East Friesland. His successor, Anton Günther (1603–67), continued improving the nascent Oldenburg breed and generally is credited with its establishment as such. In the seventeenth and eighteenth centuries, the Oldenburg was very popular among the European nobility for use as an elegant carriage-horse. The state stud responsible for the Hanoverian breed was established in 1735 at Celle in the kingdom of Hanover. Local stock was crossed with imported horses, primarily Thoroughbreds, to produce a robust horse for military, agricultural, and carriage use. In 1732, King Friedrich Wilhelm I of Prussia established a royal stud at Trakehnen in East Prussia. There he began to develop the Trakehner breed by crossing the small native Schwaike horse with various imports, mostly Thoroughbreds and Arabians. His goal was to develop a new and better type of cavalry horse, one that was lighter and had more speed and endurance than the type of horse needed to carry the armored heavy cavalryman of earlier periods.[49]

Beyond the confines of Western Europe, new breeds did their work as well. When Europeans first began to establish foreign colonies, the mere presence of horses and the simple ability to ride one—regardless of the style of riding, the breed of horse, or the associations either one did or did not have with a certain social rank or gender—in many cases served to differentiate colonials from indigenous peoples. Everyone is familiar with the story of the initial impact of mounted men on the native populations of South and Central America, where the horse long had been extinct at the time of the first Spanish conquistadores. In instances such as these, however, horse culture was simply one of numerous factors differentiating European colonists from the preexisting inhabitants of newly colonized territories.

Where the horse played perhaps its most interesting and complex role in the colonial context was in the creation—whether deliberate or inadvertent—of an identity that was distinct from that of the colonists' homeland. In the vast majority of cases, European colonists brought the culture of their home countries with them, and many probably would have been delighted to maintain their native cultural traditions in their new environment. Colonial environments, however, inevitably were different from the colonists' home environment, and colonial culture thus was forced to adapt and evolve. In terms of horse culture, this adaptation or evolution could manifest itself in terms of riding style, type of horse, or both.

For purely practical reasons, local conditions and, if there were an indigenous horse culture, local equestrian traditions rapidly could influence the riding style of a group of colonists. What point would there be, for example, in retaining the type of cavalry tactics and equipment that were prevalent in sixteenth-century northern Europe if one were facing fairly primitive weapons and were operating in terrain and weather conditions that made the weight and heat of full armor a drawback rather than a benefit? Horsemanship, military and otherwise, thus could change rapidly and even rather drastically under the pressure of local demands, leading to the development of a "colonial style" of riding that could differ sharply from that of the colonists' homeland.

Horses, too, were impacted by similar factors. In colonial regions in which there was a preexisting horse culture, the indigenous breed often proved to have the advantage over horses from the colonists' homeland. Not all types of horse will thrive in all types of conditions. If horses imported at great expense from Europe tended to succumb to local diseases to which native stock was immune, or to collapse under conditions that native stock handled with no difficulty, or simply to perform badly tasks at which native stock excelled, then anyone who needed a horse eventually saw the wisdom of selecting the one that not only would survive but also would serve well. As with riding styles, the type of horse a colonist chose to ride thus could be influenced substantially by the circumstances of his locality.

In many instances, colonists created entirely new breeds to meet their needs. If there was an indigenous breed that met the demands of the locality but that did not meet European standards for size, quality, looks, and so forth, the local horse often was "improved" by crossing it with imported stock, ultimately creating a new breed of horse. In colonial areas with no existing horse culture, various types of horses often would be imported and then selectively crossbred to develop new breeds, deliberated crafted to respond to the specific demands of a given colonial environment. In either case, these breeds often were dramatically different from those that prevailed in the colonists' home countries. Over time, they could come to be associated with, or even representative of, the colonial culture that created them. As a specifically colonial product, such horses could help to differentiate colonial cultures from homeland cultures. Ultimately, when colonies became independent, these breeds contributed— admittedly, along with many other factors—to the development of a sense of national identity and self-definition.

In the American colonies, for example, the breed now known as the American Quarter Horse had its origins in a specifically colonial need for a short-distance speed horse—a need that sharply differenti- ated colonial horseracing, at least in some regions, from horseracing in Britain. In the seventeenth and eighteenth centuries, much of the eastern seaboard in colonial America was covered with dense forest. Clearing land required an immense effort and therefore was too valuable for agricultural purposes for it to be squandered on English-style oval racetracks. On the other hand, narrow tracks, wide enough for only two horses and no more than a quarter mile in length, could be cut through the forest without too much difficulty. Horses also could be raced on village streets, country lanes, level stretches of pasture—virtually any relatively flat, straight, cleared piece of land would do. Because of these topological factors, such races tended to be short, and horses with the ability to sprint were privileged over those with the ability to run longer distances. Through selective breeding of horses that excelled at short-distance racing, many of them Thoroughbreds imported from England, the American colonists developed a horse that responded very specifically to their local needs. Rather than adapting all colonial racing to the type of racehorse developed by the British in response to British needs, the colonists created a new breed of racehorse that reflected a different, specifically local racing tradition. When the American colonies eventually achieved their independence in the late eighteenth century, this specifically colonial horse and the specifically colonial horse culture that had spawned it helped the Americans to differentiate themselves from the British and thus contributed, if only in a small way, to the creation of a new national identity.[50]

A similar trajectory may be traced for the Peruvian Paso, a breed that was developed in response to conditions in colonial Peru. The Paso is a "gaited" horse, a term generally used to describe a horse that walks and canters just as non-gaited horses do but whose intermediate gait between these two is not the trot. In most cases, this intermediate gait is some form of amble, in which the horse's legs move in broken lateral pairs to create a smooth ride with a four-beat rhythm. The amble contrasts sharply with the trot, in which the legs move in diagonal pairs to create a highly stable but very jarring ride with a two-beat rhythm. During the Middle Ages, horses that ambled were greatly prized for general-purpose riding, because their smooth gait covered ground at a reasonable rate of speed while allowing the rider to travel in relative comfort. With the advent of wheeled travel and with the increasing popularity of racing and jumping in Western Europe from the seventeenth century on, however, the need for gaited horses declined. Trotting horses are more efficient at pulling vehicles than ambling horses, and amblers generally do not excel at racing or jumping. Trotting horses thus were privileged over gaited horses and ultimately became the norm, and the gaited riding-horse eventually disappeared almost entirely from Western Europe. In colonial Peru, on the other hand, different needs resulted in a different fate for the gaited horse. The Peruvian Paso, developed from as early as the sixteenth century, was based on Barb and Iberian stock—including horses that ambled—brought to Peru by the Spanish. These animals then were selectively bred to produce horses with comfortable gaits and a naturally long stride, both essential qualities in an area where long distances had to be covered and the only way to do so was on horseback. By the time other alternatives for traveling became routinely available in Peru, the Paso horse was firmly established as part of a specifically Peruvian culture and identity. Unlike its gaited European ancestors, the Peruvian Paso did not vanish when its practical usefulness declined, quite possibly because of its associations with colonial and, from 1824, national identity.[51]

The chapters in this section all show how notions about identity and self-definition shifted over time, whether their context was specific to a limited group circumscribed by social status and gender or concerned a much larger and more diverse group or even a nation. They each use horses and horsemanship as a lens through which to view a cultural process that was in many ways a reflection of much larger (and more thoroughly studied) military, political, economic, social, and cultural changes.

Karen Raber uses the arguments and illustrations in the mid-seventeenth-century work of William Cavendish, Duke of Newcastle, to show how horsemanship served as a means to create English national identity. Through gestures of containment, Cavendish establishes a specifically English form of *haute école*, which separates those who practice it from members of other nations and races. This English manège becomes the perfect way to infuse English culture with national and racial Other-ness without being colonized or dominated by it in turn.

Richard Nash's chapter presents the Thoroughbred, a breed developed by the English during the eighteenth century for a sport that enjoyed particular popularity in England, as a cultural metaphor. Nash argues that the myths associated with the development of this peculiarly English breed reflect similar attitudes and circumstances associated with the development of British national identity and that both the breed and the sport for which it was created therefore could serve in a number of pervasive cultural metaphors about the nature of Englishness.

Treva Tucker's chapter discusses the role of horsemanship in shaping the identity and self-definition of French noblemen from the mid-sixteenth to the mid-seventeenth century. Over that period, the nobility shifted from an essentially medieval warrior-knight identity to an early modern courtier–aristocrat one. Tucker argues that manège horsemanship, and in particular the dramatic "airs above the ground," facilitated this transition by allowing noblemen simultaneously to display both their martial qualities and their capacity for courtly grace and elegance.

Sandra Swart examines the sociocultural role of the horse in colonial Dutch South Africa from the late seventeenth through the nineteenth centuries. For the Boers, horses were the centerpiece of an identity that was masculine, martial, land-based, and distinct from that of their Dutch homeland. The breed developed by the Boers in response to their colonial environment, the Cape Horse, in particular reflected the development of a specifically settler identity that was independent of and different from that of the Dutch.

Finally, Donna Landry analyzes the "invention" and popularization of the "forward seat" on the English hunt field during the eighteenth century. The forward seat, whose shortened stirrups and forward position allowed the horse to move more freely, was transformed by English hunting riders into a discourse about "native" values of freedom and liberty. This seat became a metaphor for national cultural

superiority over those whose continental or dressage seat, with its long
stirrups, upright posture, and restricted motion, reflected their lack of
these values. Landry's chapter, while grounded in the early modern
world, points toward the continuing effect changes in the eighteenth
century had in the nineteenth and even the twentieth centuries.

*   *   *

From Europe to Russia and Africa, the chapters in this volume range
the globe in much the same way as did their equine subjects, and with
something of the same contingent irregularity. We nonetheless hope
that the volume will persuade readers of the force of one of our primary arguments: that a far more complete understanding of horses
and horsemanship and the roles they played is absolutely crucial to
our understanding of the early modern world. Our goal has been
both to reintroduce scholars to the significance of the horse during
the early modern period and to suggest future directions for criticism
and scholarship on the many and multifaceted domains in which it
had an impact. We also hope that this book will help to bridge at least
partially this gap in our knowledge of the early modern world and
perhaps will restore to its study some part of the crucial impact of
horse culture—an impact that seems somehow to have gotten lost in
the intervening centuries.

NOTES

1. William Shakespeare, *Richard III*, 5.4.13, in *Complete Works of Shakespeare*, ed. David Bevington (New York: Longman, 1997).
2. In the medieval and early modern periods, the terms "farrier" and "marshal" were used to refer both to those who today would be called veterinarians and to those who put shoes on horses—stilled called far-riers to this day.
3. If one includes only book-length treatments devoted entirely to horses in the early modern period and written in English by trained scholars within the last 30 years, the exceptions are rare indeed. They include Joan Thirsk, *Horses in Early Modern England: For Service, for Pleasure, for Power* (Reading, UK: University of Reading Press, 1978); Anthony Dent, *Horses in Shakespeare's England* (London: J.A. Allen, 1987); Peter Edwards, *The Horse Trade in Tudor and Stuart England* (Cambridge, UK: Cambridge University Press, 1988); Walter Liedtke, *The Royal Horse and Rider: Painting, Sculpture, and Horsemanship, 1500–1800* (New York: Abaris Books, 1989).
4. It is important to note that recent interest in human–animal studies takes as its target the problematically humanistic orientation of most criticism

of early modern "nature" (including animals that inhabit nature or those, such as the horse, that straddle the boundary between human culture and the natural world). Critics have become concerned with, and have attempted to remedy the "speciesism" of most such discussions, including many of the earlier sources cited here. Examples of this kind of work are found in *Representing Animals*, ed. Nigel Rothfels (Bloomington, IN: Indiana University Press, 2002), and in *At the Borders of the Human: Beasts, Bodies and Natural Philosophy in the Early Modern Period*, ed. Erica Fudge, Susan Wiseman, and Ruth Gilbert (New York: Palgrave Macmillan, 2002). While our work stresses the importance of the horse for human culture, we do acknowledge the value of opening up the debate over the theoretical position of our approach.

5. Liedtke, *The Royal Horse and Rider*, 14.

6. Dent, *Horses in Shakespeare's England*, 5.

7. A pastured horse requires more than an acre to sustain its nutritional needs. A horse that does not wish to be caught and that has a large space at its disposal can evade the person trying to catch it almost indefinitely, so simply getting one's hands on a pastured horse can be very time-consuming. A horse kept outside always is far dirtier than its stabled counterpart, thus requiring substantial grooming time before it is ready to be used. During the winter months, grooming time is increased by the fact that the horse grows a long, shaggy, greasy coat in order to protect it from the cold and the wet. A horse with a heavy winter coat sweats profusely when worked, so even on an ideal winter day, when the horse has refrained from festooning itself with mud, grooming the dried sweat from the previous day's work out of the horse's long coat requires a substantial amount of additional time and effort. Finally, in cold weather the horse kept outside requires special care after being worked. If the horse is not walked until its sweat has dried completely—called "cooling out"—but is returned to its pasture while still hot and sweating in cold, wet, or windy weather, the chances that it will get sick are quite good.

8. One reason horses were slow in replacing oxen as Europe's favorite farm animal was the cost of feeding them. Unlike bovine creatures, the horse when worked hard cannot maintain baseline health and fitness on hay or grass alone but requires a supplemental source of concentrated calories in the form of grain.

9. Although some women did ride during the early modern period, the vast majority of riders, owners, breeders, and trainers were men. We have therefore chosen to use masculine pronouns throughout this volume.

10. To "tack up" and "untack" a horse refers to the act of putting on and taking off its saddle and bridle—its "tack." If the horse were being readied to pull a vehicle, one would "harness" and "unharness" it instead.

11. Citing the *Equitium* accounts of Giles of Toulouse, R. H. C. Davis says, "Some idea of the running costs involved can be gained from the fact

that in 1315, when the daily wage of a skilled man was 4d., it cost between 6d. and 7d. a day to maintain one of the king's horses at Kennington Park near London"; see R. H. C. Davis, "The Medieval Warhorse," in *Horses in European Economic History*, ed. F. M. L. Thompson (Reading, UK: British Agricultural Society, 1983), 8. While these precise numbers certainly would not be applicable across time and place, they nonetheless offer at least some perspective on the costs of (admittedly very high-end) horse ownership in relation to the larger economy and to the ability (or not) of most people to support a horse.

12. Literally, the enclosed space in which the horse was schooled in the movements of the *haute école*, the precursor to modern dressage. See below for more on this type of horsemanship.

13. Job 39:19–25 (Revised Standard Version).

14. Quoted in Stuart Piggot, *Wagon, Chariot and Carriage: Symbol and Status in the History of Transport* (London: Thames and Hudson, 1992), 69. Ruffus, a Sicilian knight, served as farrier to Holy Roman Emperor Frederick II (emperor 1220–50; king of Naples and Sicily 1197–1250).

15. Quoted in Arthur Vernon, *The History and Romance of the Horse* (New York: Dover, 1974), 159.

16. Edmund Spenser, *The Faerie Queene*, ed. Thomas P. Roche (London: Penguin, 1987), II.V.46 and II.VI.2. For additional examples of texts, dating from antiquity to the present, that refer to the connections between horses and elite social status, see Paul Morand, *Anthologie de la littérature équestre* (Paris: Olivier Perrin, 1966), and Anthony Dent, *The Horse through Fifty Centuries of Civilization* (London: Phaidon, 1974).

17. Spenser's verb "ménage" has its roots in the French and Italian nouns for the school or arena in which the horse was trained in the *haute école*, the *manège* or *maneggio*. These terms also were employed as verbs to refer to the act of riding in such a space. In early modern English, we thus get not only "ménage" but also (and more commonly) "manage" as verbs describing the rider's interaction with his horse in this context. These terms do not imply management in the modern sense but refer instead to the training of the horse in the movements of the manège.

18. Important Italian contributions to the early literature include Cesare Fiaschi, *Trattato dell'imbrigliare, maneggiare, et ferrare cavalli* (1556), and Claudio Corte, *Il cavallarizzo* (1562). Fiaschi, a contemporary of Grisone's, also founded an important riding academy in Ferrara in the 1530s. A final key figure in this first generation of Italian horsemen was Gianbattista Pignatelli, a student of Fiaschi who subsequently established his own highly influential academy in Naples. Although Pignatelli appears to have left no treatise, he taught some of the most influential horsemen of what might be called the

second generation, including Salomon de la Broue and Antoine de Pluvinel (see n. 20) among numerous others.

19. The French preempted the Italians so thoroughly that the movements of dressage (itself a French word) are to this day rendered in French terminology rather than Italian.

20. A more complete version of Pluvinel's book appeared in 1625 under the title *L'Instruction du roy en l'exercice de monter à cheval*. The 1623 edition is prized for its magnificent plates, while the 1625 edition is considered to contain the more definitive text. Other important French contributions to the early literature include Salomon de la Broue, *Le Cavalerice françois*, part 1 (1602) and parts 2 and 3 (1608); René de Menou de Charnizay, *La Pratique du cavalier* (1612); Pierre de la Noue, *La Cavalerie françoise et italienne* (1620); Delcampe [no first name given], *L'Art de monter à cheval* (1658).

21. Cavendish actually had made an earlier contribution to the literature with a text written in French, *La Méthode et invention nouvelle de dresser les chevaux* (1657/58), but his later text was one of the first important original contributions written in English. Prior to Cavendish, English-language treatises on horsemanship tended to be inspired by earlier texts: Thomas Blundeville's ca. 1560 *Newe Book Containing the Arte of Ryding* was a translation and adaptation of Grisone; John Astley's 1584 *The Art of Riding* claimed to "interpret" the works of Xenophon and Grisone; Thomas Bedingfield's 1584 *The Art of Riding* was a translation and adaptation of Corte; Gervase Markham's numerous treatises, including *A Discourse of Horsemanshippe* (1593) and *Markham's Maister-peece or What Doth a Horse-man Lacke* (1610), also borrowed most of their material from previous authors.

22. Formally documented equine breeds as we know them today did not exist in Western Europe until fairly late in the early modern period. Contemporaries did refer, however, to certain types of horses (e.g., Barbs, Turks, Arabians, Spanish genets, Neapolitans, and so forth) in ways that implied that all (or most) horses in that group were believed to have certain common characteristics. For the sake of simplicity, such horse groups will be discussed in this introduction as breeds, even when that term technically may be anachronistic.

23. Davis, "The Medieval Warhorse," 8, estimates that at large establishments the services of one stablelad were required for every one to two horses.

24. Lucy Worsley and Tom Addyman, "Riding Houses and Horses: William Cavendish's Architecture for the Art of Horsemanship," *Architectural History* 45 (2002): 194–229; quote from 217. For evidence of a similar trend in seventeenth- and eighteenth-century France, see the magnificent volume, *Les Ecuries royales du XVIe au XVIIIe siècle*, ed. Daniel Roche (Paris: Association pour l'académie d'art équestre de Versailles, 1998). This collection includes several

essays on the stables of the French monarchy and of high-ranking French noblemen, as well as two essays on the stables of the English monarchs during the sixteenth and seventeenth centuries.

25. Quoted in Pia F. Cuneo, "Beauty and the Beast: Art and Science in Early Modern European Equine Imagery," *Journal of Early Modern History* 4 (2000): 269–321; quote from 269.

26. Quoted in Vernon, *The History and Romance of the Horse*, 157. In this bill, the breeding of "great horses" under 15 hands in height is prohibited. In mid-sixteenth-century England, the term "great horse" generally referred to a horse suitable for heavy cavalry service—a horse large and strong enough to carry an armored rider into battle. As for the height restriction, horses are measured in "hands," one hand being 4 inches; the measurement is made from the ground to the withers, the highest point of the horse's back, where the shoulder blades meet at the base of its neck. A 15-hand horse thus stands 60 inches at the withers.

27. Lisa Jardine and Jerry Brotton, *Global Interests: Renaissance Art between East and West* (Ithaca, NY: Cornell University Press, 2000), 145.

28. Jardine and Brotton, *Global Interests*, 149; see also 145–51 for a brief outline of horse trade negotiations between various early modern states, including Portugal, Spain, Italy, India, Persia, and the Ottoman empire.

29. Jardine and Brotton, *Global Interests*, 152–54. Henry and François exchanged among others coveted horses from the Mantuan stud whose "bloodstock was made up of Barbary and Arabian lines." Obtaining these horses became an increasing priority for both rulers, but especially for Henry. As early as 1514, the gift of horses from the Marquis of Mantua prompted Henry to say, "Had the marquis given him a kingdom he could not have been more delighted" (quotes from 152).

30. Karen Raber, " 'Reasonable Creatures': William Cavendish and the Art of Dressage," in *Renaissance Culture and the Everyday*, ed. Patricia Fumerton and Simon Hunt (Philadelphia: University of Pennsylvania Press, 1999), 42–66.

31. This shift from the dressage seat to the forward seat, why it happened first in England, and how that shift both shaped and reflected notions of a specifically English national identity are addressed in further detail in Ch. 12.

32. On the horse in European art from 1500 to 1800, without doubt the best single source is Liedtke's *The Royal Horse and Rider*; the book also covers, albeit in considerably less detail, classical and medieval equestrian art. Although the text is not entirely free of errors in terms of the history of horses and horsemanship, it is nonetheless quite good overall, and the number and quality of the images are priceless for anyone interested in this topic. Much of what follows relies on those images and, where noted, incorporates Liedtke's interpretation of them.

33. Roy Strong, *Van Dyck: Charles I on Horseback* (New York: Viking Press, 1972).

34. An interesting hybrid in equestrian art is the portrayal of riderless horses performing the movements of the *haute école*, in particular the airs above the ground. Clearly, these images are intended to signify the elite status of the owner of the horse portrayed and even could be read as saying something about his noble control *in absentia*, e.g., the horse is so well trained, obedient, and submissive that it performs even without its master's presence in the saddle. On the other hand, these images also begin to gesture toward the appreciation of the horse for its own sake. See Liedtke, *The Royal Horse and Rider*, 293, for one example from a series of six life-size equine portraits painted in 1700 by Johann Georg von Hamilton (1672–1737).

35. Liedtke, *The Royal Horse and Rider*, 83. He emphasizes the contributions to this genre from ca. 1650 onward of various Dutch painters, especially Thomas de Keyser and Aelbert Cuyp (80–83).

36. Liedtke, *The Royal Horse and Rider*, 85.

37. Liedtke notes that "post-Romantic" rulers still might be portrayed mounted, but their relationship with their horses is different. Horses in such portraits are at best sympathetic, often indifferent, and sometimes openly willful (*The Royal Horse and Rider*, 13).

38. Ken Keffer, "Riding out the Renaissance in Montaigne," *Romance Notes* 37 (1997): 339–45. According to Keffer, rational direction is exactly what Montaigne has trouble achieving in his writing. Like the wayward horse, the wayward writer seizes the opportunity for wandering off his path, defeating the bounds of strictly curbed narrative.

39. Liedtke, *The Royal Horse and Rider*, 14–16.

40. Liedtke suggests a corollary to this point: "The discipline, patience, and pride required to master the horsemanship of the *haute école* could not but have had some refining effect upon a courtier's character" (*The Royal Horse and Rider*, 13).

41. The work of Norbert Elias is seminal in this context. See *The Civilizing Process: The History of Manners*, trans. Edmund Jephcott (New York: Urizen, 1978; first published in 1939); *Power and Civility*, trans. Edmund Jephcott (New York: Pantheon, 1982; first published in 1939); *The Court Society*, trans. Edmund Jephcott (New York: Pantheon, 1984; first published in 1969, although written in the 1930s).

42. This list includes only the major players and could be expanded almost infinitely if we were to add all the rulers of smaller but nonetheless autonomous territories in areas such as Italy and Germany. A fascinating corollary to the royal equestrian portrait is the many paintings (but never monuments, it should be noted) of high-ranking noblemen. Outstanding examples include Velázquez's portrait of the Count-Duke Olivares (ca. 1636) and Rubens's portraits of the Duke of Lerma (1603) and the Duke of Buckingham (1627).

43. Liedtke devotes much of the second chapter of *The Royal Horse and Rider*, "Symbolic Themes in Equestrian Portraiture from 1550 to

1650," to the theme of riding ability as a metaphor for ruling ability, especially as manifested in depictions of rulers riding horses in *levade*.

44. Liedtke, *The Royal Horse and Rider*, 73. On page 79, he makes a similar juxtaposition between a statue of Louis XIV of France (1643–1715) executed at the very end of the seventeenth century and one of Peter the Great of Russia (1689–1725) executed in 1770. "Peter seems to ask the people for support. Louis commands it—or did, until the statue was destroyed in the Revolution."

45. Blundeville, *Fowre Chiefest Offices Belonging to Horsemanshippe* (London, 1566), 8.

46. In the seventeenth and eighteenth centuries, English topography changed in ways that impacted on the sport of hunting and ultimately led to the development of the sport of steeplechasing. During this period, England experienced both substantial deforestation and the enclosure of much agricultural land. The former changed hunting from a dense woodland activity to an open field activity, while the latter added obstacles between fields, which either had to be jumped or gone around. All of these changes combined to impact on the qualities deemed desirable in a hunter (the horse used for hunting). Qualities such as speed, stamina, and agility became increasingly important—all qualities that also were necessary in a racehorse or steeplechaser. See "The Legacy of the Horse: 1660–1840" (Lexington, KY: International Museum of the Horse, 1998), at http://www.imh.org/imh/kyhpl3b.html (accessed April 22, 2003).

47. Unsurprisingly, as time passed and notions of freedom and liberty became important beyond the confines of England, the English style of riding and forms of sport grew in popularity throughout Western Europe. It is, we believe, no accident that this occurred at the same time that Europe began to experience the first upheavals that would eventually undermine traditional monarchical government. Democracy and fast riding have something in common: both resist strict adherence to traditional forms; both involve liberty, setting free "natural" impulses, and an implicit rejection of boundaries for individuals. While one does not lead to or necessarily predict the other (Cossacks, after all, rode "freely" while coexisting with fairly repressive forms of government both internal and external to their immediate cultural group), in Western Europe they do seem to point to an emerging value system that can explain and bolster them both.

48. The Iberian breeds, most commonly known today as the Andalusian (Spain) and the Lusitano (Portugal), are not mentioned in this context because horses identified as coming from the Iberian peninsula are mentioned in sources that long predate the early modern period. The same may be said of the Friesian (from Friesland, in the northern Netherlands). This does not mean, however, that in a later context such ancient breeds could not satisfy a sense of national pride.

49. Breed histories were drawn from the websites "Horse Breeds of the World" (Lexington, KY: International Museum of the Horse, 1999–2002), at http://www.imh.org/imh/bw/home2.html; "Breeds of Livestock: Horses" (Stillwater, OK: Department of Animal Science, Oklahoma State University, 1995–2002), at http://www.ansi.okstate.edu/breeds/horses; "Breed Profile" (Lexington, KY: American Hanoverian Society, n.d.), at http://www.hanoverian.org/breed.htm; "The Breed" (Chicago: Oldenburg Registry North America, n.d.), at http://www.isroldenburg.org/Oldbg.htm; "The Trakehner Horse: A History" (Newark, OH: American Trakehner Association, 1998–2001), at http://www.americantrakehner.com/The%20Breed/history.htm (all accessed April 22, 2003).

50. On the history of the American Quarter Horse, see the websites "Horse Breeds of the World," "The Legacy of the Horse: 1660–1840," and "Breeds of Livestock: Horses." The first racecourse in America was created in 1668 in Long Island. It was two miles long, possibly due to topological factors: it was built on an existing plain rather than reclaimed from dense forest. The first recorded quarter-mile horserace was in 1674 in Virginia. Both long- and short-distance racing thus seem to have been very popular in the colonies; which type of racing, and thus which type of horse, dominated seems to have depended on local culture and on local geography. It would appear that racing in the northern colonies tended to follow the English pattern, while short-distance racing flourished in the southern regions; it was most popular in Virginia and North Carolina. The blending of bloodlines aimed specifically at producing a short-distance speed horse can be traced back to before the Revolutionary War. The biggest early influence on the development of the Quarter Horse was the English Thoroughbred stallion Janus (1746–80/81), imported into Virginia in 1756.

51. On the history of the Peruvian Paso, see the websites "Horse Breeds of the World" and "Breeds of Livestock: Horses."

PART I

POWER AND STATUS

CHAPTER 1

CULTURAL CONVERGENCE: THE EQUINE CONNECTION BETWEEN MUSCOVY AND EUROPE

Ann M. Kleimola

Is Russia Europe? The question divided the nineteenth-century Russian intelligentsia, and has returned to haunt the post-1991 society of the New Russians. Westerners who visited the Muscovite Russian state in the sixteenth and seventeenth centuries described a fascinating but alien place. By the late eighteenth century, however, Russian aristocrats living in the empire shaped by Peter the Great (1682–1725) and Catherine the Great (1762–96) inhabited a world increasingly like that of their European counterparts. Muscovite "horse culture" both contributed to this process of convergence and reflected its progress.

The economic and military significance of horses has received considerable scholarly attention, but the equine role in shaping the social and cultural parameters of elite society has been little remarked. In France the horse stood "at the center of aristocratic pleasures: the tournament, the hunt, the riding-school, pomp and ceremony."[1] The Renaissance courts of Italy and France set the tone in horseflesh as in other areas of cultural life. "To speak of horses was a pleasant and cultured thing to do like talking of books, paintings, and philosophy, and the most elegant of all was conversation about bloodlines and breeding."[2] In Muscovy elite life was perhaps even more centered on "horse culture" than was the case in the early modern West. The majority of Muscovite mounts, like the majority of horses more generally, were not distinguished by their size or beauty. Foreigners visiting Rus' in the sixteenth and seventeenth centuries found the Nogai and Russian horses notable only for stamina and hardiness. Their appraisals largely reprise the estimate of the Roman veterinary surgeon Vegetius Renatus centuries earlier regarding the horses of the Huns:

> For the purposes of war the Huns' horses are by far the most suitable, on account of their endurance, working capacity and their resistance to cold and hunger . . . one forgets the ugly appearance of these horses as this is set off by their fine qualities: their sober nature, cleverness and their ability to endure any injuries very well.[3]

The steeds of the elite, however, presented a sharp contrast.

The horse of choice for the Muscovite aristocracy was the *argamak*, a fine horse of Asiatic type usually acquired through Poland or Turkey.[4] The term is first recorded in the 1483 testament of the Muscovite aristocrat I. I. Saltyk, who instructed his executor (later a leading boyar) Mikhailo Rusalka Morozov personally to transfer this horse to Volk Ukhtomskii.[5] *Argamaki* served as valuable gifts prized by grand princes and abbots of monasteries, and may have been introduced as elegant saddle horses, although they are mentioned as warhorses from the second half of the sixteenth century.[6] Agents of Vasilii III (1505–33) bought *argamaki* in the steppe,[7] and one of the earliest foreign visitors to write about Muscovy, the Austrian diplomat Herberstein, after seeing *argamaki* from the Grand Prince's stable during a royal hunt in the 1520s, concluded that Vasilii III's horses "were better bred than the Turkish."[8] Ivan IV (1533–84) evidently shared his father's preference, putting *argamaki* at the top of his "wish list" when the Polish ruler Stephen Batory asked what Ivan would like in return for a gift of gerfalcons.[9] The horses were equally appreciated in Hungary and Poland, where they were often acquired as ransom for Turkish prisoners of war, and Eastern Europe became one of the sources of Russian *argamaki*. Isaac Massa, a Dutchman who was in Moscow in the early seventeenth century, witnessed the arrival of Marina Mniszek, the Polish bride of the first False Dmitrii, and was deeply impressed by the spectacle of the Polish cavalry accompanying her: "But what I could not admire enough were the magnificent horses on which they were mounted, cantering all the time and splendidly harnessed. Several of them had painted wings, so it appeared that these horses flew rather than walked. Most of them were from Hungary."[10]

The *argamak* was a luxury item. These horses set the standard of equine beauty, as reflected in the Russian iconography of Saints Florus and Laurus, patrons and protectors of horses. The horses depicted in the icons suggest the range of size and quality found in Muscovy, with *tabun* (Tatar for "herd") horses often resembling the tough, wiry, but unlovely steppe ponies; the mounts presented to the Archangel Michael, however, are usually large, handsome steeds with proud necks and leaping hooves, suitable for the head of the heavenly host.[11] Utility was another matter. Marcus Fugger, the German merchant banker and author of a sixteenth-century book on horse breeding, concluded that Turkish horses were not of much use to ordinary people, since they could not stand a cold and raw climate or deep roads.[12] Prices reflected the status attached to *argamak* ownership. In the seventeenth century the median price for all horses was roughly 4 rubles (prices rose at the rate of 0.219 percent per year), at a time when the average craftsman earned 4 kopeks per day and the price of a slave was 3 rubles.[13] The *argamaki*, however, were much more expensive. The French mercenary captain Margeret was not particularly impressed with the qualities of these horses, but noted the cost of owning a status symbol: "A very beautiful and good horse of Tartary or of Russia can be bought for twenty rubles. This horse will do more service than a Turkish *argamak* horse, which costs fifty, sixty, up to a hundred rubles."[14] Members of the Russian elite, however, had other priorities. When the boyar Prince M. V. Skopin Shuiskii handled the public sale of M. I. Tatishchev's estate in 1608, for example, he kept for himself the two horses appraised at the highest value, both *argamak* stallions, one with a Georgian brand and the other with a Lithuanian. Tatishchev had owned a Russian horse of good breeding, appraised at 30 rubles, but the Georgian *argamak* was valued at 65.[15] Prices for such horses remained high throughout the seventeenth century. While average horses went for 2–4 rubles, warhorses of European and Asiatic breeding were particularly expensive. A Turkish warhorse went for between 50–60 and 100 rubles, a Tatar mount for 20, a Bashkir for between 6 and 10.[16] In the late seventeenth century a Kizylbash (Persian) went for 100 rubles.[17]

Over the course of the sixteenth and seventeenth centuries the "stables section" (*koniushii put'*) of the royal household was transformed into the complex bureaucracy of the Stables Chancellery (*koniushennyi prikaz*), whose extensive staff handled equine matters of all sorts, ranging from the grooming of the ruler's mounts and organization of ceremonial events to the administration of lands set aside to support the growing horse establishment and the supervision of the horse trade. The staff grew from roughly 400 in the 1570s to about 700 a century later.[18] The value of goods and properties administered by the chancellery is shown, at least relatively, by the size of its losses during the Time of Troubles (1589–1613, a period of turmoil, foreign invasion and civil war). Looting in the capital in 1611–12 brought not only the theft of horses from the royal stables but also the disappearance of tack, sleighs, coaches, carriages, and other items and supplies, to a total value of 30,000 rubles.[19] Recovery from the Troubles led to resumed expansion, and in 1673 a new brick, two-storied building with a tower over the entrance gates and a covered staircase on the right-hand side leading up to the saddlery was erected to house the chancellery.[20]

The royal stables ran the largest breeding program in the country. Unfortunately documentation from before the seventeenth century is sparse and provides only hints. The testaments of the early Moscow princes, beginning with Ivan I Kalita (probably written about 1339), bequeath horses and horse herds to their heirs.[21] Later grand princes generalized, leaving to the heir "whatever is in the custody of my Master of Horse (*koniushii*)."[22] Ivan III perhaps had already established a breeding program at Khoroshevo, near Moscow, by the end of the fifteenth century.[23] "Presentation" horses from abroad (stallions from Austria, Turkish or Hungarian horses sent from Poland, Holstein horses, *argamaki* from Central Asia and Persia) enriched the breeding stock.[24] Aleksei Mikhailovich (1645–76) had a reputation as a horse fancier and received lavish gifts of stallions from his eastern neighbors. The list of stallions dispatched to the royal stud at Shekshovskaia in 1664 included Georgian and Kizylbash (Persian) as well as German horses and homebreds, and one of the stud horses at the royal stable at Kolomenskoe was described as a "light bay stallion with its mane on the left, bred by Shingirei, the Circassian *murza*."[25]

After the end of the Time of Troubles and election of the new Romanov dynasty in 1613, the traces of a planned royal breeding program become more evident. In the reign of Mikhail Fedorovich (1613–45) special breeding stables were established in royal towns, villages, and settlements to supply horses for the sovereign and his court. Rather than "stud farms" they were called "mares' stables" (*kobylich'i koniushni*), to set them apart from the *Argamak* and Great Stables (*argamach'i* and *bol'shiia koniushni*) in Moscow, which were occupied primarily by stallions. During the spring breeding season the best specimens of both *argamak* and drafthorse stallions were taken to the "mares' stables" (located in at least 13 villages and settlements in Mikhail's reign, with at least 16 more added in the following reign).

EQUINE CONNECTION OF MUSCOVY AND EUROPE   49

Some data indicate that by the mid-seventeenth century no fewer than 100 stud horses and 1,500 broodmares were being used each season.[26] Aleksei Mikhailovich was willing to pay for quality, as is evident from his ordering "the best solid-color stallions" from England at 300 rubles apiece.[27] By the end of Aleksei's reign in 1676, there were 1,829 head in the royal stable villages near Moscow.[28] Aleksei's son Fedor shared his father's passion for horses as well as his keen interest in falconry. During his brief reign he gave considerable attention to the stables, building a larger complex in Moscow and arranging inspections of the provincial studs, despite his sickliness and lack of strength for riding.[29]

The royal stables led the way, but other elements of Muscovite society were not far behind. Many West European studs were founded and owned by cloisters and monasteries. By the mid-to-late sixteenth century many Russian monasteries had likewise built substantial stables. The Iosif-Volokolamsk Monastery had 385 horses, and the prices the brethren were able to command for the relatively few horses that they sold would suggest that the animals were high-quality stock.[30] In the 1560s the Krasnokholmskii Anton'ev Monastery had an extensive stable from which the monks systematically sold horses and foals.[31] St. Cyril's Monastery in the Beloozero region had a large and well-differentiated stable complex by the beginning of the seventeenth century. The 1601 inventory lists a total of 1,086 head, including 619 mares, and growth continued thereafter. Unfortunately the monastery suffered devastating losses during the Time of Troubles, including, the monks estimated, 1,500 head, not counting animals commandeered for state service.[32] Horses came to play a larger part in the economy of the neighboring Spaso-Prilutskii Monastery near Vologda during the seventeenth century. The account book for 1637 lists "stallions, warhorses, *argamaki*, and geldings, 'great' horses and workhorses and broodmares and young horses, colts and fillies, four-year-olds, three-year-olds, two-year-olds, and yearlings," a total of 179 head. When taken together with the stock in the monastery's villages, there had been a four-fold increase since the low point during the Time of Troubles.[33] Inventories from the mid-seventeenth and beginning of the eighteenth centuries record that the Trinity–Sergius Monastery near Moscow had two stable complexes near the monastery, one housing between 130 and 145 riding-horses belonging to the monastery and to guests, the other holding between 237 and 286 workhorses. In addition the monastery had stable complexes in three nearby villages to accommodate its breeding stock, which in 1701 consisted of 377 head including colts and broodmares with foals.[34]

Monastic stables also benefited from the donations of lay patrons. Muscovites who wished to enter religious life or provide eternal prayers for themselves or relatives frequently included horses, along with money, land, and various precious objects, in their donations. Over the years the Holy Trinity–St. Sergius Monastery, for example, received numerous valuable additions to its stables: a new entrant donated an *argamak* worth 40 rubles; a contribution for memorial prayers included 54 horses, among them 24 mares, valued at 189 rubles; a gift of 5 horses included a German stallion and an *argamak* mare; another donation brought 2 German stallions worth 200 rubles and 19 German and Caucasian mares valued at 500 rubles.[35] The stream of donated mounts varied in quality and breeding, but helped build monastic equine stock.

The royal breeding program, however, had its most direct impact upon members of the Moscow elite. Even in the sixteenth century the presence of stables was one of the elements that set a landlord's residence apart from those of his peasants.[36] In the first half of the seventeenth century the stables complex on a country estate usually consisted of several structures, including grooms' quarters, barns, feeding pens for daytime use, stalls, sheds, granaries, and haylofts.[37] Similar arrangements are found for the second half of the century.[38] Some members of the Muscovite elite built substantial private stables including *argamaki*, drafthorses, and driving-horses for sleighs, and were paying considerable attention to their stock, including keeping registers of the animals at various villages that detail the color, age, and particular markings of each.[39] The immense holdings of boyar B. I. Morozov, one of the wealthiest Muscovite aristocrats in the mid-seventeenth century, included 7 stud farms and 13 livestock stables, and he wrote to his stewards personally to inquire about horses or give specific instructions regarding care and treatment.[40] Elite landholders, like the rulers, employed special personnel to look after the livestock on their properties. Grooms frequently handled administrative and supervisory activities, and provided a pool from which stewards and other agents were recruited.[41]

Horse ownership, breeding, and participation in equine-dependent activities played an integral role in the emergence of aristocratic "society" in sixteenth- and seventeenth-century Muscovy, closely tied to the development of the estate culture that came to dominate the imperial Russian landscape in the eighteenth and nineteenth centuries.[42] Country lodges, especially for hunting, had always been valued possessions of the Muscovite elite, even more so if they were located near a royal residence and enabled the holder to attend the monarch during his "amusements." After 1564 members of Ivan IV's short-lived special corps of trusted servitors, the Oprichniki, followed in the tradition of the boyar clans and established lodges of their own in the countryside around the capital. The German Oprichnik Heinrich von Staden, for example, acquired the village of Spitsyno, a mile from Moscow, "for recreation"; as he explained in his account of his Russian experiences, "I kept horses in this village so I would have them on hand when I needed them."[43] These estates provided a relaxed atmosphere in which the elite could gather and converse at leisure—about horses and breeding, among other things.

During the second half of the seventeenth century the "country estate loses its utilitarian purpose and gains its showplace role."[44] A few holdings—such royal villages as Izmailovo and Kolomenskoe, and the residential estates of some aristocrats—gained such foreign elements as European-style gardens, ponds and fountains, gazebos and walks, and beds of tulips and peonies.[45] By the 1680s the leading representative of the new elite lifestyle was Prince V. V. Golitsyn, a close advisor and favorite of Peter the Great's half-sister, the regent Sofiia, until she fell from power in 1689. One of the consuming interests of the Golitsyns, both Vasilii and his son Aleksei, was their stables. At Spasskoe, evidently one of his stud farms, Golitsyn kept 3 stallions and 2 warhorses along with a herd of 24 mares. He owned a variety of breeds—*argamaki*, German and Kabardinian and Polish horses, and possibly even Lipizzaner.[46] Medvedkovo, with its luxurious buildings, "reflects his desire for comfortable living."[47]

Between the mid-sixteenth and mid-seventeenth centuries Muscovy changed significantly, even in the area of horse gear. The early foreign visitors were struck by the contrasts between Russian and West European tack, remarking particularly on the relative simplicity and utility of Muscovy's unshod horses, "simple bits," small saddles, and preference for whips rather than spurs.[48] The so-called Hussar (*gusarskii*) saddles, probably Hungarian in origin, had appeared in Moscow by 1600, if not earlier, when they were included among the gifts brought by a Polish diplomatic mission. The Russian version of these saddles had much in common with those used in Western Europe, and the new equipment came into more general use with the Muscovite military reforms of the mid-seventeenth century and the development of a Western-style cavalry.[49] By the time Olearius, secretary to embassies from the Duke of Holstein to Muscovy, arrived in the 1630s the Russians had become more familiar with foreign styles and had acquired some items for their own use. Tack held by the Stables Chancellery included West European and Turkish

equipment.[50] Members of the Moscow elite had access to a variety of
equipment and apparently enjoyed displaying as much of it as possible.
By the late seventeenth century horse tack even formed part of dowries.
In 1687, for example, the dowry of Anna Kondrat'evna Zagriazhskaia,
who was engaged to Prince Petr Ivanovich Khovanskii, included in
addition to landed property, clothing, jewelry, books, and household
goods a carriage, two grooms, a saddle with niello and silver gilt
adornment, bridles and headstalls decorated with rubies and emeralds
on gold braid and Turkish niello work, and a silver curb-bit.[51]

Proper display of this finery required appropriately impressive
mounts, and Russian aristocrats acquired them in substantial numbers.
Elegant horses fit the elite lifestyle Olearius observed in the 1630s.
Baron Mayerberg, envoy of the Austrian Emperor in the
mid-seventeenth century, likewise noted that members of the
Muscovite elite had no shortage of Persian horses, which they decked
out in the most stylish tack and rode to any sort of public event.[52] The
Stables Chancellery played a crucial role in the two types of festivities
most frequently described by foreign observers, the reception of
diplomatic embassies and the occasion of royal processions. Its staff
had to provide the requisite mounts, vehicles, and attendants, properly
equipped; it had to line up the participants, and then coordinate the
movements of the various units. But however complicated the event,
horses were central to the production. And by all accounts the staging
of public spectacles was an activity at which the Muscovites excelled.[53]

In the realm of "horse culture" the worlds of the European and the
Muscovite elites were rapidly converging in the early modern period.
The Russians' stables appear comparable in size to those of their
English contemporaries. Henry VIII and Elizabeth I had between 100
and 300 trained horses at any time, while aristocrats had from 80 to
100.[54] Tsar Aleksei Mikhailovich in the mid-seventeenth century had
about 150 horses in the royal stables for riding and carriage use, about
50 for the coaches and sleighs of the royal ladies, and about 100 for the
use of ambassadors and for presentation as gifts.[55] In
mid-century the stables of boyar Boris Morozov at just one of his
villages, Kotel'niki near Moscow, had 48 horses.[56] Members of elite
society in Muscovy and Europe were increasingly looking for the same
qualities in a horse. One facet of the so-called military revolution was
the development of new cavalry techniques that shifted emphasis from
weight and size to speed and mobility. To meet changing needs,
European breeders turned to Eastern and North African stock (Arabs,
Turks, Barbs).[57] In large measure they were looking for horses with
qualities already long prized in Muscovy. On another question, riding

geldings, West moved toward East much more slowly. The Russians, like contemporary Tatars, Turks, and Hungarians, rode almost exclusively geldings on campaign. This was in sharp contrast to prevailing European practice at the beginning of the early modern period, when the stallion was considered the only suitable mount for a warrior. But European views were changing, and the advantages of riding geldings came to be recognized by an ever-growing segment of elite "horse people."[58]

The "great advances made in veterinary medicine and surgery, and the rediscovery of Xenophon's short but powerful tract *Hippike* (On Horsemanship)" were the two developments of the Renaissance that concerned horses most directly.[59] Both of these areas mark additional points of convergence between Europe and Russia. Muscovites were exposed to the new ideas through Polish and German intermediaries, in much the same way that they came into contact with other aspects of Westernization. Traditionally, Muscovite veterinary practitioners, like those of the West, were farriers who learned their craft through experience and contact with others who had a reputation for special skill. But Russians were becoming interested in more academic sources of assistance. The government's Apothecary Chancellery, established in 1581, introduced European physicians and medicines, initially operating narrowly within the parameters of the court, but gradually expanding its range of services. As early as 1629 it was supplying medicinal substances to the royal stables for treating horses. Medicaments for equine use included fenugreek, laurel oil, oak-gall, alum, green vitriol, turpentine, wax, white vitriol, camphor, popolium (*unguentum popoleum*, a narcotic salve made from poplar buds), asafoetida, and deer tallow.[60] By the late seventeenth century Muscovites were also coming into contact with Western veterinary medicine through translations into Russian from Polish and German sources. V. V. Golitsyn, Sofiia's favorite who was among the best educated members of the Moscow elite, had a substantial library including a medical advice manual for the treatment of horses (*konskii lechebnik*).[61] A. S. Matveev, the noted Westernizer and close associate of Tsar Aleksei Mikhailovich, also had a "horse manual" (*konskaia kniga*) in his personal library.[62] Surviving manuscript copies of a number of translated manuals from the late seventeenth and the eighteenth centuries attest to significant interest in European veterinary medicine.[63]

Such influences likewise contributed to a growing appreciation among the Muscovite elite for the aristocratic equine activities of dressage and coaching. In the mid-seventeenth century the Austrian envoy Mayerberg was impressed with the quality of Russian horses and the "showiness" of turned-out riders, but found equestrian technique sadly lacking. Muscovites had no riding masters (*bereitors*) and "neither horse nor rider was acquainted with the beautiful, or trained, steps."[64] In the 1670s and 1680s, however, probably directly connected first with Tsar Aleksei's and then with his son Fedor's even more passionate enthusiasm for horses, Muscovite courtiers took up riding in the European style. Taras, son of Elisei Poskochin, gained a reputation as a riding master.[65] Instruction manuals from abroad became available in Russian. Xenophon reached Muscovy, at least in modified form, in *Gippika*, a treatise dedicated to the "military reader," translated from Polish.[66] Russians could study the art of horsemanship in Pluvinel's *Le Maneige royal*, translated as *Korolevskaia ezdnaia shkola* in 1670 from a 1653 German version of the 1623 French original.[67]

During the seventeenth century new pursuits among the elite were extending the "social utility" of horses in recreation and leisure activities. Hunting and hawking had long been aristocratic pastimes in Russia as well as Europe.[68] The Russian elite began to take up dressage. Coaching rapidly gained great popularity, as reflected in the Kremlin Armory Museum's large collection of sixteenth- and seventeenth-century coaches and carriages. Late-seventeenth-century inventories of the Stables Chancellery record English, Polish, German, and Dutch carriages as well as many of Russian workmanship manufactured by the court master craftsmen. The Russian rulers received carriages as gifts from West European rulers, and in the 1660s the tsar sent 2 carriages made in the Stables Chancellery and 16 carriage-horses among other presents with an embassy to Iran.[69] When M. I. Tatishchev's property was confiscated in 1608, he had a single carriage that "must have been a cheap, worn-out thing with wheels." In contrast, Golitsyn's confiscated property, lost to the crown after the overthrow of Sofiia in 1689, included 20 carriages, one of which, valued at 500 rubles, was described as a

> large gilt carved Northern European carriage, upholstered in black leather along the windows, with large panes of glass in the windows and doors. Along the panes were red silken, braided tassels. Inside, the carriage was upholstered with red velvet and gold edging. . . . [Inside] it was upholstered with braided lace and had merlons and tassels of scarlet silk and gold. . . .[70]

Golitsyn had the most luxurious conveyances in Moscow, but his enthusiasm for driving was not unique. By the late seventeenth century the streets of Moscow could not handle the growing traffic, and a decree of 1682 limited the use of coaches to people from the higher levels of society, and even they were restricted to two horses on weekdays and four on holidays.[71] Apparently the decree was a response to the growing popularity of "competitive coaching" in Moscow society.

Interest in selective breeding for specific purposes was clearly widespread in Russia by the early eighteenth century. The royal stud at Bronnitsy, southeast of Moscow, specialized in breeding horses intended for pleasure and dressage. Considerable attention was given to bloodlines, and the stables produced horses of several breeds (Arab, Spanish, English, Persian, Italian, Circassian, and Kabardinian).[72] And the Russian Enlightenment produced the man who "put Russia on the map" in the horse world, Count A. G. Orlov-Chesmenski (1737– 1807). Orlov had long thought about setting up a breeding stable, but his military career precluded such activities. While commanding the Russian fleet in the Mediterranean during the Russo-Turkish War (1768–74), he acquired not only his sobriquet as the victor at Chesme but also a number of excellent Arab horses, including the silver gray stallion Smetanka, purchased in Arabia for the fantastic sum of 60,000 rubles. As his family lost favor at court, Orlov retired from service and settled in Moscow. In addition to the Arabs he had acquired in the Mediterranean, he also purchased almost a hundred English horses, including offspring of Derby and St. Leger winners. He admired the Arabs and the famed English racehorses of the day for much the same qualities that his Muscovite predecessors had prized in the *argamaki*. The goal of his breeding program was to produce strong trotters that could handle the great distances of the Russian Empire and still be winners on the racetrack. He succeeded so rapidly that he astonished the English, the preeminent breeders of the period. Crossing Arab with Danish and Dutch bloodlines, in 1784 he produced Bars I, foundation sire of the breed that soon brought the Russian Empire international acclaim. Thus, during the same century in which the Thoroughbred was being developed in England, he created the Orlov, the breed that became the dominant trotter in the world down to 1900.[73]

Interest in equine matters provided a common ground for members of the elite, whether Russian or European. The increased attention focused on both royal and aristocratic stables in the decades before Peter the Great's reign paved the way for the rapid adoption of Westernized equestrian practices in the eighteenth century. Clearly the horse world was a matter of greater interest to a majority of the Muscovite elite than many of the more elevated tastes usually discussed in connection with cultural Westernization in early modern Rus'. It was also an area in which Russian society "took off" very quickly. Despite a relatively late start and unfavorable geographic and climatic conditions, the "horse world" was one in which the Russian Empire rapidly gained a competitive edge. The foundations for this achievement, however, were firmly laid during the Muscovite period.

NOTES

1. Jacques Mulliez, *Les Chevaux du royaume: Histoire de l'élevage du cheval et de la création des haras* (Paris: Montalba, 1983), 8.
2. Luigi Gianoli, *Horses and Horsemanship through the Ages*, trans. Iris Brooks (New York: Crown Publishers, 1969), 95.
3. Quoted in S. Bökönyi, *History of Domestic Mammals in Central and Eastern Europe* (Budapest: Akadémiai Kiadó, 1974), 267–68. For the comments of foreign observers in Muscovy, see Sigmund von Herberstein, *Description of Moscow and Muscovy*, ed. Bertold Picard, trans. J. B. C. Grundy (London: Dent, 1969), 76; Jacques Margeret, *The Russian Empire and Grand Duchy of Muscovy: A 17th-Century French Account*, trans. and ed. Chester S. L. Dunning (Pittsburgh, PA: University of Pittsburgh Press, 1983), 47–48; Adam Olearius, *The Travels of Olearius in 17th-Century Russia*, trans. and ed. Samuel H. Baron (Stanford, CA: Stanford University Press, 1967), 330.
4. G. F. Odintsov, *Iz istorii gippologicheskoi leksiki v russkom iazyke* (Moscow: Nauka, 1980), 31; D. Ia. Gurevich and G. T. Rogalev, *Slovar'-spravochnik po konevodstvu i konnomu sportu* (Moscow: Rosagropromizdat, 1991), 12; see the illustration of "an *argamak* from the Tsar's Stables," in Nikolai Kutepov, *Velikokniazheskaia i tsarskaia okhota na Rusi s X po XVI vek*, 2nd edn. (St. Petersburg: Ekspeditsiia zagotovelniia gos. bumag 1896), after 174. "Argamak," a Tatar word, was used in old Russian as a collective term for purebred Eastern horses (as distinct from "nemetskii" or "German," which referred to horses from Western Europe; the term originally meant "dumb" or "mute" and so may refer to any and all non-Russian speakers). By the 1400s *argamaki* were being treated as a distinct breed. References to Tatar, Polish, and Turkish *argamaki* suggest that they were also being bred elsewhere, and traded back into Russia.
5. *Akty iuridicheskie, ili sobranie form starinnago deloproizvodstva, izdany Arkheograficheskoiu Kommissieiu* (St. Petersburg: Tipografiia II-go otdeleniia Sobstvennoi E. I. V. Kantselarii, 1838), no. 413.
6. Odintsov, *Iz istorii gippologicheskoi leksiki*, 105–6.
7. *Sbornik Imperatorskago russkago istoricheskago obshchestva* 95 (St. Petersburg: Obshchestvo, 1895), no. 2 (1508).
8. Herberstein, *Description of Moscow and Muscovy*, 69.

9. N. Zeziulinskii, *Istoricheskoe izsledovanie o konnozavodskom dele v Rossii*, I (St. Petersburg: Tipo-lit. Iu. Ia. Rimana, 1889), appendices to ch. III, no. 1.

10. Isaac Massa, *A Short History of the Beginnings and Origins of These Present Wars in Moscow under the Reign of Various Sovereigns down to the Year 1610*, trans. and ed. G. Edward Orchard (Toronto: University of Toronto Press, 1982), 128–29; Miklós Jankovich, *They Rode into Europe: The Fruitful Exchange in the Arts of Horsemanship between East and West*, trans. Anthony Dent (London: Harrap, 1971), 94–97, 158. Seventeenth-century engravings of Polish hussar officers with wings attached to their saddles are reproduced in Jan K. Ostrowski, Thomas Dacosta Kaufmann, and the Walters Art Gallery, *Land of the Winged Horsemen: Art in Poland, 1572–1764* (Alexandria, VA: Art Services International, in association with Yale University Press, 1999), 72–73. The False Dmitri appeared after the death of the "real" Dmitri, youngest son of Ivan the Terrible, and Fedor, Dmitri's half-brother, to challenge the rule of Boris Godunov; he was killed in a coup in May 1606.

11. For illustrations, see the striking icons of Novgorod masters from the late fifteenth and sixteenth centuries. The portrayal of horses in later icons reflects the growing popularity among the elite of larger, heavier West European breeds. On the cult of the horse guardians, see Ann M. Kleimola, "Visions of Horses: The Evolution of the Russian Cult of Florus and Laurus," *Mesto Rossii v Evrazii/The Place of Russia in Eurasia*, Ruszisztikai Könyvek vol. IX (Budapest: Eötvös Loránd University, 2001), 86–95. Although there are no written records to confirm that the horses depicted in the icons are *argamaki*, I believe they most likely are: the icons clearly show a difference between the saints' steeds and the more common *tabun* horses.

12. Daphne Machin Goodall, *A History of Horse Breeding* (London: Robert Hale, 1977), 204.

13. There are 100 kopeks to the ruble. On horse prices in the seventeenth century, see Richard Hellie, *The Economy and Material Culture of Russia 1600–1725* (Chicago and London: University of Chicago Press, 1999), 40–45, 574–78.

14. Margeret, *Russian Empire*, 48.

15. "Opis' i prodazha s publicnago torga ostavshagosia imeniia po ubienii narodom obvinennago v izmene Mikhaila Tatishcheva vo 116 godu," *Vremennik Obshchestva istorii i drevnostei rossiiskikh pri Moskovskom universitete* 8 (Moscow: Universitetskaia tipografiia, 1850), 24.

16. L. N. Vdovina, "Zemledelie i skotovodstvo," in *Ocherki russkoi kul'tury XVII veka*, pt. I (Moscow: Izdatel'stvo Moskovskogo universiteta, 1979), 54.

17. Odintsov, *Iz istorii gippologicheskoi leksiki*, 178, 183.

58   Ann M. Kleimola

18. cf. A. A. Zimin, "O slozhenii prikaznoi sistemy na Rusi," *Doklady i soobshcheniia instituta istorii AN SSSR* 3 (1954): 166–67, and Grigorii Kotoshikhin, *O Rossii v tsarstvovanie Alekseia Mikhailovicha*, 4th edn. (St. Petersburg: Izd. Imp. Arkheograficheskoi kommissii, 1906), ch. VI; Zeziulinskii, *Istoricheskoe izsledovanie*, I, 64–68; M. M. Denisova, "Koniushennaia kazna," in *Gosudarstvennaia oruzheinaia palata moskovskogo kremlia* (Moscow: Iskusstvo, 1954), 250–51; *Gosudarstvennaia oruzheinaia palata* (Moscow: Sovetskii khudozhnik, 1988), 373–74. By 1666 the Saddle Treasury maintained a separate branch at the *Argamak* Stables to handle the sovereign's excursions and campaign transport; Rossiiskii Gosudarstvennyi Arkhiv Drevnykh Aktov, f. 396, op. 1, d. 10504, l. 2.

19. *Russkaia istoricheskaia biblioteka*, II (St. Petersburg: Pechatnia V. I. Golovina, 1875), no. 95, col. 231.

20. Denisova, "Koniushennaia kazna," 252–53. The building was demolished in 1848 and replaced in 1851 with the Armory.

21. *Dukhovnye i dogovornye gramoty velikikh i udel'nykh kniazei XIV–XVI vv.*, ed. L. V. Cherepnin and S. V. Bakhrushin (Moscow–Leningrad: Izdatel'stvo Akademii Nauk SSSR, 1950), nos. 1 (Ivan Kalita), 3 (Semen), 4 (Ivan II), 8, and 12 (Dmitrii Donskoi).

22. For example, the will of Ivan III (1462–1505); *Dukhovnye i dogovornye gramoty*, no. 89.

23. I. Merder, *Istoricheskii ocherk russkago konevodstva i konnozavodstva* (St. Petersburg: Tipografiia E. Metsiga, 1868), 22; E. V. Kozhevnikov and D. Ia. Gurevich, *Otechestvennoe konevodstvo* (Moscow: Agropromizdat, 1990), 14.

24. *Pamiatniki diplomaticheskikh snoshenii Drevnei Rossii s derzhavami inostrannymi*, II (St. Petersburg: v Tip. II-go Otdeleniia Sobstvennoi E. I. V. Kantseliarii, 1852), 518; N. M. Karamzin, *Istoriia gosudarstva rossiiskago* (St. Petersburg: v. Tip. Imperatorskoi akademii nauk, 1842), XI, 79; Massa, *Short History*, 49; Zeziulinskii, *Istoricheskoe izsledovanie* I, 37 (n. 2) and appendices to ch. V, no. 5.

25. Zeziulinskii, *Istoricheskoe izsledovanie*, I, 44–46.

26. Zeziulinskii, *Istoricheskoe izsledovanie*, I, 31 (and n. 2), 32–45; M. E. Lobashev, *Ocherki po istorii russkogo zhivotnovodstva* (Moscow–Leningrad: Izdatel'stvo Akademii Nauk SSSR, 1954), 28.

27. Vdovina, "Zemledelie i skotovodstvo," 54; A. I. Zaozerskii, *Tsarskaia votchina XVII v.* (Moscow: Sotsekgiz, 1937), 114.

28. E. I. Indova, "Dvortsovoe zhivotnovodstvo v pervoi polovine XVIII v.," *Materialy po istorii sel'skogo khoziaistva i krest'ianstva SSSR*, V (Moscow: Nauka, 1962), 105.

29. Zeziulinskii, *Istoricheskoe izsledovanie*, I, 59–60, and appendices to ch. VI, nos. 4 and 5.

30. M. N. Tikhomirov, "Monastyr'-votchinnik XVI v.," *Istoricheskie zapiski* 3 (1938), 139–41.

31. N. A. Gorskaia, "Zemledelie i skotovodstvo," in *Ocherki russkoi kul'tury XVI veka*, pt. I (Moscow: Izdatel'stvo Moskovskogo universiteta, 1977), 92 n. 267; *Materialy po istorii krest'ian v russkom gosudarstve XVI veka*, ed. A. G. Man'kov (Leningrad: Izdatel'stvo Leningradskogo universiteta, 1955), nos. 3, 5, and 8.

32. Nikolai Nikol'skii, *Kirillo-Belozerskii monastyr' i ego ustroistvo do vtoroi chetverti XVII veka (1397–1625)*, vol. I, pt. 1 (St. Petersburg: Sinodal'naia tip., 1897), 265–68, appendix 6 (pp. LXXXV–XC), and pt. 2 (St. Petersburg: Sinodal'naia tip., 1910), 107 and n. 1.

33. A. S. Prokof'eva, *Votchinnoe khoziaistvo v XVII veke* (Moscow–Leningrad: Izdatel'stvo Akademii Nauk SSSR, 1959), 9, 25–28.

34. K. A. Filimonov, "Iz istorii koniushennogo khoziaistva Troitse-Sergievoi lavry XV–XIX vv.," *Trudy po istorii Troitse-Sergievoi lavry* (Sergiev-Posad: Izdatel'skii dom "Podkova," 1998), 113.

35. E. N. Klitina, T. N. Manushina, and T. V. Nikolaeva (eds.), *Vkladnaia kniga Troitse-Sergieva monastyria* (Moscow: Nauka, 1987), 59, 68, 88, 110, 139.

36. V. I. Kuznetsov, "Dvorianskaia usad'ba v strukture sel'skikh poselenii rossiiskogo gosudarstva XVI–XVII vv." *Vestnik moskovskogo universiteta*, Seriia 8, Istoriia, no. 6 (1989), 53.

37. V. D. Nazarov and Iu. A. Tikhonov, "Pomeshchich'e imenie v Rossii v pervoi polovine XVII v. (Osnovnye demograficheskie i khoziaistvennye cherty)," *Ezhegodnik po agrarnoi istorii vostochnoi Evropy 1971 g.* (Vilnius: Izdatel'stvo Mintic, 1974), 72.

38. Iu. A. Tikhonov, "Podmoskovnye imeniia russkoi aristokratii vo vtoroi polovine XVII–nachale XVIII v.," in *Dvorianstvo i krepostnoi stroi Rossii XVI–XVIII vv.* (Moscow: Nauka, 1975), 140–41, 146–47, 149–51, 154–55; *Rozysknyia dela o Fedore Shaklovitom i ego soobshchnikakh*, IV (St. Petersburg: Izd. Arkheograficheskoi kommissii, 1893), col. 347.

39. See, for example, A. A. Vvedenskii, *Torgovyi dom XVI–XVII vekov* (Leningrad: kn-vo "Put' k znaniiu," 1924), 30–31, 45, 47–48, 50; Nazarov and Tikhonov, "Pomeshchich'e imenie," 76 and n. 36; *Akty khoziaistva boiarina B. I. Morozova*, ed. A. I. Iakovlev, pt. I (Moscow–Leningrad: Izdatel'stvo Akademii Nauk SSSR, 1940), no. 74, and pt. II (Moscow–Leningrad: Izdatel'stvo Akademii Nauk SSSR, 1945), nos. 331, 421, 536.

40. D. I. Petrikeev, "Zemel'nye vladeniia boiarina B. I. Morozova," *Istoricheskie zapiski* 21 (1947), 65; *Akty khoziaistva B. I. Morozova*, pt. II, nos. 230, 254, 286, 306, 331.

41. See Nazarov and Tikhonov, "Pomeshchich'e imenie," 67–69; A. A. Zimin, "Khoziaistvennyi god v s. Pavlovskom (seredina XVII v.)," *Materialy po istorii sel'skogo khoziaistva i krest'ianstva SSSR*, VI (Moscow: Nauka, 1965), 68–69; *Kniga kliuchei i dolgovaia kniga Volokolamskogo monastyria* (Moscow–Leningrad: Izdatel'stvo Akademii

Nauk SSSR, 1948), 14, 16 ff.; "Rospis' vsiakim veshcham, den'gam i zapasam, chto ostalos' po smerti boiarina Nikity Ivanovicha Romanova," *Chteniia v Imperatorskom obshchestve istorii i drevnosti rossiiskikh pri Moskovskom universitete*, bk. III (1887), 34–35.

42. On estate culture see Priscilla Roosevelt, *Life on the Russian Country Estate: A Social and Cultural History* (New Haven, CT: Yale University Press, 1995).

43. Heinrich von Staden, *The Land and Government of Muscovy*, trans. and ed. Thomas Esper (Stanford, CA: Stanford University Press, 1967), 115.

44. Kuznetsov, "Dvorianskaia usad'ba," 53–54.

45. D. S. Likhachev, *Poeziia sadov: K semantike sadovo-parkovykh stilei— Sad kak tekst*, 2nd edn. (St. Petersburg: Nauka, 1991), 110–26.

46. A. A. Stepanov, "Kniaz' V. V. Golitsyn kak khoziain-votchinnik," *Doklady Akademii Nauk SSSR* (1926), 45–48; Lindsey A. J. Hughes, *Russia and the West, the Life of a Seventeenth-Century Westernizer, Prince Vasily Vasil'evich Golitsyn (1643–1714)* (Newtonville, MA: Oriental Research Partners, 1984), 5, 12; Tikhonov, "Podmoskovnye imeniia," 146–51; *Rozysknyia dela o Fedore Shaklovitom i ego soobshchnikakh*, III (St. Petersburg: Izd. Arkheograficheskoi kommissii, 1888), nos. 24, 29. The text (no. 24) refers to *tsesarskii* and *imeretinskii*, both of which indicate "imperial"—in Europe the "Emperor's" breed referred to horses from the stud of the Holy Roman Emperor at Lipizza, established in 1580; see R. H. C. Davis, *The Medieval Warhorse: Origin, Development and Redevelopment* (London: Thames and Hudson Inc., 1989), 121.

47. Tikhonov, "Podmoskovnye imeniia," 149–50.

48. Herberstein, *Description of Moscow and Muscovy*, 76, 78; Lloyd E. Berry and Robert O. Crummey (eds.), *Rude and Barbarous Kingdom: Russia in the Accounts of Sixteenth-Century English Voyagers* (Madison: University of Wisconsin, 1968), 71, 76, 82.

49. Denisova, "Koniushennaia kazna," 259, 290–91; Jankovich, *They Rode into Europe*, 97–100; *Nyeregbe! In the Saddle! Exhibition at the Museum of Ethnography 22 March–10 September 2002* (Budapest: Néprajzi Múzeum, 2002), 84–85; Ostrowski et al., *Land of the Winged Horsemen*, plates 71–74. On the origins of the hussars, see Gyula Rázsó, "The Mercenary Army of King Matthias Corvinus," in *From Hunyadi to Rákóczi: War and Society in Late Medieval and Early Modern Hungary*, ed. János M. Bak and Béla K. Király (Brooklyn, NY: Brooklyn College Press, 1982), 125–40.

50. Gift horses from abroad usually came well-dressed in expensive saddles, jeweled headstalls, and the like. Both horses and tack, after their "presentation" to the ruler, were immediately appraised and handed over to the Stables Chancellery; Denisova, "Koniushennaia kazna," 276. An early eighteenth-century inventory of the Stables Chancellery treasury provides detailed descriptions of tack and

equipment, noting the date and origin of items as well as an appraised value; see A. Viktorov, *Opisanie zapisnykh knig i bumag starinnykh dvortsovykh prikazov 1613–1725 g.* (Moscow: S. P. Arkhipov, 1883), II, 495–504. For examples of Polish horse gear, see Ostrowski et al., *Land of the Winged Horsemen*, plates 70–72; for Russian and Turkish examples, see *Treasures of the Czars from the State Museums of the Moscow Kremlin, Presented by Kansas International Museum* (London: Booth-Clibborn Editions, 1995), 100–2, 104–9, and *Paradnoe oruzhie i konskoe ubranstvo XVII–XVIII vv./Ornamental weapons and horse accoutrements of the 17th and 18th centuries,* ed. O. I. Mironova and E. V. Tikhomirova (Moscow: Izdatel'stvo "Izobrazitel'noe iskusstvo," 1986).

51. "Spisok s rospisi pridanago Anny Kondrat'evny Zagriazhskoi, vyshedshei zamuzh v 1687 godu za Kniazia Petra Ivanovicha Khovanskago, dvoiurodnago plemiannika nachal'nika strel'tsov, Kniazia Ivana Andreevicha Khovanskago," in *Izviestiia Imperatorskago russkago arkheologicheskago obshchestva,* 10 (1884), 27–33.

52. "Puteshestvie v Moskoviiu barona Avgustina Maierberga," in *Chteniia v Imperatorskom Obshchestve istorii i drevnostei rossiiskikh pri Moskovskom universitete,* bk. II, pt. 4 (1873), 58.

53. See, for example, Massa, *Short History,* 127–29; Olearius, *Travels of Olearius,* 57–58, 70–74; Guy Miege *A Relation of Three Embassies from his Sacred Majestie Charles II to the Great Duke of Muscovie, the King of Sweden, and the King of Denmark. Performed by the . . . Earle of Carlisle in the years 1663 and 1664* (London: Printed for John Starkey, 1669), 127–32; Lindsey Hughes, *Sophia, Regent of Russia, 1657–1704* (New Haven, CT and London: Yale University Press, 1990), 42.

54. Joan Thirsk, *Horses in Early Modern England: For Service, for Pleasure, for Power,* Stanton Lecture 1977 (Reading, UK: University of Reading, 1978), 7.

55. Kotoshikhin, *O Rossii,* ch. VI, art. 6.

56. Petrikeev, "Zemel'nye vladeniia," 76.

57. Peter Edwards, *The Horse Trade of Tudor and Stuart England* (Cambridge, UK: Cambridge University Press, 1988), 12, 20, 38–51.

58. Davis, *Medieval Warhorse,* 18, 135–36; Jankovich, *They Rode into Europe,* 14.

59. Davis, *Medieval Warhorse,* 99–100.

60. "Opis' stolptsov aptekarskago prikaza," *Materialy dlia istorii meditsiny v Rossii,* I (St. Petersburg: Tip. M. M. Stasiulevicha, 1881), nos. 5, 191, 228, 237; N. Novombergskii, *Ocherki po istorii aptechnago diela v do-Petrovskoi Rusi* (no publisher, n.d.), 18.

61. *Rozysknyia dela o Fedore Shaklovitom i ego soobshchnikakh* (St. Petersburg: Izd. Arkheograficheskoi kommissii, 1888), IV, col. 56; S. P. Luppov, *Kniga v Rossii v XVII veke* (Leningrad: Nauka, 1970), 107–10; Hughes, *Sophia, Regent of Russia,* 48, 161.

62. Luppov, *Kniga v Rossii*, 102–6.
63. N. N. Nazarenko, "Nekotorye rukopisnye istochniki po zootekhnii XVII–XVIII vekov," *Voprosy istorii estestvoznaniia i tekhniki* 1 (1956): 236–41; A. I. Sobolevskii, *Perevodnaia literatura moskovskoi Rusi XIV–XVII vekov* (St. Petersburg: Tip. Imp. Akademii nauk, 1903–8), 112–15.
64. "Puteshestvie," 58–59.
65. Zeziulinskii, *Istoricheskoe izsledovanie*, I, 53–54 n. 4.
66. Sobolevskii, *Perevodnaia literatura*, 112.
67. Nazarenko, "Nekotorye rukopisnye istochniki po zootekhnii," 235; Sobolevskii, *Perevodnaia literatura*, 112–15.
68. Nikolai Kutepov, *Velikokniazheskaia i tsarskaia okhota na Rusi s X po XVI vek*, 2nd edn. (St. Petersburg: Ékspeditsiia zagotovleniia gos. bumag, 1896) and *Tsarskaia okhota na Rusi tsarei Mikhaila Feodorovicha i Alekseia Mikhailovicha XVII vek* (St. Petersburg: Ékspeditsiia zagotovleniia gos. bumag, 1898).
69. Denisova, "Koniushennaia kazna," 294–99.
70. Hellie, *Economy and Material Culture*, 577–78.
71. Denisova, "Koniushennaia kazna," 298.
72. Indova, "Dvortsovoe zhivotnovodstvo," 117.
73. Oleg Ivanov, *Graf Aleksei Grigor'evich Orlov-Chesmenskii v Moskve* (Moscow: Svarog i K, 2002); Goodall, *History of Horse Breeding*, 208–9; Merder, *Istoricheskii ocherk*, 150–57; Vladimir Plugin, *Alekhan, ili Chelovek so shramom: Zhizneopisanie grafa Alekseia Orlova-Chesmenskogo* (Moscow: Mezhdunarodnye otnosheniia, 1996), 352–56; Kozhevnikov and Gurevich, *Otechestvennoe konevodstvo*, 29–41; Gurevich and Rogalev, *Slovar'-spravochnik po konevodstvu*, 131–34. In 1867 Beduin, a great-great-great-great-great grandson of Bars I, broke the world speed record for trotters at the Paris Exhibition.

CHAPTER 2

THE *PALIO* HORSE IN RENAISSANCE
AND EARLY MODERN ITALY

Elizabeth Tobey

On the first Saturday in May 2002, a black horse sped to the front of the pack in the 128th running of the Kentucky Derby, winning America's most important race by four lengths. The horse, War Emblem, though American-bred, became the first winner of the Derby to be owned by an Arab owner, the late Prince Ahmed Salman of Saudi Arabia, who unfortunately passed away a few months after War Emblem's historic victory.

Saudi Arabia, a longtime ally of the United States, came under severe criticism and suspicion when it was discovered that some of the terrorists who participated in the September 11 attacks on the United States were Saudi citizens. When the heirs of Prince Salman heard this criticism, they responded by offering War Emblem as a gift to the families of the September 11 victims as a gesture of goodwill and sympathy. Although the offer was never finalized, it demonstrates how even in the modern world, the gift of a horse may be used diplomatically to strengthen relations between two countries.

The international nature of horseracing, and the utilization of horses for diplomatic means, is not a new concept. In Renaissance and early modern Italy, the *palio*, named for the precious banner award to victors, marked important occasions in the life of a city. Horses from a number of breeds competed in the *palio*, and the importation of these animals forged contacts and trade between Europe and the Islamic kingdoms in North Africa and Ottoman Turkey. Italian nobles used horses as diplomatic gifts to gain favor with the most powerful European courts of England, Spain, and France. Lastly, the portraiture of individual horses not only reflected the prestige that these animals brought to their owners, but also showed changing attitudes toward the horse and its individual merits.

THE *PALIO* RACE IN RENAISSANCE ITALY

In order to understand the significance of the *palio* horse, one must first understand the origins and significance of the *palio* race. At least one sixteenth-century writer, Claudio Corte, attributes the origin of the *palio* to the chariot races of Roman antiquity. Whether this viewpoint is correct or not needs further proof, but it is an interesting hypothesis.[1] Much like the chariot races that celebrated the festival days of the Roman deities, the majority of *palio* races honored the feast days of a city's patron saint or a particular religious observation. The *Palio* of the Assunta or Assumption of the Virgin Mary in Siena (the August *palio*) dates back to the 1230s. The *Palio* of San Giorgio in Ferrara began in 1279.[2] The *Palio* of San Giovanni Battista in Florence (run in late June) paid tribute to Florence's patron saint, and the various races run in Rome were part of the pre-Lenten festival of Carnevale. Other *palio* races honored anniversaries of events in a city's history, welcomed the visits of foreign rulers or dignitaries, celebrated marriages, and commemorated military victories. In 1480, when Siena regained lost territory from the Florentines, the city marked the occasion with a *palio* race, jousting, and a Catharine wheel.[3]

The term *palio* comes from the banner awarded to the victor, made from precious material such as velvet, ermine, and silk, and often emblazoned with the coats of arms of prominent families or rulers. The word *palio* derives from the Latin *pallium*, or cloth. The fourteenth-century Florentine chronicler Gregorio Dati describes the *Palio* of San Giovanni Battista, Florence's patron saint to whom an annual feast day was dedicated, as being drawn by two horses on a triumphal cart bearing the symbol of the civic government.[4] This *palio* cloth described by Dati, made of red velvet with a symmetrical frieze of gold calf-skin and border of ermine fringed with silk, cost 300 gold florins and was thus an extremely expensive object.[5] By comparison, in 1354, the wealthy Strozzi family paid the painter Andrea Orcagna only 200 gold florins for creating a polyptych for their chapel in the church of Santa Maria Novella.[6] In the northern Italian city of Ferrara, *palii* of differing colors, such as red, white, and green, were awarded to the winners of the various races.[7]

Figure 2.1.   Giovanni Toscani, *The Race of the Palio on the Streets of Florence* (1418).
With permission of the Cleveland Museum of Art, Holden Collection.

Palio banners were emblazoned with the symbols of those in power.
A description from 1316 of a Sienese *palio* banner mentions that the
city's coats of arms were displayed on the standard surmounting the
palio cloth itself. By the early seventeenth century, Sienese *palio*
banners always carried an image of the Virgin Mary as well as the arms
of various families.[8] On a 1418 *cassone*, or marriage chest, painted by
the Florentine artist Giovanni Toscani (now in the Cleveland Museum
of Art; Figure 2.1), one can see clearly the *palio* cloth on the viewing
platform at the finish point of the *Palio* of San Giovanni Battista.[9]
Visible in the central band of the cloth are several indecipherable crests
or coats of arms. Early Florentine *palii* included mostly symbols of the
comune and of noble families, but following the appointment of
Cosimo I de' Medici as Grand Duke of Tuscany in the mid-sixteenth
century, the San Giovanni *palio* cloth began to include the coats of
arms of rulers to whom Florence held allegiance (including the emblem
of Emperor Charles V).[10] Heraldry on the *palio* cloth could vary
according to who currently held power; for example, when Siena was
ruled by the Visconti of Milan in 1395, the family's insignia showing a
golden apple and silver zigzag replaced the *comune*'s golden lion.[11]
    The races were staged through the most revered streets and public
spaces of the city. Most Renaissance era *palii* were run *alla lunga*, or
linearly, along a prescribed route through city streets, often beginning
at a city gate and ending in a *piazza*. According to Claudio Corte, the
longest *palio* race at the end of the sixteenth century was the *Palio* of
Bologna, run for a distance of 2 miles.[12] In the late sixteenth century,
the Sienese *contrade* began holding races *all tonda* (in the round) in
the shell-shaped Piazza del Campo.[13] In Florence, the *Palio* of San
Giovanni Battista began at the western gate, the Porta al Prato, and
followed a path through the most ancient part of the city, ending at

the Piazza di San Pier Maggiore. The Cleveland *cassone* depicts the finish of the race, in which the running horses approach the cart carrying the *palio* banner. Onlookers incline their bodies toward the approaching horses, which are ridden bareback by helmeted jockeys (*fantini*) wearing silks. In the background, spectators view the race from the windows of a *palazzo* from which banners or carpets hang, while jubilant youths cling to timbers waving branches, or what appear to be horseshoes, in their hands. Viewing the *palio* was almost as much of a sport as participating in it: in Florence, even the nobility vied for invitations to watch the *palio* from the "courts" or viewing platforms of the *potenze*, neighborhood groups of working-class citizens who assumed mock titles such as "Emperor" and "King" during the Festival of San Giovanni Battista.[14]

In the case of Florence and Rome, the *palio*'s course evoked the cities' Roman pasts. A portion of Florence's *Palio* of San Giovanni Battista followed the ancient *decumanus*, or east–west artery, of Roman Florence, which acquired the name Via del Corso, after the race itself.[15] Along the route, the horses would have passed the *palazzi* of Florence's wealthy families, including the Palazzo Strozzi (on the present-day Via Tuornabuoni) and the many edifices along the Corso and the Borgo degli Albizi. Rome's Carnevale races took place in the Testaccio neighborhood across the Tiber and later along the Via Lata from the Porta del Popolo to Piazza Venezia, which was renamed the Via del Corso in the sixteenth century.[16] The Corso was an ancient Roman thoroughfare later transformed by Pope Sixtus V into a major artery in the late sixteenth century.[17]

In sixteenth-century Florence, the Medici grand dukes appropriated the Piazza of Santa Maria Novella for the reenactment of a Roman imperial sport—the chariot race. Cosimo I, the first Grand Duke of Tuscany, saw himself as heir to the Roman emperors of antiquity, and employed imperial symbolism in art and architectural commissions and public spectacles.[18] In 1563, Cosimo initiated the *Palio dei Cocchi*, a chariot race that took place around wooden obelisks in the *piazza* in front of the church. Like his ancient predecessors who presided over chariot races in Rome's Circus Maximus, Cosimo watched the careening two-horse chariots from a viewing stand set up in the loggia of San Paolo directly across from the church. Wooden obelisks mimicked those of the Circus Maximus, and were later replaced by stone obelisks supported by bronze turtles, sculpted by Giambologna.[19] Although the *Palio dei Cocchi* never replaced the regular *palio* race in Florence, it reinforced the almost imperial authority of the Grand Duke.[20]

Palio racing continues to play an important role in the cultural life of some Italian cities: the *Palio* of Siena, the most famous surviving race, is run twice annually, on July 2 and August 16 (during the Feast of the Assumption). In it, 10 horses, sponsored by 10 of the 17 different *contrade* or neighborhood organizations, race 3 times around Siena's Piazza del Campo. The victorious *contrada* wins a decorative banner painted with the image of the Virgin Mary, the protector of the city.[21] *Palio* races are still run annually in at least five other Italian cities, and include the *Palio* of San Giorgio in Ferrara (at the end of May) and the *Palio* of Asti (in late September).

Although the horses in the modern Siena *palio* are owned privately and assigned to the various *contrade*, horses competing in Renaissance *palio* races belonged almost exclusively to members of the nobility.[22] The Gonzaga family of Mantua was perhaps the most dominant player in *palio* racing. Lorenzo the Magnificent of Florence was an avid competitor, as was the Este family of Ferrara. The Aragonese King of Naples had a powerful stable and was a supplier of fast horses to the rest of Italy. Families such as the Gonzaga maintained breeding farms for raising and training their horses, and horses were also imported directly from Sicily, North Africa, Eastern Europe, and Turkey.

During the Renaissance and early modern period, *palio* racing impacted the Italian city on many levels, marking important days in the city's religious and cultural calendar, providing a "safe" arena for rivalry with families from other parts of Italy, and, on the international level, bringing noble families into contact with foreign, including non-Western, cultures in the pursuit of a fast *palio* horse.

THE *PALIO* HORSE: OBJECT OF TRADE AND DIPLOMACY

In today's world of horseracing, Middle Eastern owners buy Thoroughbred racehorses not from their own nations, but from the stud farms and sales pavilions of the United Kingdom and the United States. Similarly, the Renaissance and early modern Italians sought *palio* horses primarily from Turkey and North Africa.

Occasionally an un-pedigreed horse of Italian origin would be victorious. Claudio Corte recalls in particular a roan bred by the Vetrallo stud, as well as a bay owned by the Duke of Udine:

> Although one finds that other bastard and ill-bred horses in Italy at this craft [racing] are the most perfect; and they win races over any type of

Barb; but these are rare, and I myself have not seen any of them in my life, with the exception of two; these were of greatest perfection in racing, and each one of them won the *palii* in Bologna, Florence, and in Rome, having always as competition Barbs and other very excellent horses, and the most excellent that there were in Italy.[23]

Although the occasional native horse would turn out to be a successful runner, the most popular breeds were of foreign origin, such as the *Barberi*, or Barbs, of North Africa; the *Cavalli Turchi*, or Turkish horses; and the Irish *Ubini*, or Hobby horses.[24]

Modern-day Sienese still refer to their *palio* horses as *barberi*, even though the horses are usually pure or half-Thoroughbred in breeding. However, the *Barberi* of the Renaissance were part of a distinct breed. The North African Barb, one of the oldest surviving breeds, is a compact animal with the ability to run fast over longer distances.[25] Barb horses are fairly small, measuring from 13.2 to 15 hands at the withers (shoulder),[26] and are short-backed, having 16 or 17 rather than 18 pairs of ribs. The croup (the downward-sloping part of the rump) is long and the tail set low.[27] Sometimes confused with another ancient breed, the Arabian horse, the Barb is distinguished from the Arabian in that the profile of its head is straight or convex, lacking the fine "dished" profile of the latter.

Representations of *Barberi* horses in European art seem to confirm a general Barb type. Morel Favorito, one of the stallions depicted on the walls of the Sala dei Cavalli (Room of the Horses) in Mantua's Palazzo Te (Figure 2.2) has a compact frame, a fairly plain head, and a sloping croup. The roan Barb stallion named Paragon in a group portrait (ca. 1657–58) of horses belonging to the English Duke of Newcastle has similar conformation and appears to be quite a diminutive animal.[28]

What little we know about the Barb horse during the Renaissance and early modern period comes from references and descriptions by sixteenth-century writers. Pasquale Caracciolo, in his encyclopedic work on the horse, *La gloria del cavallo*, explains that all African horses are referred to as *Barbari*, because they come from the region known at the time as Barbaria, and he describes them as slender-legged, courageous, and high-stepping due to their sandy and hot environs.[29] In another chapter of this book, Caracciolo notes that the *Barbari* are the horses best suited for racing.[30]

Sixteenth-century authors described the Numidian Barbs as particularly swift. The North African-born writer Leo Africanus makes a distinction between Barb horses and other horses bred by nomadic tribes.[31] One type of Barb, raised by the Hafsid princes and

Figure 2.2. South wall, Sala dei Cavalli, Palazzo Te, Mantua, Italy. Painted by Giulio Romano and assistants in 1527. Shown in the photograph are two Barb stallions, an unnamed gray (on the left), and Morel Favorito (on the right). In the middle above the fireplace is the figure of Vulcan. Photograph taken by Elizabeth Tobey in 1996, used by permission from the Museo Civico.

the Arabian nomads living between the Atlas Mountains in Tunisia and the coast, is heavier but not as swift as its desert-bred counterpart. The Arabians who rove the Numidian and Libyan deserts east of Tunisia "have likewise a great store of horses, which in Europe they call horses of Barberie." These horses, which Leo Africanus calls Arabian, are used for travel and warfare, and are "nimble, lively, and of spare flesh," and are fed on camel's milk. He mentions that some of the Arabian horses run wild, and that the fastest can outrun an ostrich.[32] Caracciolo mentions a Numidian horse that belonged to Lorenzo de' Medici and was celebrated in a verse by Poliziano. Its speed "surpassed the angels and the winds; only ceding to Cillarus and Pegasus; because in the middle of the race one could not even see him with the naked eye, either at the start at the head of the Carrera,[33] or when he had reached the finish."[34]

But the *Barbero* was not the only successful racing breed; the fleet *Cavallo Turcho* bred in territories belonging to the Ottoman Empire was another source of speed. By the early sixteenth century, the Ottoman Turks had captured Syria and a good part of the Middle East. Control over this region gave them easy access to purebred

Arabian horses, renowned for their ability to maintain speed over a distance. The Ottoman sultans forbade the export of purebred Arabians, and instead developed a breed of light horse that carried a large portion of Arabian bloodlines (known as the Turk or Turcoman) for export and as diplomatic gifts. Because of their Arabian blood, the Turkish horses had enough stamina to compete successfully in the longer *palio* races.[35] Caracciolo notes that although almost all horses from the East are referred to as Turkish, they vary in quality and type. The best, coming truly from Turkey, are large, pretty, and swift, while there are less agile but gallant horses produced from crosses with horses from the areas conquered by the Turks—Croatia, Albania, and the southern Mediterranean. He observes that the Turkish horses are not very high-stepping, have a bumpy trot, and move with their heads held high, due to the severe bit used.[36] As for color, most are white, though some are chestnut and bay and a few rare ones, brown.[37]

Although the *Cavalli Turchi* served primarily as light cavalry horses, they also excelled as racehorses. In the Gonzaga's correspondence, the *Turchi* are repeatedly referred to as *corredori*, or runners.[38] A letter from 1492 from the Doge of Venice, Agostino Barbarico, sends his representative, Alexio Becauti, to Constantinople to buy "boni cavali turchi corredori" (good Turkish running horses).[39] Giovanni Menavino, a Genoese ambassador at the Turkish court, describes the Turkish horse as a "buon corridore" (good runner) and notes its fine legs and hard, black hooves. He describes the Turkish horse as a light animal with a small head with large eyes, a long, high-crested neck, short ears, and a long tail.[40] Ottaviano Bon, a Venetian ambassador to the Ottoman court, describes the Sultan's stable of racehorses:

> He hath also stables of stallions for race in Bursia, Adrianople, and in divers other places; from which are brought to Constantinople very stately colm; besides such as are continually sent him for presents from Cairo, Damascus, Bagdat [Baghdad], and other places by the *Bashaws*. He hath also many which fall to his share by the death of great persons: all which are horses of great price, and kept for his own use.[41]

Whereas the African *Barberi* and the *Turchi* excelled at longer distances, the *Ubini*, or Irish Hobby horses, were excellent sprinters known for their ambling or pacing gait.[42] The *Ubini* were quite popular with the Italian nobles: Duke Francesco Sforza of Milan and Ercole and Alfonso d'Este of Ferrara sent representatives abroad to purchase *Ubini* from the kings of England, and the Gonzaga received several gifts of *Ubini* from King Henry VIII.[43] The presence of *Ubini* horses in Gonzaga stud books implies that they were part of their racing dynasty.

The importation of horses was part of a larger trade between Italy and Hafsid North Africa and Ottoman Turkey. Despite the cultural and religious differences and the ongoing war between the Ottoman Empire and Europe, bilateral trade existed and even thrived from the late Middle Ages onward.

During the thirteenth through sixteenth centuries, the Islamic Hafsid dynasty controlled most of North Africa and conducted trade with cities in Italy. The Hafsid dynasty established trade relations with Italy's major ports in the thirteenth century: commercial relations with Venice began as early as 1231, with Pisa in 1234, and with Genoa in 1236.[44] Under the Hafsid ruler Abu Faris, the region completed a trade treaty with Florence in 1423.[45] Cosimo de' Medici of Florence signed a 30-year trade contract in 1445 with the Hafsid dynasty.[46] Italian ships sailed out of the ports at Tunis, Oran, and other coastal cities. Unfortunately, trade in the Mediterranean during this period could be quite dangerous; both Turkish and Christian pirates plagued Hafsid ports with their attacks,[47] and European and North African ships faced dangerous travel conditions throughout the Mediterranean.

The area that is now known as Tunisia exported a number of products to Europe, including polychrome ceramic ware, coral harvested by divers off the coast, animals (including camels, mules, and horses), salt, spices, and alum (a substance used in the fixing of dyes in fabric, especially important to the textile industry in Tuscany).[48] Owing to the decline in domestic agricultural production (which resulted in periodic famines in the thirteenth and fourteenth centuries), Hafsid North Africa imported oil, wheat, and other grains from Europe, and it relied considerably on the income from taxes and duties on European exports.[49] Gifts of exotic animals, including horses, were utilized by the Hafsids to maintain positive relations with their Italian trading partners. The Hafsid ruler Abu Amir Utman regularly sent animals to Italy as gifts: in 1460, he sent *Barberi* horses to Sigismondo Malatesta of Rimini.[50] An anonymous Florentine chronicler mentions four horses, two camels, and eight falcons that the ambassador of the king of Tunisia presented to Emperor Charles V in Florence on May 2, 1536 as part of an annual tribute.[51]

The Gonzaga family of Mantua dispatched many representatives to Hafsid North Africa to purchase horses.[52] The emissaries of Marchese Francesco Gonzaga imported *Barberi* for his racing stable. A license from the Hafsid rulers was required in order to export horses, and the sale of mares and fillies theoretically was forbidden. Yet some letters do indeed mention the exportation of mares: for example, a letter from 1496 from the Gonzaga's emissary in Tunis notifies the Marchese that a license has been obtained from the King of Tunisia to export "tante cavalle" (some mares).[53] Importation continued into the sixteenth century; in 1525, Francesco's son Federico Gonzaga used the political influence of his brother Ferrante, who was an ambassador at the Spanish court of Charles V, to obtain a license for his agent to import horses from Oran, even though it was quite dangerous at that time.[54]

During the Renaissance and early modern period, the Ottoman Empire, which took over control of North Africa in 1574,[55] was considered a grave threat to Christianity. During the Counter-Reformation, the Catholic Church encouraged Christian rulers to fight the westward advance of the "heathen" empire. The sixteenth century saw some major conflicts between Europe and the Ottoman sultans, with the most important European victory occurring at the Battle of Lepanto in 1571. But few history books emphasize the trade and cultural exchange that took place between Italy and the Ottoman Empire. Turkey supplied Europe with large amounts of grain and alum, and the Ottoman Empire obtained from Europe finished cloth and wine, among other products.[56] Cultural exchange also flourished. The Venetian artist Gentile Bellini spent time at the court of Sultan Mehmet II around 1480 and even painted the monarch's portrait.[57] Turkish carpets appear repeatedly in Italian painting (including in images of the *palio* races), and ceramic wares, such as Iznik pottery, influence the development of painted terracotta in Italy.[58]

Families such as the Gonzaga at times enjoyed favorable relations with the Turkish sultan, which worked to their advantage in acquiring horses. Francesco Gonzaga came to the aid of an ambassador of Sultan Bayezid II. The ambassador, named Dauzio, was robbed in Ancona on his way to Rome to deliver money to Bayezid's imprisoned brother, Djem.[59] Francesco Gonzaga heard of Dauzio's plight and helped him complete his mission. He invited the ambassador to Mantua, and then assisted him in his return to Constantinople. The Sultan thanked the Marchese by sending him a boatload of Turkish horses. The Marchese responded by sending a boatload of Mantuan cheese to the Sultan! When the Venetians imprisoned Gonzaga in 1509, accusing him of treason, Sultan Bayezid intervened to free the Marchese.[60]

Sultan Bayezid's name appears in the Gonzaga correspondence pertaining to the importation of *Turchi*. Like the Hafsids, the Ottomans had strict rules about the selling of horses and in certain cases did not permit export.[61] Francesco's friendship with Bayezid II helped his representative, Bernardino Missaglia, to obtain a license to purchase eight mares and one stallion in September 1491.[62] The Gonzaga continued to receive other gifts of horses from the Ottomans; in a letter of May 22, 1492 the Governor of Herzegh (Bosnia-Herzegovina), Mustafa Begh, gave Francesco Gonzaga a gift of two horses as a token of friendship.[63] Though the letter is composed and signed in Italian, it is signed also with the governor's name in Arabic script.

Some *Turchi* were obtained not through diplomacy, but as spoils of war. Federico Gonzaga received two letters from one of his military captains, Niccolo Rali, from Zava (Sava) in April and May of 1525. The Sava river is in Serbia, where in 1521 the Ottoman Sultan Suleyman the Magnificent conquered the city of Belgrade as part of his campaign of westward expansion.[64] Gonzaga mercenary troops appear to have joined Imperial forces in the fight against the Turks. Rali mentions horses taken from Turkish prisoners, including a horse that he hopes to send the Marchese that is "el frate de quello Cavallo che l'anno passato mandai a Tuo Sig[ria]" (the brother of that horse that I sent you last year).[65]

RACEHORSE AS GIFT HORSE

Breeding programs became a source of pride and prestige for Italian noble families throughout Italy. Once they had obtained these valuable bloodlines from North Africa and Turkey, noble families established studs where they perpetuated breeding programs for horses of various breeds. According to Caracciolo, the Gonzaga of Mantua were the largest producers of horses on the Italian peninsula.[66] Stud books in the Archivio di Stato in Mantua show that the Gonzaga bred several kinds of horses, including Barbs, Turks, and *Zannette* (Spanish jennets) and kept careful records of the mares of each breed, the covering sires, and the colors and markings of the resultant foals.[67] Books published in the sixteenth and seventeenth centuries reproduce hundreds of the brands used to designate the horses of various families' or kingdoms' breeding programs.[68] Brands not only were breed specific, but were family specific as well: for example, the brand used for the jennets of the Marchese of Sant'Eramo of Puglia looked completely different from that used by the Gonzaga for their jennets.[69] The brands functioned as "coats of arms" for certain breeding programs, which were an extension of a noble family's prestige and glory. Families showed great pride in their horses, and were concerned to make a distinction between the horses from *their* breeding programs and those from others. In a letter to an unidentified "Cavalier de la Volta," Marchese Francesco Gonzaga bragged about his breed of *Barberi*, offering to send him an illuminated manuscript, the *Codice dei palii gonzagheschi*, in which his top runners were portrayed:

> My breed of *Barberi* is good not only in comparison with Italian horses, but with Turkish, Moorish, and Indian horses, and to prove that this is true, I send to you Zohan Iacomo, my assistant and present trainer, with the book of *palii* won with my horses so that you may see if my breed deserves to be discounted as it seems to have been in the past; that this breed is praised and desired by the very King of France, the Catholic king [the King of Spain], [the kings of] England, of Turkey, of Hungary, and by many others, and finally by whomever else has knowledge of them. . . .[70]

The stud books and brands promote and maintain "good breeding," and in a sense, the horse becomes a vessel for a family's own political ambitions.

Therefore, their horses were the ideal gift for Italian nobles to present to foreign sovereigns in order to advance their own political standing. Families such as the Gonzaga and the Este of Ferrara made their money as mercenary fighters, so their potential employment depended upon their relationships with the courts of Europe.

The Gonzaga used their horses to gain favor with the French, Spanish, and English courts. When Francesco Gonzaga's teenage son Federico Gonzaga spent time at the French court of Francis I in the early sixteenth century learning how to be a courtier, much of the correspondence between father and son mentions the French king's desire for Mantuan horses.[71] The Gonzaga also presented horses to Emperor Charles V, for whom Federico later fought as a mercenary fighter, and at whose court Ferrante Gonzaga served. One letter mentions a bay Turkish horse of Gonzaga breeding that so pleased the Emperor that Ferrante gave the horse to him as a gift.[72] But perhaps their most influential gift of their horses were those sent to

the English court. In a letter of June 1, 1516, Francesco describes to
Federico Gonzaga a colt born on the day of San Giorgio:

> I tell you that *razza nostra* [our breed] is in fuller flower than it has
> ever been and up until now we have eighty-one colts born this year, the
> most beautiful that we've ever had. . . . Among these there is one very
> beautiful colt born on Saint George's Day. This one we want to give to
> the King of England because he was born on the day of that saint that
> is principally venerated in England. . . . [73]

The Gonzaga exchanged horses with the English King Henry VIII,
sometimes as gifts, and sometimes in exchange for Irish *Ubini*. In
1532, Federico made a historic gift of a stallion named Argentino and
a band of *Barbero* broodmares to King Henry VIII, who wished
to found a stud in his country.[74] The incorporation of the Gonzaga
Barberi into the royal studs of England may even have contributed
to the development of the Thoroughbred racehorse. Historians of
the breed such as noted twentieth-century breeder Federico Tesio have
theorized that the foundation mares of the Thoroughbred breed were
descended in part from the horses the Gonzaga sent to England.[75]

Just as a well-negotiated marriage could advance the political
standing of an Italian noble family, likewise the presentation of gift
horses could also spread the family's fame and gain them favor with
the rulers and courts of early modern Europe.

PORTRAITS OF RACEHORSES AND THE RECOGNITION OF THE HORSE AS AN INDIVIDUAL

The Italian nobility put incredible effort into their horses, so it is not
surprising that they also hired artists to portray their most illustrious
animals for posterity. Both texts and images identify individual *palio*
horses by name. Not only does this equine portraiture indirectly glorify
a noble family, but it also points to an increased cultural recognition
during the sixteenth century of the horse as an individual.

Francesco Gonzaga commissioned the aforementioned *Codice* to
show his most illustrious *Barberi* and the various *palii* they won. The
manuscript is a small, intimate work, intended for the Marchese's own
personal enjoyment and, as his letter attests, for lending to other
nobles as a "brag book." We know from a letter from 1512 in the
Archivio di Stato in Mantua that the Marchese commissioned
Silvestro da Lucca, a debt collector, to organize the production of the

book and hire the illuminator, Lauro Padovano.[76] The frontispiece shows a framed portrait of a chestnut horse, Daino Sauro, who stands against a backdrop of a cityscape (probably the center of Mantua) wearing only a red bridle with a curb bit.[77] The framed portrait hangs beneath a classical arch inscribed with the Marchese's name and supported by two marble columns with gilded pilasters. Two *putti* (cherubs) below flank a shield emblazoned with an emblem. Displayed on a plaque that appears tied to the two columns is a list of three *palio* races won by Daino Sauro—the gold *Palio* of San Giovanni in Florence, the *Palio* of San Giorgio in Ferrara, and the *Palio* of San Leonardo in Mantua—three of the most important and competitive races in Italy.

On each page of the *Codice* is a gilt-framed portrait of an individual horse, shown in profile with a placard displaying its name above. Silvestro da Lucca's letter states that the Marchese desired the *Barberi* to be portrayed "dal naturale" (from life). Each horse wears a red bridle with a curb bit, and stands within a landscape, often on a road passing through mountainous countryside or by a body of water (this choice may be determined by the fact that Mantua was surrounded by lakes). At least one horse, El Bayo Perla, has an "F" branded on his flank, to indicate Francesco's ownership. In the portrait of Isdormia Secondo, a gray horse is held by a jockey wearing striped pants, a red jacket, and a red helmet. The artist appears to have used some profiles for multiple portraits. Around the outlines of some of the horses appear small pricks in the paper, which indicates that the artist may have traced various profiles many times, altering only the horses' coat color, markings, and direction of travel.

Despite the repetition of poses shown in the *Codice*, the artist has made some attempt to show distinguishing characteristics. Some of the gray horses are dappled, while others have uniform coat colors. The chestnut Serpentino has a luxuriant (possibly braided) mane, and El Falchon has four white stockings. The list of victories below each horse records the place of victory, the type and color of *palio* won, the day, and the year. Gonzaga horses triumphed in races in cities throughout the Italian peninsula, including those in Padua, Cervia, Cesena, Imola, Bologna, Florence, Pistoia, and the Roman Carnevale. Some horses appear to have run over a period of several years; for example, for El Turcho de la Raza, victories are recorded as early as 1508 and as late as 1511.

The Gonzaga also had their *palio* horses portrayed in the frescoes decorating the Palazzo Te in Mantua. The Palazzo Te was designed and built by the Roman artist and architect Giulio Romano for his patron, Federico Gonzaga, as a suburban residence on the Isola del Te just outside the city. Romano built the palace using the old walls and foundations of an existing villa and stable complex, and the Sala dei Cavalli occupies the main nucleus of the old complex.[78]

There are portraits of six horses frescoed on the wall of the Sala dei Cavalli. The horses, like the animals in the *Codice*, are framed by landscape vistas, and are placed amidst a trompe l'œil backdrop of classical Corinthian pilasters, colored marble panels, and imaginary statues of Roman gods and goddesses, reliefs showing the labors of Hercules, and portrait busts depicting members of the Gonzaga family as members of the Roman imperial family. We know the names of two of the horses—Dario and Morel Favorito—from faded names painted on the plinths upon which the stallions stand, and the names of two others—Battaglia and Glorioso—appear in sixteenth-century drawings of the Sala by the artist Ippolito Andreasi.[79] The four horses on the long walls wear bridles with plumes in their head-stalls, and some also wear a *celata*, or diamond-shaped headpiece. These horses I have identified as *Barberi*, since their headgear matches descriptions of bridles designated for the *Barberi* in a letter from 1509 that lists "le robe de li barberi" (the adornments of the *Barberi*).[80] The two horses on the short walls appear to be *Zannette*, or jennets, a type of riding-horse originating in Spain and also bred at the Gonzaga studs.[81]

The portraits of the *Barberi* may allude to passages from the Roman poet Virgil's *Georgics*, which describe the qualities of the ideal stallion for siring warhorses and racehorses. Virgil was originally from Mantua, and a portrait bust rising from a fountain—identified as Virgil—appears in the adjacent Loggia of the Muses, within a painted lunette above the entrance to the Sala dei Cavalli.[82] The juxtaposition of the portrait busts with the equine portraits suggests that the Gonzaga saw their animals as "heirs" to the champions of the ancient Circus Maximus, just as they saw themselves as "heirs" to the Roman imperial family. The images do not show generic animals, but are portraits of named individuals to whom the Gonzaga could point proudly. The fact that the Sala dei Cavalli, as the main reception hall, often welcomed foreign dignitaries (including Emperor Charles V) shows how important the Gonzaga's horses were to the spreading of Mantuan fame. Thus, the Sala dei Cavalli functions as a gallery of *viri illustri* (the Gonzaga as rulers from antiquity) presiding over *equi illustri* (the *palio* horses in the guise of Roman circus horses). The fresco cycle belongs to the same tradition as the portraits of famous philosophers and thinkers in Federico da Montefeltro's *studiolo* in Urbino's Palazzo Ducale, or the Medici's collection of artist self-portraits in the Vasari Corridor of the Uffizi.

The *palio* horses appear to have achieved a certain level of fame and would have attracted the attention of the citizens of the cities in which they competed. A late-sixteenth-century panel painting in the National Gallery of Ireland, "The Return from the *Palio*" by Giovanni Maria Butteri (ca. 1540–1606),[83] shows the victorious horse, Il Seicento (Figure 2.3). According to the sixteenth-century humanist Vincenzo Borghini,[84] Francesco de' Benci paid 600 gold coins for Il Seicento, spawning the phrase "gli par essere il seicento" (he thinks he is worth six hundred), signifying someone who parades in sumptuous clothing.[85] Early in his artistic training, Butteri, who trained in the workshop of Mannerist artist Alessandro Allori, painted works on canvas to decorate ephemeral monuments for public festivals, for which Borghini devised the *invenzioni* (written descriptions).[86] Owing to the large size of the canvas, it is conceivable that Borghini commissioned the painting from Butteri as decoration for a public festival such as the feast day of San Giovanni Battista, thus commemorating this famous racehorse's victories in *palio* races. A groom leads Il Seicento down the crowded street, while spectators peer from windows to get a glimpse of the victorious steed. The horse appears to wear a special saddlecloth or mantel on its back with a coat of arms (too vague to be deciphered) and a border of gold lilies, the symbol of the city of Florence.

The naming of individual racehorses in the *Codice*, in the Sala dei Cavalli, and in Butteri's painting reflects an increasing celebration in the early modern period of the horse as an individual possessing and expressing almost human qualities. In his chapter on *palio* horses, Corte paints a verbal portrait of a particular winning horse of native stock:

> I don't know from which stud he came—but he was owned by a Count of Udine. That horse had in the middle of the arch of his neck a *cerro* of braided mane, that circled round his neck one time, and from there yet almost touched the ground: and he was of such great speed that when I saw him the day of San Giovanni Battista in Florence in the race pass all the other horses, and Barbs, in the middle of the running, I speak of that when they ran the *palio* that day; there were not only the Barbs of Mantua, but those of the Duke of Florence, and Il Bonzaga, the famous Barb of the Duke of Urbino.[87]

Corte describes the luxuriant mane of the victorious horse as one might praise the hair of a beautiful woman. The horse has been able to overcome his ignoble beginning by defeating the pedigreed Barb,

Figure 2.3. Giovanni Butteri, *The Return from the Palio* (late sixteenth century), oil on canvas, cat no. 1021. With permission of the National Gallery of Ireland.

Il Bonzaga, belonging to the Duke of Urbino. Luca Landucci, in his chronicle of Florence, enthusiastically recorded for posterity the victories of a North African *Barbero* named Draghetto (Little Dragon), who won twenty *palio* races for his brother, the spice-seller

Costanzo Landucci.[88] A poem in the Gonzaga *Codice* goes even further in praising the victorious Mantuan horse Daino Sauro in verse.

> Neither Dayno [doe] nor Pardo [leopard] nor wild thing
> nor arrow from a bow in fury shot
> nor radiance from the sky through the colored air
> ever passed so soon morning or evening
>
> Neither Phoebus whose charger [*de la sua spera?*]
> whose speed has not yet ever been surpassed
> nor wind that every force has ever extinguished
> ever showed such ferocity
>
> As in running did the fleet Sauro
> passing in the midst of the city of the Flower [Florence]
> to win of the Baptist [*Palio* of San Giovanni] the prize of gold
>
> Glory of my Francesco, eternal honor
> for which the Gonzaga from the Indian Ocean to Mauritania
> will always have fame of his great bravery
>
> Put on the feathers and the wings on your back
> You have proven yourself, Sauro
> that always it will be told from Indian Ocean to Mauritania
> and the one and the other heaven be struck . . .
>
> The virtue that God entrusts in you
> is spread with the clamoring among many people
> Turcho, Turcho, all of Italy cries[89]

The anonymous poet compares Daino Sauro to the mythical winged Pegasus, and like a victory in battle, his winning of the prestigious *Palio* of San Giovanni Battista in the rival city of Florence brings fame to the Gonzaga. It is noteworthy not only that this poem is being addressed to a horse, but also that God entrusts the horse with "virtue," thus acknowledging that an animal is capable of possessing positive human qualities.

The glorification of the *palio* horse is part of the individualization and even humanization of the horse that has its parallel in equestrian treatises of the early modern period. The publication in Naples in 1550 of Federico Grisone's treatise on horsemanship, *The Rules of Riding*,[90] marks the flowering of the art of classical horsemanship. Grisone and his followers based their philosophies of horse training on the work of the ancient Greek general Xenophon, who advocated training the horse through gentle persuasion. Although some of Grisone's training methods were quite harsh and even cruel, at the same time, he expresses the interdependent relationship of man and horse: the horse should become one, in mind and body, with its rider.[91] Subsequent sixteenth- and early-seventeenth-century works on riding acknowledge the horse's ability to think and to learn. In discussing methods of training, riding masters such as the Neapolitan Pirro Antonio Ferraro recall in depth experiences of working with individual horses, often mentioning them by name.[92] Many such authors spend a considerable time listing and describing courageous horses from history and the qualities they possessed.[93]

Horses, therefore, even in some sixteenth-century minds, share many physical and emotional qualities with humans. As Caracciolo expresses so poignantly toward the beginning of *La gloria del cavallo*,

> It is not surprising that the horse resembles Man in many things, being animals subject to all the same feelings and diseases that we have, and they dream, as we do, and like us in their old age, many become white-haired. . . . And although this and other conditions horses share with Dogs, such as faith, love, and memory; nevertheless they show these openly more than anything else, and they not only are participants, but conform to our natures. This conformity is perhaps the reason that they [horses] are such good friends of humans. . . . [94]

Caracciolo expresses what seems like a radical idea for the sixteenth century, one that is supported by the portraiture of *palio* champions—that these horses, in spirit and nature, possess human characteristics.

Through their participation in urban spectacle, *palio* horses attained celebrity for themselves, even while bringing fame to their owners. They served their owners by acting as gifts or by starring in a tradition of equine portraiture, but they also became individuated and valued personalities as a result. *Palio* horses were a point of connection between vastly different cultures because their beauty and speed were valued by civilizations in Catholic Italy and Muslim Africa and Turkey. It seems fitting that the exchange of horses among these cultures led ultimately to the development of the modern breed of racehorse, the Thoroughbred, which continues to be a common passion for so many different nations because of its perceived courage, intelligence, and personality.

NOTES

Translations from the original Italian into English are mine unless otherwise noted.

1. Claudio Corte, *Il cavallarizzo* (Venice: Giordano Ziletti, 1562), 98ʳ. "But first, you must know, that the Emperor Verus had a horse called

Volucrus of incomparable speed, of greatest excellence. In honor of
this horse they began to first run *palio* races; being at first a race of
chariots" (Ma prima devete anco sapere, che Vero Imperatore hebbe
un cavallo chiamato Volucro della velocità sua incomparabile, di
somma eccellenza. In honore del qual cavallo si cominciarono prima
à correre i palii; essendosi prima corso con le carrette). Sixteenth-century writers certainly knew about the history and even the appearance
of the Roman circus, based upon the unearthing of archaeological
sites and surviving writings by Roman authors such as Ovid. Pasquale
Caracciolo devotes over six pages to descriptions of the ancient
Roman chariot races. Pasquale Caracciolo includes a section on
ancient Roman chariot races in his book, *La gloria del cavallo* (Venice:
Gabriel Giulito de' Ferrari, 1566), 6–10.

2. The statute establishing the *palio* is in the Archivio di Stato in Modena,
libro II, col. 117. See Nico Franco Visentini, *Il Palio di Ferrara*
(Rovigo, Italy: Istituto Padano di Arti Grafiche, 1968), 12–13.

3. Giovanni Cecchini and Dario Neri, *The Palio of Siena*, trans. Elisabeth
Mann Borgese (Siena: Monte de Paschi, 1958), 63.

4. From Gregorio Dati, *La storia di Firenze 1380–1405*, in Luciano
Artusi, "Il Palio dei Barberi," *Le feste di Firenze* (Rome: Newton
Compton Editori, 1991), 186–87.

5. A sixteenth-century manuscript known as the *Codice dei palii gonzagheschi* owned by Marchese Francesco Gonzaga lists *palio* cloths won
by his horses; fabrics are specified as *raso* (satin), *damasco* (damask
silk), *veluto* (velvet), and *brochato d'oro* (gold brocade). The original
manuscript is in a private collection. The *Codice* is illustrated in the catalog of David Chambers and Jane Martineau's exhibition, *Splendours
of the Gonzaga* (Milan: Amilcare Pizzi, S.p.a., 1981), 147 and is also
illustrated and discussed in Giancarlo Malacarne, *Il mito dei cavalli
gonzagheschi: Alle origini del purosangue* (Verona: Promoprint, 1995).

6. Gert Kreytenberg, *Orcagna's Tabernacle in Orsanmichele, Florence*
(New York: Harry N. Abrams, Inc., 1994), 33.

7. Dino Tebaldi, Luigi Vincenzi, and Stefano Lolli, *Ferrara e il Palio:
Storia, poesia in dialetto attualità* (Ferrara, Italy: Giovanni Vicentini
Editore, 1992), 25.

8. See Duccio Balestracci, "Alle origini del palio. Da festa come tante
altre a festa come nessun'altra," in *Pallium: Evoluzione del drapellone
dalle origini ad oggi*, ed. Luca Betti (Siena: Betti Editrice, 1993),
9–10; Christina Ciampoli and Caterina Palmiera, "Il drapellone:
Nascita ed evoluzione stilistica fino al 1800," in *Pallium*, ed. Betti, 10.

9. Mark Christopher Rogers, *Art and Public Festival in Renaissance
Florence: Studies in Relationships* (Diss., University of Texas at
Austin, 1996), 212–16. The *cassone* is reproduced as fig. 7.51 in Paula
Vetrone (ed.), *Le tems revient, 'l tempo si rinuova: Feste e spettacoli
nella Firenze di Lorenzo il Magnifico* (Florence: Silvana Editoriale,
1992), 251.

10. For more on the heraldry of Florentine *palio* banners, see Luigi Borgia, "Vicende di alcuni stemmi del Palio di San Giovanni," in *La festa di San Giovanni nella storia di Firenze: Rito, istituzione, e spettacolo*, ed. Paolo Pastori (Florence: Edizioni Polistampa, 1997), 243–56.

11. Alessandra Gianni, "Araldica e allegoria nel drapellone," in *L'immagine del Palio: Storia cultura e rappresentazione del rito di Siena*, ed. Maria A. Ceppari Ridolfi, Marco Ciampolini, and Patrizia Turrini (Siena: Monte dei Paschi di Siena, 2001), 131.

12. Corte, *Il cavallarizzo*, 99^r.

13. In 1581 the *contrade* began organizing donkey and buffalo races in the Piazza del Campo, as well as horseraces *alla lunga*; cited in Marco Ciampolini and Sonia Corsi, "Repertorio delle principali feste e cortei nei secoli XVI–XIX," in *L'immagine del Palio*, ed. Ceppari Ridolfi et al., 222–23 and described in Domenico Tregiani, "Trattato sopra le belle e sontuose feste fatti ne la magnifica città di Siena cominciate de la prima domenica di maggio per tutto il di XVII d'agosto di l'ano 1581," MS. B.V.42, Biblioteca Comunale Siena, fos. 12–20^v. But the first documented instance of a horserace in the Campo occurred on August 15, 1633 for the Feast of the Assumption, as illustrated in a print by Bernardino Capitelli. See Patrizia Bonaccorso, *Bernardino Capitelli 1589–1633*, catalog published in conjunction with the Capitelli exhibition at the Museo Civico, Siena, June 15–September 30, 1985 (Siena: Edisiena, 1985), 71–72 and Document 123, "Repertorio documentario sulle contrade e sulle feste senesi," *L'immagine del Palio*, ed. Ceppari Ridolfi et al., 541.

14. Heidi Chrétien, *The Festival of San Giovanni: Imagery and Political Power in Renaissance Florence*, American University Studies, series IX: History 138 (New York: Peter Lang, 1994), 65. For more on the history of the *potenze* in Florence, see Roberto Ciabani, *Le potenze di Firenze: Una pagina inedita di storia fiorentina* (Florence: Casa Editrice Bonechi, 1994).

15. Rogers, *Art and Public Festival in Renaissance Florence*, 212–13.

16. Richard Joseph Ingersoll, *The Ritual Use of Public Space in Renaissance Rome* (Diss., University of California at Berkeley, 1985), 271–74. See also Peter Partner, *Renaissance Rome, 1500–1559* (Berkeley: University of California Press, 1976), 101.

17. For more on the history of the Corso, see Marina Moriconi, "Il Corso: Dal Carnevale alla festa politica," in *La festa a Roma dal Rinascimento al 1870*, ed. Marcello Fagiolo (Rome: Umberto Alledmandi & Co., 1997), vol. I, 168–81.

18. For more on the imperial iconography of Cosimo's reign, see Janet Cox-Rearick, *Dynasty and Destiny in Medici Art: Pontormo, Leo X, and the Two Cosimos* (Princeton, NJ: Princeton University Press, 1984).

19. One of many engraved representations of the *Palio dei Cocchi* was made by the French printmaker Jacques Callot. In 1617, Callot made a series of 50 etchings known as the *Capricci*, which he dedicated to

Don Lorenzo de' Medici, the younger brother of Grand Duke Cosimo II of Florence. H. Diane Russell, *Jacques Callot: Prints and Related Drawings* (Washington, DC: National Gallery of Art, 1975), 19–21. Prints from the *Capricci* showing *palio* races are scattered throughout various print collections worldwide, including the Gabinetto Disegni e Stampe at the Uffizi and the National Gallery of Art in Washington, DC.

20. Chrétien, *The Festival of San Giovanni*, 44–45.

21. For more on the modern Siena *palio*, see Alan Dundes and Alessandro Falassi, *La Terra in Piazza: An Interpretation of the Palio of Siena* (Berkeley: University of California Press, 1975).

22. There were exceptions—the Sienese artist Sodoma owned the horse that won the August 1514 Siena *palio*. See Cecchini and Neri, *The Palio of Siena*, 70.

23. Corte, *Il cavallarizzo*, 98^{r,v}. "Benche si trovino alcuni cavalli bastardi, & villanotti in Italia à questo mestiere perfettissime; & che vincano anco nel corso ogni sorte di Barbaro; ma sono rari; & io per me non n'ho veduti se non due in vita; li quali erano di somma perfettione nel corso, & ciascuno di loro vinse i palii in Bologna, Fiorenza, & in Roma, havendo sempre al contrasto barbari & altri cavalli eccellentissimi, & i più eccelenti che fossino in Italia. Et questi furono un caval leardo rotato della razza di Vetrallo: & l'altro baio non so di che razza si fosse, ma era di un Conte da Udine."

24. According to Corte, *Il cavallarizzo*, 98^{r}, the Barbs belonging to the Duke of Mantua were the best runners, but the Sorian (Spanish) and Scythian horses were also fast.

25. Alexander MacKay-Smith, *Speed and the Thoroughbred* (Lanham, MD: The Derrydale Press, 2000), 117.

26. The hand, a unit used for measuring horse height, is equal to 4 inches.

27. Robert Painter and Louise Painter, *International Society for the Preservation of the Barb Horse and Barb Horse Registry* (Midvale, ID, 1997), 7–8.

28. This painting, by the Flemish artist Abraham van Diepenbeck (ca. 1596–1675), is reproduced in MacKay-Smith, *Speed and the Thoroughbred*, 76.

29. Caracciolo, *La gloria del cavallo*, 315.

30. Caracciolo, *La gloria del cavallo*, 103.

31. Leo Africanus, whose Arabic name was Hassan Ibn Muhammad al-Wazzin al Zayyati, knew the last of the Hafsid sultans. After converting to Christianity, published a *Description of North Africa* in Bologna in 1524. Giancarlo Pizzi, *Tremila anni di storia in Tunisia* (Vibo Valentia (Milan): Jaca Book, Qualecultura, 1996), 279.

32. "The most certain triall of these horses is when they can overtake the beast called the Lant or the Ostrich, in a race, which if they be able to performe, they are esteemed worth a thousand ducats or a hundred camels." Leo Africanus, *The History and Description of Africa and of*

the Notable Things Theirin Contained, Written by Al-Hassan Ibn Muhmammed al-Wezaz al-Fasi, a Moor, Baptised as Giovanni Leone, but Better Known as Leo Africanus, trans. John Pory, reprint of the original edition of 1600 (New York: Burt Franklin, n.d.), 156–57, 942–43.

33. This may refer to the start of the *Palio* of San Giovanni Battista in Florence, which once started near the Ponte alla Carraia.

34. Caracciolo, *La gloria del cavallo*, 103.

35. MacKay-Smith, *Speed and the Thoroughbred*, 122–24.

36. In many sixteenth- and seventeenth-century treatises on horsemanship and bitting, certain bits are prescribed to correct the naturally high head carriage of the Turkish horse.

37. Caracciolo, *La gloria del cavallo*, 309.

38. Although *barberi* seems to be the most prevalent term in correspondence to describe *palio* runners, horses are also referred to more generically as *corredori* or runners. A letter of August 1, 1512 discusses choosing a *buon cavallo corridore* (good running horse) for the *Palio* of San Leonardo. See Malacarne, *Il mito dei cavalli gonzagheschi*, 76.

39. "Littere Serenissimi Augustini Barbarico Ducis Venetiarum directe nobili viro Hieronimo Bayulo in Constantinopoli pro auxilio et favore prestando spectabili Domino Alexio Beccaguto nuntio Illustrissimi Domini Marchionis Mantuae in aquirendo et conducendo equos," Letter of May 12, 1492, Archivio di Stato in Mantua, busta 1423, Archivio Gonzaga, also cited in Malacarne, *Il mito dei cavalli gonzagheschi*, 54.

40. Giovanni Menavino, *I costumi et la vita dei Turchi* (Florence: Appresso Lorenzo Torrentino, 1551), 85–86. On pp. 112–13 and 123, Menavino describes the organization of the Sultan's stables in Constantinople in vivid detail.

41. Ottaviano Bon, *The Sultan's Serraglio: An Intimate Portrait of Life at the Ottoman Court (from the Seventeenth-Century Edition of John Withers)*, ed. Godfrey Goodwin (London: Saqi Books, 1996 [1625]), 113.

42. MacKay-Smith, *Speed and the Thoroughbred*, 30–31. Hobbies contributed much of the speed to the Thoroughbred bloodlines, and five Hobbies were exported to Jamestown, Virginia, in 1666, where they contributed to the establishment of the American Quarter Horse, which is the fastest horse in the world at a quarter-mile distance.

43. MacKay-Smith, *Speed and the Thoroughbred*, 24–26.

44. Jamil M. Abun-Nasr, *A History of the Maghrib* (Cambridge, UK: Cambridge University Press, 1971), 140. Patricia Kozlik Kabra, *Patterns of Economic Continuity in Early Hafsid Ifrîqiya* (Diss., University of California at Los Angeles, 1994), 74.

45. Abun-Nasr, *A History of the Maghrib*, 148.

46. Pizzi, *Tremila anni di storia in Tunisia*, 267.

47. Pizzi, *Tremila anni di storia in Tunisia*, 272.

48. Kabra, *Patterns of Economic Continuity*, 197–99, 311.
49. Kabra, *Patterns of Economic Continuity*, 294–308.
50. Pizzi, *Tremila anni di storia in Tunisia*, 268.
51. Luca Landucci, *Diario fiorentino dal 1450 al 1516: Continuato da un anonimo fino al 1542*, ed. Antonio Lanza (Florence: Sansoni Editori, 1985 [1883]), 372. Landucci died in 1516, but an anonymous chronicler continued his chronicle. The editor notes that a contract between Mulay Hassan, king of Tunisia, and Charles V established that every year the king was to give Charles V a tribute of six *Barberi* horses and twelve falcons.
52. The Gonzaga were not the only family to import horses from North Africa: Lorenzo de'Medici is known to have sent his representative Martino d'Arezzo to Tunis to buy horses; see Michael Mallett, "Horse Racing and Politics in Lorenzo's Florence," in *Lorenzo the Magnificent: Culture and Politics*, ed. Michael Mallett and Nicholas Mann (London: The Warburg Institute, 1996), 258. The most extensive documentation of the importation of Barb horses that I have been able to find, however, are the letters of the Gonzaga family in the Archivio di Stato of Mantua. Excerpts and entire letters appear in Malacarne's *Il mito dei cavalli gonzagheschi* and in Carlo Cavriani's *Le razze gonzaghesche dei cavalli nel mantovano e la loro influenza sul puro sangue inglese* (Mantua, Italy: Adalberto Sartori Editore, 1974 [1909]). I have cited these transcriptions in this chapter.
53. Malacarne, *Il mito dei cavalli gonzagheschi*, 51–52.
54. R. Tamalio, *Ferrante Gonzaga alla corte spagnola di Carlo V* (Mantua, Italy: Gianluigi Arcari Editore, 1991), 54, also cited in Malacarne, *Il mito dei cavalli gonzagheschi*, 39–40 n. 15.
55. Abun-Nasr, *A History of the Maghrib*, 169.
56. For more on trade between Europe and the Ottoman Empire, see Kate Fleet, *European and Islamic Trade in the Early Ottoman State* (Cambridge, UK: Cambridge University Press, 1999).
57. See Patricia Fortini-Brown, *Narrative Painting in the Age of Carpaccio* (New Haven, CT: Yale University Press, 1988), ch. 4.
58. For more on the mutual cultural influences between Italy and Ottoman Turkey, see Charles Burnett and Anna Contadini (eds.), *Islam and the Italian Renaissance* (London: Warburg Institute, 1999).
59. Djem, who tried to gain the Ottoman throne from his brother, was sent into exile in France and later in Italy, where Bayezid II paid the Papacy to have him held prisoner in Rome. See Sydney Nettleton Fisher, *Sultan Bayezit II and the Foreign Relations of Turkey: An Abstract of a Thesis* (Diss., University of Illinois, 1935).
60. Malacarne, *Il mito dei cavalli gonzagheschi*, 96 n.14.
61. Fleet, *European and Islamic Trade*, 29–30.
62. Letter from Bernardino Missaglia to Francesco Gonzaga, September 25, 1491, Archivio di Stato in Mantua, busta 795, fos. 33–35, also cited in Malacarne, *Il mito dei cavalli gonzagheschi*, 52.

63. Archivio di Stato in Mantua, busta 795, fo. 37, also cited in Malacarne, *Il mito dei cavalli gonzagheschi*, 53.
64. Paul Coles, *The Ottoman Impact on Europe* (London: Thames and Hudson, 1968), 82–83.
65. Letter of May 16, 1525, Archivio di Stato in Mantua, busta 795, fo. 127.
66. Caracciolo, *La gloria del cavallo*, 323.
67. Stud book of 1540, Archivio di Stato in Mantua, busta 258, Archivio Gonzaga.
68. Pages of brands appear in Francesco Liberati's *La perfettione del cavallo* (Rome: Francesco Corbelletti, 1639). Several books were published in the sixteenth and seventeenth centuries reproducing the horse brands of various prominent Italian families. Other books are devoted entirely to the subject of brands, such as the *Libro de marchi de cavalli con li nomi di tutti li Principi, & privati Signori, che hanno razze di cavalli* . . . (Venice: Bernardo Giunti, 1589).
69. Liberati, *La perfettione del cavallo*, 93, 106.
70. "La mia raza de barberi è bona per rendere conto non solum a cavalli italiani, ma a turchi, mori, et indiani, et in fede che ciò sia vero gli mando Zohan Iacomo mio alveo, presente exibitore, col libro di palii viti con li mei cavalli a fine che la veda se la mia raza merita d'esser svilata come fa fece pare; che è laudata et desiderata per una de la singulari dal re di Francia, re Catholico [re di Spagna], d'Inghilterra, de Turchia, de Ungaria et da multi Reverendissimi Cardinali Illustrissimi Signori, et finalmente a qualunche altro che n'habbia cognitione. . . ." Letter from Francesco Gonzaga to a Cavalier de la Volta, March 4, 1517, Archivio di Stato in Mantua, busta 2924, fo. 250, 2^v, 3^r, Archivio Gonzaga, also cited in Malacarne, *Il mito dei cavalli gonzagheschi*, 86.
71. R. Tamalio, *Federico Gonzaga alla corte di Francesco I di Francia nel carteggio privato con Mantova (1515–1517)* (Paris: Honoré Champion Editeur, 1994), 86.
72. R. Tamalio, *Ferrante Gonzaga alla corte spagnola di Carlo V*, 153.
73. "Ti avvisamo come la razza nostra è in maggior fiore che lo fosse mai et fin qui havemo 81 cavalli maschi nati quest'anno, gli più belli che uscessero mai . . . tra gli altri ne uno che nacque il dì di S.Zorzo beliss.o. Quello volemo donar al Re d'Angliterra per esser nato il dì di quel Santo che precipuamente è in veneratione in Anglia." Carlo Cavriani, *Le razze gonzaghesche dei cavalli*, 23. The letter is in the Archivio di Stato in Mantua, although I do not have the precise archive reference.
74. The correspondence surrounding the trading of horses with England is cited and discussed in Malacarne, *Il mito dei cavalli gonzagheschi*, 106–29.
75. Federico Tesio, *Breeding the Racehorse*, trans. Edward Spinola (London: JJ Spinola, 1994 [1958]), 2–3. Tesio, who studied and wrote about the genetics of the Thoroughbred racehorse, was also

one of the most influential breeders of the twentieth century. Many of the prominent racehorses of the modern day are descendants of two stallions, Nearco and Ribot, whom Tesio bred at his Dormello stud on the shores of Lago Maggiore in Italy. Tesio maintains that the prevailing theory that the Thoroughbred was produced from three Oriental foundation sires (the Godolphin Barb, the Darley Arabian, and the Byerley Turk) crossed with native English mares is incorrect; he argues that at least some of the mares also were descendants of horses of Oriental blood, including the Gonzaga imports.

76. Letter from Silvestro da Lucca in Mantua to Marchese Francesco Gonzaga, September 20, 1512, Archivio di Stato in Mantua, busta 2485, Archivio Gonzaga, also cited in Malacarne, *Il mito dei cavalli gonzagheschi*, 87–88.

77. Although Daino Sauro is portrayed with a curb bit, which was the most popular bit at the time, Claudio Corte (*Il cavallarizzo*, 98ᵛ) mentions a *filetto*, or snaffle bit, in his chapter on training and conditioning a *palio* horse.

78. For more on the conversion of the villa into a palace, see Amadeo Belluzzi and Walter Capezzali, "Le scuderie dei Gonzaga sul Te," *Civiltà Mantovana* 42 (1973): 378–94 and Amadeo Belluzzi and Walter Capezzali, *Il palazzo dei lucidi inganni: Palazzo Te a Mantova* (Mantua, Italy: Centro Studi Architettura Ouroboros, 1976).

79. See Amadeo Belluzzi, *Palazzo Te a Mantova*, 2 vols. (Modena, Italy: Franco Cosimo Panini Editore S.p.a, 1998), figs. 215–17.

80. The trappings of the *Barberi* are described in a list that appears in a letter from Isabella d'Este Gonzaga (Federico's mother) to Berardo Ruta, May 26, 1509, Archivio di Stato in Mantua, busta 2416, letter 205, 58, Archivio Gonzaga, also cited in Malacarne, *Il mito dei cavalli gonzagheschi*, 230. The letter is entitled "Nota de le robe de li barberi de veluto cremesino e verde, tempestati de tremolanti cum la impresa del Crosolo" (Note on the Adornments of the *Barberi* of Crimson and Green Velvet, Studded with Shining Ornament with the Crest of the Crosolo). The item, or list number, that describes the *pennacchi*, or feathers, reads "penachii sei verdi e rossi, cioè 3 celate e 3 per li testeri da li cavalli" (six red and green feathers, that is, three [attached to] headpieces and three for the headstalls of the horses). The letter lists as an item "brille 3 da barberi de tesuti de seta verde e cremesina cum li sonagli" (three bridles of the *Barberi* of crimson and green silk fabric with bells).

81. The faint brand visible on the rump of the chestnut *Zannetta* stallion, as well as the brand visible on Glorioso in the Andreasi drawing, resemble illustrations of *Zannetta* brands in a Gonzaga stud book. The brands, found in documents in Archivio di Stato in Mantua, busta 258, Archivio Gonzaga, are reproduced in Malacarne, *Il mito dei cavalli gonzagheschi*, 102–3.

82. The identification of this bust as the head of Virgil was made by Egon Verheyen, *The Palazzo del Te in Mantua: Images of Love and Politics*

(Baltimore, MD and London: Johns Hopkins University Press, 1977), 15. Other examples of this Virgil bust are given in Belluzzi, *Palazzo Te a Mantova*, vol. I, 362.
83. The undated painting ($51\frac{1}{2} \times 40$ in.) is no. 1021 in the National Gallery of Ireland in Dublin; it was purchased from the collection of Captain R. Langton Douglas in 1940.
84. Vincenzo Borghini was a humanist and philologist at the Medici court and was one of the first lieutenants of the Academy of Design. Karen-edis Barzman, *The Florentine Academy and the Early Modern State: The Discipline of Disegno* (Cambridge, UK: Cambridge University Press, 2000), 28–29.
85. Vincenzo Borghini, *Della moneta fiorentina*, in *Discorsi di Monsignore Vincenzo Borghini* (Florence: P.G. Viviani, 1755 [1584–85]), 167. This is mentioned by Federico Zeri in "La percezione visiva dell'Italia e degli italiani nella pittura," in *Storia d'Italia, VI: Atlante* (Turin: Einaudi, 1976), 72. I would like to acknowledge Margaret Donnelly of the National Gallery of Ireland for sending me this excerpt from Zeri's article.
86. Rick Scorza, "Borghini, Butteri and Allori: A Further Drawing from the 1565 'Apparato,'" *Burlington Magazine* 137/1104 (1995): 172–75.
87. Corte, *Il cavallarizzo*, 98ᵛ: "non so di che razza si fosse, ma era di un Conte da Udine. Il qual cavallo havea nel mezzo dell'inarcatura del collo un cerro di crini fatto à treccia, che ce lo rivolgevano d'interno al collo una volta, & dipoi anco l'avanzo andava quasi à toccar terra: & era di sì grande velocità ch'io lo vidi il giorno di San Giovanni Battista in Fiorenza nel corso avanzan tutti gli altri cavalli, & barbari, di mezza carriera, dico di quella dove correvano tal giorno il palio; & pur c'erano barbari di Mantua, quelli del Duca di Fiorenza, & il Bonzaga barbaro famossissimo del Duca d'Urbino."
88. Landucci, *Diario fiorentino*, 39, 50, cited in Mallett, "Horse Racing and Politics in Lorenzo's Florence," 254, 259.
89. Non Dayno o Pardo o fuggitiva fera
nè sagitta da chorda a furia spinta
nè fulgare dal ciel per l'aria tinta
passò sì presto mai mattina ò sera

Nè Febo cho destrier de la sua spera
la cui velocità gia mai fu vinta
nè vento che ogni forza ha sempre extinta
mostrò furia nel mondo mai sì fiera

Come correndo fece il legier Sauro
passando in mezzo la città del fiore
per vincer del Baptista il premio dauro

Gloria del mio Francesco eterno honore
per cui Gonzaga dal mar Indo al Mauro
phama harà sempre del suo gran valore

Ponendoti le piume e l'ali adosso
tu hai fatto di te tal pruova Sauro
che sempre sen dirà dal Indo al Mauro
e l'uno e l'altro ciel ne sia percosso
Tu non fosti dal segno così presto mosso
che teco ti portasti il premio dauro
che tu sii vera gloria e ver restauro
del Duca mantuan dir non tel posso
Tu fusti honor di tutti li altri armenti
nel correre, e nel corso senza guida
vincesti senza dubbio tutti i venti
La virtù del Signor ch'in te si fida
s'è sparsa con rumor fra tante genti
che Turcho, Turcho, tutta Italia chrida.

(*Codice dei palii gonzagheschi*, p. 6, in Malacarne, *Il mito dei cavalli gonzagheschi*, 229.)

90. Federico Grisone, *Gli ordini di cavalcare* (Naples: Giovan Paolo Suganappo, 1550).

91. Grisone, *Gli ordini di cavalcare*, 12[r,v]. "Et volete cavalcare, & star sopra di esso, non solo con animo grande, senza tema di lui: Mà far concetto, che egli sia con voi un'istesso corpo, di un senso, & di una voluntà" (And you want to ride and stay upon him, not only with a grand spirit, without fear of him: but think also that he is together with you of the same body, of the same spirit, and the same will).

92. Pirro Antonio Ferraro, *Cavallo frenato* (Naples: Antonio Pace, 1602).

93. Some examples provided by Caracciolo are Alexander's horse, Bucephalus; the human-handed horse of Julius Caesar; and Boristene, who belonged to the Emperor Hadrian. Caracciolo, *La gloria del cavallo*, 11–12.

94. Caracciolo, *La gloria del cavallo*, 7–8. "Ne maraviglia se n'è da prendere, havendo in molte cose il Cavallo somiglianza con l'Huomo, stando questi animali soggetti a tuttie que' medesimi affetti e morbid, a' quali noi stiamo; Eglino si sognano, come noi, & come noi nella vecchiezza manifestamente più che altri canuti divengono. . . . Et benche questa & alcune altre conditioni, comuni habbiano ancor co' i Cani, come la fede, l'amore, & la memoria; tutta via dimostrano apertamente, ch'essi piu che altri, della natura nostra non solamenti partecipi siano, ma conformi. La qual conformità forse è cagione, ch'eglino sian de gli huomini tanto amici. . . ."

CHAPTER 3

SHAKESPEARE AND THE SOCIAL
DEVALUATION OF THE HORSE

Bruce Boehrer

This chapter pursues a simple argument: that Shakespeare's plays enact a downward displacement of the horse's character as a social signifier. I believe that this displacement, in turn, may be loosely correlated to the decline of the armigerous gentry's identity as a military class, which decline is closely mirrored by the horse's own emerging obsolescence as an instrument of warfare in early modern England. In other words, Shakespeare associates the horse preeminently with chivalry, and—as Ralph Berry has argued—he presents chivalry primarily as "a defunct ideology."[1]

My thesis gains compact illustration through a brief exchange from *The Merchant of Venice* (ca. 1596). There, in the scene that first introduces Portia to the play's audience (1.2), her waiting-woman Nerissa asks her opinion of her various suitors, beginning with "the Neapolitan prince" (1.2.39).[2] Portia's response conveys much disdain in little compass:

> Ay, that's a colt indeed, for he doth nothing but talk of his horse, and he makes it a great appropriation to his own good parts that he can shoe him himself. I am much afeard my lady his mother play'd false with a smith. (1.2.40–44)

This observation marks a classic failure to communicate. A quality that the Neapolitan prince considers "a great appropriation to his own parts" (his expertise as a horseman) strikes Portia as precisely the opposite: as evidence not of his distinction but rather of his baseness. Thus her insulting suggestion that the prince's mother has "play'd false with a smith" speaks to the vast disparity between her and her suitor's understandings of the horse as a marker of social status, and if the play as a whole endorses one view of this matter over another, it is clearly Portia's. Like Slender in *The Merry Wives of Windsor* (1597), who fails to comprehend that his efforts to woo Anne Page with talk of bear-baiting confirm neither his sophistication nor his masculinity but only his idiocy (1.1.281–99), the Neapolitan prince fails to grasp how utterly his sense of the attributes of social distinction falls short of Portia's reality.

However, one might conceivably object that this passage says less about horses than about one particular horseman: that the problem here is not the Neapolitan prince's love of equitation but rather its expression in activities (such as the shoeing of horses) that are manifestly inappropriate to his station in life. This complaint strikes me as misguided for at least two reasons: first, because within the context of Portia's speech the offending behavior is clearly the prince's general obsession with his horses, of which his fascination with horseshoes is merely the most egregious expression ("he doth nothing but talk of his horse"); and second, because it is unwise to promote the social baseness of the blacksmith's work to the status of a transcendent historical principle, as if there were not potentially times and places in which the ability to shoe a horse could signify something other than meanness of rank. Clearly it means nothing of the sort to the prince, and this fact may bespeak his immersion in a competing social code just as easily as it might indicate some fundamental wrongness of personal character.

I shall return to this point later; in the meantime, however, let me offer another, more extended instance of the social devaluation to which Shakespeare subjects his horses. This second example comes from *Henry V* (1599), in which the most prominent discussion of horsemanship is assigned to the French Dolphin, the Duke of Orleans, and the Constable of France, all in high spirits preceding the Battle of Agincourt:

> DOL.   Nay, the man hath no wit that cannot, from the rising of the lark to the lodging of the lamb, vary deserv'd praise on my palfrey . . . . 'Tis a subject for a sovereign to reason on, and for a sovereign's sovereign to ride on; and for the world, familiar to us and unknown, to lay apart their particular functions and wonder at

him. I once writ a sonnet in his praise and began thus: "Wonder of
    nature"—
ORL.   I have heard a sonnet begin so to one's mistress.
DOL.   Then did they imitate that which I compos'd to my courser, for my
    horse is my mistress.
ORL.   Your mistress bears well.
DOL.   Me well, which is the prescript praise and perfection of a good and
    particular mistress.
CON.   Nay, for methought yesterday your mistress shrewdly shook your
    back.   (3.7.31–49)

Perhaps the most prominent feature of this passage is its association of horsemanship with history's losers, Henry V's French opponents, whose boasting rings particularly hollow in retrospect, after the
defeat that they are destined to suffer. Here, very clearly, we
encounter a Shakespearean representation of the aristocratic culture
of the horse, and it is not a pretty picture. This vignette, in turn, is
composed out of various recurring gestures that serve as base motifs
in Shakespeare's treatment of equestrian society. First, there is the
association of horses with foreignness; while it is certainly true
that some of Shakespeare's English characters (notably Hotspur in
1 Henry IV, to which I will return) exhibit a fondness for horsemanship, it is equally true that the ethnic Otherness of characters such as
the Neapolitan prince and the French Dolphin is lent particular
expression through their obsession with horseplay. Second, it is precisely horse*play* that acquires prominence in such passages; the
Dolphin and Orleance discuss horsemanship as if it were an end unto
itself, and this fact exposes the degeneracy of their fondness for equitation, which no longer exists in the context of military training but
has devolved instead into a form of pastime and social display. The
Dolphin's horse, coupled with his mistress as an object of sonnetry,
emerges from this exchange more as an accessory of courtly love than
as a weapon. And third, this particular juxtaposition of horses with
women forms one of the most notable and persistent features of
Shakespeare's treatment of the animal. Horse and woman appear
repeatedly in Shakespeare's works as a dyad at once antithetical and
complementary; in the case of Portia and the Neapolitan prince, the
oppositional quality of the relationship is foregrounded, while the
Dolphin and his companions suggest something of the complemen-
tarity through their equation of horse and mistress.
    These are some of the most distinctive features of the complex of
associations that Shakespeare creates around the figure of the horse,

and that this chapter seeks to explore. In working through their sig-nificance, I will proceed first to an account of the extraordinary ten-sions and ambivalences ascribed to this wondrous necessary beast by early authors, qualities that Shakespeare as a playwright necessarily inherited and that gain illustration from widely dispersed passages in his work. Then, to conclude, I will concentrate particularly upon the symbolic function of the horse within *Antony and Cleopatra* (ca. 1607), a play in which it is assimilated with especial clarity into a discourse of military decline. In proceeding thus, I will argue that Shakespeare constructs something we might anachronistically describe as an incipient bourgeoisification of the horse: a literary idiom in which the animal's traditional aristocratic associations are exposed as effete pretense, and in which, instead, the horse comes to be identified most persistently with figures of social abjection such as the woman, the child, the base-born, and the ethnic Other.

HORSES AND TENNIS BALLS

Historically, of course, the horse has proven perhaps more central to a broader range of social endeavor than has any other domesticated animal. This centrality was, if anything, more pronounced than ever before in early modern England, as horses became subject to "grow-ing and increasingly diversified demand," especially in the carting and farming sectors.[3] As a result of its indispensability, the horse has acquired a particularly rich range of social connotations in the literature that deals with it; since it proves essential to such diverse activities as travel, trade, exploration, agriculture, hunting, warfare, and sport, it signifies somewhat differently in each of these contexts. For this very reason, the horse has served from classical times forward as a particular focus of what I would call the anxiety of composite forms; as the domesticated animal par excellence, half in nature and half in culture, the horse is itself a composite creature, and this fact is only further compounded by the exceptional, sometimes self-contradictory, range of its human usefulness. Thus when Shakespeare inherits the horse as symbol, he inherits a particularly chaotic set of competing identifications, some in the process of becoming anachro-nistic, and all partaking of the horse's own irreducible ambivalence as both a natural and a human construct.

At heart, this ambivalence derives from the composite nature of cultural activity in general, which has recently been summarized by Douglas Bruster as entailing an irresistible confusion of "process [with] product," as well as with "producing faculty, place, [and] agent."[4] Perhaps the most influential classical image of this confusion (and the anxiety to which it gives rise) may be found in Plato's *Phaedrus*,[5] with its famous comparison of the soul to a chariot:

> We will liken the soul to the composite nature of a pair of winged horses and a charioteer. Now the horses and charioteers of the gods are all good and of good descent, but those of other races are mixed; and first the charioteer of the human soul drives a pair, and secondly one of the horses is noble and of good breed, but the other quite the opposite in breed and character. Therefore in our case the driving is necessarily difficult and troublesome . . . for the horse of evil nature weighs the chariot down, making it heavy and pulling toward the earth the charioteer whose horse is not well trained.   (246a–b, 247b)

Figuring the dual and variable potential of the human spirit, Plato simultaneously illustrates the capacity of the horse to signify both for good and for ill, as an emblem of nature well managed and conversely as an exemplar of human dependence upon qualities that are never entirely manageable or absolutely dependable. Similarly, the horse/man amalgam of the centaur emerges from classical sources as a peculiarly mixed creature, capable both of extraordinary wisdom and equally remarkable depravity. Thus Ovid's *Metamorphoses* presents Chiron, the son of Philyra and an equiform Saturn, as honored with the charge of raising Apollo's son Aesculapius (2.626–34); yet the very same passage of the *Metamorphoses* depicts Chiron's daughter Ocyrhoe, punished for exercising her power of prophecy, as degenerating entirely into equine form (2.636–75).[6] Likewise Nessus, entrusted by Hercules with the care of his wife Deianira, betrays that trust in a rape for which Hercules rewards him with the epithet "biformis" (9.121); in parallel fashion, Eurytus begins the battle of the Lapiths and centaurs by seizing Hippodame, the bride of Pirithous, at her wedding celebration, thus encouraging his fellow-centaurs to a mass rape (12.210 ff.). Here, as in the Platonic metaphor for the soul, the horse figures forth both a disturbing propensity for baseness (especially sexual baseness) and an equally disturbing sense of that baseness as somehow intrinsic to human behavior. Nor are these classical sources foreign to Shakespeare; recall that in *A Midsummer Night's Dream* (ca. 1596), Theseus is invited to hear "The battle with the Centaurs, to be sung, / By an Athenian eunuch to the harp" (5.1.44–45), while in *Antony and Cleopatra* Antony, betrayed by Cleopatra, complains that "The shirt of Nessus is upon me" (4.12.43).[7] Such moments in Shakespeare arguably coincide with the broader pattern of equine reference surveyed in this chapter.

If the horse thus serves from classical times as an emblem of mythic duality, that duality settles into the beast's diverse social significations in a variety of different ways, some exalted, others less so. Predictably enough, the most distinguished of equestrian associations tend to be martial in character. Hector's Homeric cognomen, "breaker of horses" (7.38),[8] bespeaks not only his Trojan foreignness (the best Greek cavalry were introduced from abroad),[9] but also his military prowess (Patroclus is given the same epithet, 16.839). Xenophon's two widely dispersed treatises on horse-management, *The Cavalry Commander* and *The Art of Horsemanship*, both take for granted the identification of cavalry service with "those who are most highly qualified by wealth and bodily vigor";[10] likewise, Xenophon declares that "no action of man bears a closer resemblance to flying" than does riding,[11] and he insists that "I know not why any art should be more assiduously cultivated than the arts of war."[12] Here already is the conjunction of martial heroism, horsemanship, and social privilege that, relayed through the equestrian order of classical Rome, eventuates in the knightly and aristocratic ranks of medieval and early modern Europe. Thus William Harrison can observe in 1577 that the order of English knights "seemeth to answer in part to that which the Romans called *equitum Romanorum*," with the signal difference that

> whereas the *Equites Romani* had *equum publicum* of custom bestowed upon them, the knights of England have not so but bear their own charges in that also, as in other kind of furniture, as armory meet for their defense and service.[13]

Harrison likewise extends this wholly conventional view of social privilege to the ranks of the temporal peerage, which he defines primarily in terms of their relationship to military affairs; thus dukes derive their title from the facts of their "valor and power over the army," marquises from their responsibility for maintaining "a marching [border] province upon the enemy's countries . . . to keep and defend the frontiers," and barons from the fact that they are "*robur belli* [that is, the best in war]."[14]

This classic understanding of horses as instruments of warfare, representative of a military distinction that in turn licenses social privilege, of course provides the foundation for the Dolphin's equestrian enthusiasm in *Henry V*, and it arguably also informs the Neapolitan prince's passion for riding in *The Merchant of Venice*. (Indeed, we should note in connection with the latter case that Xenophon, for one, instructs his readers in the performance of such tasks as currying a horse (5.5–10) and cleaning and examining its hooves (6.1–3), and while he makes it clear that these menial activities should be delegated to a groom, he nonetheless clearly believes that the horse's owner should also know how to perform them properly. The Neapolitan prince's interest in shoeing horses may thus be viewed as roughly adhering to the spirit of Xenophon's advice to gentleman equestrians.) But of course, there is also something very wrong with the language of equestrian privilege as invoked by these Shakespearian characters. Most obviously, the horse's military associations are undercut in both *Henry V* and *The Merchant of Venice*. In the former case, the French lords' braggadocio stands in ironic contrast to their fecklessness in battle. In the latter, the horse seems to have no martial associations whatever, as if the military expertise that traditionally mediated between horsemanship and social privilege had simply ceased to exist. In its absence, both Shakespearian passages provide a wholly different set of associations: between the aristocrat as gentleman of fashion, the horse as fashionable accoutrement, and the mistress as a comparable ornament of the fashionable life. Shakespearian characters such as the Dolphin and the Neapolitan prince thus mark an important moment of transformation in the history of equestrian symbolism.

As it happens, this symbolic shift parallels a material one, which occurs more or less simultaneously on two levels. First, the traditional military character of the aristocratic ranks gives gradual way to a notion of group identity based less on martial *virtus* than on conspicuous consumption. Second, the horse itself, rendered increasingly irrelevant on the battlefield, comes instead to serve—and hence to signify—as a beast of sport, luxury, and social display. In a recent essay on the *Henry VI* plays, Gregory Colón Semenza has persuasively argued that Shakespeare's earliest histories enact the degeneration of warfare into aristocratic sport, and that this degeneration is compounded by the plays' tendency to present sport itself as a vice endemic to the privileged ranks.[15] My argument here may be understood to extend Semenza's thesis while rendering it simultaneously more general and more particular: more general in that I locate a similar process of aristocratic degeneration not only in the early histories but in widely dispersed places throughout the Shakespeare canon; more particular in that I regard the figure of the horse as a distinctive synecdoche for that process. I consider it no accident, for instance, that the Dolphin of *Henry V* praises his horse so lavishly in the midst of a play that in turn dramatizes one of the most brutal demonstrations in early modern military history of cavalry's emerging obsolescence as a weapon. The great English victories at Poitiers, Crécy, and finally

Agincourt were made possible precisely by the vulnerability of heavy French mounted warriors in the face of massed English archery. By Shakespeare's day, this vulnerability had, if anything, grown still more marked with the introduction of gunpowder to the battlefield. Thus, increasingly emptied of its military utility, the horse begins to exist for the privileged ranks less as a practical implement than as a symbol, less as a tool of business than as an accessory of pleasure.

Indeed, in its capacity as an aristocratic signifier, the horse attests to the fact that pleasure has increasingly *become* the business of the privileged ranks. Hence it is again appropriate that the Dolphin, *Henry V*'s horse-lover par excellence, should first irrupt into the play's action through his insulting gift to Henry of a set of tennis balls (1.254–63). In effect, the French equestrians of this play embody the same courtly ethos that afflicts the battlefield in *1 Henry IV* when Hotspur, fresh from victory at Holmedon, is commanded to deliver his prisoners into the keeping of "a certain lord, neat, and trimly dress'd" (1.3.33), who discourses "like a waiting-gentlewoman / Of guns, and drums, and wounds" (1.3.55–56). For his part, Hotspur may well be Shakespeare's most prominent representative of the traditional military aristocracy, and he is every bit as fond of his horse as is the Dolphin in *Henry V*. To this extent, he may initially seem to contradict the train of equestrian associations I am pursuing in this chapter; unlike the Dolphin and the Neapolitan prince, Hotspur, at least, takes warfare seriously, is good at it, and values his horse accordingly.

Yet Hotspur, too, unquestionably has his problems. And concomitant with those problems, his horse operates in symbolic capacities markedly similar to those we have already identified elsewhere in Shakespeare's plays. Consider, for instance, *1 Henry IV* 2.3, in which Hotspur prepares to take the field against Henry IV. When his wife inquires, "For what offense have I this fortnight been / A banish'd woman from my Harry's bed?" (2.3.38–39), her question initiates a lengthy parallel between woman and horse reminiscent of the Dolphin's banter with Orleance:

> LADY. What is it carries you away?
> HOT.   Why, my horse, my love, my horse.
> LADY. Out, you mad-headed ape!
>   A weasel hath not such a deal of spleen
>   As you are toss'd with. . . .
> HOT.   Away,
>   Away, you trifler! Love, I love thee not,
>   I care not for thee, Kate. This is no world

> To play with mammets and to tilt with lips.
> We must have bloody noses and crack'd crowns,
> And pass them current, too. God's me, my horse!
> . . .
> Come, wilt thou see me ride?
> And when I am a' horseback, I will swear
> I love thee infinitely.   (2.3.75–79, 89–94, 100–2)

Whereas Hotspur, unlike the Dolphin, seems consciously determined not to confuse women with horses ("This is no world / To play with mammets and to tilt with lips"), his very insistence on their separateness nonetheless suggests their potential equivalency. Moreover, it points in the process to Hotspur's own celebrated defects of character; Lady Percy chastises him as a "mad-headed ape," a "weasel," and a "paraquito" (2.3.85), and her question "What is it carries you away," answered flippantly by Hotspur, enforces the contrast between his skill at managing his horse and the ease with which he is figuratively carried away through his ineptitude at managing himself. The result is a character whose equestrian obsessions bespeak weakness as much as strength, pointing as they do to a glaring deficit in his reserves of personal discipline and wisdom.

The existence of this deficit is of course no news to Shakespeareans; the playwright goes out of his way in *1 Henry IV* to foreground the inadequacy of Hotspur's approach to life. As a result, this play activates a series of traditional equestrian images of social abjection and applies them to Hotspur in more or less deliberate ways. It is as if the aristocratic horse-and-rider image of martial heroism to which he lays conscious claim had become so enfeebled that it could not police its own semiotic boundaries but repeatedly found itself overrun by other, less exalted, social associations. Thus the epithets of ape, weasel, and parrot, applied to Hotspur in frustration by Lady Percy, are summarized in Northumberland's despairing appraisal of him as a "wasp-stung and impatient fool" (1.3.236): one who, in the metaphorical language of Plato's *Phaedrus*, is a poor charioteer, allowing his better instincts to be governed by his worse. On the structural level, Shakespeare revised his source in Holinshed specifically so as to render Hotspur twenty-odd years younger than he actually was, and this revision forcefully associates his passion for horses with the heat of ungoverned youth—an association made memorable by the charactonymic properties of his nickname and likewise embodied in the traditional elision of child-rearing and horse training effected by educational discourse from Plato's *Republic* (413d)[16] to Ascham's *Scholemaster*.[17] As for Hotspur's ineffective

efforts to distinguish himself from women and identify himself with
horses instead, they do not prevent his father from denouncing his
propensity for the "woman's mood" of railing (1.3.237).

Such patterns of association are all of ancient lineage, and they
become irresistibly available to Shakespeare's horse imagery when the
more elevated conjunction of equestrian language and martial heroism
is weakened. Of them all, perhaps the most ubiquitous and interesting
in Shakespeare's plays is the affiliation of the horse with notions of
feminine sexuality. As Ovid's centaurs illustrate, the horse had already
acquired connotations of sexual excess in classical times; as I have
argued elsewhere,[18] medieval bestiaries, devotional manuals, and
morality plays assimilated these connotations particularly into feminine
sexual behavior, thus manufacturing the specific bond of equestrian
association exploited by Shakespeare in his treatment of characters
such as Hotspur and the Dolphin. Jeanne Addison Roberts has related
Shakespeare's use of this imagery to popular woodcut representations
of inverted domestic discipline in which the shrewish wife is depicted
as riding her saddled and bridled husband.[19] This same pattern of association, when applied to a character such as Hotspur, arguably activates
the tensions inherent in the horse's status as a composite creature,
suggesting the extent to which the aggressively masculine military aristocrat is enfeebled, despite his own protests to the contrary, by a
traditionally feminine failure of self-governance. Nor is Hotspur an
isolated instance of this enfeeblement. It emerges again in the figure
of Coriolanus, another outspoken representative of patrician military
culture whose exploits on the battlefield, manifested in part through a
profound emotional attachment to his horse, are accompanied by an
equally spectacular capacity for social self-sabotage.[20]

Interestingly enough, one of the most admirable military figures in
the entire Shakespeare canon, Othello, expresses no such preoccupation with horses. Indeed, by promoting the "great arithmetician"
(1.1.19) Cassio to the position of his lieutenant and overlooking the
more conventionally trained Iago in the process, Othello seems to
signal his investment in cutting-edge military science of the sort that
in the seventeenth century was already challenging the military
supremacy of cavalry. It is Iago, *Othello*'s most vocal proponent of a
traditional military order founded upon the "old gradation" of sen-
iority (1.1.37), who employs the most memorable equestrian imagery
in *Othello* when he warns Brabantio that his daughter, having eloped
with the Moor, will be "cover'd with a Barbary horse" (1.1.111–12)
and will furnish her father with "coursers for cousins, and gennets for
germans" (1.1.113). These images, perhaps partly embodying the

ancient Homeric association of horses with foreignness, likewise absorb a more recent vocabulary of racial hatred and teratological abnormality into the nervousness that Shakespeare's horse imagery expresses toward notions of the composite. Hence it is particularly appropriate that Othello and Desdemona should elope to an inn with the sign of "the Sagittary" (1.3.115). Nor, for all its ugliness and self-serving, is Iago's bigoted language entirely unwarranted; at the very least, it serves to encourage in Othello himself the sense of alienation and alterity that will eventuate in his murder of Desdemona. As Iago famously remarks to him, "I know our country disposition well: / In Venice they do let God see the pranks / They dare not show their husbands" (3.3.201–3); this suggestion of cultural relativism, followed by Othello's own nervous recognition of his blackness as an impediment (3.3.263–67), suggests the extent to which Othello himself emerges as the outstanding composite creature of his play, participating uneasily in the very conjunction of nature with culture that Iago's horse imagery figures at its ugliest.

Thus, if characters such as Hotspur and Coriolanus represent a residual body of equestrian symbolism associated with the aristocratic social ranks through the mediating term of martial activity, characters such as the Dolphin, the Neapolitan prince, and Iago give us some sense of the semiotic that takes its place in Shakespeare's plays. The heroism of Hotspur and Coriolanus, splendid as it is, remains impossibly self-impaired, always already compromised by a febrile determination to shun the contaminating influence of social inferiors (women, the plebeians) and a concomitant failure to recognize the greater danger arising from one's own defects of character. These representatives of a declining chivalric aristocracy, in turn, are supplanted by figures like the Dolphin, the Neapolitan prince, and Iago. Iago, on the one hand, represents the turn to a tragic equestrian language associated with bigotry and vengeful intrigue. The Dolphin and his Neapolitan counterpart, on the other hand, emerge as fundamentally comic characters for whom the horse's old martial associations survive, if at all, as empty and self-serving rhetoric. In each case, the composite nature of the horse as a social symbol obstructs its deployment as an emblem of aristocratic triumphalism.

O Happy Horse

However, this schematic appraisal of Shakespeare's horse imagery would be incomplete without a reasonably sustained reading of at least one play, and *Antony and Cleopatra* makes an ideal candidate for

such analysis. Its governing binarisms—Rome and Alexandria, masculine and feminine, war and love, and so forth—are sufficiently well
recognized to need no exposition here, and they lend themselves well
to a reading that emphasizes the disjunction between ideals of nobility predicated upon warfare and upon conspicuous consumption,
respectively. Likewise, this play's particular treatment of remote historical matters cries out for further application to the contemporary
affairs of early Jacobean England, affairs that attest to the decline of
the military ideal among the knighthood and peerage of
Shakespeare's day.

Antony and Cleopatra has provided audiences with one equestrian
image of exceptional prominence, noted again and again by commentators on the play.[21] That, of course, would be the image of
Cleopatra herself as horse to Antony's rider; as she ponders her absent
lover's possible whereabouts, her language indulges a compensatory
fantasy that would place him specifically on top of her:

> O Charmian!
> Where think'st thou then [Antony] is now? Stands he, or sits he?
> Or does he walk? Or is he on his horse?
> O happy horse, to bear the weight of Antony!   (1.5.18–21)

These lines compactly illustrate what is tempting—and wrong—about
Cleopatra and Egypt. The association of women with horses here, by
now familiar, obviously works to supplant martial activity with sexual
intercourse, thus speaking to the weakness of "ne'er lust-wearied
Antony" for the latter (2.1.38). Likewise, the image of Antony riding
Cleopatra implies its reverse: the conventional iconographic trope in
which the husband is saddled and ridden by his shrewish wife.
Transforming Antony into the plaything of her fantasy, Cleopatra suggests the extent to which, as Canidius remarks of him later, "our
leader's led, / And we are women's men" (3.7.69–70). The obvious
function of such imagery is to specify the erotic character of Antony
and Cleopatra's mutual attraction, and to depict it as a threat to
Antony's military identity and masculine self-sufficiency. In this respect,
Cleopatra's daydream speaks directly to a much later remark by
Enobarbus, made before Antony and Cleopatra enter together into
battle at Actium: "If we should serve with horse and mares together, /
The horse were merely lost; the mares would bear / A soldier and his
horse" (3.7.7–9). Here the conventional precedence of rider over horse
is reversed, with the obvious implication that "the soldier and his horse
cannot attend to the business of war in the presence of females."[22]

But this echo of Cleopatra's daydream comes relatively late in the play; as it happens, Shakespeare employs equine imagery to render the opposition between her erotic caprices and the business of warfare even more immediate and manifest. Within 15 lines of Cleopatra's fantasy, news arrives of Antony's actual circumstances, brought by a courier who also bears Cleopatra the gift of a pearl and an accompanying message:

> "Good friend," quoth [Antony],
> "Say the firm Roman to great Egypt sends
> This treasure of an oyster; at whose foot,
> To mend the petty present, I will piece
> Her opulent throne with kingdoms. All the East,
> Say, thou, shall call her mistress." So he nodded,
> And soberly did mount an arm-gaunt steed,
> Who neigh'd so high that what I would have spoke
> Was beastly dumb'd by him.   (1.5.42–50)

Most immediately, this vision of Antony provides counterpoint to Cleopatra's erotic fantasy. Removed from her presence, Antony at least temporarily reachieves some measure of his martial identity, and the most obvious signal of this fact, his movement from woman to horse, is underscored by a variety of other textual markers as well. The steed Antony mounts is so high-spirited as to drown out human conversation, thus providing an implicit contrast to Antony and Cleopatra's most recent scene together (1.3.13–41), where, as he attempted to take his leave of the queen, Antony found himself overborne by the torrent of Cleopatra's invective. Antony mounts the steed "soberly," his demeanor an explicit rejection of the "lascivious wassails" for which Octavius Caesar has taxed him in the preceding scene (1.4.56). And the horse that he mounts is itself described as "arm-gaunt." This phrase has been subject to a good deal of scholarly emendation,[23] but it has the authority of the 1623 folio behind it, and moreover it sorts well with the broader range of associations accruing to the figures of Antony and Cleopatra in Shakespeare's play. This last point, in turn, deserves some prolonged attention.

First, of course, the steed's gauntness stands in overt opposition to the luxury characteristic of Cleopatra's regime. But in so doing, it also invokes a particularly sustained pattern of alimentary reference in Shakespeare's play, a pattern of discourse that leads us to yet another celebrated horse image. This time the speaker is Octavius, who summarizes Antony's reputation for military prowess in an oft-quoted apostrophe:

> Antony,
> Leave thy lascivious wassails. When thou once
> Wast beaten from Modena, where thou slew'st
> Hirtius and Pansa, consuls, at thy heels
> Did famine follow, whom thou fought'st against
> (Though daintily brought up) with patience more
> Than savages could suffer. Thou didst drink
> The stale of horses and the gilded puddle
> Which beasts would cough at; thy palate then did deign
> The roughest berry on the rudest hedge;
> Yea, like the stag, when snow the pasture sheets,
> The barks of trees thou brows'd. On the Alps
> It is reported thou didst eat strange flesh,
> Which some did die to look on. . . .   (1.4.55–68)

Thus the horse's gauntness connects with Antony's own fortitude in the face of starvation. Indeed, if we imagine the "arm-gaunt steed" in question to have also been Antony's warhorse in Modena, beast and rider share a very visceral bond; Antony partakes literally of his horse's emaciation as he consumes its urine, and this fact contributes to his heroic status, which is inversely proportional to the physical comfort he permits himself.

Needless to say, the fare in Egypt is of another order altogether. Maecenas, questioning Enobarbus about Antony's life in Alexandria, repeats rumors of the notorious gourmandizing associated with the place, rumors that Enobarbus derides as understatement:

> MAEC.   Eight wild boars roasted whole at a breakfast, and but twelve
>   persons there; is this true?
> ENO.   This was but as a fly by an eagle; we had much more monstrous
>   matter of feast, which worthily deserv'd noting.   (2.2.179–83)

Here and elsewhere, Shakespeare's play juxtaposes competing economies of luxury and austerity, with Antony splayed out, as it were, between the two. If, as this chapter argues, Shakespeare's equestrian imagery dramatizes the replacement of a residual notion of nobility grounded in military heroism with an emergent model of aristocratic conspicuous consumption, Antony emerges as both an embodiment and a casualty of that very transition. Hence it becomes particularly appropriate that the horse images associated with him should figure a dichotomy between martial prowess and abstemiousness, on the one hand, and effeminacy and sensual indulgence, on the other.

This opposition may be read, at least superficially, to the disadvantage of all things Egyptian in Shakespeare's play, and the play itself may thus be read as an indictment of the aristocratic ethos Egypt represents. However, one should temper any impulse to view *Antony and Cleopatra* simply as a traditional misogynist diatribe, for the very qualities that problematize life in Shakespeare's Egypt appear, when viewed from a slightly different historical perspective, as distinctively Roman, and even as distinctively English. The matter of feasting provides a classic case in point; the very same Lucullan extravagance that typifies Alexandrian dining in *Antony and Cleopatra* can reappear, in a play such as Middleton's *Game at Chess* (1624),[24] as a defining feature of the Roman temperament:

> We do not use to bury in our bellies
> Two hundred thousand ducats and then boast on't,
> Or exercise th'old Roman painful-idleness
> With care of fetching fishes far from home. . . .   (5.3.6–9)

As for Shakespeare himself, his own *Timon of Athens* (ca. 1608)—a play drawing on the same principal source as *Antony and Cleopatra* and deriving from the same period of Shakespeare's career—identifies "feasts, pomps, and vainglories" (1.2.242–43) very clearly with the dominant social ethic of classical Greece. Any association of culinary excess with Egypt thus neglects the broader historical process whereby classical Greece and Rome develop their own epicurean reputations.

When it comes to Jacobean England, moreover, a very similar situation meets the eye. On the one hand, Jonathan Goldberg has documented the deliberateness with which King James and his court adopted classical Roman iconography and symbology in celebration of their own regime.[25] Yet on the other hand, Lawrence Stone and others following him have focused in gruesome detail upon the growth of conspicuous consumption (not least of all in its gastronomic form) among the peerage and gentry in King James's England.[26] These stories are sufficiently well documented to need no rehearsal here, and between them they produce what is, in the terms provided by *Antony and Cleopatra*, a peculiarly ironic spectacle: an English monarchy that adopts Roman rhetoric and Egyptian behavior more or less simultaneously. If Shakespeare's play offers a single exemplary figure for this conjunction, it is Antony, and his play's horses, operating as they do in two concurrent and competing symbolic registers, give compact expression to the resulting irony.

Indeed, not only can Antony's horses be read as an expression of his own predicament; Antony, in turn, can be viewed as illustrating the

process of social devaluation to which Shakespeare subjects his horses
in general. As he encounters the exotic East, he comes away from the
encounter a changed man, changed in ways that represent the future
of Rome—and of England—at least as well as does the behavior of
the triumphant Octavius. Antony's transformation from "the triple
pillar of the world" into "a strumpet's fool" (1.1.12–13) parallels the
transformation of the chivalric ranks in early modern England from a
military body, via what Rosalie Colie has called "the passing of aristocratic military power" in early modern England,[27] into a leisure class.
This transformation inevitably affects the symbolic status of the horses
associated with chivalric virtue and aristocratic privilege; like their
owners, horses gradually metamorphose from a military necessity into
a social excrescence. Concomitantly, Antony's own association with
this metamorphosis helps to explain the recurrent strain of comic dialogue associated with Egypt in Shakespeare's tragedy. Through the
insistent sexual jesting that typifies the Alexandrian court—and that
asserts itself in Cleopatra's fantasy of herself as Antony's horse—the
comedy of the Dolphin and the Neapolitan prince reappears in *Antony
and Cleopatra*, where it is allied with a very similar social ethic.

A CLOUD IN'S FACE

But if Cleopatra and the Egyptian court represent the comic valence
of equestrian imagery in Shakespeare, one might reasonably wonder
what happens in *Antony and Cleopatra* to the tragic counterpart of
such language: that strain of equine metaphor associated—as in the
case of Iago discussed above—with intrigue and duplicity and prejudice. In the event, one can glimpse it, I believe, in a brief remark by
Enobarbus, uttered on the occasion of Antony's last amicable meeting with Octavius Caesar. There (3.2), as Antony leaves Rome for
parts East, taking with him Octavius' sister, whom he has wedded for
political purposes, brother and sister exchange farewells and Octavius
seems to shed tears:

ENO.   [*Aside to Agrippa*] Will Caesar weep?
AGR.   [*Aside to Enobarbus*] He has a cloud in's face.
ENO.   [*Aside to Agrippa*] He were the worse for that were he a horse,
         So is he, being a man.
AGR.   [*Aside to Enobarbus*] Why, Enobarbus?
             When Antony found Julius Caesar dead,
             He cried almost to roaring; and he wept
             When at Philippi he found Brutus slain.

ENO.   [*Aside to Agrippa*] That year indeed he was troubled with a rheum;
What willingly he did confound he wail'd.   (3.2.50–58)

As editors regularly note,[28] a cloud (or dark spot) on the face of a
horse was proverbially a mark of bad temper, and when Enobarbus
conflates Caesar's tears with such a mark, he not only suggests
Caesar's treacherous nature, but also assimilates him into the very discourse of equine hybridity we have considered earlier in this chapter.
As horselike man, Octavius acquires overtones of the quintessential
bad horse from Plato's *Phaedrus*: untrustworthy and ill tempered,
prepared to appeal to and exploit one's baser instincts, despite all
appearances and assurances to the contrary. In this sense, Octavius is
Antony's Iago. And concomitantly, we may read Antony as trapped
between two opposed but complementary worlds, one tragic and one
comic, representing between them the devalued social contexts
within which Shakespeare's equestrian imagery typically operates. To
this extent, indeed, Antony may figure the impossibility of the very
chivalric ideal to which he aspires.

But if this is the case, there remains one final irony. For in con-
struing Caesar's tears as a mark of his duplicity, Enobarbus relies for
precedent upon the behavior of no less a worthy than Antony himself, who, like Caesar, has lamented "What willingly he did confound." This suggestion of Antony's own capacity for intrigue
echoes, in turn, the opinion of his officer Ventidius, for whom Antony
and Caesar are more alike than not. Having just defeated a Parthian
army, Ventidius refuses to consolidate the victory, observing that

> [A] lower place . . .
> May make too great an act. . . .
> Caesar and Antony have ever won
> More in their officer than person. Sossius,
> One of my place in Syria, [Antony's] lieutenant,
> For quick accumulation of renown,
> Which he achiev'd by th' minute, lost his favor.
> Who does i' th' wars more than his captain can
> Becomes his captain's captain. . . .   (3.1.12–13, 16–22)

One is accustomed to associating Antony with the sensual indulgence
of Alexandria, and so moments such as these that align him instead
with the politic hypocrisy of Rome may easily pass unremarked. But
their presence suggests the extent to which Antony in fact partakes of
both worlds, while recognizing neither as his proper province. So
where, if not in Egypt or in Rome, lies Antony's true kingdom, the

realm of chivalric heroism to which he aspires and in which the horse might conceivably regain its symbolic status as an emblem of martial *virtus?* For Antony's play, at least, that realm appears to be located precisely in the regions of fantasy. As for Shakespeare's England, it seems to have lain no closer to the realm of heroic chivalry than did Egypt or Rome. Instead, Shakespeare's homeland provided him and his contemporaries with a heroic vocabulary whose key signifiers registered the very remoteness of the chivalric values to which they ostensibly referred. The notorious Jacobean inflation of honors, for instance, made it virtually impossible to locate any vestige of the medieval ideal of knighthood in the parade of ninnies, ne'er-do-wells, and nobodies upon whom King James bestowed that distinction. The collapse, under King James, of the Tudor sumptuary proclamations attested to the growing realization that clothing could no longer be effectively regulated as a marker of social position. Likewise, as prosperous merchants and citizens dressed like their betters, the Jacobean peerage seemed increasingly to degenerate into comic Dolphins or (in the case of an Essex, a Somerset, or a Buckingham) into scheming Iagos. In the process, their horses, too, partook of the general transformation, surviving in Shakespeare largely as markers of a lost social semiotic.

NOTES

1. Ralph Berry, *Shakespeare and the Awareness of the Audience* (London: Macmillan, 1985), 105.
2. All references to Shakespeare's works are drawn from the Riverside edition: William Shakespeare, *The Riverside Shakespeare.* ed. G. Blakemore Evans et al. (Boston: Houghton Mifflin, 1997).
3. Peter Edwards, *The Horse Trade of Tudor and Stuart England* (Cambridge, UK: Cambridge University Press, 1988), 13. For an overview of the increasing demand for horses in Elizabethan and Jacobean England, particularly within the relatively humble spheres of transportation and agriculture, see pp. 1–20. For a discussion of the culture of the warhorse in medieval Europe and England (where it declined rapidly after the fourteenth century), see R. H. C. Davis, "The Medieval Warhorse," in *Horses in European Economic History: A Preliminary Canter,* ed. F. M. L. Thompson (Leeds, UK: The British Agricultural History Society, 1983), 4–20.
4. Douglas Bruster, "Shakespeare and the Question of Culture," unpublished ms., 15. Bruster's discussion of culture is predicated upon the groundbreaking work of Raymond Williams in *Keywords: A Vocabulary of Culture and Society* (New York: Oxford University Press, 1976), 76–82. Williams traces the term's etymology to "early

uses [as] a noun of process: the tending *of* something, basically crops or animals," 77. Obviously the horse's exemplary status as domesticated animal renders it particularly representative of such processes.

5. Plato, *Euthyphro, Apology, Crito, Phaedo, Phaedrus*, trans. Harold North Fowler (London: William Heinemann, 1923).

6. Ovid, *Metamorphoses*, trans. Frank Justus Miller, 2 vols. (Cambridge, MA: Harvard University Press, 1984).

7. For recent commentary on Antony's reference to the shirt of Nessus, see Coppelia Kahn, *Roman Shakespeare: Warriors, Wounds, and Women* (London: Routledge, 1997), 129.

8. Homer, *The Iliad*, trans. Richmond Lattimore (1951; reprint, Chicago: University of Chicago Press, 1974).

9. Xenophon, *Cavalry Commander*, 9.4; in Xenophon, *Scripta Minora*, trans. G. W. Bowersock (Cambridge, MA: Harvard University Press, 1984).

10. Xenophon, *Cavalry Commander*, 1.9.

11. Xenophon, *Cavalry Commander*, 8.6.

12. Xenophon, *Cavalry Commander*, 8.7.

13. William Harrison, *The Description of England*, ed. Frank Edelen (New York: Folger Shakespeare Library and Dover Publications, 1994), 102.

14. Harrison, *The Description of England*, 95–96.

15. Gregory M. Colòn Semenza, "Sport, War, and Contest in Shakespeare's *Henry VI*," *Renaissance Quarterly* 54/1 (2001): 1251–72.

16. Plato, *The Republic*, trans. H. D. P. Lee (Harmondsworth, UK: Penguin, 1955).

17. Roger Ascham, *The Scholemaster*, ed. R. J. Schoeck (Don Mills, Ontario: J. M. Dent and Sons, 1966), 30. For the conventional association of horse breaking with the education of children, see Keith Thomas, *Man and the Natural World: Changing Attitudes in England 1500–1800* (London: Allen Lane, 1983), 45. Thomas claims, "it was no accident that the emergence in the seventeenth and eighteenth centuries of more humane methods of horse-breaking would coincide with a reaction against the use of corporal punishment in education."

18. Bruce Boehrer, *Shakespeare among the Animals: Nature and Society in the Drama of Early Modern England* (New York: Palgrave, 2002), 44–45.

19. Jeanne Addison Roberts, *The Shakespearean Wild: Geography, Genus, and Gender* (Lincoln: University of Nebraska Press, 1991).

20. For a discussion of the association of women with horses in *Coriolanus* and in *1 Henry IV*, see Michele Willems, "'Women and Horses and Power and War': Worship of Mars from *1 Henry IV* to *Coriolanus*," in *French Essays on Shakespeare and His Contemporaries: "What Would France with Us?"* ed. Jean-Marie Maguin and Michele Willems (Newark: University of Delaware Press, 1995), 189–202, esp. 192–93.

21. For representative commentary on this passage, see Rosalie L. Colie, *Shakespeare's Living Art* (Princeton: Princeton University Press, 1974), 187; Frankie Rubinstein, *A Dictionary of Shakespeare's Sexual Puns and Their Signification* (London: Macmillan, 1984), 129; Gordon Ross, "Enobarbus on Horses: *Antony and Cleopatra* 3.7.7–9," *Shakespeare Quarterly* 31/3 (1980): 386–87; David Bevington (ed.), *The Complete Works of Shakespeare* (New York: HarperCollins, 1992), 1293.

22. Robert Miola, *Shakespeare's Rome* (Cambridge, UK: Cambridge University Press, 1983), 138.

23. As Derek Traversi has noted, "The Folio text, which produces this adjective, has been questioned here; but the alternatives suggested scarcely carry conviction," *Shakespeare's Roman Plays* (Stanford, CA: Stanford University Press, 1963), 105 n.

24. Thomas Middleton, *Women Beware Women and Other Plays*, ed. Richard Dutton (Oxford: Oxford University Press, 1999).

25. Jonathan Goldberg makes the argument that from the start of his reign, King James I "presented himself in the Roman image, stamped with the Roman stamp," *James I and the Politics of Literature: Jonson, Shakespeare, Donne, and Their Contemporaries* (Baltimore, MD: Johns Hopkins University Press, 1983), 46. This argument, in turn, bears some affinity to Frances Yates's earlier claim that medieval and Renaissance monarchs—including those of the Tudor dynasty in England—depicted their regimes as in fact representing "the Roman empire itself through the theory of the translation of the Empire," *Astraea: The Imperial Theme in the Sixteenth Century* (1975; reprint, London: Ark, 1985), 2.

26. Lawrence Stone presents the thesis that James I's inflation of titles of honor encouraged conspicuous consumption by requiring "a symbolic justification for the maintenance or acquisition of status," *The Crisis of the Aristocracy 1558–1641* (Oxford: Clarendon Press, 1965), 185. In conjunction with this phenomenon, Stone argues, the Stuart "landed classes were particularly idle. In the Middle Ages war was a time-absorbing and honourable occupation"; however, by the early seventeenth century "nobles and squires found that the end of military service left time lying heavily on their hands," and they responded with a ruinous orgy of conspicuous consumption. For the gastronomic dimensions of this behavior, see *The Crisis of the Aristocracy*, 555–62; for horses as an element of conspicuous consumption, see *The Crisis of the Aristocracy*, 566–67.

27. Rosalie L. Colie, "Reason and Need: *King Lear* and the 'Crisis' of the Aristocracy," *Some Facets of "King Lear": Essays in Prismatic Criticism*, ed. Rosalie L. Colie and F. T. Flahiff (Toronto: University of Toronto Press, 1974), 209.

28. For the term "cloud" as referring to a dark blaze on the face of a horse, see the *Oxford English Dictionary* entry for "Cloud" sb. 6b,

where *Antony and Cleopatra* 3.2.50–51 provides the earliest illustration of the usage. For typical scholarly commentary on the line in question, see John Wilders (ed.), *Antony and Cleopatra* (London: Routledge, 1995), 3.2, n. 52; Bevington (ed.), *The Complete Works of Shakespeare*, 3.2, n. 53. For another, comparable Shakespearean usage, see *The Two Noble Kinsmen*, 5.4.50–53.

CHAPTER 4

"FAITH, SAY A MAN SHOULD STEAL YE—AND FEED YE FATTER": EQUINE HUNGER AND THEFT IN *WOODSTOCK*

Kevin De Ornellas

In a letter written on December 31, 1594, John Carey, the Acting Governor of Elizabeth I's military garrison at Berwick, pleads to William Cecil, the Lord High Treasurer, for urgent assistance with supplies:

> On St Stephen's day the whole horse garrison came to my house, saying they must either sell their horses or let them starve, for they could neither get in "the palace" oats, pease, beans or money—which last they have always hitherto had on a dearth to shift with. "But where there is nothing, it is hard shiftinge."[1]

Carey is careful to construct himself as a messenger bearing the complaints, rather than as a discontented instigator. He even distances himself from the disquiet by using a proverb in his last quoted comment, separating himself from the hubbub by unleashing a common and banal truism. The soldiers are themselves seen as single-minded military men first, and self-interested citizens second: their primary concern is for the effectiveness of their horses. The scarcity of their own food only becomes apparent in proximity to equine feeding issues—"oats, pease, beans" are elaborated as products that are not distinguished in terms of their potential consumers. They are all foods that can be eaten by both humans and horses. What Carey does not say explicitly is that if horse rations are short, then human rations are as well; citing the horses' condition allows a subtle, indirect criticism of the Crown's treatment of Berwick's soldiers.

This conjunction of horse and human food reinforces a fundamental early modern material reality: when animals suffer, humans are affected, and when humans decline, horses follow a similar course. In Carey's letter, this suffering is not one of sentiment, but of the nation's defensive necessity; if the horses are not fit, then they cannot be expected properly to work in tandem with the soldiers manning this Elizabethan frontier with Scotland.[2] In times of dearth, horses and humans become partners in hunger. The two forms are locked in an essentially symbiotic relationship. Anxieties of healthy consumption and healthy nationhood become inextricably linked within a cross-species vacuum of food supply.

His own age and decrepitude notwithstanding, the Lord Treasurer had problems other than provisioning Berwick. As Peter Clark has shown, supplying food to the English border guards provided Cecil with just another resource drain and a logistical headache that added to other problems—dreadful harvests, an escalating London population, civil unrest, and military expenses accrued in the related fights against Ireland and Spain.[3] Less than two months earlier, Cecil had received another depressed missive, this time from almost the opposite end of Elizabeth's home territory, from the Lord Mayor of London. The November 1591 letter conveys the Mayor's horror at the prospect of another playhouse being opened at Bankside. The Mayor condemns the present playhouses' patrons, writing that "the qualitie of such as frequent the sayed playes beeing . . . all vagrant persons & maisterless men that hang about the Citie, theeues, horsestealers whoremoongers coozeners conneycatching persones practizers of treason & such other lyke."[4] Plays, then, attract cheats, fornicators, and horse stealers. Despite the perceived prevalence of crimes such as conning and even treason, the national government— Cecil's Privy Council and the monarch—according to the letter, seems unaware and indifferent. It is "hir Ma[ties] people" and local dignitaries, not the distant Lord Treasurer or queen, who suffer the iniquities of the criminally inclined playgoers.[5] Taken together, the Berwick and London documents offer an argument that England is rent asunder with a chaos that is summarized by the condition of improperly controlled horses: military animals go hungry, while city, civilian horses are prone to illegal expropriation.

Late-Elizabethan England was indeed a land of hunger and theft, riot and revolt. These interrelated ills operate within a fluid, unfixed structure of mutually needy components—civil disorder and civil hunger not only fall hard upon one another, but thrive under the other's magnetic, energizing pull. This chapter is concerned with a moment in a play that is historically situated in the epicenter of the crisis of the 1590s, a moment that I interpret as a belligerent, campaign episode that calls for engagement with the time's malaise. The authorless, *dénouement*-less, nameless, early printed edition-less drama of the downfall of Thomas of Woodstock, the Duke of Gloucester, Richard II's uncle, was probably written some time between 1591 and 1595.[6] In the play, horse hunger and horse theft act as metaphors for discontent within Elizabethan society.

The twin ills of dearth and stealing are addressed in one particular scene in *Woodstock*. With an approach that has led to a trivializing of this individual scene, critics have been united: when Woodstock talks to a hungry horse, nothing happens except comic diversion. The twentieth-century editor of *Woodstock*, A. P. Rossiter, does not include the episode in a lengthy summary of the action; further, he gently paints the comments of Richard's uncle to the horse as insubstantial by using the informal adjective "chat."[7] Oddly, Rossiter includes the animal in his editorially created "Dramatis Personae," calling it "A Horse from Hackney."[8] Rossiter's annotations indicate that this specific equine moment has been treated with a humorous lightness by critics of the play. I seek to reverse this handling of a most dramatically vital, hippodramatic conceit.

After this introduction, I assess the intellectual and material background of the early modern convergence between animal and human food consumption: horses and humans in the period participated in a sort of commensalism. This material convergence between the two species and their symbiotic dependency form the basis for the discussion of the first section below, and provide a context for the later discussion of Woodstock's sympathetic engagement with a hungry animal. This identification is crucial, for the unique moment when a character speaks to a horse becomes less strange through its engagement with issues of economics, politics, and social relations. In short, the familiarity of the anxieties works to make the quirky dramaturgy appear less remote. Then, in the second section, I argue that in the 1590s there was a clear link between the threats to order in the state that were brought on by food shortages (for horses and people) and horse stealing. Conflicts of the Middle Ages are replayed on the late Elizabethan stage; the parallels between the two eras are manifest. When Woodstock talks to the hungry horse, he ponders becoming an outright rebel. A disenfranchised medieval nobleman becomes thematically confused with a lowly dissident of the

Renaissance. He talks of rebellion to his only listener—the horse—
and eventually shies away from revolt. The scene where Woodstock
talks to the hungry animal is explicated at length in the third section.
My decision on whether or not Woodstock's critique of Ricardian
misgovernment affords radical potential depends upon the disgruntled statesman's comments to the beast. For the horse is not a character. This is not a "normal" conversation between two figures on
stage. The animal, of course, cannot speak or even listen.
Woodstock's speech to the horse is effectively a soliloquy. It is
through this *solus* staging that a character's constructed characteristics
can be discovered. Thomas is only a would-be revolutionary figure.
His campaigns to ease the spur directed at the animals and people
under an exploitative government fail—he talks to and about
the lowly beasts and lowly humans, yet ultimately fails to change their
harsh lot. *Woodstock* is not a revolutionary text; instead, it is one that
dramatizes a narrative of decision making—to revolt or not to revolt.
Woodstock is constructed and presented as a nuanced and slippery
representative of a 1590s troubled English patriot.

BEHOLDING TO MAN: THE EARLY MODERN
DIETARY UNDERSTANDING BETWEEN
HORSES AND HUMANS

Woodstock's expression of sympathy for the hungry horse can be
placed within a historical context of interdependence between horses
and humans. In the first book of *Kings*, Ahab's immediate response
to rain after a three-year drought is to order Obadiah to seek good
pasture: "peradventure we may find grass to save the horses . . . that
we lose not all the beasts."[9] In this narrative, a human leader must
find ways to feed the horses as well as the human underlings. In the
Middle Ages, beasts fell as human luck fell. As Ann Hyland shows,
English horses suffered terribly during the bad harvests of 1310–14,
the drought of 1325–26, and the catastrophic flood of 1327.[10] Quite
simply, if excessive rains, for example, rot crops for humans, the same
excessive rains will molder and rot hay. Horses also suffer in such
times of want because, as fewer of them survive, those remaining
must be ever more demandingly used for burdensome tasks. Horses
are partners in the human quest for food—they are not eaten
themselves in early modern England. They help to assimilate food;
they do not provide it intrinsically.

Horsemeat was outlawed by Rome. The scriptural basis for the ban
(which was first asserted by Pope Gregory III ca. A.D. 732) is obscure.

Perhaps it is easy to ban the consumption of a product that is rarely consumed anyway. Laura Mason posits a number of theories to "explain the English aversion to horsemeat . . . the perception of horses as noble creatures, their role as pets, their value as draught animals, and dislike of the flavour."[11] Of these four possible reasons for the English rejection of hippophagy, only two seem relevant for the Renaissance. I have found no historical or literary evidence to suggest that horses were treated as pets in the Renaissance. They can be represented as trusty servants or as impressive possessions, but there is little sign that individual horses were treated in sentimentally companionate ways. Mason's last comment, that horsemeat does not taste pleasant, does not seem like a wholly serious remark. Traditionally, dearth- or famine-ridden communities have had to eat whatever is available, not what is appealing to taste. Mason's most salient point involves the use of the animal as a draught (load-dragging) creature. The early modern English work their horses hard, they will not eat them, however harsh the prevailing circumstances may be. However, in *Woodstock*, the hungry horse is worked too hard.

The neglect of the horse is analogous to Richard's disregard for Woodstock. His capacity for offering good advice on legal precedents, on financial care, and on probity is ignored. Woodstock's intellectual resources and the physical resource of the horse are neglected equally by Richard. Neither aged counselor nor four-footed beast are managed effectively by Richard's government. In addition, the lower sorts of the play are also undernourished, a failure of government that stirs up public agitation and Woodstock's ire. The failure to feed the horse properly parallels the failure to feed the country's citizens. The equine body and the human body need to be controlled equally. In portions of Elizabethan England, particularly in the early 1590s, human bodies could not be maintained because of bad harvests that led to dearth. Equally, horses were suffering because of the shortages of money and provender. Loss of state control over bodies was also made clear through the prevalence of horse theft. Before examining the scene in *Woodstock* where these anxieties from the 1590s congregate, it is appropriate to reinforce the inseparability of human hunger, equine hunger, and the retention of horses as rightful property.

Hunger, Riot, and Horse Theft: The 1590s Context of *Woodstock*

In March 1593, Elizabeth called one of her infrequent, short-lived parliaments. As ever, the Queen and Privy Council had one requirement: money. As Christopher Haigh writes, the speaker stressed, with an expression of apology, to the members of 1593's parliament, that "the threats to national security [from] Catholic Spain . . . and the risk of treason by discontented minorities, had forced the Queen to ask for taxation."[12] The response of one member of parliament, Francis Bacon, was surly—he spoke against the imposition of further taxation under the government's hoped-for "Triple Subsidy Bill." As A. G. R. Smith notes, the precarious state of "the government's financial situation in the 1590s made it possible for the members of the Commons to make their voices heard in no uncertain terms."[13] Bacon may have been heard, but he was not heeded. His own career under Elizabeth suffered—within two years even the backing of the still-favored Essex failed to procure him the posts of, first, attorneyship and, later, the solicitor-generalship.[14] Bacon's stand has been read favorably by some commentators. Showing something of a disregard for the public's limited rights of franchise for selecting members of the Elizabethan Commons, Brian Vickers writes that Bacon was "fulfilling his duties to his constituents by outlining the hardships that would follow if Queen Elizabeth's demands for extraordinary taxes were met."[15] This portrays Bacon as a proto-democrat, an egalitarian crusader who stands up to insatiable, princely summonses. Lisa Jardine and Alan Stewart admiringly report that Bacon's objections were "fought in the name of his conscience"; and W. A. Sessions, with an equally positive air, insists that Bacon's "brilliant opposition" emanated from "his deepest self."[16] These perspectives on Bacon provide one contextual bridge to the situation of Woodstock in the play, and offer further purchase on the 1590s and its preoccupied milieu.

The figure "plain Thomas" of Woodstock, speaking on stage at a temporal moment that coincides roughly with the controversial parliament of 1593, justifies his decision to wear plain clothes rather than the elaborate outfits favored by Richard II and his cronies. In his plain clothes, he will "do the realm more good / Than these that pill [pillage] the poor, to jet in gold" (2.2.36–37). This aligns Woodstock with a homespun local economy as opposed to the foreign ethos of Ricardian splendor. Thrifty and modest with clothing, the central figure can be seen to be reacting to the demonstrative consumption of the continental-influenced showmen who rule England. If we accept that the Reformation of the sixteenth century involved a reaction against the showy excesses of garish Catholic clerical dress, then Woodstock's homely, modest attire becomes a Protestant signifier. Echoes of religious divide thus further accentuate the division of plain

Thomas from lurid Richard. Woodstock's cloth is reformed and simple; Richard II's dress is unreformed and decadent. Divergent codes of personal deportment reflect the sobriety or otherwise of differently inclined characters' dress.

Previously, Woodstock has condemned the licentious, unthrifty predilections of the king, calling him "a wild-head" and a "headstrong youth" (1.3.25, 4.3.189). This is a king that—like a horse that cannot be held back with the bridle—is not influenced by noblemen such as Woodstock. It is perhaps too tempting to draw parallels between the Baconian concerns of March 1593 and the dramatically manufactured complaints of Richard II's uncle in *Woodstock*. There is, however, another point of connection between the Bacon who can be reconstructed from surviving documents and the drama's character of Woodstock. Both assert that their primary concern is with preventing rebellion. Neither is in any way committed to a radical course of action against the perceived tyrannies of their regal tax raisers. But there is one differentiated nuance between the Baconian and Woodstockian oppositions: when Woodstock talks to the hungry horse, he does, briefly, like many historical figures of the 1590s, contemplate revolt. He does this through the suggestion that he should steal, feed, and use this inconsiderately treated horse of the state. Woodstock questions the uncomprehending horse: "Faith, say a man should steale ye—and feed ye fatter, could ye run away with him lustily?" (3.2.172–73). The horse is a symbol of the hungry masses of Richard's England. Woodstock pictures a seizure of the reins of control, a coup, the outcome of which would be a more generous awarding of animal and human provender for servants of the state. This would lead to a society, that would, in Bacon's phrase, offer the permanent "Remedy" of removing "that materiall Cause of Sedition . . . Want and Poverty in the Estate."[17] It is a fleeting moment, a rare instance where Woodstock quietly conceives of a program of open revolt. In seeking to feed the lower sorts more generously, he is working to the same agenda as the food rioters of the early 1590s; and, with consideration of stealing horses, he is replicating a tactic used by numerous outcasts and rebels of the period.

A statute from 1589 reveals the Elizabethan executive's incredulity at the prevalence of horse stealing—so common is this form of theft that "neither in Pastures or Closes nor hardlie in Stables the same [horses] are to be in safety from stealinge."[18] An English horse's stable is not his castle, for the beast is not safe even in that cosseted sanctuary. Previous proclamations and statutes had attempted to limit the damage caused by horse robbers who operated outside of, and in competition with, officially sanctioned trade. But the wording of the 1589 statute concedes that these "have not wrought soe good effecte for the repressinge or avoydinge of Horsestealinge as was expected."[19] Patience is wearing out, as the drafters of the legislation acknowledge the failure of previous clampdowns. Success this time is not to be "expected," it is suggested, for this is an endemic, widespread problem—this blight concerns "most Counties of this Realme."[20] The statute's words maintain a steady air of disgruntled agitation, defending the validity of its law-enforcing predecessors; there is an evident outrage that citizens can repeatedly ignore such "sondrie good Ordinaunce."[21] Confronted with the seeming omnipotence and permanence of horse theft in the landscape, the statute can only respond with muted threats and weary recantations of the nuisance caused by the thieves and their horse-selling allies.

Horse stealers, in much prose of the period, are depicted as some sort of racially distinct tribe. Dictionaries and guides to the supposed linguistic codes of underground thieving cultures frequently translate this canters' tongue. John Awdeley writes of one breed of villain as "co[m]monly a stealer of horses, which they terme a Priggar of Paulfreys."[22] Such horse stealers possess a unique tenancy in the allotments of the English language. In a 1628, first-person verse story about a highwayman's conversion to morality, one John Clavell narrates, from a lonely King's Bench cell, a long section where he insists that even the way people ride can reveal the indisputable fact that they steal horses.[23] For early modern commentators, horse thieves are presented as a recognizable blight; they are a mobile, almost racially Other, alien presence in England.

The 1589 statute condemns the "Horscorsers" who collaborate with thieves by selling on the stolen livestock. Like the actual thieves, these horse dealers are constructed as a beastly infestation. In Samuel Rid's *Martin Mark-All* (1610), the preface is consciously presented as a sales pitch that should not be accepted at face value. Together with dedicatory verses, the word of a preface is "farre worse than a Horse-coursers commendation of a Smythfield Iade."[24] This satiric comment on the book trade compares the publishing business to horse selling—in Elizabethan terms, this is an excoriating comparison. Again, we see that some twentieth-century commentators and their early modern counterparts have a similarly coruscating attitude. J. A. Sharpe describes the Elizabethan horse coursers as people who "displayed the same standards of honesty and fair-dealing popularly attributed to used-car dealers in modern Britain."[25] Sharpe goes on to discuss allegations that horses' appearances could be changed to disguise their criminally acquired provenance: "the early modern equivalent of false number plates."[26] By relating early modern annoyances to our own, this sort of criticism sympathizes with the law-abiding classes in late Tudor England, while attacking and homogenizing all those who operate outside legally sound structures of commerce. Peter Edwards shows his respect for early capitalists by emphasizing that "horse thieves can clearly be distinguished from the reputable dealers who did so much to develop the trade during the course of the Tudor and Stuart period."[27] So, honest, proper horse dealers were a vital cog in the progression of a mercantile economy—they are epoch-making. Edwards separates corrupt horse coursers from honest sellers on caste lines: unrighteous dealers "came from lower social classes than the legitimate dealers . . . [they were] less responsible members of society than their respectable counterparts."[28] Dishonest dealers are illegitimate bastards, then, lumped together with other squads of England's criminal fraternity. When Woodstock talks to the animal about horse stealing, he is associated with these lower, arguably criminal, classes—groups that have been sometimes crudely castigated by both Elizabethan and subsequent observers. Horse theft was sometimes seen as more than a mere nuisance: occasionally, equine skulduggery can be seen to threaten the very existence of the Elizabethan state. Woodstock, when he speaks of stealing a kingly horse, reverts to the camp of the revolutionary thief. In this brief moment of theater, Woodstock is aligned with the hungry classes who would steal horses and attack the very structures of early modern government.

The perception of a connection between illegal horse procurement and anti-state agitation is established in a proclamation, issued under Edward VI's name, in April 1549. This is concerned with security on the Scottish borders. For the main part, the proclamation's text is aimed against captains of English companies of soldiers, some of whom had, apparently, been misappropriating the Tudor regime's equine resources. It is announced that if any "captain of lighthorsemen or soldier of his band be so hardy as to sell, give, exchange or otherwise, by any fraud . . . any horse, mare, or gelding, to be taken or come into the possession of any Scottishman or other stranger being his majesty's enemy . . . [he] shall . . . incur the danger . . . [of] execution."[29] Here, strict retention of horses becomes a racial imperative. Ethnically and nationally different, the Scottish are demarcated as racially Other through the term "strangers," a loaded term that argues for their exotic foreignness (*Oxford English Dictionary n* 2.a). Draconian measures are threatened to quash any equine-configured cooperation between English troops and Scottish Others. Misappropriation of horses, in the period, is often linked with hunger. One of Robert Greene's numerous picaresque tracts depicts a "certaine Priggar, a horse-stealer," ripe with excitement as he sees a vulnerable, spotless "blacke" specimen.[30] "The horse was so faire and lustie, wel proportioned, of a high crest, of lusty countenance, well buttockt, and strongly trust [reliable, sound], which set the Priggars teeth a water to haue him," Greene relates.[31] The horse, to the thief, is presented in language that at once stresses the appetitive and the criminally seductive. The thief's mouth waters as he contemplates the "well buttockt" animal, the Otherness of which is enhanced by its blackness. So appealing is this magnetic beast, that it is almost good enough to eat. The rogue loses water orally as his competing appetites come together in the vision of a supreme, satisfying equine prize. Robert Payne, in a 1589 advertisement for the bounties of Ireland, offers potential English planters an equally mouth-watering supply of food and horses. Payne forms a long list of the availability of wild birds, including "Swannes, Cranes, Pheasantes . . . & al other fowles much more plentiful then in England."[32] Coming in 1589, a couple of years after dearth had caused numerous fatalities in some parts of England, this Cockayne-like vision of a country stuffed with game birds can be seen as an archly constructed temptation. Within the same short paragraph, Payne tells us that Irish "carthorsses, mares, and little hackneyes are of very small price."[33] Avian foodstuffs and equine tools are roughly sandwiched together in what amounts to a call for the colonial theft of Ireland's abundant resources.

Other connections between horses and food theft occur in representations of fraud in the period. With immense sarcasm, John Awdeley notes that there are types of servant who will "make his Maisters horse eate pies and rybs of beefe, and drinke ale and wyne."[34] Of course, the animal does not enjoy this fine drink and food: by misappropriating funds that are ostensibly procured to nourish the quadruped, the worker serves his own greedy inclinations. Neglect of the master's equine property will ensue; animal welfare will suffer in this manifestation of theft. Plain Thomas's disgust at the sorry circumstances of the hungry horse of *Woodstock* is aimed at the state's hierarchy—the ownership of the horse—rather than attendant staff. Resources that should feed the horse and the lower human sorts are plundered for kingly excess. Woodstock, fleetingly, then, might be characterized as a horse-stealing and food-rioting figure who may claim jurisdiction over all beastly and human minions, thus inspiring a more humane distribution of sustenance.

"A Very Indifferent Beast": Woodstock's Equine Revolutionary Colleague

At the court of Richard II, plain Thomas is discovered in down-to-earth dress. His homespun clothing is not commensurate with ostentatious government—it is suited to country, not court. Even his family ally, York, expresses his disquiet that the "coarse and vulgar" laud Woodstock for his humble habit (1.2.198). York uses two derogatory adjectives to describe the lower sorts when one adjective would suffice: simply, he stresses the perceived baseness of Thomas's support. Coming from a kinsman, this underlines Woodstock's isolation from the mainstream of national politics. Woodstock is figured as an outsider, one who is uncomfortable with the obsequiousness of princely courts. This is significant because a later incident of misidentification—when Woodstock is wrongly supposed to be a horse-holding servant—is thereby facilitated. It sends the character on a trajectory that moves him away from courtly trappings, marking him as more common man than stately totem, a figure more likely to shovel a horse's dung than ride pompously in display. Woodstock is constructed as the consistent earth to Richard's changeable fire.

Thomas's plain dress is repeatedly contrasted with Richard II's opulence. At the king's wedding, Woodstock's usually simple appearance is amended to rich magnificence in a demonstrative concession to the new regime. With self-lacerating language, Thomas tells the court that "For once I'll sumpter a gaudy wardrobe" (1.1.211). As a verb, "sumpter" means to wear, but it also has equine connotations. A sumpter-horse is a packhorse, a solid, reliable, unexcitable beast of burden. Thomas is seen as a reluctant beast of burden, a sumpter-horse whose homely inclinations are compromised by a monarchy that demands splendor. Woodstock's staid fortunes are quickly contrasted with the upwardly mobile successes of Richard's followers. Tresilian becomes the Lord Chief Justice. His back-slapping colleague Bagot tells him that he is "already mounted on [his] footcloth" (1.2.25). Whereas Woodstock is presented increasingly as a disenfranchised, unwilling horse, the rising follower of Richard is semantically elaborated as a rider who is getting a monarchical leg-up to the higher saddle of influence over government. A "footcloth" is a "large richly-ornamented cloth laid over the back of a horse . . . a mark of dignity and state" (*Oxford English Dictionary*). The play's dramatic rhetoric, then, which summons up images of shiny equine decoration, is a linguistically formulated marker for the rise in influence of the parasites of the state. In contradistinction to this, Woodstock's equine finery for the wedding hangs on him like a synecdoche for shame, an evident sign of his subjection to Richard's visually ornate rule. Richard is content to spend money to solidify the appearance of luxury. For him, a horse is not just a tool, but also a backdrop to project his splendor onto—he will "ride through London only to be gazed at" (3.1.81). This hedonistic appropriation of equine potential is couched in response to a homoerotically charged invitation to Richard from another hanger on, Greene: "Prithee sweet king, let's ride / somewhither an it be but to show ourselves" (3.1.75–76). The "sweet" couple will "ride" together. The language of horse riding is wrapped in a tender frame of romantic sounds. The soft, whispering vowel sounds—"Prithee sweet king"—echo the sounds of intimate affection, not stern, statesmanlike vigor. The riding will be a little adventure for the couple. The problem for government is that the king and parasite's intimacy will be paradoxically apparent to all who see their progress. Richard provocatively courts the malign awe of a put-upon public—he agrees with his minion that they should "ride through London only to be gazed at." Richard is not dramatically presented as a firm leader. He is seen to respond to rather than to direct suggestions about horse-backed splendor. Metaphorically, he is discovered as a passive type, as he is ridden by Greene and other self-serving, unworthy agents of greed and misappropriation.

The rejection of manly virtues of active strength and sacrifice is seen by Woodstock as destructive of English leadership. The following exchange focuses attention on the combative vitality of horse imagery in the play:

> KING RICHARD.   But, noble uncle,
>   I did observe what I have wondered at.
>   As we today rode on to Westminster
>   Methought your horse, that wont to tread the ground
>   And pace as if he kicked it scornfully,
>   Mount and curvet like strong Bucephalus,
>   Today he trod as slow and melancholy
>   As if his legs had failed to bear his load.
> WOODSTOCK.   And can ye blame the beast? Afore my God,
>   He was not wont to bear such loads, indeed.
>   A hundred oaks upon these shoulders hang
>   To make me brave upon your wedding-day,
>   And more than that, to make my horse more tire,
>   Ten acres of good land are stitched up here.
>   You know, good coz, this was not wont to be.   (1.3.84–99)

At an immediate level, Richard mocks his uncle for riding a slow, unspectacular horse. Woodstock, however, retaliates with a complicated, politically rich and metaphorically laden allegory of his nephew's plunder of England. He elaborates a pathetic fallacy whereby the horse itself is ashamed of his unnecessarily ostentatious dress. The animal is given agency for thought—"can ye blame the beast?" The formerly proud beast is reduced to a creature of pointless burden.

Here, in continuing with the discourse of Woodstock as a type of wronged horse, it is pertinent to acknowledge that the historical figure, Thomas of Woodstock, is exhibited as a gulled sot in Tudor chronicles. Paul Strohm points out that Richard II was not necessarily the profligate spendthrift that Lancastrian critics and the author(s) of *Woodstock* allege. Richard was very much solvent at the time of his 1399 deposition, but, as Strohm insists, "he was widely *perceived* as profligate, squandering the resources of his realm."[35] Equally, it should be argued, in Tudor propaganda that slights Richard II, Thomas of Woodstock merely becomes *perceived* to be a righteous campaigner against excessively autocratic and extravagant kingship. The historical figure was no friend of the revolting poor. In fact, he was heavily involved in the storming of a rebel fortification at Billericay, Essex during June 1381. By the mid-1380s, Woodstock had become one of the Lord Appellants, vocally, hawkishly opposed to Richard's commitment to pursuing peace with France, amongst other policy wranglings. Though spared the wrath of the state's ultimate hierarchy at this time, Thomas's influence progressively dwindled. As Richard II's recent biographer, Nigel Saul, states, by 1397 Woodstock's opinion was "being disregarded and ignored . . . marginalized politically, Gloucester was of little or no account in the king's counsels."[36] Whatever luck Woodstock had previously had, it ran out in July 1397. He was arrested by Richard and his allies and brought to Calais, expiring before being tried for treason. He may or may not have been murdered. For the Lancastrian and Tudor chroniclers, though, keen to discredit Richard and beatify any potential heroes of resistance, there was no doubt about the kingly brutality that ushered in Woodstock's death.

In John Hardyng's phrase, Thomas was "the duke y^t was ful clene."[37] This spotless nobleman was treated with clandestine brutality: "he [was] sent, to Calyce secreately" and "murthered."[38] The "clene," open, upfrontedness of a blunt objector is contrasted with the deceitful machinations of a mendacious government. Holinshed, in his *Chronicles*, argues that there is no doubt that Richard II

decided to have his uncle killed; it is claimed, indeed, that "the K[ing]
wold haue it done with all expedition."[39] However, this proponent of
the Tudor myth highlights the essential textuality of his history.
Holinshed writes that Thomas Mowbray, a Ricardian favorite at the
time, "caused his seruantes to cast fetherbeddes vpon him
[Woodstock], and so to smoother him to death, or otherwyse to
straungle him with towels (as some write)."[40] Different accounts offer
different explanations of Thomas's end. Some of these sources conflict, as Holinshed's text acknowledges: if one aspect of Woodstock's
fall differs from speaker to speaker, then other aspects of the fall must
also be competitive in their alternative narrative offerings. Woodstock
is, in short, manufactured through a selection of contradictory voices.

All historians who relate the events of July 1397, however, agree
on one element of the arrest of Woodstock: the necessary role of
horses in the operation. In terms of place of residence alone, there is
a great physical distance between Richard II and Woodstock. The
king resides at the palace of Westminster; his uncle's estate is at
Plashy, a small town in Essex. The play retains this topographical gulf
between the quarreling king and neglected counselor. Horses are
needed for any journey between the two locations. Indeed, this
dependence on equine transport forms a thematic fissure: it is repeatedly stated that characters, in their imagined existence off the stage,
would have to "ride down to Plashy," to "ride home to Plashey
house" (4.1.90–91, 2.3.72). This attention to the material need for
horses underpins the metaphorical preeminence of the animal in
Woodstock. (Also, on a more practical level, it justifies the need for one
of the state's horses to be ridden to Woodstock's home by a courtly
worker, facilitating the horse-holding scene.) Yet the horse-back journey from Westminster into Essex also forms one of the cruxes in the
Tudor historians' depiction of a benign Thomas.

May McKisack describes the arrest of the historical Woodstock as
a mammoth, kingly task. Richard II, she writes, accompanied by "a
large number of household troops and Londoners . . . rode down to
Pleshey by night."[41] The king and his followers are depicted as the
riders, the determined agents of action. "When Gloucester
[Woodstock] came out to meet them," McKisack writes, "his nephew
told him that, since he would not heed his invitation, he had come to
fetch him."[42] The mounted monarch personally seized Thomas, as a
competent horseman would seize a recalcitrant horse. In the
Dictionary of National Biography, it is noted that the journey from
Westminster to Plashey took place throughout the night, before
"Richard with his own hand arrested him [Thomas]." Richard II is

constructed in these narratives as a hands-on leader, a ruthless bridler of even familial malcontents. Richard's control, and Thomas's immersion in ridden victimhood, are furthered more bitterly in Richard Grafton's *Chronicle* (1569). The king himself is absent, but his staff are very much in control over an unsuspecting Woodstock. Here, the colorful account of Thomas's arrest reads almost like an episode from one of the cony-catching, prose fiction pamphlets that were becoming common:

> And when he was a horsback, with a merry cheere, he sayd, vnto the Lordes that abode for him Nowe, whether shall we go? And who shall be our guide? I or one of you? They aunswered with reuerence. Nay syr, it becommeth you to leade, and we to folow. Then sayde he, let vs set forth a Gods name . . . and so he was conueyed to Calice, and thus taken and arrested.[43]

In this representation, Woodstock is envisaged as a sot who has been gulled into participating in his own capture. Believing that the future captors are on conventional business, he cooperates readily. Here, Thomas is an English Everyman—he even utters mild oaths ("Gods name" here signifying impatience) like an exasperated, lowly citizen. Being on "horsback," holding the reins, should symbolize a measured, assured control over the situation. But the gulling "Lordes," with their exaggerated politeness ("reuerence"), mock an unknowing Woodstock. It is the agency of Thomas that is stolen, not his horse. Now more like a horse than a rider, he has become deprived of the discourse of horsemanship—the "Lordes" offer him the chance to "leade," even as they are leading this blind, naive horse into the halter held by Richard's camp. A noteworthy innovation in Grafton's text is the introduction of a similarly fooled populace (the "Commo[n]s"). The masses had, according to the chronicler, "great hope" in the Francophobic, nationalist champion Thomas. They had, it is suggested, regarded Woodstock's position as secure, since "by his prosperitie the same was safe from all inward and outward enemies."[44] The populace has been gulled out of its patriotic champion; its leader has been cozened into submission. These "Lordes" of Richard—and by extension, their families' descendants, some of whom retained sway in Tudor times—share a similar technique to horse stealers. Horse stealing can be a subtle art in the Renaissance, and is not always an action of ham-fisted force. Woodstock, crude in dress and demeanor, is also crude and monosyllabic ("Faith, say a man should steal ye") when he ponders horse theft. The originality of

Woodstock resides in its complication of the Tudor myth of a spotless Thomas. However, before examining his key speech to the beast, it is necessary to reflect on one practical, theatrical issue: on stage, is Woodstock talking to a real horse? *Woodstock*'s editor and commentator, A. P. Rossiter, offers little help about the beastly credentials of the equine "character" that Thomas has that "chat" with: "I have no idea whether this can have been anything less than a real horse," he concedes.[45] W. J. Lawrence speculates intelligently, but without evidence, that the play may have been performed in one of the many inn yards that staged Elizabethan theatrical events. "The stables of these inns were seldom without a lean old horse or two," he writes.[46] In this formulation, any haggard animal could become an actor. But there is no convincing indication that a real horse ever stood on a purpose-built, professional theater stage before the Restoration. Whether or not Woodstock is talking to a real horse is not a matter of mere theatrical antiquarianism. In performance, the appearance of the animal could have very important interpretive consequences. If there is a horse, and it does indeed look starved, then an audience could respond with either comic contempt for its sorry state or sympathetic acknowledgment of Thomas's outrage at the beast's treatment. However, if this notional "actor" seems like a well-provisioned-for creature, then this would undercut Woodstock's criticisms of the Ricardian order: Thomas's complaints about mishandling and neglect of the state's resources would appear discreditable and hyperbolic should the beast appear healthy and lively like the attractive horse from Greene's pamphlet. So, on a performance level, it does matter whether this is a real horse (and whether such a horse is fat or thin). For our purposes, though, it is not absolutely essential to know whether a horse was or was not on stage. Rather, the meeting between Woodstock and the horse, and the points of contact between the meeting and the crises of the 1590s, take on greater significances as mythological constructions: in short, the scene discharges an ideological purpose and touches, in particular, on Woodstock's own potential for confrontation with the hegemony of the ruling regime.

Margot Heinemann says of the horse-holding scene that it presents

comic history in the popular tradition. In a memorable stage image . . . a groom tips Woodstock sixpence to hold his horse . . . with which the great man carries on a sympathetic political discussion. This prepares the way for a grimmer confrontation. [47]

This insightful reading moves critical dialogue away from the perception that the scene's effects are limited to comic diversion. There is only one aspect of Heinemann's comment that I differ from: for that critic, the horse-holding scene "prepares the way" for a grim confrontation; I, on the other hand, consider this scene to be one of the play's most abrasive interludes. When Thomas comments on the leanness of a courtier's horse, he is descrying the entire mismanagement of England. The scene's consequence—which transcends questions of elusive theatrical history—lies in its function as an allegory of kingly misrule, of the murderously unequal distribution of England's resources by a corrupt political organization.

It is correct, however, to note that there is a comic energy in the horse-holding scene. This does not contradict my argument that the scene is profoundly serious: cold exposure of harsh issues seems tougher when they follow hard on high spirits raised by uproarious entertainment. A courtier arrives at Plashy to speak to Woodstock. He will not dismount from his horse until he is received within the house's fortifications (3.2.120–23). Thomas will receive the visitor, ruefully noting that, unlike other Ricardian agents, this one at least "brings no blank charters with him" (3.2.118)—these iniquitous taxing devices have been used in the play to fund Richard's elaborate feasts, in what Garrett A. Sullivan, Jr. calls "the subordination of hospitality to the wilful pursuit of the Crown's prerogatives and pleasures."[48] Tension rises, though, as one of Woodstock's servants, speaking candidly to his master, castigates the demanding guest as "some fine fool. He's attired very fantastically" (3.2.127). The artificiality of the servant's alliterative phrase draws attention to the artificial, ostentatious dress and manner of the horseman. The trope of the ridiculous is compounded by the fact that a lowly servant feels able to describe a knight in such a dismissive manner to his lord, Thomas, the Duke of Gloucester. This represents a breakdown in the conventions of deference and respect. The servant proceeds to reject the courtier's haughty request to hold the horse. It is a ridiculous situation when a figure on the king's business is hindered by uncooperative servants ("a rude swain") of the host (3.2.136). To borrow the terminology of Northrop Frye, as adapted by Bruce R. Smith, this servant belongs to the "low mimetic" type. Such lowly figures have a small "range of possibilities open" to them.[49] It is unconventional and absurd, therefore, for a servant to hinder a superior, "mid-mimetic" type such as the courtier. By definition, a servant is emplaced to assist, not to impede.

The silliness continues when the visitor mistakes plain Thomas for a groom, asking him—"prithee walk my horse"—to take charge of

the tired steed (3.2.141). The supercilious front of the courtier has
been pricked. Now, he has to ask for favors, not just receive them.
This disparity in his behavior is itself a pointed criticism of the
Ricardian regime: the courtier is ready to accept favor and lush hospitality as a given inevitability, but, in the appellant-inclined house of
Woodstock, he must compromise his taste for arrogantly expected
luxury. Woodstock does not reveal his identity to the courtier, and
proceeds to walk the horse around the yard (or stage). This case of
mistaken identity becomes a matter of disguise and illusion, as the
"high mimetic" type performs the role of a "low mimetic" type.
Woodstock's manipulation of the courtier's mistake may appear to
offer an opening of powerful potential for Thomas—he is, after all,
figured to be holding the reins. But Woodstock is constructed as a
victim here. In holding the horse, he becomes a "low mimetic" type,
suffering, exhibiting meekness to complement a developed, princi-
pled social conscience. Woodstock presents himself as a figure working for all of England. In a twist that further enhances the challenged
conventions and morals of Richard's England, he modulates into a
cipher who considers horse stealing to be a possibly legitimate course
of political action.

Theologically charged imagery envelops the horse-holding incident in *Woodstock*. Within 50 lines, we hear remarks citing "heaven,"
"mercy," "ifaith" (in faith), "rood" (Christ's cross), "By th'Mass,"
"Sfoot" (God's foot), and "graces" (3.2.136–83). The prominence
of Christian imagery at a superficially comic moment heightens our
receptiveness to more sober processes of anxiety at work. The tone,
though already complicated by the theological allusions, drops its
comical flavor when Woodstock is left alone with the horse.

The courtier leaves the stage, ironically to look for Woodstock.
With the flashy outsider gone, Thomas speaks in conventional soliloquy at first, and then directly to the horse: the two parts of the speech
maintain a striking seriousness of content and tone. This is
Woodstock's entire (prose) speech to the horse:

> Come on, sir, you have sweat hard about this haste, yet I think you
> know little of the business. [*Walks the horse.*] Why so I say? You're a
> very indifferent beast; you'll follow any man that will lead you. Now
> truly, sir, you look but e'en leanly on't. You feed not in Westminster
> Hall a-days where so many sheep and oxen are devoured. I'm afraid
> they'll eat you shortly if you tarry amongst them. You're pricked more
> with the spur, than the provender, I see that. I think your dwelling be
> at Hackney when you're at home, is't not? You know not the duke

neither, no more than your master, and yet I think you have as much wit as he. Faith, say a man should steal ye and feed ye fatter, could ye run away with him lustily? Ah, your silence argues a consent, I see. By th'Mass, here comes company. We had both seen taken if we had, I see. (3.2.159–75)

Woodstock identifies the animal as a victim of the courtier's hasty business dealings. These activities are carried out on behalf of King Richard II. It follows, then, that the beast starves and sweats because it gives so much and receives little in return from the ungrateful tyranny that it serves. It accepts great spurs of demands from its master, while receiving little foodstuff or rest, Woodstock argues. The relationship between horses and humans is violated by Richard's staff. Ideally, they would be colleagues in a partnership of convenience, with one thriving alongside the other. But Woodstock sees the ruthless exploitation of the horse as a path that could lead even to the animal itself being eaten, "devoured" by the savage overeaters at Westminster. The harsh, unnecessary treatment of the animal is seen to be suspect and foolish. So, for Woodstock, the poor treatment meted out to the courtier's horse is not just a matter for sentimentality about animal welfare, but an instance of common sense being ignored in the frenetic usages of all available objects, animal or otherwise.

The identification of the horse with Woodstock is embodied in his poor pay. Thomas is given a "tester" by the courtier, who remains unaware of his hostler's noble status. This is a coin (sometimes called the "testoon") that had been devalued during the reigns of Henry VIII and Edward VI, and again in Elizabethan times.[50] Once worth a shilling, a "tester" had become worth only a sixpence. The coin's very name, indeed, became a pejorative term, as the coin became known for being "debased and depreciated" (*Oxford English Dictionary* 3). Woodstock's remuneration for his chore is evidently paltry; he receives a coin that was originally valuable, but is now tarnished. The noun "tester" has another early modern resonance—it could refer to a "piece of armour for the head of a horse" (*Oxford English Dictionary* 2). The act of giving Thomas a "tester," then, draws a linguistic analogy between him and the horse—Woodstock gets a "tester," just as the courtier's mount might. During this episode of "topsy-turvy" carnival, where a horse gets called "sir" by a king's uncle, the animal and Woodstock join together on the same, deprived side. For the period of this role-playing pantomime, both are revealed as harshly done-by beasts of burden.

When the courtier returns and Woodstock's identity is revealed by a furious Cheney—the mood of comedy having now completely passed—Thomas orders a servant to take the horse to a stable and to "meat [feed] him well" (3.2.196). The indifferent visitor does not express any desire for the animal under his charge to be fed. Concern for the animal's welfare—and more importantly, its longevity as a useful tool—prompts Woodstock to feed the animal. This might be seen as a demonstration of how a government should reward its faithful followers. To strengthen his self-fashioning as a more generous leader, Thomas takes the derisory "tester" he is offered for walking the horse and increases it, giving twelve pence to his servant. This is not a huge financial improvement from a sixpence, but at least demonstrates Woodstock's belief that workers should receive more than the Ricardian regime allows.

Woodstock seizes the reins and comes to express his cohesion with the people of England, a link that is perpetrated by and maintained through a similarity of harsh treatment from the careless, self-absorbed political world. Woodstock asks whether it is a good idea to steal the horse and feed it and its colleagues more effectively. But he does not steal the horse. He does not make a move to challenge Richard's misgovernment. Rather, Woodstock snipes from the sidelines. Only one "character" hears his comments on horse stealing: the beast. In practice, Woodstock offers no revolutionary agenda. In *Woodstock*, Richard's regime is seen as directionless and unfocused, and without any effective opposition (Bolingbroke, the future Henry IV and Richard's historical nemesis, is not mentioned in the play). It sounds rather like the disillusioned 1590s England of an aging Cecil and heirless Elizabeth. Rebels in late Elizabethan England often made tactical efforts to steal horses and to feed the poor with proceeds gained through throwing over perceived oppressors. But no successful interior rebellion occurred in the period. Contemporary audiences of *Woodstock* may have looked to Thomas as a figure of nostalgic yearning, a righteous hero who stands up to a king that the Tudor chroniclers had taught everyone to despise. But Woodstock disappoints. He articulates outrage at the effeminizing of Englishmen and economic wastage, but without occasioning any effective counterbalancing maneuver. Articulated through the familiar medium of the history play, Woodstock's failure to curb the excesses of Richard II becomes an acute symbol of the perceived lack of focused dissidence in Renaissance England; the 1390s are appropriated to comment on the 1590s. Woodstock loses metaphorical control of the reins. When he does seize control of the courtier's horse's bit, it is fleeting and transient, a demonstration of Thomas's ultimate impotence. The revolutionary moment passes, and Woodstock's standing continues to plummet. Rather than as an insurrectionary icon, he winds up as a powerless, downtrodden sot. With Woodstock's demise, hopes for material gains for the exploited public also disappear. It is a depressing ending for an Elizabethan audience who may well have looked to Thomas as a symbol of opposition to unpopular governments.

CONCLUSION

In 1562, a proclamation was issued, descrying what it presents as two related problems: "the monstrous abuse of apparel almost in all estates, but principally in the meaner sort. The other is the decay and disfurniture of all kind of horses for [military] service within the realm."[51] An explicit link is forged between overelaborate human dress, the declining quality of horses suitable for the state's work, and the loss of quality in horse-management equipment. The proclamation's text goes on to lament "the decay of horses within the realm, which partly riseth by stealing and carrying numbers of horses, geldings, mares, and colts out of the realm."[52] The stress on the varied ages and sexes of the disappearing horses works to convey a sense of numerically large herds of animals being surreptitiously moved away from Elizabeth's use. Although the proclamation is alarmist and exaggerated in tone, its embedded anxieties about excessively expensive human dress and the national imperative to maintain an effectively maintained bloodstock anticipate some of those in *Woodstock*.

Like most Elizabethan proclamations, that of 1562 had little effect in practice. A similar text was issued for the monarch 35 years later. The July 1597 proclamation complains that "the meanest sort [of humans] are as richly appareled as their betters, and the pride that such inferior persons take in their garments [is] driving many for their maintenance to robbing and stealing by the highway."[53] The text attributes crime to vanity, not to hunger. Highway robbery (often, of course, including horse theft, and always involving mounted felons) is inspired by the drive for showy clothes. Human bodies are treated coterminously with equine bodies in this proclamation. Subjects are told that "none shall have in their saddles, bridles, stirrups, trappings, harness, footcloth, or other furniture of their horse any velvet, guilding, damasking with gold or silver, silvered, under the degree of baron's son."[54] If a rider is not a nobleman, then finding a lawful item to decorate the animal's equipment with, and finding a legal part of horse gear to fasten the gimmick onto, will take some creative ingenuity. Again, we find that the fortunes of horses and humans mingle together. The problem with these proclamations about accoutrements of clothing is that they address only external concerns—it is the outside of horses' and humans' bodies that are (theoretically, at least) regulated and controlled.

Woodstock shares some anxieties with the writers of these proclamations—the necessity to regulate the treatment of English horses, the unmanly inclination to present oneself gaudily—but the play insists that the ultimate problems of the English body are internal. In 1597, when the last proclamation cited was produced, people had literally been starving because of dearth and consequent high food prices. Both the crotchety Woodstock constructed in the play and the 1590s would-be opponents or rebels he represents fail greatly to amend governmental policy so that burdens on poorer sorts are lessened. But at least the dramatic Thomas sees the disparity between opulent presentation and internal emptiness. For Woodstock, ineffective though he is, offers a voice for the internal bodily needs of late Elizabethan subjects, human and equine.

Notes

Research for this essay was conducted at the Huntington Library, San Marino, California and at the British Library, London, enabled by a Huntington Fellowship and by Arts and Humanities Research Board travel grants. Mark Thornton Burnett, Richard Dutton, Ewan Fernie, and Sarah Hatchuel commented usefully on earlier versions.

1. Joseph Bain (ed.), *The Border Papers: Calendar of Letters and Papers Relating to the Affairs of the Border of England and Scotland, 1560–94*, 2 vols. (Edinburgh: H. M. General Register House, 1894–96), vol. II, 554.
2. Berwick-upon-Tweed is located close to England's east coast, just south of the current border with Scotland.
3. Peter Clark, "A Crisis Contained? The Condition of English Towns in the 1590s," in *The European Crisis of the 1590s*, ed. Peter Clark (London: Allen and Unwin, 1985), 48.
4. E. K. Chambers and W. W. Greg (eds.), "Dramatic Records of the City of London: The *Remembrancia*," in *The Malone Society Collections, Part One* (Oxford: Oxford University Press/Malone Society, 1908), p. 75.
5. Chambers and Greg, "Dramatic Records."
6. As the title of a diplomatic transcript of the manuscript edition (*The First Part of the Reign of King Richard the Second, or Thomas of Woodstock*, ed. Wilhelmina P. Frijlinck, Oxford: Oxford University Press/Malone Society, 1929) indicates, there is no standard title for the play. I call the work *Woodstock*, which is the most commonly used

title. There have been three modern-spelling editions of the text: ed.
A. P. Rossiter (London: Chatto and Windus, 1946), ed. G. Parfitt and
S. Shepherd (Nottingham, UK: Nottingham Drama Texts, 1977),
and ed. P. Corbin and D. Sedge (Manchester, UK: Manchester
University Press, 2002). All of the citations in my essay derive from
Corbin and Sedge's recent edition. The consensus that the play dates
from the early 1590s has been broken by Macdonald Jackson, who
asserts that the play was actually written ca. 1606–10, "Shakespeare's
Richard II and the Anonymous *Thomas of Woodstock*," *Medieval and
Renaissance Drama in England* 14 (2002): 17–65. Jackson also speculates that the author was Samuel Rowley. The play's preoccupations
with food shortages, unpopular government, and civic unrest are
clearly influenced by experiences of the 1590s. So, it is appropriate to
call *Woodstock* a 1590s play, even if it was not put on paper during that
exact period.

7. For this summary of the play, see Rossiter, *Woodstock*, 21–23; for the
"chat" remark, see 76.

8. Rossiter, *Woodstock*, 77.

9. Robert Carroll and Stephen Prickett (eds.), *The Bible: Authorized King
James Version* (Oxford: Oxford University Press, 1997), 1 Kings 18.5.

10. Ann Hyland, *The Horse in the Middle Ages* (Thrupp, UK: Sutton,
1999), 12–13.

11. Laura Mason, "Horses," in *The Oxford Companion to Food*, ed. Alan
Davidson (Oxford: Oxford University Press, 1999), 387.

12. Christopher Haigh, *Elizabeth I* (London: Longman, 1988), 108.

13. A. G. R. Smith, *The Government of Elizabethan England* (London:
Edward Arnold, 1967), 41.

14. Haigh, *Elizabeth I*, 103.

15. Francis Bacon, *The Essays, or Councils Civil and Moral*, ed. Brian Vickers
(Oxford: Oxford University Press, 1999), "Introduction," p. xii.

16. Lisa Jardine and Alan Stewart, *Hostage to Fortune: The Troubled Life
of Francis Bacon* (London: Victor Gollancz, 1998), 144; W. A.
Sessions, *Francis Bacon Revisited* (New York: Twayne, 1996), 7, 8.

17. Francis Bacon, *The Essayes or Counsels, Ciuill and Morall*, ed. Michael
Kiernan (Oxford: Clarendon Press, 1985), 47.

18. Alexander Luders (ed.), *Statutes of the Realm*, 12 vols. (London:
G. Eyre and A. Strahan, 1810–28), IV.ii, p. 810.

19. Luders, *Statutes of the Realm*, IV.ii, p. 810.

20. Luders, *Statutes of the Realm*, IV.ii, p. 810.

21. Luders, *Statutes of the Realm*, IV.ii, p. 810.

22. John Awdeley, *The Fraternitye of Vacabondes* (London, 1575; STC
994), sig. A3[r].

23. John Clavell, *A Recantation of an Ill Led Life* (London, 1628; STC
5369), sigs. B2[r], D2[v]–E1[v].

24. S[amuel] R[id], *Martin Mark-All, Beadle of Bridewell* (London,
1610; STC 21028.5), sig. ¶2[r].

25. J. A. Sharpe, *Crime in Early Modern England, 1550–1750* (London: Longman, 1984), 106.
26. Sharpe, *Crime in Early Modern England*, 106.
27. Peter Edwards, *The Horse Trade of Tudor and Stuart England* (Cambridge, UK: Cambridge University Press, 1988), 139.
28. Edwards, *The Horse Trade*, 139.
29. Paul L. Hughes and James F. Larkin (eds.), *Tudor Royal Proclamations*, 3 vols. (New Haven, CT: Yale University Press, 1964–69), vol. I, 448.
30. Robert Greene, *The Second Part of Conny-Catching* (London, 1591; STC 12281), sig. A2ᵛ.
31. Greene, *The Second Part of Conny-Catching*, sig. A2ᵛ.
32. Robert Payne, *A Brief Description of Ireland: Made in This Yeare, 1589* (London, 1589; STC 19490), sig. A3ʳ.
33. Payne, *A Brief Description of Ireland*, sig. A3ᵛ.
34. Awdeley, *The Fraternitye of Vacabondes*, sig. C1ʳ.
35. Paul Strohm, *Theory and the Premodern Text* (Minneapolis: University of Minnesota Press, 2000), 189.
36. Nigel Saul, *Richard II* (New Haven, CT: Yale University Press, 1997), 372.
37. John Hardyng, *The Chronicle of Jhon [sic] Hardyng, from the Firste Begynnyng of Englande* (London, 1543; STC 12767), sig. A8ᵛ.
38. Hardyng, *The Chronicle of Jhon Hardyng*, sig. A8ᵛ.
39. Raphael Holinshed, *The First Volume of the Chronicles of England, Scotlande, and Irelande* (London, 1577; STC 13568), sig. Uu2ᵛ.
40. Holinshed, *The First Volume of the Chronicles*, sig. Uu3ʳ.
41. May McKisack, *The Fourteenth Century, 1307–1399* (Oxford: Clarendon Press, 1959), 478.
42. McKisack, *The Fourteenth Century*, 479.
43. Richard Grafton, *A Chronicle at Large and Meere History of the Affyres of Englande* (London, 1569; STC 12147), sig. Ll4ʳ.
44. Grafton, *A Chronicle at Large*, sig. Ll4ʳ.
45. Rossiter, *Woodstock*, 233.
46. W. J. Lawrence, "Horses on the Elizabethan Stage," *Times Literary Supplement*, June 5, 1919, 312. Lawrence's acceptance of the use of a live horse in early productions of *Woodstock* is supported by Louis B. Wright, "Animal Actors on the English Stage before 1642," *Publications of the Modern Language Association* 42 (1927): 656–69.
47. Margot Heinemann, "Political Drama," in *The Cambridge Companion to English Renaissance Drama*, ed. A. R. Braunmuller and Michael Hattaway (Cambridge, UK: Cambridge University Press, 1990), 81.
48. Garrett A. Sullivan, Jr., *The Drama of Landscape: Land, Property, and Social Relations on the Early Modern Stage* (Stanford, CA: Stanford University Press, 1998), 89.
49. Bruce R. Smith, *Shakespeare and Masculinity* (Oxford: Oxford University Press, 2000), 120.

50. J. J. North, *English Hammered Coinage*, 2 vols. (London: Spink and Son, 1991–94), vol. II, 17.
51. Hughes and Larkin, *Tudor Royal Proclamations*, vol. III, 193.
52. Hughes and Larkin, *Tudor Royal Proclamations*, vol. III, 193.
53. Hughes and Larkin, *Tudor Royal Proclamations*, vol. III, 175.
54. Hughes and Larkin, *Tudor Royal Proclamations*, vol. III, 176.

PART II

DISCIPLINE AND CONTROL

CHAPTER 5

JUST A BIT OF CONTROL: THE HISTORICAL SIGNIFICANCE OF SIXTEENTH- AND SEVENTEENTH-CENTURY GERMAN BIT-BOOKS

Pia F. Cuneo

While recently engaged in research at the Herzog August Bibliothek in Wolfenbüttel, Germany, I stumbled across an intriguing source the likes of which I had never seen before. It was an enormous book, published in folio format first in 1562 and then again in 1591, and comprised of over 400 pages, almost each one of which was lavishly illustrated with finely detailed copper engravings.[1] The subject of this extravagant production came as a surprise to me: it was almost exclusively about bits, the metal mouthpieces attached to the bridles of horses and used to control the animals when riding. All in all, over 382 different bits were illustrated, one to a page (ca. 16 × 14″), with a brief explanatory text appearing below each illustration (figures 5.1 and 5.2). Each bit was an exquisitely and often astonishingly decoratively wrought piece of metalwork, its likeness lovingly rendered in the graphic medium that had itself developed out of the metalworking tradition, namely copperplate engraving. The book, written by the Augsburg spur-maker Hans Kreutzberger, was originally dedicated to the Hapsburg archduke and future Holy Roman Emperor, Maximilian II.[2]

Figure 5.1. Title page of Hans Creutzberger (also Kreutzberger), *Eygentliche/ Wolgerissene Contrafactur und Formen der Gebiß* (Vienna, 1591). Wolfenbüttel, Herzog August Bibliothek, 15.1 Bell. 2°.

Although I had been generally aware of the importance of the horse in early modern history and culture (a subject that the chapters in this book seek to demonstrate and clarify), I was nonetheless astounded by the book's rich opulence and the patron's high rank for what seemed like little more than a catalog of bits. I soon realized, however, that Kreutzberger's book had seemed utterly unique only because it had taken me by surprise. Additional research revealed a number of different catalogs of bits that had been produced and published in the sixteenth and seventeenth centuries, constituting a category of what I am here referring to as bit-books. While my initial

Figure 5.2. Bit #108, in Hans Creutzberger (also Kreutzberger), *Eygentliche/ Wolgerissene Contrafactur und Formen der Gebiß* (Vienna, 1591). Wolfenbüttel, Herzog August Bibliothek, 15.1 Bell. 2°.

fascination with these books stemmed from my own physical activities as a rider, my subsequent research has revealed their significance to the interpretive activities of a historian. It is this significance that I wish to explore in this chapter. I will argue that these sixteenth- and seventeenth-century bits, as illustrated and explicated in bit-books, not only functioned as the mouthpieces of bridles to be used by Renaissance riders for greater control of their horses, but can also function as mouthpieces for the late Renaissance to be used by contemporary historians for greater understanding of an age.

My argument will assume concentric dimensions; after first considering the production of German bit-books in general it will proceed from the bits themselves and what they can tell us about their most immediate context—the history of riding—to ever-wider areas of historical inquiry for which they provide potential illumination, including the histories of technology, art, and the Renaissance itself. There is no secondary literature on Kreutzberger's 1562 book of bits; one or two other books belonging to the same genre have been cursorily considered in terms of the history of riding, but a serious analysis of sixteenth- and seventeenth-century German bit-books in terms of the histories of science and culture has yet to be undertaken. In taking this first step, this chapter draws on the methodological inspirations of microhistory, which accords even so-called minor events and objects the potential for major historical signification.[3]

WHAT ARE BIT-BOOKS?

We first need to establish the category of bit-books to which Kreutzberger's book belongs. In researching the collections of Wolfenbüttel and the Staatsbibliothek in Munich, two of the main repositories for sixteenth- and seventeenth-century German printed materials, I found 17 different bit-books, printed between 1532 and 1689.[4] Most of these went through at least two separate editions.[5] Sometimes the entire book is dedicated to the subject of bits; other times this subject is included in broader discussions of the care and training of horses. While we cannot exactly speak of bit-books flooding the sixteenth- and seventeenth-century German markets, my preliminary findings suggest that there was indeed a kind of niche market for this material. And although the books cohere as a group in terms of their common subject matter, their production and thus also their cost and price indicate that a variety of audiences was targeted.

For example, at one end of the production/audience spectrum, we would find the book bearing the descriptive title *Bits Included Here Clearly Demonstrate How Each and Every Horse Should Be Bitted* (Augsburg?, ca. 1530).[6] This book is actually little more than a pamphlet. Eighty-five bits are individually illustrated, one to a page, by extremely simple woodcuts and explicated by a single brief sentence (figure 5.3). There is no dedication or even a colophon indicating when and where the book was printed. Because of the evident simplicity of production, and thus because of what must have been a relatively modest price, we can assume that this booklet would have

Figure 5.3. Bit, in *Hier inn begriffne pis zaigen clärlich an/wie ain yedeß Roß . . . soll gezämbt [werden]* (Augsburg?, ca. 1530). Wolfenbüttel, Herzog August Bibliothek, 108.14 Quodlib. (3).

been available to horse owners of more modest means and/or to those who desired a simple, straightforward presentation of information.

Other, what we could call mid-range, bit-books also picture a number of bits with minimal text, but the illustrations are somewhat finer and more detailed. An example of this type of book is *Hippiatria: On the Treatment, Education, and Training of Horses* (Frankfurt, 1550), which went through numerous editions in the course of the second half of the sixteenth century.[7] On each page, woodcuts depict an entire bit, a mouthpiece, and a curb chain arranged vertically so that the bit is on top, the mouthpiece is on the bottom, and the curb chain is in the middle (figure 5.4).[8] The woodcuts use a system of parallel lines to indicate areas of shading, thus helping to give the impression of the bit and its elements as three-dimensional objects, although on the whole the woodcuts are

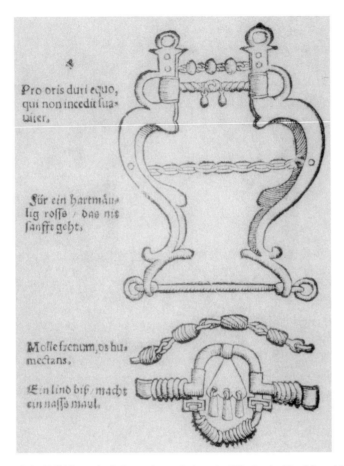

Figure 5.4. Full bit, curb chain, and mouthpiece, in *Hippiatria* (Frankfurt, 1550). Wolfenbüttel, Herzog August Bibliothek, HN 106.

still fairly rudimentary. On the outside of the page—that is, either to the left or the right of the illustration depending on whether it is on a left- or a right-hand page—paired inscriptions state briefly the level of the bit's severity (whether it is gentle or harsh or somewhere in between) and the problems it is supposed to solve. The inscriptions are paired because one is written in Latin and the other in German. This dual-language edition probably indicates not only an educated but also an international audience.

At the other end of the production/audience spectrum are luxury tomes such as Kreutzberger's and, another example, Mang Seutter's *Book of Bits* (Augsburg [1584], 1614; figure 5.5).[9] These are large,

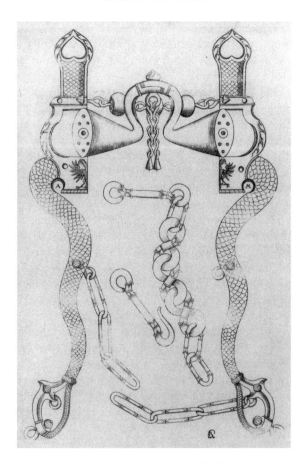

Figure 5.5. Master A. M., Bit, in Mang Seutter, *Bißbuch* (Augsburg [1584], 1614, fol. K recto). Wolfenbüttel, Herzog August Bibliothek, 6 Bell. 2° (2).

folio-sized books with minimal texts and copious illustrations that are as finely crafted as the actual bits themselves must have been. In these books, the more expensive medium of copperplate engraving is used for the illustrations of literally hundreds of bits, as opposed to the cheaper medium of woodcut used in the lower- and mid-range books discussed above, for example. These latter books picture bits that are markedly less ornate, and one would assume also less costly, than the luxury books, which display on their pages bits highly decorated with geometric, vegetal, and even human forms.

Besides the assumed cost of a book based on its production, another indication of audience can be found in the book's dedication.

Although a dedication does not firmly and hermetically circumscribe a book's audience, it nonetheless gives us an idea of the kind of audience the author ideally was hoping to reach. Not surprisingly, the lower- and mid-range books lack dedicatory texts and thus seem to have been aimed at the open market, a conclusion that is reinforced by the nature of their production, based on the obvious indicator of the amount and quality of their illustrations. However, the more expensive and expansive books and those produced into the seventeenth century are dedicated to the likes of the wealthy merchant Marx Fugger of Augsburg; the city council of Strasbourg; the Saxon dukes Johann Casimir, Johann Ernst, and Johann Georg the Elder; the Bavarian duke Albrecht; the dukes of Braunschweig and Lüneburg Heinrich Julius, Friedrich Ulrich, and August Wilhelm; Christian IV, king of Denmark; and the Hapsburg archduke and future emperor Maximilian II.[10] Thus the audience for these bit-books must have consisted of a wide range of people, from those who could afford only the simple pamphlets to members of the highest nobility.

Correspondingly, the authors of bit-books range from anonymous writers through local stable-masters and craftsmen to members of the lower aristocracy. The lower- and mid-range books often have no indication of identifiable authorship, but as the books increase in size and cost, and as they continue to be produced into the seventeenth century, the authors are not only named but their professions are also often given.[11] This may well indicate a growing sense of professionalism within the ranks of men working with horses. Kreutzberger, we remember, was a spur-maker from Augsburg; according to documentation, including information provided by the bit-books, the craftsmen who actually made the bits were "Sporer" or spur-makers, whose specialized work in metal evidently included the manufacture of both these equestrian accessories.[12] Mang Seutter was the stable-master to Marx Fugger, another citizen of Augsburg and one of the city's wealthiest inhabitants. Humanistically educated, Fugger was heir to the family fortune, director of the Fugger banking and trading concerns, and himself an enthusiastic hippologist and author who wrote a highly influential book on horse breeding.[13] Another author, Caspar Reuschlein, was the official civic stable-master for the free imperial city ("freie Reichsstadt") of Strasbourg. The office of stable-master ("Stallmeister"), especially when connected with the management of stables owned by the nobility, was often occupied by members of the lower aristocracy, some of whom also wrote bit-books, such as Georg Engelhard von Loehneysen, stable-master to

Heinrich Julius, Duke of Braunschweig, and Ernst Abraham von Dehnen-Rothfelser, stable-master to the Saxon princes in Dresden. Other members of the aristocracy with no ostensible employment connections to noble stables also authored bit-books, such as Hörwart von Hohenberg, Gundaker zu Troppau, and Wolf Helmhardt von Hohenberg.

At this point we should stop to consider not only the authorship of the book's texts but also the manufacture of their images. In most instances, we do not know who designed or made the illustrations. However, some of the bit books include tantalizing hints as to the images' production. Although in almost all of the bit-books the illustrations are unsigned, a few illustrations in two of the books include initials most likely of the artist who had made the woodcuts/engravings. These are in Mang Seutter's *Book of Bits* (Augsburg, 1584), where the initials A. M. appear on the title page and on one engraving of a bit (figure 5.5), and in Johann Geissert's *A Knightly and Noble Book of Art* (here referring to the art of riding; Coburg, 1615), where woodcuts illustrating six different bits include the initials B. G., usually placed in the middle of the bit's mouthpiece (figure 5.6).[14] The artists referred to by these initials are not known, a fact that is not very surprising as work of such a highly technical nature as these illustrations would most likely have been carried out by the kind of specialized craftsmen not usually studied in the history of art, with its typical focus on the so-called fine arts.

A number of other sources indicate that, in some cases, the author himself was involved in the book's illustration. In the dedication to the 1562 edition, Kreutzberger describes his role in the book's production, stating that it was "to draw and to describe" the material covered in the book. Kreutzberger in fact emphasizes his role as a draftsman by maintaining that all of the elements necessary to riding that are illustrated and discussed in the book "were originally drawn by my own hand."[15] In Mang Seutter's introduction to his *Book of Bits*, he describes how he has studied other bit-books, in both manuscript and printed forms, only to find that many of the bits illustrated are incorrectly fashioned. However, he has particular praise for a book of bits made by Fugger's former stable-master and Seutter's own teacher, Veit Tufft. These illustrations are particularly good, he says, because they "are correctly drawn by hand and are rendered in correct proportion and geometry." The implication here is that the illustrations stem from Tufft himself. In praising the exactitude of these illustrations, Seutter helps us to understand exactly how they were meant to function: namely, as designs to be shown to

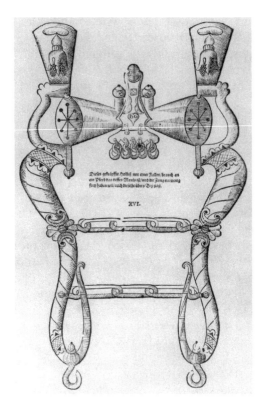

Figure 5.6. Master B. G., Bit #16, in Johann Geissert, *Ein Ritterlich und Adelich Kunstbuch* (Coburg, 1615). Wolfenbüttel, Herzog August Bibliothek, 2 Bell. 2°.

spur-makers, who would then actually manufacture the bits. Tufft's drawings are so good, Seutter says, "that even a simple spur-maker can make a flawless bit, as it should be made, by copying the drawing."[16] Ernst Abraham von Dehnen-Rothfelser also makes this striking connection between art- and equine-related crafts in *A Short but Thorough Description of the Training and Bridling of Horses* (Dresden, 1637). The first chapter of his book is titled "What Kind of Qualities a Horseman Should Have" and here the author states that "He [the horseman] should also be a kind of painter or he should at least be able to draw on paper every kind of bit that might be needed by a horse in order to have the bit made."[17]

Although it seems clear that in some instances the spur-maker or stable-master/horseman might be responsible for initial drawings, the actual transfer of these drawn designs into the medium of woodcut or engraving was probably done by specially trained artists. In the foreword of an earlier book authored by Mang Seutter, he discusses the progress of his other project, the *Book of Bits*. He bemoans the fact that progress is so slow "because every piece [i.e., each illustration of a bit] is being assiduously and carefully engraved in copper, which takes a long time. Often a week goes by and hardly one piece has been completed. In order to design a proportionately correct piece, to draw it, and then engrave it, takes time."[18] The implication here would seem to be that a number of different craftsmen are active in the different stages involved in the production of the illustrations. Somewhat more specific information is given in the public sermon, subsequently published, given at the funeral of the stable-master and bit-book author Georg Engelhard von Loehneysen. Here it is mentioned that "the dearly departed had a particular inclination for drawing and painting; he was able to give instructions to his engravers and draftsmen about how to set things up in a proportionately correct manner."[19]

In considering the category of bit-books and their production and audience, we discover an unusual kind of book that is at this level already historically revealing. The books straddle a wide range of authors and audiences, they indicate a growing professionalism among horsemen, and they blend skills and crafts not usually associated with one another into cooperative publishing ventures, namely, spur-making, horsemanship, engraving/woodcutting, and printing.

BIT-BOOKS AND THE HISTORY OF RIDING

Although the amount and the quality of text and images vary, the books typically illustrate individual bits accompanied by explicative text. This combination allows us to draw conclusions about the history of riding, which is generally delineated in the secondary literature as follows.[20] The first written evidence we have of a systematic method of riding that was also sympathetic to the horse and to modern-day objectives is found in the writings of Xenophon in the fourth century B.C.E. Following that there is nothing in the West until the publication in 1550 of the Neapolitan Federico Grisone's work *Gli ordini di cavalcare*. Pupils of Grisone's successor in Naples, Pignatelli, then transplanted the art of riding to other parts of Europe, particularly France, and it is here and in England in the seventeenth and early eighteenth centuries that the classical art of dressage flowered under riding masters such as Antoine de Pluvinel, William Cavendish Duke of Newcastle, and François de la Guérinière. Interestingly, this narrative directly mimics standard histories of art and culture in general, with the initial paradigm found first in classical

Greece, then reappearing in Renaissance Italy, and then moving on to France and England. According to this scheme, Germany certainly had no role to play whatsoever, other than slavish imitation of everybody else in Europe. Although it is beyond contest that the writings of Grisone did indeed have an important influence on later sixteenth-century German discussions of riding and training techniques, numerous sources that I have found paint a detailed picture of a very rich and independent hippological culture in Germany before, during, and after Grisone's influence. It becomes clear, then, that the history of riding as traced in the secondary literature has been constructed so as to follow a thoroughly generalized trajectory of cultural development and thus is in need of serious revision. The chapters in this volume make a major contribution to this important project.

But even the work of Grisone is dealt with in a rather embarrassed fashion by historians of riding. I believe that this is the case because, despite the fact that he was living geographically and chronologically in the middle of Renaissance Italy, Grisone does not really fit the Renaissance paradigm very well. How, indeed, does one reconcile an age described since Jacob Burckhardt[21] as the epitome of European civilization and refinement with the following often-cited passage from Grisone?

> If your horse won't go forward or even goes backward, get someone to stand behind him holding a long pole with a cat tied to it in such fashion that the cat is lying belly up and has full use of its claws and jaws. Your helper should hold the cat right next to the disobedient horse's thighs so that the cat can scratch and bite them.[22]

Grisone not only misused horses through his equally abusive handling of cats, he also recommends the use of extremely harsh bits, as did many of the sixteenth-century German bit-books.

In advocating this technique of severe bitting, these sixteenth-century sources are in fact closely following medieval techniques that also used bits with extremely long shanks to control large-boned and heavily armored horses in their lumbering charges in war or in tournaments.[23] Although the use of art as evidence is methodologically tricky, sixteenth-century imagery indicates that these kinds of bits illustrated in the bit-books were indeed employed, as can be seen, for example, in Albrecht Dürer's famous engraving of *Knight, Death, and the Devil* (1513), which features a mounted knight who controls his steed by means of a long-shanked curb bit.[24] The deployment of such crass and often brutal methods also does not fit the Renaissance paradigm of an age of subtlety and discernment. In thus advocating some decidedly medieval techniques of Renaissance equestrianism the bit-books also reveal some of the cracks in the edifice of Renaissance history as constructed by scholarly discourse.

Yet the goals of riding had in fact changed in the course of the sixteenth century from those of medieval times. Due to developments in warfare technologies, heavy horses bearing armored knights touting lances and acting as living juggernauts were no longer effective as the main component of battlefield combat. Although cavalry continued to play a role in warfare in the sixteenth century, it was very much subsidiary to the deployment of infantry increasingly armed with gunpowder.[25] Thus the rigorous training given to horses by Grisone and others, emphasizing lightness, obedience, flexibility, and agility, although purportedly for military purposes, in fact functioned for aristocratic display.[26] The breeding of different kinds of horses that were lighter and more agile was a response to these new goals. So was the endless designing of different bits, as riders struggled to reach these goals with animals, techniques, and equipment that were still in the process of catching up.

HISTORIES OF TECHNOLOGY AND ART

In their promulgation of a dizzying array of bits, the bit-books also tell us not only about the history of riding, but also about the history of technology, and by extension, about sixteenth- and seventeenth-century attitudes regarding nature. If we define technology as "the application of science to practical problems,"[27] then it is clear that bits belong to this category. Although not designed in a scientific laboratory, their operation on the horse's mouth nonetheless follows scientific precepts to do with leverage and pressure. The longer the shank, the greater the leverage when the rein is activated, and the greater the pressure that is exerted on the horse's sensitive oral tissues. The greater the pressure, the greater the pain, and that was what solved the practical problem of regulating a horse's pace.[28]

As the brief texts of the bit-books make clear, different bits were implemented according to different training and behavioral problems. For example, let us consider a page from the 1539 edition of *Bits Included Here Clearly Demonstrate How Each and Every Horse Should Be Bitted* (Regensburg, 1539). Page C2 verso illustrates two different bits side by side (figure 5.7). The one on the left is supposedly a gentle bit that will encourage the horse to salivate, whereas the one

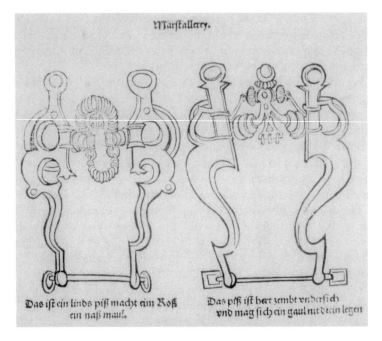

Figure 5.7. Two bits, in *Hierein begriffne Pis/zaygen klärlich an* . . . (Regensburg, 1539), C2 verso. Later edition of Figure 5.3. Wolfenbüttel, Herzog August Bibliothek, 38.2 Bell.

next to it is a severe bit meant to restrain the horse from leaning on it and becoming heavy in the rider's hand.[29] A page from the 1550 edition of *Hippiatria* shows a similar juxtaposition; the fully rendered bit is severe, to be used on a horse that will not "go softly" or yield to the rider's hand, whereas the partially illustrated bit below is mild, to be used to get a horse's mouth wet, an indication that the horse is accepting the bit and the rider's aids (figure 5.4).[30] What this indicates is a great confidence in, and indeed a sole reliance on, technology to fix a problem. The issue becomes that of identifying the incorrect behavior of the horse and then finding the appropriate bit to address that behavior. The corollary of this attitude is that the horse, as a living being with a will of its own but one that lacks reason, is there to be controlled and subjugated by man through his reasoned manipulation of technology. As Karen Raber has demonstrated, later attitudes about the horse and training techniques were much more like our own; these included a greater sensitivity to the horse's needs and accorded a more important role to the use of positive reinforcement.[31] Especially for the sixteenth century, however, it is clear that nature was there to be dominated by man and it was technology that provided him the means to do so.

Because the bit-books were illustrated, they also impinge upon our understanding of the history of art. While no one other than perhaps a sixteenth-century spur-maker would view such images as works of art,[32] these technological illustrations do address the issue of how it is that images communicate information and provide authority. In a fascinating study published in 1996, Bert Hall used medieval and Renaissance scientific and technological illustrations to consider this very issue. Although he does not seem to have been aware of the genre of bit-books, their illustrations function exactly as do the others Hall describes. In distinguishing between illustrations to, for example, literary texts and technological illustrations, Hall maintains that

> Images usually serve as adjuncts to words; images depict what is described elsewhere. In technology, the priorities are reversed: the image is the primary object of the viewer/reader's attention, while words of explication serve to illuminate details that might not be apparent at first glance. By displaying how things work . . . technical drawings [read pictures of bits] persuade the viewer to accept whatever is being illustrated as a possible machine [functioning mechanism]. In that sense, technological illustrations are self-authenticating. . . . In seeking to grasp the complex process by which images came to be vested with the ability to create conviction, we must see these self-authenticating technological drawings as pioneers.[33]

The illustrations of bits function in exactly this manner. While the text explains what the bit is for, it is the image itself that provides the fundamental information, namely, of what elements this mechanism is comprised and how it is put together. We have already mentioned the passage from the introduction to Seutter's *Book of Bits* in which he indicates that the illustrations were to be used as designs for spur-makers to follow in the manufacture of bits. This example clearly demonstrates the primacy of the image and the secondary role of text. For the discipline of art history, many of whose methodologies automatically grant the textual hermeneutic authority over the visual, the dominating role of the illustrations in the bit-books serves as a useful counterpoise to logocentric assumptions.

Also something to consider in terms of art history is the relationship between bit-books and artworks that feature bits and bridles. Since classical antiquity, parallels have been made between the horse and human passions.[34] This longstanding tradition of equating the overthrow of reason by passion with an unrestrained horse must certainly explain the appearance of bridles and bits—or, in some cases, the pointed absence of these—in particular iconographic schemes of the Renaissance. Usually, the bridle and bit in images signify self-control that is socially and even morally beneficial. The virtue of Temperance, for example, is sometimes depicted as a female personification who actually wears a bridle, such as in Pieter Bruegel the Elder's engraving from his series on *The Seven Virtues* from 1560.[35] The need for the passions to be subject to Prudence is exemplified by a man restraining an unruly horse by firmly grasping the lead rope attached to the horse's halter as illustrated in Bocchi's *Symbolicae questiones* from 1574. In 1559 the Dutch artist Maarten van Heemskerck completed an eight-plate series on the *Triumph of Patience*; plate four represents King David riding a bridled lion while holding aloft a banner upon which another bridle is depicted. The print's inscription describes how David's victories were accomplished by the "fraeno rationis" (the bridle of reason).[36] The bridle is actually the identifying attribute of the personification of Ratio in several paintings from the late sixteenth century by the Netherlandish artist Hans Vredeman de Vries.[37] And the figure of the goddess Nemesis holding a bridle, who is represented, for example, in Dürer's engraving from ca. 1502 and in Andreas Alciatus' *Book of Emblems*, is meant to signal the desirability of cautious circumspection in words and actions.[38]

The absence of appropriate restraining mechanisms *mutatis mutandis* usually indicates undesirable and/or dangerous situations, such as in Hans Baldung Grien's enigmatic *Bewitched Groom* from 1544. Here an unbridled horse seems in some way related to the figure of a witch, and both seem to have exercised some kind of malevolent power that has left the stricken groom in the foreground utterly senseless.[39] In another series by Maarten van Heemskerck, *The Allegory of the Unbridled World* from 1550, unhappy consequences await even positive forces such as Justice, Knowledge, and Love, which cannot be effective if society is completely unrestrained.[40] Heemskerck personifies all three in his four-part print series, and they each meet disaster in their individual encounters with the unbridled horse, consistently identified in the accompanying inscriptions as "the foolish world"; Justice gets bucked off, and Knowledge and Love get dragged into the abyss.

Sometimes, however, the reins of the bridle wind up in the wrong hands, and the bridle turns from a positive force of reason and restraint into an instrument of enslavement. Heemskerck again provides an example. In the first plate of a 14-part series on *Jacob's Ladder or the Allegory of the Road to Eternal Bliss* (1550), the devil grasps in his fist the reins of a bridle worn by a man whose feet and hands are also tied with ropes, the ends of which are held by the devil in his other hand. The inscription states, "A slave of sin is also a slave of Satan."[41] Similar implications of sinfulness as enslavement resonate in another group of images, in which a man is bitted and bridled and the reins are held in the hands of a woman. This is the depiction of the courtesan Phyllis's seduction of the great philosopher Aristotle, in which she is usually shown riding him as if he were a horse. Phyllis's ride on Aristotle began to be depicted in the Middle Ages but became increasingly popular in the late fifteenth and early sixteenth centuries with the advent of prints.[42] Northern artists who represented this image in prints include Master M. Z. (engraving, ca. 1500), Hans Baldung Grien (woodcut, 1513), Lucas van Leyden (woodcut, 1514), and Hans Burgkmair (woodcut, 1519). This scene is part of the so-called "power of women" topos, which featured a variety of situations in which women had the upper hand over men, usually due to the men's sinfulness and foolishness (rather than through the women's virtue and intelligence).[43] Phyllis's ride also represents the world turned upside down; topsy-turvy indeed when a woman controls a man and when a philosopher, the ultimate man of reason, is brought down to the level of an irrational animal. In such images, Aristotle usually sports a bridle, holds a bit between his teeth, and smiles lecherously as the lovely Phyllis delicately brandishes her whip in one hand and holds the reins in the other. Here Aristotle is not guided by reason but by passion. Brought low by the sin of lust he is more than willing to debase himself and become Phyllis's slave; her complete control over him is signified by her eager and competent wielding of bridle and bit.[44]

HISTORY OF THE RENAISSANCE: ISSUES OF CONTROL

When we consider the images discussed above in terms of their dates of production, we will notice that they fall for the most part rather conspicuously into the course of the sixteenth century. Such images, with the exception of Aristotle and Phyllis, are not characteristic of the Middle Ages or even of the fifteenth century. How is this to be interpreted? Certainly one could rightly say that such images belong generally to the trend of increasingly secular subject matter in art and, of course, more specifically to the developing markets for prints. Nonetheless, these images, along with the genre of bit-books, seem to indicate an increasing interest in the topic of control. I am not arguing here that artists looked at bit-books or that spur-makers studied artworks. What I am postulating is that congruently the images and the books articulate a concern with issues of control; and here is where I would like to link this discussion of bit-books to the widest of my concentric circles, the history of the Renaissance.

Just recently, William Bouwsma's book *The Waning of the Renaissance 1550–1640* was published by Yale University Press.[45] In a deliberate echo of Johann Huizinga's study about a century earlier of *The Waning of the Middle Ages*, Bouwsma also focuses not on the origins of a period but on its closure. He quite rightly notes the paucity of work in a variety of disciplines on the second half of the sixteenth century, when the Renaissance is no longer new, as opposed to plentiful work done on the beginning and early phases of the Renaissance in the fifteenth and early sixteenth centuries. Bouwsma's theory is quite straightforward. Culture moves back and forth between two poles, one formed by the desire for intellectual freedom and complete liberation, the other formed by the desire for order and control. The motor driving culture from one pole to the other is human anxiety. In describing the dominant culture of the Middle Ages, Bouwsma notes that

> the indefinite multiplication of categories, distinctions, and boundaries, however necessary to human existence at one stage, is ultimately suffocating. . . . The result is a reaction toward cultural liberation, as in the Renaissance. . . . But the creativity made possible by liberation from habitual and stultifying modes of cultural expression is itself only temporarily satisfying; the dissolution of old boundaries, old categories, old certainties, in the short run liberating, is in the long run destructive and frightening. The result is a movement in the opposite direction. . . . In the later Renaissance, the impulses toward liberation seem to have become unendurable, and thus to have set in motion a reaction in the opposite direction.[46]

While I am skeptical about the simultaneously linear and cyclical assumptions in Bouwsma's theory and about its overarching application, I nonetheless find his ideas helpful in thinking about the sixteenth century. Instead of picturing a pendulum forever swaying first toward freedom and then, upon arriving at that pole, swinging back the other way, eventually attaining the opposite pole, it is perhaps more defensible to think about a dialectic that is always and immediately present, to think about culture as in a constant state of dynamic flux, where the forces of liberation and control are perpetually caught up in a struggle for dominance. Instead of the first half of the sixteenth century being more free and the second half more controlled, as Bouwsma generally postulates, it is probably more accurate to grant the entire century a greater degree of entropy that nonetheless exists—but in a messy state—between a number of different paradigms, including those of freedom and control.

According to this idea, the bit-books, combined with the images discussed above, would together argue for an increasing concern with control that would seem to parallel broader developments in the Renaissance. But the bit-books have more to tell us. Those produced in the course of the seventeenth century, in particular, suggest that it is not just the issue of control that might be a significant characteristic of an age, but also the method of control.

Conclusion: The Demise of the Bit-Book

The production of bit-books does not last long, historically speaking. The great burst of activity along these lines occurs in the second half of the sixteenth century and continues into the early part of the seventeenth. These roughly sixty years witness the production of those enormous books that include sumptuous, full-page illustrations of hundreds of different bits. In 1599, Caspar Reuschlein in fact makes specific mention of the plethora of bit-books that have appeared recently on the market.[47] But things begin to change quite quickly in the course of the seventeenth century. Johann Geissert's *A Knightly and Noble Book of Art* (Coburg, 1615 and reissued in 1625) is the last of the big picture books, illustrating 98 different bits (figure 5.6). The next bit-book to be published is Christoph Jacob Lieb's *Book of Bits* (Dresden, 1616), which, like Geissert's, comes from the realm of courtly Saxon production. Lieb was a horse trainer ("Bereutter") for Christian II, electoral duke of Saxony, and dedicated his book to three members of the Saxon court. The emphasis is now clearly more textual. In discussing the different kinds of mouthpieces, Lieb includes only one or two illustrated examples. At the end of this discussion, 19 bits are illustrated in full, 2 to a page, a far cry from the hundreds pictured in earlier books. The same is true of Gundaker zu Troppau's *On the Bridling of Horses* (Vienna, 1625); 48 pages of text are completely dedicated to discussing the relevant features of the horse's mouth and how to make and fit bits correctly. Although some figures are included (figures 5.8 and 5.9), at the

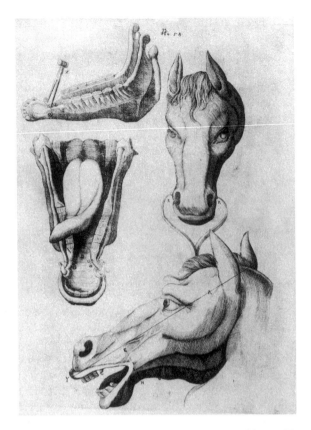

Figure 5.8. The horse's mouth and its measurement, in Gundaker zu Troppau, *Von Zaumung der Pferde* (Vienna [1609], 1625), figure #58. Wolfenbüttel, Herzog August Bibliothek, 3.2 Bell. 2° (1).

end of the book, only 19 bits are illustrated. Both Ernst Abraham von Dehnen-Rothfelser's *Description of the Training and Bridling of Horses* (Dresden, 1637) and Johann Misselhorn's *On Bridling* (Celle, 1685) are completely unillustrated.

How should we understand this rather dramatic reduction in the illustration of bits? Earlier in this chapter it was assumed that books with fewer illustrations printed in the first part of the sixteenth century were less expensive and were probably made that way in order to target a more modest group of purchasers. But the later books discussed above are mostly authored by and dedicated to men within a courtly milieu, so a conscious marketing strategy aimed at a lower-end audience would not apply in their cases. Certainly the Thirty Years' War (1618–48) had a devastating effect on the central European

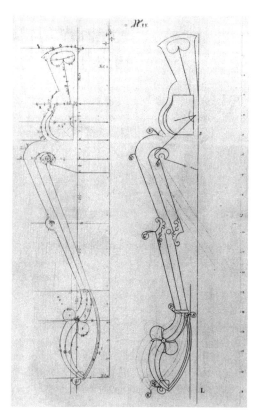

Figure 5.9. Measurements of shanks, in Gundaker zu Troppau, *Von Zaumung der Pferde* (Vienna [1609], 1625), figure #55. Wolfenbüttel, Herzog August Bibliothek, 3.2 Bell. 2° (1).

economy, and the Saxon realms, where many of these books were produced, were hit hard by the war.[48] In general, luxury commodities and nonessential expenditures would have been curtailed as a result, and perhaps to some extent the lavishly illustrated bit-book might be regarded as one more casualty of the war.

I think, however, that there were also other factors at play. Not only does the amount of illustration in the bit-books change during the course of the seventeenth century, but so do the assumptions regarding the horse's training as revealed in the text. Generally, the texts in the sixteenth-century bit-books are minimal. After several pages of dedication, foreword, and introduction, the matter at hand quickly turns to illustration with only brief textual explication. But beginning in the seventeenth century, the amount and content of the text start to change. Now there is much more text, and in the text there is a much greater emphasis on the training of the horse. To effect change in the horse's manner and gaits, it is no longer a matter of just finding the right bit; it is a matter of correct training based on a thorough knowledge of the individual horse. In a suggestive passage, von Dehnen-Rothfelser likens the horse trainer to a physician who must know his patient, identify the ailment, and use the right medicine to cure it.[49] Indeed, the trainer must have a thorough understanding not only of the horse's physical characteristics but also of its mental abilities and its moods. Several sources talk about the horse's "fantasy" and how, if it is ridden unfairly, it experiences "desperation."[50] This is new. What these sources recognize is the interior, emotional life of the animal. In terms of the rider, more and more emphasis is placed on patience, understanding, mercy, and compassion.[51] Bits are to be implemented with reason, and the use of those that are overly harsh is condemned outright.[52] Horses that lean on the bit and are heavy in hand exhibit this behavior not just because they are lazy or have the wrong bit in their mouths, but because of a wide variety of factors that influence their performance, ranging from conformational deficiency and physical weakness of the horse to emotional ineptitude and physical incompetence of the rider.[53] Therefore, the rider's sensitivity, knowledge, and talent are key to the health and happiness of the horse—in most cases an expensive and treasured resource for which the trainer bears professional responsibility.

Not everything was rosy in the riding ring, however. Some authors still promulgate rather brutal elements in their descriptions of training. Johann Misselhorn, for example, heartily recommends rubbing a horse's face raw with a cavesson if that is what it takes to get the message across. If a horse persists in sticking its tongue out (as a way of avoiding the bit), Misselhorn advocates a method that he has practiced on numerous occasions: simply cut off that part of the tongue that protrudes.[54] Von Dehnen-Rothfelser warns against those "heathens" of antiquity who loved their horses too much. For a horse that bucks, he recommends simultaneously and energetically whipping it between the ears, across the chest, and under the belly near the testicles, spurring its flanks, and shouting at it "so that it doesn't know where to defend itself, is terrified, and becomes frightened. . . . Then it will become obedient."[55] Nonetheless, even these authors also recommend immediate positive reinforcement by praising the horse as soon as it behaves in the desired way. They stress that it is the rider's job to enhance the horse's nature, not to violate it, through the use of reason and wisdom, and that the horse should ideally be taught to fear but also to love its rider.[56]

Clearly, issues of control have not gone away in the seventeenth-century bit-books. But the implementation of control has become more subtle, nuanced, and pervasive. Instead of control of the horse's body focused on the mouth through use of an appropriate bit, the rider now needs to affect the horse's mental as well as its physical state. He has to attend to the horse's moods as well as to the various parts of its body, and not just the mouth, but everything between that and its tail. The rider must also control himself—both his own body and his emotions.[57] Control is thus implemented not only through the use of exterior, physical mechanisms, but also by the adoption and maintenance of inner states of being—of calm reason on the part of the rider, and trusting obedience on the part of the horse. In short, notions of control have become internalized.[58] Perhaps this does indeed mark the transition between the end of one phase of history and civilization and the beginning of another.

As historical documents, sixteenth- and seventeenth-century German bit-books can be surprisingly rich. They provide information about an unusual form of book production that combines the professional forces of printers, artists, and horsemen/spur-makers; they indicate techniques and assumptions that play key roles in the history of riding; they reveal the uses of and attitudes toward early technology; they constitute an important context for the iconography of bits and bridles in works of art; and they can offer a way of thinking critically about historical periods defined according to changes in attitudes about mechanisms of control. Regarded in combination with other historical and cultural evidence, sixteenth- and seventeenth-century German bit-books can speak to a variety of significant historical issues and conditions. In so doing, they provide the historian with a unique kind of information, as it were, straight from the horse's mouth.

NOTES

1. Hans Kreutzberger, *Warhafftige und Eygentliche Contrafactur / und Formen der Zeumung und gebiß / zu allerley mängel unnd Undterichtung der Pferdt . . . Durch Hansen Kreutzberger Sporern un burgern zu Augspurg mit sonderem fleyß erst gantz newlich zusamen getragen* (Augsburg, 1562; Wolfenbüttel, Herzog August Bibliothek, 15.2 Bell. 2°); Hans Creutzberger, *Eygentliche / Wolgerissene Contrafactur und Formen der Gebiß / für allerley mängel / auch underrichtung der pferdt . . . Durch Hansen Creutzberger / Rö. Kay.*

M. etc. Hoffsporer gemacht . . . (Vienna, 1591; Wolfenbüttel, HAB 15.1 Bell. 2°). This edition is also in Munich, Staatsbibliothek Res. 2° A. vet. 3.

2. Maximilian II, 1527–76. The dedication of the 1562 edition refers to Maximilian as the archduke of Austria and the king of Hungary and Bohemia. Maximilian did not become emperor until two years after the book was published, 1564. See Paula Sutter Fichtner, *Emperor Maximilian II* (New Haven, CT: Yale University Press, 2001). Kreutzberger identifies himself on the title page as "Sporern und burgern zu Augspurg," or "spur-maker and citizen of Augsburg" (all translations from the German in this chapter are my own). Evidently, Kreutzberger was not only successful in his craft but also received recognition for it in the highest circles; the 1591 edition of his book, published posthumously, refers to him as "Rö. Kay. M. etc. Hoffsporer" (imperial court spur-maker) and also includes two portraits of him, one on the title page and a second on p. iii^v picturing him full-length standing next to a horse. The 1591 edition, although also dedicated to "Archduke Maximilian" must actually be referring to Maximilian II's son (1558–1618) of the same name. Maximilian II had been dead for fifteen years by the time the 1591 edition was published. The dedication also mentions Rudolph (1551–1612), Ernst (1553–95), and Matthias (1557–1619), all of whom were brothers of Archduke Maximilian.

3. For microhistory, see Florike Egmond and Peter Mason, "A Horse Called Belisarius," *History Workshop Journal* 47 (1999): 241–52.

4. These books are as follows: (1) Laurentius Rusius, *Hippiatria sive marescalia Laurentii Rusii . . . plures quam in priore editione comodissime frenorum formae excusae sunt . . .* (Basel, 1532; Wolfenbüttel, HAB, Hn 4°31); (2) *Hier inn begriffne pis zaigen clärlich an / wie ain yedeß Roß / . . . sol gezämbt . . .* (Augsburg?, ca. 1530; Wolfenbüttel, HAB, 108.14 Quodlib (3)); (3) *Frenorum nova et varia exempla* (Frankfurt, 1546; Wolfenbüttel, HAB, 218.13 Quod. (17)); (4) *Hippiatria: De cura, educatione & institutione equorum, una cum uariis ac novis frenorum exemplis* (Frankfurt, 1550; Wolfenbüttel, HAB, Hn 106); (5) Kreutzberger, *Warhafftige und Eygentliche Contrafactur* . . . (see n. 1); (6) *Des Edlen Hochberuembten und Rittermessigen Friderici Grisoni Neapolitani / kuenstlich beschreibung/ unnd gründtliche ordnung . . .* (Augsburg, 1566; Munich, SSB, Res. 2° Gymn. 17); (7) Hans Friedrich Hörwart von Hohenberg, *Von der Hochberhuembten / Adelichen und ritterlichen Kunst der Reyterey* (Tegernsee, 1577; Munich, SSB, Res. 2° Gymn. 20); (8) Mang Seutter, *Bißbuch* (Augsburg, 1584; Munich, SSB, Res. 2° Gymn. 48); (9) Georg Engelhard von Loehneysen, *Grundliche Bericht des Zeumens* (1588; Wolfenbüttel, HAB, Hn 2° 5); (10) Caspar Reuschlein, *Hippiatria. Grundlicher und eigentlicher Bericht . . . allerhand Zeumung* (Straßburg, 1593; Wolfenbüttel,

HAB, 7 Bell. 2°); (11) Johann Geissert, *Ein Ritterlich und Adelich Kunstbuch: Darinnen von Reiten / Zeumeun / auch Roßartzney* (Coburg, 1615; Wolfenbüttel, HAB, 2 Bell. 2°, and Munich, SSB, Res/2 Gymn.11); (12) Christoph Jacob Lieb, *Gebißbuch* (Dresden, 1616; Wolfenbüttel, HAB, 3.2 Bell. 2° (3)); (13) Gundaker zu Troppau, *Von Zaumung der Pferde* (Vienna, 1625; Wolfenbüttel, HAB, 3.2 Bell. 2° (1)); (14) Ernst Abraham von Dehnen-Rothfelser, *Kurze doch eigendliche und gründliche Beschreibung von abrichtung und zäumung der Rosse* . . . (Dresden, 1637; Wolfenbüttel, HAB, Alv.: Nn 399); (15) Johann Misselhorn, *Von der Zeumung* (Celle, 1685; Wolfenbüttel, HAB, N 210 Helmst. 4° (2)); (16) Wolf Helmhardt von Hohenberg, *Die vollkommene Pferd- und Reitkunst* (Nürnberg, 1689; Wolfenbüttel, HAB, Xb 4° 357); (17) Johann Misselhorn, *Die Bey dem Hause Braunschweig-Lüneburg anjetzo übliche Bereit-Kunst* . . . (Celle, 1692; Wolfenbüttel, N 210 Helmst. 4° (1)). This represents a survey primarily of German texts; this list could be expanded to include further texts in Latin, French, Spanish, and Italian.

5. Using the item numbers in n. 4, the different editions are (1) Venice, 1543 and 1559; (2) Regensburg, 1539; (4) Frankfurt, 1555, 1560, 1565, 1570, 1582; (5) Vienna, 1591; German translations of Grisone after (6) Augsburg, 1570, 1573, 1580, 1599; (8) Augsburg, 1614; (9) Augsburg, 1610 (as *Della cavalleria*, which includes different material and an expanded section on bits); (10) Strasbourg, 1599 (with a slightly expanded bits section); (11) Coburg, 1625; (12) Leipzig, 1665, ca. 1670, Frankfurt, 1668, 1674.

6. See n. 4, item 2.

7. See n. 4, item 4. For different editions, see n. 5.

8. What are mostly illustrated in these books are sixteenth-century examples of a curb bit. This is technically made up of two different elements: the mouthpiece, which lies inside the horse's mouth, and the shanks, the two vertical elements attached at right angles to either end of the mouthpiece that lie outside the horse's mouth, one on each side. Reins are attached to rings at the bottom end of the shanks, and the headstall of the bridle is attached to the top ends. When the reins are activated, the shanks move, which then also move the mouthpiece, and its action on the bars, tongue, and/or roof of the horse's mouth encourages the desired response. A curb chain is an element that can be attached to the shanks, passing under the horse's chin. When the reins are activated and the shanks move, the curb chain tightens underneath the horse's chin and augments the effect of the reins. For definitions of these various pieces, see Mary Ann Belknap, *Horsewords: The Equine Dictionary* (London: J.A. Allen & Co. Ltd., 1997).

9. See n. 4, item 8.

10. Using the item numbers in n. 4, Seutter's book (8) is dedicated to Fugger; Reuschlein's (10) to the Strasbourg city council; Geissert's

(11) to Johann Casimir and Johann Ernst of Saxony; von Dehnen-Rothfelser's (14) to Johann Georg the Elder of Saxony and Christian IV of Denmark; Hörwart von Hohenberg's (7) to Albrecht of Bavaria; Loehneysen's (9) to Heinrich Julius of Braunschweig and Lüneburg (his second edition, 1610, is dedicated to Friedrich Ulrich, also of Braunschweig and Lüneburg); Misselhorn's (15) to August Wilhelm of Braunschweig and Lüneburg; and Kreutzberger's (5) to Maximilian II. Kreutzberger's posthumous 1591 edition (see nn. 1, 2) was dedicated to Maximilian's son of the same name but not the successor to the throne.

11. The following discussion indicating the professions of the various authors is based on the 17 sources listed in n. 4, in which information about the authors is indicated either on the title pages or mentioned in the dedications and/or forewords. In the case of Georg Engelhard von Loehneysen, additional information can be found in the published sermon held at his funeral: Martin Vedemeiern, *Christliche Leichpredig / Bey dem Begräbnis des weiland woledlen / Gestrengen Vesten und Mannhafften Georg Engelhart Löhneyss*... (Remlingen, 1623).

12. See n. 32.

13. Marx Fugger, 1529–97. For basic information on Fugger, see Gode Krämer, "Markus (Marx) Fugger," in *Welt im Umbruch: Augsburg zwischen Renaissance und Barock*, vol. 2 (Augsburg: Augsburger Druck- und Verlagshaus, 1980), 120–21. Fugger's book on horse breeding is *Von der Gestüterey* (Frankfurt, 1584).

14. Seutter (n. 4, item 8), K i^r; Geissert (n. 4, item 11), illustrations 13, 26, 57, 60, 70, and 85.

15. Kreutzberger (n. 4, item 5), A i^r: "So hab ich derhalben E.K.W. zu undtertheniqstem gefallen / mich gehorsamlich unterfangen / dises Werck für die hand zunemen / und gegenwertigs Bißbuch... zureyssen / und zubeschreyben... Inn welchem nicht allein die biß ordentlicher weyß / sonder auch allerley arten der Naßbender / Cavezoni / Maulkorb / Stegrayff / Sporn / unnd andere rüstungen zur Reyterrey dienstlich / durch mein aygne Hand anfängklich gerissen... seind...."

16. Veit Tufft was also known as Veit Forster, and he was one of the people responsible for the first German translation of Federico Grisone's *Gli ordini di cavalcare* (Naples, 1550), which was made at Fugger's request (Augsburg, 1566). The entire quote by Seutter from *Bißbuch* regarding Tufft's drawings and their use as designs is as follows (A i^v): "Under ermelten Büchern aber hab ich meines alten Zucht und Lehrmaisters / bey wellichem ich vierzehen Jar gewest / des Veit Forsters oder Duffts (mit welchem Nam er baser bekandt geweßt...) Buch auch gefunden / welliches er E.G. als er in derselben dienst vor mir gewest / mitgetheilt / und dasselb ist / meines erachtens / das fürnemste unter allen / dann dieselben Biß seind gar schön unnd gerecht von der Hand abgerissen / in die recht Proportz und Zirckel

gebracht / als das ihnen nichts abgeht / derwegen sie auch ein schlechter Sporer mit Stangen und Mundstucken / wie sie an inen selbst sein sollen / nach demselben gemahl abmachen kan / ohn alle mängel."

17. Von Dehnen-Rothfelser (n. 4, item 14), "Das 1. Capitel: Was ein Roßbereuter vor qualiteten billich haben soll," 1–4; "Muß er auch etwas ein Mahler geben / oder so viel können / daß er iedes Gebiß / was einem Roß dienstlich / auff Pappier abreissen / und darnach kan machen lassen," 3. Misselhorn, *Bereit-Kunst* (n. 4, item 17), also describes what it is necessary to know for those who want to make, riding their profession in his fourth chapter, "Was der jenige / welcher von dem Reiten Profession machen wil / wissen muß," 18–23, which includes "Er muß auch nicht alleine die Zeumunge verstehen / sondern muß noch da zu einen guten Abriß machen können. . . ." (He must not only understand all methods of bridling [a horse]; he must also be able to make a good drawing), 19.

18. Mang Seutter, *Hippiatria* (Augsburg, 1599), written 1583: "Was aber das Bißbuch betrifft / da bin ich gleichwol in stetter Arbeyt / Ich trag aber Sorg . . . / es werde noch so bald nicht außgemacht werden / die Verhindernuß ist aber an dem / daß alle die Stuck mit grossem Fleiß und Mühe in Kupffer gestochen werden / welches lange weyl bedarff / also daß offt in einer gantzen Woche kaum ein Stuck fertig wird / Dann biß ein Stuck nach der Proportz recht gestellet / hernach abgerissen / und letzlich in das kupffer gestochen wirdt / das brauchet zeit . . .," v^r.

19. Vedemeiern, *Christliche Leichpredig* . . . (n. 11): "Es ist aber keines Weges mit stillschweigen vorbey zu gehen / daß S. Gest. ein besondere Inclination zu reissen und mahlen / wie er darin seiner Kupfferstechern und Reissern hat seine Anleitung geben können / wie sie nach der Proportion solten stellen," 26.

20. For the history of riding, see Michaela Otte, *Geschichte des Reitens von der Antike bis zur Neuzeit* (Warendorf: FN-Verlag der Deutschen Reiterlichen Vereinigung GmbH, 1994). Vladimir Littauer's *The Development of Modern Riding: The Story of Formal Riding from Renaissance Times to the Present* (New York: Macmillan, 1991 [1962]) is limited in terms of history and almost unlimited in matters of personal opinion.

21. I am referring here specifically to the Swiss cultural historian Jacob Burckhardt's (1818–97) highly influential book *The Civilization of the Renaissance in Italy*, published originally in 1850.

22. Cited in Otte, *Geschichte des Reitens von der Antike bis zur Neuzeit*, 62; the translation is my own.

23. See Elwyn Harley Edwards, *Bitting in Theory and Practice* (London: J.A. Allen, 1990), 10–17.

24. For a discussion of the intelligent use of art as evidence, see Peter Burke, *Eyewitnessing: The Uses of Images as Historical Evidence*

(Ithaca, NY: Cornell University Press, 2001). Albrecht Dürer (1471–1528) was a printmaker and painter from Nuremberg. For a discussion focusing on the role of the horse in Dürer's print, see Pia F. Cuneo, "Practicing Art: Dürer's *Knight, Death, and the Devil* (1513) as Praxis and Performance," in *Essays on Albrecht Dürer*, ed. Larry Silver (Philadelphia: University of Pennsylvania Press), forthcoming.

25. Making an eloquent case for the continuing role of cavalry is Larry Silver, "Shining Armor: Emperor Maximilian, Chivalry, and War," in *Artful Armies, Beautiful Battles: Art and Warfare in Early Modern Europe*, ed. Pia F. Cuneo (Leiden: Brill, 2002), 61–86. For a fascinating example of how warfare strategists attempted to blend the use of horses and hand-held firearms, see Johann Jacobi Wallhausen, *Kriegskunst zu Pferd* (Frankfurt, 1616).

26. Treva J. Tucker, "Eminence over Efficacy: Social Status and Cavalry Service in Sixteenth-Century France," *Sixteenth Century Journal* 32/4 (2001): 1057–95; see also Helen Watanabe-O'Kelly, *Triumphal Shews: Tournaments at German-Speaking Courts in Their European Context 1560–1730* (Berlin: Gebrüder Mann Verlag, 1992), esp. 65–84.

27. This is the definition given to technology in Bert Hall, "The Didactic and the Elegant: Some Thoughts on Scientific and Technological Illustrations in the Middle Ages and Renaissance," in *Picturing Knowledge: Historical and Philosophical Problems Concerning the Use of Art in Science*, ed. Brian S. Baigre (Toronto: University of Toronto Press, 1996), 3–39; here 29.

28. Edwards, *Bitting in Theory and Practice*, 10–17.

29. The texts accompanying these bits are as follows: (left) "Das ist ein linds biß macht ein Roß ein naß maul" and (right) "Das piß ist hart zembt undersich und mag sich ein gaul nit drein legen."

30. The texts here are as follows: (above) "Für ein hartmäulig ross / das nit sanft geht" and (below) "Ein lind biß / macht ein nass maul."

31. Karen Raber, " 'Reasonable Creatures': William Cavendish and the Art of Dressage," in *Renaissance Culture and the Everyday*, ed. Patricia Fumerton and Simon Hunt (Philadelphia: University of Pennsylvania Press, 1999), 42–66.

32. That spur-makers were the ones to make bits, as indicated in the sources, makes some sense in that they were highly skilled in working in metal. These craftsmen differed from saddlers, who made saddles, harnesses, and riding boots, and from smiths, who made horseshoes, nails, and sometimes also iron wagonwheels. See *Der Stad leipzig allerley Ordungen* (Leipzig, 1544) for a contemporary listing of products and prices made by the "Schmide" (Eii^v–iii^r) and the "Sattlher" (Eiiii^v–iiii^v); see Hans Sachs, *Eygentliche Beschreibung Aller Stände* (Frankfurt, 1568) for discussion of "Der Sporer" (Riii^r), "Der Schmidt" (Tiiii^r), and "Der Sattler" (Y). In the woodcut illustration

of the spur-maker's workshop, Jost Amman depicts the spur-maker at his forge and anvil with a large metal file in his hand, speaking to a fashionably attired gentleman. Bits, stirrups, and metal curry combs are placed on his workshop table and are also suspended from a pole running horizontally above the table.

33. Hall, "The Didactic and the Elegant," 36.

34. Margaret Sullivan, "The Witches of Dürer and Hans Baldung Grien," *Renaissance Quarterly* 53/2 (2000): 333–401; here esp. 382–92.

35. Pieter Bruegel the Elder (1524/30–1569) was a Flemish printmaker and painter. For Bruegel's series, see H. Arthur Klein, *The Graphic World of Peter Bruegel the Elder* (New York: Dover Books, 1963), 213–45.

36. For Heemskerck and the *Triumph of Patience* series, see Ilja Feldman, *Maarten van Heemskerck and Dutch Humanism in the Sixteenth Century* (Maarsen, The Netherlands: Gary Schwartz, 1977), esp. 65.

37. Hans Vredeman de Vries (1526–1609) was a Netherlandish printmaker and painter. One painting, dated 1586, illustrates the surrender of Antwerp to Philip II (1527–98). The clearly labeled figure of "Ratio" holds a bridle in one hand and, together with the personification of "Clementia," crowns Philip II with a laurel wreath. The artist's other figures of "Ratio" appear repeatedly in a cycle of oil paintings made between 1594 and 1595 for the city hall in Danzig. See Heiner Borggrefe, Vera Lüpkes, Paul Huvenne, and Ben van Beneden (eds.), *Hans Vredeman de Vries und die Renaissance im Norden* (Munich: Hirmer Verlag, 2002), cat. no. 147, 306–7, ill. p. 309 and cat. no. 168, 323–31, ill. pp. 326 (168a) and 328 (168e), respectively.

38. For Dürer's print, see H. Diane Russell, *Eva/Ave: Woman in Renaissance and Baroque Prints* (New York: The Feminist Press, 1990), cat. no. 139, 212–13. Dürer's monumental nude female is depicted holding a goblet in one hand and a bridle with massive curb bit in the other. For Alciatus' *Book of Emblems*, see Andreas Alciatus, *Emblematum Libellus* (Darmstadt, Germany: Wissenschaftliche Buchgesellschaft, 1991), which is a reprint of the 1542 Paris edition. Here Nemesis appears as emblem number 13 (pp. 42–43) under the rubric "injure no one either through word or deed" (Niemand verletzen, mit wort noch that) since, the text goes on to explain, the goddess Nemesis will avenge such bad behavior. She is pictured as well as described as holding a bridle in her hand.

39. Hans Baldung Grien (1484/5–1545) was a Strasbourg printmaker and painter. For a recent discussion of this print, with extensive bibliography, see Sullivan, "The Witches of Dürer and Hans Baldung Grien," 378–92. For a discussion of this print in terms of the consequences for its interpretation of the fact that the horse is clearly female, see Pia F. Cuneo, "Mad Mares and Wilful Women: Ways of Knowing Nature—and Gender—in Early Modern Hippological

Texts," in *Ways of Knowing: Ten Interdisciplinary Essays*, ed. Mary Lindemann (Leiden: Brill, 2004), 1–21.

40. See Veldman, *Maarten van Heemskerck*, 70–74, ills. 47–50. The four plates of this series have the following inscriptions: (1) "Good justice wants to ride the foolish world, but it will not permit her to do so." (2) "Foolish knowledge, together with foolish love, want to restrain the world, which is acting irrationally, from bolting; but the world mocks them." (3) "One seldom sees anything that begins foolishly ending well. Even if it is done out of love it will still harm them." (4) "He who, without understanding, wishes to check the course of an irrational being increases his own disadvantage in a way that brings much disgrace upon himself."

41. Veldman, *Maarten van Heemskerck*, 57.

42. For discussion of images of Phyllis and Aristotle, see Russell, *Eva/Ave*, 149–50.

43. For the power of women topos, see Susan L. Smith, *The Power of Women: A Topos in Medieval Art and Literature* (Philadelphia: University of Pennsylvania Press, 1995).

44. Yet another avenue of exploration one could traverse with the bit-book material is the issue of gender, which this essay only briefly touches upon. For an initial foray into this field, see Cuneo, "Mad Mares and Wilful Women."

45. William J. Bouwsma, *The Waning of the Renaissance 1550–1640* (New Haven, CT: Yale University Press, 2000).

46. Bouwsma, *The Waning of the Renaissance*, p. x.

47. Reuschlein, *Hippopronia* (Strasbourg, 1599), 69.

48. For the impact of the Thirty Years' War on various regions in Germany and on cultural production, see Sigrun Haude, "Warfare and Artistic Production in the German Lands during the Thirty Years' War (1618–1648)," in *Artful Armies, Beautiful Battles*, ed. Cuneo, 35–58.

49. Von Dehnen-Rothfelsen, "Es gehet mit Zeumung der Rosse zu gleich mit einem Arzt und Medicum / Erstlichen muß er des Patienten seine stärcke / und schwache Natur und vermögen erkennen können. Hernacher 2. die Mängel und Gebrechen oder Kranckheiten. Nach diesen und zum 3. die Medicamenta / was sie vor wirckung haben," 160. The explicit parallel made between a horse trainer and a physician is another indication of a growing sense of professionalism among horsemen. Von Dehnen-Rothfelsen even includes a brief chapter that considers the rhetorical question "Is it difficult to train a horse?" ("Das CXII Capitel. Ist es denn auch schwer ein Roß abzurichten," 99–100). In answering this question, he says that the physical and emotional talents required to be a good horse trainer (an activity he refers to here specifically as a "Profession") are God-given and so diverse that it is easier to study at the university and get a doctoral degree than to be a good horseman! "Wann einer nicht recht darzu naturet / und gleich

von Gott darzu geschaffen von Leibe und Gemüthe / so wird er schwerlich also beschaffen werden / . . . Profession darvon zumachen / und solte einer eher studieren / und Doctorem promovieren können / denn er nicht so viel Eigenschafften haben muß. . . . Unter 40 Schülern kaum einer recht gerathen wird," 99–100. See also Misselhorn, *Bereit-Kunst* (n. 4, item 17).

50. For example, Geissert (n. 4, item 11), in the first section of his book, which discusses training (unpaginated). He gives instructions as to how to deal with a horse that has been badly ridden: "Wenn denn einem solche obgemelte übel gerittene Pferd zu handen kommen / sol man nicht unterlassen / mit grosser Gedult (weil ihnen nicht allein der Verstand mangelt / sondern nur fantaseyerischer / zorniger und verzweiffelter werden) sich der besten unnd rechten Mittel . . . zu gebrauchen" (If you get a horse that has been badly ridden, you should not cease to employ the best and correct methods [of training] and great patience, not only because the horse lacks reason, but because [otherwise] it will only become more capricious, enraged, and desperate). Von Dehnen-Rothfelser (n. 4, item 14) talks about the importance of looking at the eyes of a horse because "daran erkennestu wenn es zornig / leunisch / trawrig / lustig / fröhlich / oder fanthaseyisch ist" (from that you can recognize if it is enraged, moody, sad, frisky, happy, or capricious), 9.

51. See the quote above by Geissert in which he insists that the rider be patient. Von Dehnen-Rothfelser (n. 4, item 14) lists "merciful" as one of the necessary qualities a good horseman should have: "So sol er auch barmhertzig seyn / sich also bald des armen Thiers erbarmen / so er sich nur ein wenig in gehorsamb begiebet / die Straffen fallen lassen / un dem gutes thun. . . ." (He should also be merciful, so as soon as the horse offers even a small measure of obedience, the rider should have mercy on the poor animal and should cease his punishments and reward it), 2.

52. Von Dehnen-Rothfelser (n. 4, item 14), 159; Christoph Jacob Lieb (n. 4, item 12), 1; Misselhorn (n. 4, item 15), 12–13.

53. Von Dehnen-Rothfelser (n. 4, item 14), 180–82, gives 31 different reasons why a horse can be heavy in hand. Lieb (n. 4, item 12), 2, maintains that a horse leans on the bit if it is weak in the back, a way of thinking with which modern-day dressage riders would agree. See also Loehneysen (n. 4, item 9), 40[r].

54. Misselhorn (n. 4, item 15), "Bey einem sturrischen / verwegnen / hartnäckichten und tückischen Pferde / . . . wird ihnen die Nase erstlich und wacker / biß auff das rohe Fleisch durchgesiedelt / so kommen sie unter das Joch / und können alsdann bald demühtig werden" (with pigheaded, rank, obstinate, and malicious horse[s] . . . their noses should be first and energetically worked down to the raw flesh; then they'll learn submission and humility), 21; regarding the tongue, see p. 19.

55. Von Dehnen-Rothfelser (n. 4, item 14) explains that he has dedicated his book to the Saxon dukes and the Danish king and prince because they know a lot about horses and "Auch zu guten wohl abgerichteten dapffern lehrigen / und wendigen Rossen eine sonderbare beliebung tragen: Jedoch mit bescheidenheit / und nicht auff unbesonnene Heidnische weise / darvon man nachrichtung hat / daß die Persianer / in vorzeiten / ihre guten Pferde / aus übermässiger Liebe gegen dieselbigen / haben neben sich begraben lassen . . ." (that you have a special appreciation for well-trained, clever, and tractable horses, yet this is a moderate appreciation and not the imprudent kind displayed by the heathens such as by the ancient Persians, of whom it is said that they had their good horses buried next to them, out of an excessive appreciation for the horses), ii^r; for methods to deal with a bucking horse: "so hawe es mit der Spißrutten unter den Bauch umb die Hoden / und mit einem Creutzstreich auff die Brust / so wol mit den Sporn nach den Lancken / und schrey es mit rawer stimme an / so offt es solches thut . . . / unnd wenn die Straffen in gleicherzeit und auffeinander folgen / so weiß es nicht wo sichs wehren sol / erschricket und bekommet eine furcht . . . / so wird er gehorsam. . . . So schadet es auch nicht wenn du es . . . mit der Rutten gleich zwischen die Ohren schlegest . . .," 94.

56. Von Dehnen-Rothfelser (n. 4, item 14), "Weil aber ohne Menschliche Hülffe ein Roß nichts nütze ist / und der Mensch weit mehr als ein Thier mit Weißheit und Verstand begabet / so sol es auch der Mensch mit Verstand regieren / lernen und weisen / der Natur des edlen Thieres helffen / und nicht über Vermögen die Natur zwingen . . . / es also machen / daß es ihn liebet und fürchtet . . ." (Because a horse is useless without human aid, and because man has been given wisdom and reason much more than has an animal, so man should control the animal with reason, he should teach it and show it [what is correct], he should enhance the nature of this noble animal and not force it beyond its natural capacity . . . he should make it love and fear him), 18.

57. Caspar Reuschlein (n. 4, item 10), "so ist meines erachtens des fürnembste / daß ein kaltsinniger Kopff und gemuth mit einem solchen starcken rohen Thier / gleich wie mit einem schönem Glaß umbgange / damit es den Menschen lieb gewinne / dann zu gleicher weise / wie ein schön Glaß durch ein unwirsche Person bald zerstossen unnd zerbrochen wird / also bald kan ein jung schön pferd durch einen unwilligen unwirschen Reitter auch verderbet werden" (In my opinion it is most preferable that a [rider with a] cool head and calm disposition deals with a strong and unformed animal as if it were a beautiful piece of glass, so that the animal learns to love humans. Just as a beautiful piece of glass will be knocked around and broken by a surly person, so a young beautiful horse can be quickly ruined by a peevish, gruff rider), 6; Similar sentiments are uttered by von

Dehnen-Rothfelser (n. 4, item 14), 2; see also Misselhorn, *Bereit-Kunst* (n. 4, item 17), 25.

58. For a similar argument about control of the body in fencing and riding in the sixteenth and seventeenth centuries, see the suggestive essay by Georges Vigarello, "The Upward Training of the Body from the Age of Chivalry to Courtly Civility," in *Fragments for a History of the Human Body*, ed. Michel Feher, pt. 2 (New York: Zone Books, 1989), 148–99. My thanks to Diane Wolfthal for drawing my attention to this essay. For parallel observations regarding the increasing interiority of emotional and physical control in the theological/spiritual realm, see Donna Spivey Ellington, "Impassioned Mother or Passive Icon: The Virgin's Role in Late Medieval and Early Modern Passion Sermons," *Renaissance Quarterly* 48/2 (1995), 227–61. Ellington considers, among other factors, the role of Descartes' philosophy in this process.

CHAPTER 6

MAN AND HORSE IN HARMONY

Elisabeth LeGuin

[A] scholar and a horse are very troublesome to one another. . . .

Duke of Newcastle, *A General System
of Horsemanship, 1743*

It is only within the last century—very suddenly and very recently, given their long career—that horses are no longer intrinsic to the basic operations of Western society; few of us any longer rely on them for anything we consider indispensable. Horsemanship is still tightly woven into our speaking and our thinking, however, in countless figures that make up a kind of thoroughgoing metaphorical fabric. We speak of being back (or tall) in the saddle, being spurred to do something, reining in someone or something. We transpose equine experience into human terms with concepts such as "keeping pace," "hitting one's stride," "getting off on the wrong foot," "kicking up one's heels," "feeling one's oats." Such metaphors are used regularly by people who have never come near a horse to address matters of intention, control, and enactment, and they show remarkably few signs of being supplanted by automotive imagery. Given the readiness with which language adapts to social and technological change, it seems unlikely that the persistence of horsemanship metaphors in modern English is merely an odd pocket of resistance. I would instead suggest that it has to do with the intricate and as yet irreplaceable ways in which horses have represented human embodiment in Western culture.

My project here is to investigate some aspects of this representation as it evolved during the early modern period in Europe, most particularly in its association with another embodied practice, that of making music. This association—one that I first came to consider, not historically, but in daily practice as a professional musician and amateur horsewoman— is considerably less arbitrary than it might seem at first glance.

As Kate van Orden demonstrates in her essay for this volume, both practices are linked to, indeed constitutive of, the idea of physical discipline as internalized social control, as this idea developed among the upper classes in Italy and France around the sixteenth century. On the public level, music promoted bodily discipline through organizing time, and the physical traversal of time, into precise quantities whose predictable and manipulable nature was made visible through the geometrical patterning of bodies on the dance floor. On a more private level, music focused the attention of individuals discretely and discreetly onto the acquisition of socially non-threatening bodily skills: playing the lute, singing or improvising poetry to its accompaniment.

At the same time, early modern horsemen, no longer under an urgent mandate of military effectiveness, could begin to explore their work as an art—that is, in its capacity to articulate and elaborate, rather than actively defend, a status quo. The relationship of post-military horsemanship to music-making is most apparent at the public (indeed, monstrously ostentatious) level: the *balletto a cavallo* used music in the same way as the geometrical dance of which it was the equestrian transposition, as temporal and gestural organizer. However, it is the private level, that of training horses so that they could be used in the *balletti* and other endeavors, that will chiefly concern me here. The trainers involved in this were fortunate— notably more so than their counterparts in music—in the determination of the period to hearken back to classical sources, since an excellent treatise by Xenophon, *The Art of Horsemanship*, was actually preserved entire. Ancient Greek wisdom, whatever the discipline, was still enormously privileged when Cesare Fiaschi first published his *Trattato dell'imbrigliare, atteggiare, & ferrare cavalli* in 1556. To greater or lesser degree, an indebtedness to (or at least a consonance with) Xenophon may also be traced in the other, later sources I use here: treatises by Gervase Markham, prototype of the English country gentleman, whose *Cavelarice, or The English Horseman* appeared in 1607; the very influential Antoine de Pluvinel, Master of Horses to the young Louis XIII, whose instructions to his royal charge were posthumously published in 1623 as *Le Maneige royal*; William Cavendish, Duke of Newcastle, whose 1658 *La Méthode et invention nouvelle de dresser les chevaux* is a pillar of the methods of the famous

Spanish Riding School; Claude-François Menestrier, whose *Traité des tournois, ioustes, carrousels, et autres spectacles publics* appeared in 1669; and William Hope, a Scot who translated a French farriery treatise by Jacques de Solleysel, appended his own comments about riding and training, and called the whole *The Compleat Horseman*, publishing it in 1696.

For the purposes of this chapter I would like to propose that the adoption of Xenophon's humane and commonsensical approach around 1550 marks a turning point, not only in the military purposes that had dominated horse training for millennia, but in basic European understandings of how power and command work upon selfhood. Central to a Xenophonian approach is an acknowledgment of the horse as an independent intelligence, an Other, someone to be negotiated with, rather than something to be deployed. "For what the horse does under compulsion . . . is done without understanding; and there is no beauty in it either, any more than if one should whip and spur a dancer."[1] Something like this acknowledgment had been around for a long time. Metaphorically, it is of the essence that the chariot-horses of the soul in Plato's *Phaedrus* are independent intelligences, such control as their charioteer has being the product of a very uncertain negotiation indeed. Historically, there is a venerable literature of equine heroism, with early exemplars in the horse in the Book of Job who "saith among the trumpets, Ha, Ha; and he smelleth the battle afar off, the thunder of the captains and the shouting,"[2] and the famous Bucephalus. Such traditions certainly inform equestrian literature in the period in question. Menestrier tells us,

De tous les Animaux, il n'en est aucun, qui ait plus de rapport à l'Homme, & qui semble estre plus à ses usages que le Cheval. . . . Il a du cœur, il aime la gloire, & il se plait aux caresses, & aux applaudissemens.[3]	Of all animals there is not one that has more rapport with Man, and that seems better suited to his usages, than the horse. . . . He has courage, he loves glory, and he is pleased by caresses and applause.

Newcastle, in his turn, sums up the equine character warmly: "The horse [is], after man, the most noble of all animals (for he is as much superior to all other creatures as man is to him, and therefore holds a sort of middle place between man and the rest of the creation)." Greater nuance, and far greater practicality, emerge in Newcastle's characterization, however. It turns out to be as much a warning as a tribute: the horse's quasi-human, intermediate status means that "he is wise and subtile: for which reason man ought carefully to preserve his empire over him, knowing how nearly that wisdom and subtilty approaches his own."[4] Just how the horseman is to go about "preserving his empire"—that is, the practical daily science of what the horse may be said to think, why he thinks it, and how the trainer can best respond—is the explicit concern here. Shorn of sentimentality, presented with some concern for method rather than as thrilling anecdotes, treatises such as Newcastle's make a fascinating contribution to the history of discipline, in that they suggest the possibility of a dialogic relationship between trainer and trained.

It is this possibility, as it has been carried forward and amplified into the present day, that I wish to explore here. That being said, there is much in these treatises that supports a very different reading of early modern horsemanship. Much of their advice consists of what we would now consider extremely harsh training methods, methods based on pain and fear, methods that can serve as paradigmatic demonstrations of Foucault's foundational and repellent definition of *dressage*: "uninterrupted, constant coercion . . . which assured the constant subjection of [bodily] forces and imposed upon them a relation of docility–utility . . . ."[5] This is borne out in the frequent occurrence of words such as "prowess" and "subjection." William Hope expresses the perfection of the horse–rider relationship as being "to reduce horses, and bring them under a perfect subjection and obedience, and to have no other will save that of their Riders . . . [so that] there appears such a harmony and beauty, that whatever they do contrary to them is displeasing, and cannot be endured."[6] Pluvinel's advice sounds a good deal like that kind of training more lately called "breaking" a horse:

[I]l faut tousiours travailler le cheval à ce qui contrairie le plus sa volonté, pour le renger plus promptement à la parfaite obeyssance que nous desirons de tous les Chevaux.[7]	One must always work the horse toward what is most contrary to his will, to bring him most quickly toward that perfect obedience that we desire in all horses.

And Newcastle takes this a step farther, requiring of the horse not just subjection, but fear.

> It is impossible to dress a horse before he obeys his rider, and by that obedience acknowledges him to be his master; that is, he must first fear him, and from this fear love must proceed, and so he must obey. For it is fear creates obedience in all creature, in man as well as in beast. Great

pains then must be taken to make a horse fear his rider, that so he may obey out of self-love, that he may avoid punishment. A horse's love is not so safe to be trusted to, because it depends on his own will; whereas his fear depends on the will of the rider, and that is being a dressed horse. But when the rider depends on the will of the horse, it is the horse that manages the rider. Love then is of no use; fear does all; For which reason the rider must make himself feared, as the fundamental part of dressing a horse. Fear commands obedience, and the practice of obedience makes a horse well dressed. Believe me, for I tell it you as a friend, it is truth.[8]

This massively overdetermined passage is disturbing, coming as it does from the most urbane and humane of all equestrian writers; but I think it is a case of "the scholar and the horse being very troublesome to one another." There is a good deal that works against our reading Newcastle's advice as simplistically as Foucault's summing-up would encourage us to do. First, it must be said, there is the fascination value of horror. A juicy description of a physically abusive training method, a picture of a bit that must have regularly drawn blood, or even Newcastle's hypnotically insistent chant on the theme of "fear," will tend to draw scholarly and readerly attention in a way that details of dialogic interaction, which tend to be indeterminate or merely implied, cannot. My focus here is through and beyond those early modern training practices that we now find horrific; I am interested in the evidence that these treatises also provide of the beginnings of a shift, a sea change. That things were changing is suggested by the degree of inconsistency: the treatises themselves sometimes seem to militate in one place against the harshness they advocate in another. Second, I believe that these treatises suggest a crucial shift most especially when they are read with some practical, embodied knowledge of the discipline in question. In the discussion that follows I propose to maintain a dialogue between that knowledge and the points made in the treatises. Such dialogue is by its nature trans-historical: strictly documentable historicity is questionably served by reference to living praxis, yet a history of praxis, *as praxis*, is poorly served by documenta alone. Nuances, arguably essential ones, will be lost without reference to experience. As Fiaschi puts it, "No one can judge of it who is not there."[9] As a performer who is also a historian of performance, I negotiate this balancing act for a living. We can, of course, no longer be there, when "there" was 1556; but I believe that being here, now, astride, can provide a meaningful window onto that past—especially, perhaps, in a discipline as consistent and self-conscious as Western European horse training.

Molière's Fencing Master, barking commands at the hapless Bourgeois, personifies the coercive strain in early modern training:

Le Maître d'armes: Allons, monsieur, la révérence. Votre corps droit. Un peu penché sur la cuisse gauche. Les jambes point tant écartées. Vos pieds sur une même ligne. Votre poignet à l'opposite de votre hanche. La pointe de votre épée vis-à-vis de votre épaule. Le bras pas tout à fait si tendu. La main gauche à la hauteur de l'œil. L'épaule gauche plus quartée. La tête droite.[10]	The Fencing Master: Come sir, salute the swords. Body straight. Shift your weight to the left thigh. Legs not so far apart. Feet lined up. Wrist at hip level. Tip of your sword at shoulder level. Arm not quite so extended. Left hand at eye level. Left shoulder more in *carte* position. Head straight.

Clearly, the obsessive level of anatomical detail, the "attentive 'malevolence' that turns everything to account,"[11] the abrasively efficient tone are not confined to the military disciplines of which Foucault writes. But of course Molière is being ironic about such "efficiency": the Bourgeois is getting tied into terrible knots as this session proceeds. Smile at him though we may, in his hopeless confusion he represents a real problem in the dissemination of discipline, and there is little indeed in the literature of his day to rescue him. Contemporary works on fencing, dance, music, or comportment tend to present a fairly rudimentary one-way flow of information between trainer and trained; even in those written as dialogues, the pupil is a kind of straight man, rarely offering any real challenge to the method being presented. Horses, however, demand another sort of dialogue altogether: even as they exhibit extraordinary ability to adapt to human purposes, they challenge human methods through their sheer Otherness. By the time of Molière, horse training had developed very sophisticated means of managing that Otherness. The Bourgeois, wandering down to his stables and watching his Ecuyer, or Master of Horses, would have found in use there most of the strategies of which he himself stood in such sore need: the devising of appropriate goals for practice, and their modification based on results; the incremental shaping of new neurological responses through practice and reinforcement; the recognition of and working with resistance, confusion, or tension; and a full understanding of the uses of pleasure and pain in inculcating desired habits, or systematically eradicating undesired ones.

In suggesting, as I do here, a parallel between the training of horses and the training of human bodies, it would be silly to elide the profound differences between the two species. (Indeed it would be downright dangerous, given that horse bodies weigh a thousand pounds, move with startling rapidity, and are eminently capable of injuring or killing their trainers by accident, let alone by design.) Yet it would be equally silly to disallow the parallel on that basis; if nothing else, the sheer vernacular momentum of human identification with horses constitutes a kind of obligation to pursue it. These treatises succumb neither to overidentification nor to denial of commonality, but constitute a serious attempt to sort out how power and authority actually work in relation to Otherness. In so doing, they move in a particularly interesting metaphorical crosscurrent relative to the Cartesian model, taking the separation of mind and body to a kind of logical extreme by proposing the body, not as mechanism, but as a morally independent Other. (As the Duke of Newcastle, patron and friend to Descartes, Hobbes, Jonson, and Dryden, rather irascibly puts it: "If [the horse] does not think (as the famous philosopher DES CARTES affirms of all beasts) it would be impossible to teach him what he should do."[12])

What, then, are we to make of the same author's expert and strongly worded advice about maintaining fear in the horse? It is our understanding of the concept of fear, as it pertains to horses, that is key here. Fear is a central aspect of equine character, as horses are prey animals; in the wild, it is essential to their survival that they be ever ready to perceive threats and react to them. They have as a consequence a large repertoire of fear-related states, from responsive alertness through suspicion through apprehension through agitation to full-blown panic. Their reactions are similarly fine gradations of a basic response—to flee. The Ecuyer could not eradicate such a powerful instinct as this—nor indeed would he wish to, for the same swiftness that is the equine ticket to survival in the wild has recommended the horse to human purposes for millennia. But, working Aristotle-fashion with nature, the Ecuyer had much the same job as the fencing or ballet master: one of taking an unschooled (if very well-bred) body and training it to recognize and manage its own primary impulses. In one manner of speaking, this consisted of training the horse and (perhaps more importantly) the rider to a wider, more subtle, and nuanced vocabulary of fear. But the manner of speaking is important. Within an equine vocabulary, "fear" does not necessarily mean a state of abject, quaking incompetence. Newcastle's advice above reads very differently if we consider that the "fear" of which he speaks might more closely resemble that in the old injunction "Fear God," meaning the physical enactment of respect.[13]

It is this capacity for fear that most sharply differentiates horses from humans; we are not prey animals, and will forever lag behind equines in the precision and attunement of our responses to perceived danger. In learning to recognize and honor and anticipate his horse's fear, and in developing strategies for making use or even beauty out of it, the trainer, inevitably, trains himself: to an exigent level of physical reactivity, of constant receptivity, that is not peculiar to horsemanship, but beats at the heart of physical discipline in any performing art. In music-making, this same level would be called listening.

A well-managed vocabulary of fear can be most efficiently developed through strategies of reward and punishment; as William Hope says, "hope of reward and fear of punishment governs this whole World, not only Men but Horses."[14] This apparent Lockeanism harks directly back to Xenophon; particularly in its emphasis on reward, it is at the heart of his radical influence. The treatises' descriptions of rewards are interestingly detailed, sometimes offering a touching glimpse of the writer's intimacy with his animals.

> [T]he keepers greatest labour is but to procure love from the horse, so the onelie thing that is pleasant to the Horse, is love from the keeper; insomuch that there must be a sincere and incorporated friendshippe between them or else they cannot delight nor profit each other, of which love the keeper is to give testimonie, both by his gentle language to his horse, and by taking from him any thing which he shall beholde to annoy or hurt him, as moates, dust, superfluous hayres, flyes in Summer, or anye such like thinge, and by oft feeding him out of his hand, by which meanes the Horse will take such delight and pleasure in his keepers companye, that he shall never approach him, but the Horse shall with a kind of chearfull or inward neying, show the ioy he takes to behold him, and where this mutuall love is knit and combined, there the beast must needes prosper, and the man reap reputation and profit. . . .[15]

Rewards may be elaborate, or as simple as Xenophon's suggestion that the horse appreciates a rest from time to time: "[H]e will leap and jump up and obey in all the rest if he looks forward to a season of rest on finishing what he has been directed to do."[16] This use of respite as reward results in a kind of training that proceeds through frequent alternation of work and rest. This requires that the trainer have an accurate sense of his horse's particular capacities and limitations, and that in order to accomplish his goals efficiently he respect these capacities and limitations over and above any desires of his own—essentially, that he "listen" to his horse.

[H]orami par di dire, che al buon cavaliere fa bisogno . . . [temperarsi] secondo l'occasione, & tempi, si de batterli, come di farle carezze, ò di tenerli solamente in timore . . . hauendo l'occhio di continuo all'animo, & forze loro, & secondo quelle operare. . . .[17]

Hear me then when I say that the good horseman must . . . [temper] himself as the occasion requires, to beat them, make carresses, or to keep them only in fear . . . keeping an eye on the progress of [the horses'] spirits and strength, and taking these as his guide. . . .

Punishment is a more complex matter. The primary cautions here are likewise consistent among writers: it must be to the point and brief. "A good keeper therefore must know when to correct and when to cherrish, not giving either blowe or angrie word, but in the instant of the offence, nor to punish or strike the horse any longer then whilst his present fault restes in his memorie."[18] Here latter-day horse trainers can find resonance with Markham: the current understanding is that the equine upper limit for accurate cause-and-effect association is about three seconds; after this the point of punishment (or, for that matter, of reward) is simply lost. Causal associations between actions and consequences ("I balk here, and I am being punished") and the decisions they make possible ("therefore I will cease to balk") are limited to this three-second envelope. Put another way, effectively admonishing or constraining an embodied intelligence requires sharp vigilance on the part of the trainer. A tardy reprimand is simply abuse, and abuse can have endless repercussions: horses may have a very limited capacity for causality, but their long-term memories are enormously retentive and detailed. It is not unusual for a horse to react with apprehension when it is brought near a place where something bad happened, not just days, but years before.

Punishing the horse is thus a delicate business, very easily made counterproductive in its activation of equine fear, which will tend to have an energy and a logic all its own, quite independent of the trainer's purposes. Should the horse be resistant to a command because it is already afraid, Xenophon reminds us that "[c]ompulsion and blows inspire only the more fear; for when horses are at all hurt at such a time, they think that what they shied at is the cause of the hurt." In other words, the fear response has an additive tendency: "scary object" and "scary beating" will simply combine, spiraling into "doubly scary object-plus-beating." In such a situation, then, the trainer must show the horse "that there is nothing fearful in it, least of all to a courageous horse like him; but if this fails, touch the object yourself that seems so dreadful to him, and lead him up to it with gentleness."[19]

In his administration of reward and punishment the trainer must, above all, be impartial—another point on which all these writers concur, again following Xenophon: "The one great precept and practice in using a horse is this—never deal with him when you are in a fit of passion. A fit of passion is a thing that has no foresight in it, and so we often have to rue the day when we gave in to it."[20] Newcastle, for example, writes, "I have seen very few passionate horsemen get the better of a horse by their anger. . . . In this act there should always be a man and a beast, and not two beasts."[21]

For all the importance of vigilance and sensitivity, of "listening," of taking the horse's spirits as one's own guide, a crucial separation between horse and rider, mind and body, intention and execution, emerges here. In the Aristotelian view that informs the work of Xenophon and the early modern writers I discuss here, training, the dressing of nature toward excellence, cannot take place without it. The moment the trainer loses his impartiality and collapses the separation, he has lost the only thing that differentiated him from what Aristotle calls the "other animals": his ability to separate himself from his own reactions and desires, and by so doing to become an independent practical reasoner. The angry trainer and his horse are become "two beasts."

A physical intelligence, proceeding without the intervention of independent practical reason, will persist in certain traits—traits that human embodiment shares quite fully with that of horses: the "vegetative principle," as Aristotle calls it, toward growth and toward reproduction; attraction to pleasure and avoidance of discomfort; conservation of energy (i.e., laziness); and, most interestingly from the standpoint of issues of domination and subjection in training, a certain innate resistance to being told what to do. In the human soul "there is something contrary to the rational principle, resisting and opposing it";[22] as far as the equine soul, "subjection is not agreeable to a horse. . . . If the wisest man in the world were put into the shape of a horse, and retained his superior understanding, he could not invent more cunning ways (I question if so many) to oppose his rider, than a horse does. . . ."[23]

Characterizations of horses as noble and quasi-human may have something to do with this extremely resourceful resistance to subjection, a quality long associated with moral integrity in humans. However, early modern horse trainers certainly do not inflate this possibility into the full-blown romanticization so prominent in current Western culture. Horses, especially wild ones, are among our most ubiquitous and imprecise symbols of freedom, galloping with manes and tails streaming across advertisements for everything from cigarettes to mortgage plans. Wildness did not have this cachet in the period in question; it was rather more likely to be seen in a Hobbesian light, as a state of violent, unregenerate war. By these lights, resistance must and should be overcome, for only through training does the good life become possible.

Newcastle's approach to entrenched resistance, resistance to training itself, is so deeply pragmatic as to be almost metaphysical. Those who have raised children may recognize his strategy for coping with an embodied intelligence in a state of existential uncooperativeness:

> If you can't gain your point therefore in one way, you must have recourse to another: I mean, that if in his extremity the horse will not agree with you, you must agree with him in the following manner. You would make your horse advance, and he to defend himself against you runs back: at that instant pull him back with all your strength. And if to oppose you he advances, immediately force him briskly forward. If you would turn to the right, and he endeavours to turn to the left, pull him round to the left as suddenly as possible: if you would turn him to the left, and he insists on the right, turn him as smartly to the right as you are able. If you would have him go sideways to one hand, and he inclines more to the other, immediately second his inclination. If he would rise, make him rise two or three times. In a word, follow his inclinations in every thing, and change as often as he. When he perceives there can be no opposition, but that you always will the same thing as he, he will be amazed, he will breathe short, snuff up his nose, and won't know what to do next. . . .[24]

There is much in the extracts above that applies very neatly to the process of training human bodies to an art; one can imagine the Bourgeois benefiting, for instance, from the advice about doing little but often, and about the careful use of respite. Fiaschi's treatise is one place where such parallels become explicit. He directs the student of fine riding to make reference to his own musical experience—an experience naturally presumed, since music and riding were both standard parts of a nobleman's education in Italian and French academies. Fiaschi includes short extracts of musical notation as guides for coordinating rider and horse in the execution of various figures; and he gives a beautifully concise description of equestrian "listening."

[Gli] speroni, polpe, briglia, & uoce . . . non a tutti si dee oßervar un medemo [*sic*] modo, ma hor un poco piò, hor meno secōdo che si conosce il bisogno, il qual nō può niuno absente giudicare. . . .[25]	[T]he spurs, muscles, bridle, and voice . . . must not be observed in the same way toward every [horse], but now a little more, now less, following what is known of the need; no one can judge of it who is not there. . . .

Newcastle takes the parallel even further.

> The hand, thigh, leg, and heel [of the rider] ought always to go together; for example, suppose a man playing upon the lute, and he touches the strings with his left hand, without touching the others with his right, he must make but a very indifferent harmony; but when both hands go together, and in right time, the musick will be good. It is the same with respect to this excellent art; what you mark with your hand should be touched at the same time with your thigh, leg, or heel, or the musick of your work will be bad. We are at present speaking of musick, and he that has not a musical head can never be a good horseman. A horse well dressed moves as true, and keeps as regular time as any musician can.[26]

In this lovely passage, "musick" means something we all recognize, riders or no, for it is fundamental in all corporeal disciplines. We have no other concise name for it. "Musick" here means the submission and organization of embodiment to a purpose.[27] I say embodiment, and not "the body," for even the solitary lute player is many in his embodiments: there is one musick of the player's hands' intention to the purpose of a melody; another to its counterpoint; another musick, a vigilant evaluative musick, takes place as the player listens to and judges the sounds he has just produced, in order to adjust the volume or the finger placement of those now forthcoming; and another musick still, a demonstrative one, in how he has positioned himself with respect to the admiring listener across the room, and in the subtle adjustment of the plucking motions of his right hand that direct his instrument's sounds toward his idea of that listener's hearing. He plays not only upon the lute, but upon his own body, the room, and the listener too; and all of them play upon his ear and his sensibility. Such musick is momentary, fluctuating, circumstantial. No one can judge of it who is not there.

In the context of riding, where two whole bodies are involved, these overlapping circles spread yet wider and become more complex: there is "the musick of [the rider's] work," coordinating heels and hands and sense of balance to speak clearly to the horse in that kinetic and kinesthetic language the animal understands best—looking left, sinking weight into his left seat-bone, moving his right calf back a few inches along the horse's side, the rider begins to enunciate the musick of "turn left"; meanwhile the horse's body, in readiness ("fear") toward that kinesthetic speech, feels the weight-shifts of the rider's head and buttocks, anticipates the touch on its right side, and has begun the turn so that the rider need do very little more (for the horse, a reward for its readiness inheres in its rider's ceasing to insist); or, should the horse be not in readiness but in resistance (sore muscles along the right side of the neck, perhaps, due to excessive work the day before), it stiffens against the left turn; and the rider, feeling the animal shorten its stride and tense its back, hearing it swish its tail in annoyance, continues into the reinforcement of "turn left" by drawing back his left elbow, and with it the hand and rein, more or less sharply depending on the horse's degree of resistance. All of this within perhaps two seconds. Should the resistance happen a second time (the rider is vigilant here), perhaps he applies a flick of his riding whip to the horse's right shoulder at its first appearance, adding "I mean it" to "turn left." There are musicks of intention short and long. There is short-term vigilance by which the rider identifies and corrects such a resistance. (Perhaps, on another occasion, the horse's head has come up, its ears are tensely pricked toward the pile of wood over on the far side of the arena, which was not there yesterday, it holds its breath—now the rider's strategy will be quite different, he will relent with the left-turn music, and modulate instead to "it's really okay," enacting some version of Xenophon's "lead him up to it with gentleness" until the horse perceives that the pile of wood is actually quite boring—sighs, relaxes, resumes his pace.) The longer-term, overarching musick of the rider's intention for this time, this practice session, was that it center upon bending to the left, but it became perforce a session about refining fear: the release of inappropriate fear (fear of a wood-pile) in favor of that habit of trust that must underlie any left turns, any commands at all.

Finally, in sum, "musick" means that, to the observer, the purpose of all this submission and organization emerges clearly and unambiguously: that it be, simply, beautiful, or as Pluvinel puts it, *bel*, which means also effortless, easy, unaffected. Such ease is momentary, fluctuating, circumstantial. No one can judge of it who is not there.

The necessarily unwieldy blow-by-blow description of this kinesthetic musick is itself far from *bel*; the whole process is much better served by the period metaphor of sympathetic vibration. Shared vibration in the fibrous matter of the nerves was a central image for relationships among sensitive beings, and these treatises make it clear that horses were thought to have this sympathetic, musical potential quite as much as their masters. Markham describes the "Composition of Horses" in terms identical to those for the composition of human beings: horses have four humors, "choller, flegme, blood, & melancholy" (these determine the animal's color, among other things). As for their Spirit, he says, "It is the very quintessence of the blood, and being conveyed in the Arteries, gives the body a more lively and sprity Heate, and makes his feeling more quicke and tender."[28] Markham takes equine musicality as evidence of horses' special sensitivity:

> That a horse is a beast of a most excellent understanding, and of more rare and pure sence then anie other beast whatsoever, we have many ancient and rare records . . . we find it Written, that in the army of Sibaritanes, horsses would daunce to Musicke, and in their motions keep due time with musicke. . . . [29]

As here, accounts of horses responding to music intersect substantially with equine military mythology; after all, it is not just the prospect of battle that causes the horse in Job to say, "Ha, ha," but, specifically, the sound of the trumpets. Menestrier treats of the ultimate in military–musical intersections, the great outdoor spectacles so beloved of his historical moment; he quotes accounts by Pliny, Solinus, and others to demonstrate that "Ces Animaux aiment l'harmonie . . . qui les excite au Combat" (These animals love harmony . . . that excites them to combat)[30] and he devotes careful consideration to the kinds of music most likely to produce such an effect.

Accounts of sixteenth- and seventeenth-century *balletti di cavallo* typically follow a certain pattern that privileges the musical responsiveness of the horse and rider by mentioning it last. Descriptions of magnificent human and equine apparel are followed by accounts of choreographed feats of virtuoso riding; the whole closes with a reference to the obedience of this stupendous assemblage to the rhythms and phrases of the music. Thus Pluvinel, recounting an equestrian ballet composed by himself and possibly by Robert Ballard, makes the following observation:

La deuxiesme figure, les Chevaliers vis à vis l'un de l'autre Changeoient de place en faisant deux voltes à la fin, le tout à courbette en commençant, & finissant de ferme à ferme tous six en semble, tant que les cadences duroient. . . .[31]	In the second figure the horsemen, facing one another, changed places, making two *voltes* at the end, the whole having begun with *courbettes*, and finishing with the *ferme à ferme*,[32] all six in unison as long as the cadences lasted. . . .

In Vienna at the 1667 performance of *Il contesa dell'aria e dell'acqua*, the *balletto a cavallo*, choreographed by the Roman *cavaliere* Alessandro Carducci and composed by Johann Heinrich Schmelzer, opened with a Courante, a solo for the Emperor Leopold,

. . . il quale pel primo diè prova della sua alta perizia, facendo eseguire dal suo destriero corvette in aria, diritti e svolte, e fermate in cadenza secondo le note musicale.[33]

. . . who from the first proved his great prowess, making his destrier execute *corvette in aria, diritte,*[34] and *svolte*[35] all held in cadence following the musical notes.

Three hundred years later, the same privileging of certain esthetic and philosophical values persists in the Kür, or musical freestyle, that is performed as the climax of upper-level dressage competition. It is supposed to look effortlessly "natural," as if the "quicke and tender feeling" of the horse is responding spontaneously to the rhythms and gestures of the musical selections. At its best, it is easy to believe that this is in fact the case; a Kür performed by a horse trained to the highest or Grand Prix level has a rhythmic alacrity, variety, and responsiveness that would be the envy of any human dancer, and there will be no sign to the casual observer that the rider is doing anything at all to influence this.[36]

The Edenic possibility of animal training as "a sincere and incorporated friendshippe" resonates pleasantly with this idea of equine musicality, the idea that things like the Terpsichorean ferocity of the Sybaritan horses, the wondrous movements of the Kür, come from the animals' own impulse to dance to music. But once we put ceremonial descriptions aside, the dynamics of this idea in practice prove intricate and equivocal. Menestrier, for instance, uses the sympathetic vibration metaphor in order to suggest that composers and choreographers adapt their art to the animals, rather than the other way round.

Il faut donc dire que l'harmonie de certain airs, & de certains instrumens, se trouvant sympathique avec nos corps, ou les corps des animaux, de qui les muscles peuuent ester dans vne disposition semblable à celles des cordes d'un luth bien monté, dont l'vne estant touchée fait vibrer toutes les autres: il se fait de pareils tremoussemens dans ces corps au son son [*sic*] de ces instrumens. . . . Cela estant ainsi, il faut estudier la nature, & le temperament des animaux, que

One could thus say that the harmony of certain airs and of certain instruments proves to be sympathetic with our bodies, or with the bodies of animals, in which the muscles can be in a disposition similar to that of the strings on a well-strung lute, on which the one [string] being touched, all the others vibrate: a similar excitation is made in these bodies at the sound of these instruments. . . . This being so, one must study the nature and the temperament of animals if one wishes

l'on veut faire danser, & les mouvemens qui leur sont plus ordinaires, &
plus naturels, pour faire choix des
Instrumens, & des airs, qui sont plus
propres à regler ses mouvemens.[37]

to make them dance, and the movements that are ordinary and most
natural to them, in order to make that
choice of instruments and airs that
will be most appropriate for regulating their movements.

The medleys to which latter-day horses and riders move in the Kür
are painstakingly assembled by videoing the horse's movements in the
various gaits, and then finding recorded selections in tempi that fit
those movements. One can imagine the seventeenth-century
composer for one of Menestrier's *carrousels* holding in the "video" of
his mind's eye the equestrian figures devised by the Ecuyer, and
choosing from among the Baroque dance types those whose character of motion most nearly fit what he had seen. The music written,
the parts distributed, rehearsals would be much concerned with
getting the trumpeters and timpanists to pick tempi that suited
the movements of the particular horses involved. In practice, then,
the music would seem to hold in cadence following the animals, quite
as much as the reverse.

In "mak[ing] that choice of instruments and airs" the possibilities
are manifold, since equine cadence is not a simple thing. Four legs
have many more rhythmic possibilities than two. A human has only
one basic gait, with various gradations from slow to fast: a two-beat
affair in which diagonal pairs of limbs move together. The horse has
three: the walk, a four-beat gait in which lateral pairs of limbs move
hind-to-front in sequence (in so-called gaited horses, this can be
extended into a very fast, even-tempoed "flying" motion in which
only one foot touches the ground at a time); the trot, the two-beat
equine version of the human gait, with diagonals moving simultaneously; and the canter, which has a slightly irregular three-beat pattern,
and which can lead from either the left or right side. Any of these gaits
can be collected or extended, altering stride lengths and thus expressive character; in a really well-dressed horse, collection or extension
will not cause the tempo of footfalls to alter unless specific additional
commands are given.

The very diversity of shapes and sizes into which horses have been
bred is a major preoccupation of several of the treatises under consideration, notably those by Menestrier, Markham, and Hope. This
too has an impact upon matters of cadence. These authors' descriptions of the various breeds go avidly into subtleties such as length of

pasterns relative to lower leg, length of legs relative to depth of chest, amount and distribution of musculature typical to the breed, and so on—all matters with material effects upon tempo, length and loft of stride, and verging, inescapably and almost immediately, into matters of gestural character, where things such as the sex and temperament and color of the horse become factors: Markham's equine humors, musick'd.

It comes as something of a disappointment that those writers most explicitly concerned with riding to music tend to ignore this wealth of physical–musical possibility in order to extol the "airs above the ground," the fancy hopping and rearing moves that were so beloved of this period of horsemanship. Because of the strain they put on the horse's hindquarters, these moves are rarely performed anywhere today save, sparingly, at the Spanish Riding School. Reference to living praxis becomes much more problematic here, so that we must imagine all the more energetically how the Ecuyer and the Master of Music might have collaborated. The "airs above the ground" include *caprioles*, *terre à terres*, *courbettes*, and *un pas et un saut* ("a step and a jump"). The *capriole* is a motion in which the horse springs off the ground from a standstill, flinging out all four feet. Rhythmically speaking, it is a single beat, adaptable to any meter, although obviously it is a massive movement best suited to marking musical arrival points. The most beloved of the airs are also the most rhythmically complex (and therefore, one guesses, the most rhythmically adaptable), the *terre à terre* and the *courbette*, movements similar in all but degree of elevation. Menestrier describes the *courbette* as "a [hopping] movement like a crow, which has given the name Little Crow to this air."[38] Following the description given by Treva Tucker in her chapter in this volume, the rhythm of the *courbette* (and so too the *terre à terre*, to a less pronounced degree) would have been divided, the front legs' movement followed by a brief hesitation, and then the hind legs' "hopping" motion: thus 1,2-pause-3,4; 1,2-pause-3,4. The "step and a jump," a coupling of the *capriole* with the less massive *courbette*, suggests a stately triple meter articulated as LONG, short–LONG, short–LONG.

Although it is true that, as Pluvinel and others earnestly maintain, such moves occur among horses in nature, it must be mentioned that they do so only under conditions of emotional stress and agitation; a calm horse does not jump off the ground with all four feet, and the elevated posture of the front quarters used in the *courbette* is most likely to be seen in those highly charged instances when stallions fight one another. There will be some feedback from this fact: cause a calm horse to perform a motion that, in its native physical language, is associated with strong excitement, and it will become more excited.

We might interpret that excitement as military enthusiasm, as Menestrier does:

Les trompettes sont les instrumens les plus propres pour faire danser les chevaux, parce qu'ils sont loisir de reprendre haleine, quand les Trompettes la reprennent, il n'est point aussi d'instrument qui leur plaise plus, parce qu'il est martial, & que le cheval est genereux, & aime ce bruit militaire. On ne laisse pas de les dresser, & de les accoustumer à l'harmonie des violons, mais il en faut vn grand nombre, qui l'air soit de trompette, & que les basses marquent fortement les cadences.[39]	Trumpets are the most appropriate instruments for making horses dance, because they are allowed to catch their breaths when the trumpeters do so; there is also no instrument that pleases them more, because it is martial, and the horse is generous and loves such military noise. One does not let them be dressed and accustomed to the sound of violins, but a great number [of ballets] are made where the air is that of the trumpet, and where the basses mark the cadence strongly.

Buried in this fascinating tangle of cause and effect—note the coordination of the horses' and the trumpeters' very breathing—is a simple fact: loud music, especially volume and attack, the strong suit of the trumpet-and-drum corps, agitates horses; and agitation inclines them toward certain kinds of movements. In other words, "musical" responses such as this are another manifestation of equine fear.

As for other musical parameters, timbre can cause powerful responses in that it is the main means of identifying a sound; along with scent, it is central to horses' capacity for recognition of and discrimination among other beings. Horses do indeed know their masters' voices, and they can read the moods expressed or encouraged through the timbre of those voices—or, as Newcastle goes on to attest, through the timbre of instruments (he would seem here to be referring to something softer than trumpets and drums):

You may caress him as much and as often as you please: as by patting him gently with your hand: talking kindly to him: stroking him: flattering him: or sometimes by using a certain particular tone of voice, that is common to cajole skittish and unruly horses. . . . Horses take great delight in smelling to perfumed gloves, and in hearing of musick, which refreshes them very much.[40]

Timbre is inextricably linked to pitch, and while no one claims that horses find meaning in extended melody, there is good evidence for a rise of pitch being linked to excitation—trumpets are, of course, high-pitched (and timbrally piercing) instruments—as well as the reverse. Thus a trainer longeing a horse (exercising it on a long line from the ground), who is not touching the animal, and who is consequently relying on voice commands, will typically signal an acceleration—say from walk to trot—with a sharply rising inflection, "Trr-OT!," and a deceleration with a falling one, "EA-sy." Fiaschi gives a particularly succinct version of this. Most of his musical examples consist of a rhythmicized single pitch, but several—such as that for the step-and-a-jump—coordinate a rise in pitch (up a minor third) with a sharpening of timbre (from "ah" to "ahi"), and with the most athletic and agitated motion of this particular air (its *capriole* phase).

Horses clearly respond to many elements of music; but there is little to suggest, in these treatises or elsewhere, that they dance to it in the sense of spontaneously keeping time with a beat. Left to themselves with music, they just do not tap their feet or nod their heads. We do well to remember that keeping time, for all its feeling of atavistic inevitability, is in fact highly socialized and uniquely human—our species' musically reinforced version of that splendid athletic regularity of motion we see, so particularly in horses of all creatures, when they are healthy, happy, and moving freely, embodying a kind of apotheosis of rhythm, rhythm as a result, not a cause, of movement. The rider to music negotiated a delicate balance between these two musics, then, the powerful silent one of the horse's kinetic bent, and the powerfully coded audible one being played as he rode.

We come here to a strange pass, for it is no longer clear who is obeying whom. Riding to music has long been understood as a demonstration of the extent to which the horse—symbolizing not only the body, but, at least in the sixteenth and seventeenth centuries, the body politic—can be brought into control and submission; but I have been at pains to demonstrate here that it has long been equally clear in practice that both musicians and riders must know very intimately how to adapt to the horse. Its bodily intelligence calls the tune, or rather the rhythm and the gestural character, and if the rider and musicians do not listen, the display will be forced, effortful: in a word, coercive. Thus Louis XIII or the Emperor Leopold, astride magnificent horses before their noble audiences, were demonstrating to their subjects nothing so crude as a capacity for domination, but rather—and this is a most crucial distinction—a capacity for command: command as distinct from domination, command as a reciprocal condition, command as predicated upon a knowledge of when to listen as well as when to tell.

Through their own daily involvement in horsemanship, audiences at equestrian ballets would have had an intimate grasp of the terms, and the power, of this physically enacted metaphor for the equivocality of command. Even the most minimally effective horsemen among them—those multitudes who did not ride exquisitely or artistically, but who could consistently manage not to irritate or confuse the animal so much that it hurt or killed them—knew something, and knew it profoundly, in their bodies, about the importance of learning both to speak and to listen to corporeal intelligence. Depending on how one looks at it, such communication integrates, or hopelessly complicates, the mind–body split, and does so on a daily basis; its presence, undergirding the methodological details of numerous treatises, and unequivocally elevated to the status of art in the *balletto a cavallo*, needs a more nuanced explanation than it has yet received.

The flat reduction of discipline to coercion is symptomatic of the troubled relationship of the twenty-first-century West to ideas such as freedom and wildness, obedience and command. Foucault himself articulates just how poorly we deal with the necessity of discipline to the good life. We habitually conflate coercion and command; we indulge in ill-thought-out Rousseauvian fetishizations of untouched nature; we recoil from neutering our pets or training them adequately; and we worry. We worry that even those kinder, gentler visions of animal training that we find in Xenophon and his followers might, for all their reliance upon inducements, or "friendshippe," still be subtle forms of coercion. Sixteenth- and seventeenth-century horse trainers knew no such useless quandaries. By their lights, the good commander, the good listener, the horse trainer, or the emperor does not waste time in worrying, but is exceedingly vigilant, with a vigilance that is as much moral as physical. Do I command the right, the best, the good thing? Is it the right time for this thing? Is my command being followed? Why or why not? How will that influence my next command?—precisely the musick of the lutenist's vigilance as, practicing or performing, he feels the reach or press of his hands, hears the sounds he produces, forms his judgments of what to do next. For none of these arts—horsemanship, statesmanship, music, speech—is the process of physical and ethical evaluation that I have been calling musick optional. These arts resemble one another intrinsically in that they depend—and in the end, depend absolutely for the possibility of their continuation—on the incorporation of listening into the process of command.

Notes

1. Xenophon, *The Art of Horsemanship* (360 B.C.E.), trans. and with notes by M. H. Morgan (London: J. A. Allen, 1962), 62.
2. Job 39:25 (King James Version).
3. Claude-François Menestrier, *Traité des tournois, ioustes, carrousels, et autres spectacles publics* (Lyon: Jacques Muguet, 1669), facsimile edition in *The Philosophy of Images* series, ed. with introductory notes by Stephen Orgel (New York: Garland, 1979), 182.
4. William Cavendish, Duke of Newcastle, *A General System of Horsemanship*, facsimile of the 1743 J. Brindley (London) edn., with a foreword by W. C. Steinkraus (New York: Winchester Press, 1970), 122. *A General System* is a translation of the 1658 *La Méthode et invention nouvelle* mentioned earlier. All references in this chapter are to the 1743 edition but should be taken as reflecting the author's views in 1658.
5. Michel Foucault, *Discipline and Punish: The Birth of the Prison* (1975), trans. Alan Sheridan (New York: Vintage Books, 1995), 137.
6. Jacques de Solleysel, *Parfait mareschal . . . translated from the last Paris impression, by Sir William Hope . . . By whom is also added as a supplement to the first part, a most compendious and excellent collection of horsemanship . . .* (Edinburgh: George Mosman, 1696), "Some curious remarks upon Horses represented . . ." (n.p.).
7. Antoine de Pluvinel, *Le Maneige royal*, facsimile of 1626 ed., with a foreword by Alois Podhajsky (Fribourg, Switzerland: Office du livre, Bibliothèque des arts, 1969), 10.
8. Cavendish, *A General System*, 138. This and a number of other passages in Newcastle appear, closely paraphrased but not attributed, in William Hope's treatise.
9. Cesare Fiaschi, *Trattato dell'imbrigliare, atteggiare & ferrare caualli . . . opera vtilissima à precipi à gentil'huomini, à soldati, & in particolare à manescalchi . . .* 3rd edn. (Venice: Vincenzo Somasco, 1603), pt. 2, ch. XVI, 100–11.
10. Molière (Jean-Baptiste Poquelin), *Le Bourgeois Gentilhomme* (1670), trans. Stanley Appelbaum (Toronto: Dover, 1998), I.iii, opening, 210.
11. Foucault, *Discipline and Punish*, 139.
12. Cavendish, *A General System*, Introduction (n.p.).
13. I thank Susan McClary for pointing out this small intersection between horse training and religious practice.
14. Solleysel, *Parfait mareschal*, ch. XVIII, "Of rewarding and punishing Horses, that fear doth much, but love little" (n.p.).
15. Gervase Markham, *Cavelarice, or, The English Horseman, Contayning 0all the Arte of Horse-manship, as much as is necessary for any man to vnderstand . . .* (London: Edward White, 1607), bk. V, ch. 8, "Of the Passions which are in horses, and the love which their keepers should bear unto them" (n.p.).

16. Xenophon, *The Art of Horsemanship*, 49–50.
17. Fiaschi, *Trattato dell'imbrigliare*, pt. 1, ch. XXXV, 23–24.
18. Markham, *Cavelarice*, bk. V, ch. 8 (n.p.).
19. Xenophon, *The Art of Horsemanship*, 37–38.
20. Xenophon, *The Art of Horsemanship*, 37–38.
21. Cavendish, *A General System*, Introduction (n.p.).
22. Aristotle, *Nichomachean Ethics* (ca. 330 B.C.E.), trans. Richard McKeon, in *Introduction to Aristotle*, 2nd edn. (Chicago: University of Chicago Press, 1973 [1978]), bk. I, ch. 13, 1102b, 24–26.
23. Cavendish, *A General System*, Closing Remarks (n.p.).
24. Cavendish, *A General System*, 105.
25. Fiaschi, *Trattato dell'imbrigliare*, pt. 2, ch. XVI, 100–11.
26. Cavendish, *A General System*, 93.
27. For this concept of "musick" I am much beholden to Christopher Small, *Musicking: The Meanings of Performing and Listening* (Hanover, NH: Wesleyan University Press, 1998), esp. "Interlude I: The Language of Gesture."
28. Markham, *Cavelarice*, bk. VII, ch. 1, "Of the Composition of Horses . . ." (n.p.).
29. Markham, *Cavelarice*, bk. VIII, ch. 4, "Of the excellency of a Horses understanding, and other qualities" (n.p.).
30. Menestrier, *Traité des tournois*, 169.
31. Pluvinel, *Le Maneige royal*, 35.
32. Any air (including those above the ground) performed in place, without traveling forward: the ultimate in control (see the description of the airs in the text below).
33. Vincenzo Forcella, *Spectacula, ossia caroselli, tornei, cavalcate e ingressi trionfali* (Bologna: A. Forni, 1975). This is Forcella's undocumented quotation of a description of the event by its librettist, Francesco Sbarra. See also Egon Wellesz, "The 'Balletto a Cavallo,' " in *Essays on Opera*, trans. Patricia Kean (London: Dennis Dobson, 1950), 82–89.
34. Changes of lead at the canter (see the description of this gait in the text below).
35. Tight turns made with the horse's head bent to the inside.
36. There are a number of excellent videos that demonstrate the Kür, which is performed competitively. I recommend the videos of the FEI (Fedération Equestre Internationale) World Cup finals: 1998, in Gothenborg, and 1999, in Dortmund, both by Martin Bird for Equestrian Vision Productions.
37. Menestrier, *Traité des tournois*, 179–80.
38. Menestrier, *Traité des tournois*, 172.
39. Menestrier, *Traité des tournois*, 174.
40. Cavendish, *A General System*, 111.

CHAPTER 7

FROM *GENS d'ARMES* TO *GENTILSHOMMES*: DRESSAGE, CIVILITY, AND THE *BALLET À CHEVAL*

Kate van Orden

A "ROYAL" EDUCATION

In 1594, the great horseman Antoine de Pluvinel opened France's first military academy, aiming, he said, to render his students "capable of serving their Prince well, whether in peace or in war."[1] The academy filled a genuine need, as before that time young French nobles keen to fulfill the military calling of their estate had had to travel to Italy for training, where they studied at the riding school of Cesare Fiaschi in Ferrara or in Naples with Federico Grisone, Giovanni Battista Pignatelli (at whose school Pluvinel had studied for six years), or Cesare Mirabbello. After a stay that usually began no earlier than age 14 and lasted one or two years, students returned to France, where they commanded respect through their poise in the saddle.

An Italian education had certain advantages, for it allowed young nobles to pick up a useful vernacular, socialize with other elites, learn the martial arts, and especially to learn to ride in the beautiful style for which Pignatelli and others were famed. But there were dangers as well. François de la Noue, the illustrious Protestant general, warned parents to wait until their sons had achieved some fundament of piety and love of honesty before sending them to Italy, where the lures of a thousand voluptuous pleasures awaited them.[2] In 1587 he called for academies in all the French provincial capitals, beginning with Paris, Lyon, Bordeaux, and Angers, as well as in four royal châteaux (Fontainebleau, Moulins, Plessis de Tours, and Cognac), institutions that would standardize this form of higher education according to French needs.[3] The intention was to provide a comprehensive training program for aristocrats that, while it still concentrated on riding, included other subjects as well.

We do not have detailed information about the daily routines at Pluvinel's academy when it opened, but if the schedule of classes outlined in his posthumously published *L'Instruction du roy en l'exercice de monter à cheval* (1625) is any indication, students studied riding and running at the ring each morning and fencing, dancing, gymnastics, and mathematics on Monday, Wednesday, Friday, and Saturday afternoons, a time at which they likely received their instruction in drawing and music as well. On Tuesdays and Thursdays, a "man of letters" addressed the assembled students on moral virtue (with examples drawn from ancient and modern history), politics, and command.[4] Alexandre de Pontaymery declared the academy a "Parnassus to the Muses," explaining that Pluvinel

> not only instruct[s] the Gentleman in the profession of riding, but in the practice of good morals—without which all sciences are only vanity. Also, he who sees the students sees the deportment of Angels and the living images of celestial perfection. Oh happy Nobility! for whom the heavens have caused such an able governor to be born: If one has exerted himself at riding you have gymnastics, fencing, and dance, all under people who the aforesaid Monsieur happily knew to choose, and who are without argument the foremost in their art. You also have Mathematics, painting, and the lute under the most excellent masters one could desire.[5]

Riding was clearly the main preoccupation of the academy, but to it were joined ancillary subjects with more or less relevance to the military profession. Gymnastics, fencing, and dance developed strength and poise, while mathematics and the understanding of perspective and geometry gained through painting were directly relevant to ballistics and fortification. But it is harder to make sense of the role of music in the academy. How did the lute fit into a program founded upon riding? The pairing seems to generate only striking oppositions—war (equitation) versus peace (lute), action versus relaxation, summer military campaigns versus carnival-time divertissements, and even courage versus fear, at least for those who agreed with Castiglione's Signor Gaspare Pallavicino, who claimed that music made men soft, fearful, and unfit for battle.[6] To overcome these binary commonplaces and understand how music supported equitation at the academy is to strike to the heart of what made dressage *à la Pluvinel* far more than training in a martial art. Like music, it was also a moral practice and a political practice. Briefly, through a "harmonic" interpretation of Pluvinel's style of dressage—one that recovers its ideals of physical harmony and social concord—we can discover what sustained riding as a fundament of noble education during a period in which nobles began to relinquish violent behavior in favor of gentler manners.

Later in this chapter, I discuss the musical philosophies to which horsemanship appealed, as well as the spectacular combination of music and equitation in the 1612 *ballet à cheval* choreographed by Pluvinel. Here, suffice it to say that, as an educational paradigm, the pairing of music with physical exercises can be found in Plato and enjoyed significant currency in the sixteenth century. In both the *Laws*, II, and the *Republic*, III, Plato treated gymnastics and music together, maintaining that the best training in gymnastics would resemble training in music.[7] And sixteenth-century noblemen agreed. François de la Noue, in addition to a rigorous program of physical exercises, recommended music as part of a noble education, citing its ability to relax and satisfy the spirit. Michel de Montaigne included music along with running, wrestling, hunting, dance, riding, and the handling of arms in his essay "De l'institution des enfans." The objective of a complete education was to train both the body and the mind.[8] Pontus de Tyard put it well in his music treatise, *Solitaire second*, when he said that, just as wrestling, running, jumping, and fencing were essential for physical well-being, music exercised the soul.[9] In sum, the program at Pluvinel's academy suggests it was a sort of classical *gymnasium*, with—as we shall see—a political agenda advanced through neo-Platonic ideals of moral harmony. Other masters might be able to train the horse, but only Pluvinel, it was claimed, could train the man.[10]

The academy's policy of accepting only nobles, its ambitious educational program and royal support, and Pluvinel's favored position at court make it an apt case for a study of equitation and power in early modern Europe. That it opened during the civil wars and only months after Henry IV retook the capital is no coincidence, for by overseeing the education of the nobility more directly, the academy promised to foster cooperation from a class whose traditions promoted political independence, private violence (exercised through dueling and private armies), and aristocratic rebellion. If anything, the religious wars exacerbated these tendencies among an already unruly nobility. More than a riding school, we should see Pluvinel's academy as the flagship of a whole series of educational initiatives begun by

Henry, which subsequently included the restructuring of the University of Paris, the establishment of the College of Nobles at La Flèche, and the opening of provincial colleges overseen by the Jesuits, who answered directly to the king. Indeed, the conditions that precipitated the establishment of the academy and shaped its program bring into focus the political relevance of the educational enterprise more generally. Dressage, after all, explicitly targeted the nobility, for whom horsemanship was virtually synonymous with the military calling (*cheval*, *chevalier*). But dressage, in the sense in which I will use it, applied doubly to the training of the horse and its rider. Pluvinel taught the sons of a small number of tremendously powerful French aristocratic families. To the academy came precisely the young nobles who might pose the greatest threat to the monarchy in the future; there they received an education that not only furthered their own aims, but helped align their behavior with that favored at court.

Pluvinel's academy was "royal" in further ways. Louis XIII's lessons with the great master ostensibly provided the dialogue format of Pluvinel's two treatises, whose exquisite folio engravings by the drawing master at the academy showed the young king learning dressage in its palatial environs. The students there included numerous *grands* in the circle of the king, among them Richelieu and the Duke de Vendôme. Not unlike the *enfants d'honneur*, whose parents expended untold sums to have them raised with the dauphin, the academy was an institution that enabled the sons of great families to establish a future at court. The academy was *not* royal in the sense that its students would necessarily command in the royal army, for many of these same *grands* had private armies of their own. Indeed, in 1617 Louis worried that the forces mustered by the dukes of Vendôme and Mayenne gave them more direct control over the towns and forts they garrisoned than he had.[11] Military tactics learned at the academy might be turned against the king. But the academy *was* royal in that the social strategies with which it acquainted students benefited the monarchy. Like the networks of pages, *enfants d'honneur*, and ladies-in-waiting who developed personal fidelities at court from a young age, the academy nurtured political ties, familiarized students with their place in high society, and made them spectators of the social revolutions of *le monde*. As Orest Ranum has shown, the effectiveness of Richelieu's ministry rested not on institutional reform, but on the elaboration of favors, deference and preference, hierarchy, and the elevation of "creatures" to key positions.[12] Loyalty intertwined with authority in clientage systems that many young nobles first entered when they came to Paris to learn to ride.

Warhorses versus Horses for Dancing

I begin this chapter with an examination of the style of riding taught at the academy and its applicability to warfare, for surely equitation furthered the pursuit of power most directly on the field of battle. But my analysis quickly opens up to a more general consideration of riding as a cultural practice that—like dance, the lute, and painting— prepared young noblemen for other aspects of their careers. Kings, *grands*, and aristocrats continued their power struggles off the field of battle, in winter quarters and during times of peace. Sports such as jousting and Carnival tourneys and spectacles such as entries, carrousels, and equestrian ballets established social hierarchies, modeled political relationships, and, most importantly, presented opportunities for political gains that were often more permanent than those won through the fleeting and rarely consolidated victories of early modern sieges and battles. The *ballet à cheval* will provide our case in point. In it, riding claimed its power not just through its similitude to the actual practices of battle, but by rehearsing consonant relationships among nobles and between them and their king.

Unsurprisingly given its royal subventions, Pluvinel's school stood in the shadow of the Louvre, with its main building in the rue Saint-Honoré and its dressage court extending all the way to the château des Tuileries. A second academy, that of Benjamin, was opened in the rue des Bons-Enfants near the site of the Palais Royal, and by the end of the reign of Louis XIII, Paris boasted five further military academies.[13] With peace and the new academies, Frenchmen no longer had to travel to Italy, and the French academies even began to attract foreigners to Paris.[14] The establishment of Pluvinel's academy and those in its orbit formed what we can now properly call a French school of dressage, and its methods were conveyed in the treatises of Salomon de la Broue (*Le Cavalerice françois*, 1602) and René de Menou (*La Pratique du cavalier*, 1612), Pluvinel's posthumously published treatises (*Le Maneige royal*, 1623 and *L'Instruction du roy*, 1625), and the treatise of Pierre de la Noue (*La Cavalerie françoise et italienne*, 1620).

Riding lessons at the academy went well beyond the practical requirements of warfare. In fact, mounted military training was not the raison d'être of the academy.[15] Lessons included some jousting and running at the quintain, but the blunt utility of these medieval sports played a small part in a program that aimed for a more delicate symbiosis of horse and rider. Artifice triumphed over nature as comportment, equilibrium, and artistry came together in a style of dressage based on Italian techniques first developed by Pignatelli,

Fiaschi, and Grisone. This "high school" culminated in intricate footwork and leaps of a sort that epitomized stylishness but fared poorly in battle. Many of the elevated postures that were the basis for the *airs relevés* derived from natural movements such as rearing, kicking, and pivoting on the haunches, any of which could be useful in battle, but dressage transformed these useful and largely natural moves into a vocabulary that was, if not wholly extraneous to the needs of an armored knight, at least far less applicable, especially given the massive weight of armor at the turn of the seventeenth century.

Critics of the *haute école* such as Thomas Bedingfield, the English translator of a riding treatise by Claudio Corte, complained that "now adaies nothing is almost used [in the schools] but sundrie sorts of superfluous dansing and pransing, which M. Claudio calleth *corvette* & *pesatevaue* [*courbettes* and *pesades*]."[16] Nothing but a sort of dancing, *courbettes* struck him as a frivolity consistent with balls, ballets, and other decadences staged for the divertissement of elites. Whereas riding schools should be teaching the fundaments of handling the lance and sword on horseback and riders should be practicing *passades à la soldate*, instead, Bedingfield implied, schools promoted a style of equitation with little relevance to the military profession.

Bedingfield had a point. In the first place, the "prancy" horses favored by the *haute école* were unsuited for combat. As Salomon de la Broue observed, "it is a large displeasure for a knight armed to the hilt to be on a nervous horse naturally inclined to jumping . . . for a number of jumps . . . will sometimes be sufficient to put the horse out of breath and [out of] combat."[17] Warhorses were meant to stay on the ground and learn the movements of the *manège bas* or the low school. There the principal exercise was the *passade*, in which the horse passed quickly and repeatedly over a straight track, making a half-turn and switching hands at each end.[18] Since horses tend to be right or left "handed," this exercise produced greater ambidexterity.[19] The turns themselves required the horse to keep the hind legs fairly much in place, shifting its weight back, supporting it on the hind legs, and turning on a small circle. In this way, the *passade* developed strength as well as suppleness. Horses destined for the *haute école* perfected the *passade* in a succession of low leaps called the *passade terre à terre* before progressing to the *airs relevés*. Antoine de Pluvinel called the *passade* "the true proof of the horse's goodness, because in beginning one learns his speed, in stopping his good or bad mouth, in turning his skill and grace, and in beginning again several times, his force, vigor, and his loyalty."[20] But for dressage horses, no more than five turns would be attempted at a time, lest the horse tire and lose its good posture, whereas more were needed to develop the wind of warhorses, so that they would not come up short in battle.[21] Innumerable *passades* required aggressive interventions that were rarely used in the *haute école* (crop, heavy hand, or spurs) and tested the strength and good nature of the horses that would go into battle, even if the fineness of their gait and turns deteriorated toward the end of the exercise. Thus for warhorses, strength and stamina superseded precision.

Second, the *airs relevés* did indeed aim for a form of mounted dance that exuded the grace of peaceable surroundings. The *pesade* of which Bedingfield complains introduced a steed to the high airs by having him lift his forelegs off the ground while lowering his hocks, turning a rear into a more sustainable move. From the *pesade*, performed in place, students advanced to the *courbette*, a movement in which the horse alternated raising its forehand and making low, hopping strides with its hind legs. Bedingfield's association of the *courbette* with dancing is entirely appropriate, as *courbettes* emphasized evenness of cadence and tempo. According to Pierre de la Noue's *La Cavalerie française*, *courbettes* must be "diligently beaten," with "the hind legs lifting equally to the sound and the true measure of them [the *courbettes*], without having one leg or the other slow or rush by some unequal movement compared with the just cadence of the forelegs."[22] Measured in this way to a regular beat, *courbettes* were one of the most overtly musical of all the *airs relevés*, and given that they could be repeated in succession, they did indeed constitute not just prancing, but dancing, with all of its musical order. Small wonder that they were a staple of the *ballet à cheval*. This was truly a style of riding designed for princely spectacle sooner than combat.

The limited practicality of the riding taught at the academy prompts reconsideration of the *haute école* and why it became a fundament of upper-class education in the early seventeenth century. Here we should recall that Pluvinel's academy swiftly became the model for others in the provinces, all of which eventually came to be governed by the king's Grand Escuyer. This administrative arrangement shows how noble education continued to be defined by riding, even though the style of dressage taught in the academies complicates our understanding of the noble profession. Certainly the institution of the state-commission army and its tremendous expansion during the seventeenth century offered burgeoning possibilities for military careers through which nobles fulfilled the traditional calling of their estate, and, as we know, students did begin riding lessons with the *passade à la soldate*, but the tireless dedication to training in the *haute*

école indicates that the preceptors at the academy took the finishing of
a future officer or courtier to go well beyond merely attaining a firm
seat in the saddle when running at the ring.[23]

TRAINING THE MAN

Pluvinel's academy alleviated one of the great concerns of those who
argued against the tradition of sending young men abroad to school:
style. "For civility and manners, foreign schools are not appropriate
for the French,"[24] Pluvinel declared, echoing the remarks Thomas
Pelletier had made in *La Nourriture de la noblesse* (1604) when
describing the academy:

> It is therefore not an Italian that one has for instruction. It is a French
> Gentleman that one wishes, the mores, the manner, the grace truly
> French and not foreign. It is therefore only in France that [the student]
> will learn to ride, to joust for rings, to dance, to dress according to our
> style without being judged upon his return more Italian than French,
> losing in this the time and money that one should spend to erase the
> tablet and render it with a French air.[25]

Already in 1604, one senses the turn toward style for its own sake
that, by the late seventeenth century, gave rise to a culture in which
style became the essence of the nobleman—"le style c'est l'homme"
(the style is the man) was not far off. In this regard, it is worth noting that the Parisian riding academies grew upon the same social and
physical terrain as the other institutions of civility surrounding the
court: for example, Catherine de Vivonne held her salon in the Hôtel
de Rambouillet, just a stone's throw from Pluvinel's academy. Standing
cheek by jowl, military academies and the "schools" of politeness and
belles-lettres conducted in the salons shared the constituency orbiting
the court.

Indeed, the fine points of riding and a beautiful *courbette* were
themselves manners like the *révérences* and *courantes* by which nobles
presented themselves at balls, and a cavalier's grace in the saddle and
on foot were often mentioned in the same breath. "He is brave, rich,
gallant, liberal, dances well, rides well, and always has men of wit in
his employ" Gédéon Tallemant des Réaux remarked of Henry de
Montmorency, and of the Count de Cramail he said "he was always
gallant: he was decent, danced well, and rode well." Synonymy
between character and physical grace was the norm, which allowed
Tallemant to criticize François de Bassompierre for a gracelessness

that implied defects that ran more than skin deep: "he never danced well and was not a very good rider, either. He had something coarse about him, and he was not very supple."[26] External coordination was the sign of a well-balanced inner soul and the emotional restraint that defined a true nobility of spirit.

Such attention to behavior marks what Norbert Elias termed "the civilizing process."[27] What began to a large extent with Erasmus's slight manual on manners for children, *De civilitate morum puerilium libellus* (1530), and Castiglione's *Il cortegiano* (1528) had, by the early seventeenth century, grown into a vast discourse vesting gesture, bearing, and physical habit with social import.[28] In the salons and at court, the expansion of etiquette created a rhetoric of action that rejected the brutish behavior of the war years, and it is in this "polite society" that we find a connection between the explicit goal of the monarchy to monopolize the control of armed aggression and the cultural practices that contributed to it.[29] Promotion of manners and mannered behavior, Elias argued, helped to limit violence, encouraging the development of a kind of self-censorship that checked aggression before it erupted and establishing pacified social centers defined by gentle behavior.

Military academies played an important role in the civilizing process, for *haute école* dressage taught gentle lessons such as attention to detail and self-restraint. This style of riding developed character traits that were fundamental to social modes of negotiation, for the patience and aptitude for precision acquired during the long hours in the dressage court expanded the expressive range of a young nobleman's ambitions from the brutality of armed aggression to methods that required a softer touch, such as clientage, politics, and courtiership.

The emphasis on physical and emotional restraint that characterized civility shows up plainly in French equitation, where beautiful riding was equated with virtuous behavior. "It is certain that only the most beautiful minds are meant for the most beautiful exercises," remarked La Broue, adding that "the perfection of such knowledge can never be communicated to . . . weak and crude minds."[30] Here we find precisely the reflexive relationship between body and soul that made good manners so compelling. Etiquette located virtue in "just stature" and graceful movement, as La Broue termed it. Indeed, upright posture defined moral rectitude to such an extent that physical training aimed to produce spiritual benefits, and none greater than the still and balanced soul required for artful dressage. For this reason, Pontaymery could rightly claim that Pluvinel's academy was a "temple to virtue" in which gentlemen were instructed in "the practice of good morals."

HARMONIC BEHAVIOR: THE *BALLET À CHEVAL*

The moral dimension claimed for education at Pluvinel's academy suggests that it perpetuated the initiatives of an unlikely predecessor: the Academy of Poetry and Music established by Jean-Antoine de Baïf and Joachim Thibault de Courville in 1570. One need only consider the other subjects taught at the academy to see that, far more than a riding school, it was the direct descendent of the neo-Platonic academies active two decades earlier. Music is key to the connection.

The treatment of music in Plato's *Republic* placed it at the center of projects to create moral uplift in France at the time of the civil wars. Just two years before the Saint Bartholomew's Day Massacres, Baïf's academy set out to rectify the social ills of the country with a form of "measured music in the ancient style" that would produce moral order. According to the Letters Patent, the academicians believed that

> it is of great importance for the morals of the citizens of a town that the music current and used in the country should be retained under certain laws, for the minds of most men are formed and their behavior influenced by its character, so that where music is disordered, there morals are also depraved, and where it is well ordered, there men are well disciplined morally.[31]

The academy was not just "musical" in a limited sense. Masters of classical language, music, and poetry were joined by others specializing in geography, mathematics, painting, and "military prefects who taught all those things which are useful for military discipline and for the good of the body."[32] The complex of subjects, the equal attention to body and spirit, and the emphasis on military discipline reveal Baïf's academy as a possible model for Pluvinel, who served as *premier escuyer* to the Duke d'Anjou at the time of its inception and likely knew of its activities. The musical edification attempted by Baïf and Courville helps explain why Pluvinel's students received musical training and, likewise, why his academy appeared to be a "Parnassus to the Muses."

Musical affinities were the touchstone of a healthy soul, a sort of all-embracing science of proportion and measure that provided a philosophical foundation for the correspondences civility forged between the body and the soul along a continuum from good manners, physical grace, proportionality, and musicality to spiritual well-being. If man yearned to regain a lost "harmonie universelle," as Pierre de Ronsard described it, then aligning the body with the perfect pro- portions of geometrical figures brought man closer to the musical proportions from which the body's structures were formed and upon which the cosmos turned.[33]

As an art perfected through careful attention to balance, number, and measure, riding was itself harmonic or musical. For La Broue, the rider must therefore "have a lot of natural judgment, even of propor- tions: because all the airs and most beautiful exercises are composed of numbers and measures, and of many equalities that must be care- fully observed."[34] He must also know music:

> It is quite unlikely that he who cannot taste or comprehend the harmony, air, and measure of music, and consequently of instruments and of dance, could ever understand the airs and proportions of our schools well.[35]

Little separated the physical geometry of the airs from the sounding proportions of music. This, of course, had an eminently practical ori- gin, for on the one hand, La Broue is simply saying that sensitivity to beat and tempo in a horse's gait will make it easier to learn to ride well. Music is the key to coordination, a point stressed from the out- set by Fiaschi and Grisone. But there is more to it than this, for La Broue insists upon a moralized aesthetic that freighted music with the ability to bring about personal enlightenment and social harmony. Measured or "musical" behavior showed a man's sovereignty over his own, well-ordered inner life and his suitability to govern those below him, beginning with his mount.

The cooperative relationship between horse and rider demonstrated the benefits of discipline, making dressage a prime example of the proper relationship between subject and sovereign, and nowhere more pointedly than in equestrian ballets. This spectacular art form, which arose in the late sixteenth century, brought together a group of horsemen who performed synchronized dressage to music. By har- monizing the actions of a number of horsemen, the *ballet à cheval* not only showed off the disciplined footwork taught at the academy, it trained riders to work together in a genre of spectacle that exempli- fied social order. Ronsard said as much at the end of a cartel he wrote for an equestrian ballet of 1581: "these armed Centaurs are come at the renown of this high Prince of France, to instruct his people and to render them as easy as their horses are docile under the bit . . . to the end that all will learn to serve him."[36] In the *chevalier*–centaurs of the ballet, half-man, half-horse, we find the triumph of civility over nature, of obedience over willfulness, of restraint over chaos, and of the king over his subjects. The ballet promises a political grace resulting from discipline.

This propagandistic feature of ballet, whether *à pied* or *à cheval*, was part and parcel of ballet from the very beginning, and it continued to play a vital role in the organization of seventeenth-century ballets, directing choices such as the timing, themes, and participants of productions. So it was that a highly political event inspired Pluvinel to choreograph one of the most famous horse ballets of the century, a work that epitomizes the public face and political utility of the new style of "dressage" in both senses of the term.

With the assassination of Henry IV in 1610, Marie de' Medici was forced into a shaky regency that would never have survived a war with Spain, a long-time enemy of France and a significant player in the Wars of Religion. As peace was Marie's next best option, she proceeded to negotiate the double marriage of her son, Louis XIII, to the Spanish Princess Anne of Austria and of Louis' younger sister to Prince Philip of Spain. Louis was but ten and his sister younger still. The prospect of an alliance with the arch-Catholic rulers of Spain threw French Protestants into a panic—Henry IV had sympathized with the Protestants, but it looked as though Marie would be less mindful of their needs. And so she came into conflict with many nobles. With infallible political intuition, she and her advisors decided to present the marriages as a fait accompli by mounting a huge public celebration of the engagement. Thus, although the marriages would not take place for another three years, she staged a symbolic marriage of the two realms.

The celebration took the form of a carrousel combining an elaborate parade with jousting. It is of great significance indeed that its designers sought popular approval for the alliance, for unlike the private fêtes held at court, this festivity hoped to awe the whole of Paris—if not of France. One source reports that 200,000 crowded into the Place Royale (now the Place des Vosges) to witness the event.[37] The theme turned around a large "Palace of Felicity" erected in the square, which symbolized the marital happiness of the royal couples. Five Knights of Glory defended the Palace against a series of assailants: the Knights of the Sun, the Knights of the Lily, the Knights of Fidelity, the Knights of the Universe, and the Roman Conquerors. The knights made their entries in a massive pageant pitched at the taste of a broad public with triumphal carts, knights on horseback, thousands of foot-men and musicians, mythological characters, and fantastic floats. A flaming mount Etna spouted lava, "giants" processed on stilts, and lions pulled carts to the utter delight of the crowds, yet despite the car-nival atmosphere, the chivalric narrative underscored princely virtue with the parade of *chevaliers* from France's most prominent families. The carrousel came right out of Arthurian legend, with a hefty dose of classicism to include the glory days of the Roman Empire.

By this account it would seem that not much had changed since the reign of Philip the Good, when the Knights of the Golden Fleece met in Burgundy for banquets, tourneys, and vows to crusade to the Holy Lands, and to some extent this would be true, for the knights had come to face off against one another at the jousting barrier. But the procession was so elaborate that the jousting barely began before nightfall, and not only was the tourney itself overshadowed by the entries of all the knights, but the Knights of the Lily stole the show by stopping to perform a brief equestrian ballet before the royal pavilion (see figure 7.1). The printed accounts of the carrousel all lavish special

Figure 7.1.   Horse ballet, from Antoine de Pluvinel, *Le Maneige royal* (1623). With permission of the Houghton Library, Harvard University.

attention on the ballet, describing it figure by figure and even including engravings of its geometrical choreography.[38] The spectators packed into the Place Royale seem to have found it a stunningly new and wonderful thing to behold, and the queen herself requested a repeat performance in the courtyard of the Louvre three days later.[39]

Pluvinel choreographed the ballet and rode in it along with Vendôme, La Valette, the son of the Duke d'Epernon, the Baron de Pontchasteau, Benjamin, and Jean Zamet, a captain in the king's guard and son of the ultra-rich Italian financier and friend of Henry IV Sébastien Zamet. The Knights were accompanied by six squires carrying shields emblazoned with their devices, some real, some fictitious, which reinforced their social rank with emblems of military valor.[40] They wore helmets covered with plumes and feathers, jeweled belts, ruffs, silver cloaks, and white boots embroidered with silver to match the *fleurs de lys* on their skirted doublets. Their Spanish mounts were caparisoned with long saddle cloths to match, and they sported white plumes and feathers on their heads and at their tails. This synopsis, by the way, reduces page after page of description in sources that hoped to capture the magnificence of the event with detailed attention to the velvets and silks used, the braid, embroidery, and jewels encrusting the costumes, and the egret feathers, ostrich plumes, silvering, and other finery.

For all this material splendor, however, it was the musical equitation that set this entry apart from the others, giving it a sumptuousness and register of meaning surpassing other elements in the carrousel. One might even say that while the rest of the carrousel took its cues from traditional tourneys, the entry of the Knights of the Lily attempted to negotiate the terrain between the highly mythologized spectacles held at court and the more commonplace parades, floats, and processions of civic ceremonies. Like a royal entry, with its elaborate succession of triumphal arches, open-air theaters, and carts that served as ephemeral stages for lyric poetry and song, the entry of the Knights of the Lily brought an extremely humanistic commodity— *ballet de cour*—out of the court.

Here it is important to understand the theatrical function of the grand ballets that Pluvinel took as his model. They finished off court ballets, resolving the narrative strife of the first part of the ballet with a physical enactment of social harmony. In this *lieto fine*, dancers moved through geometric patterns so complex it seemed impossible that they had been memorized, and as these bodies formed one figure after another with perfect precision, spectators marveled at choreographies they often interpreted as cosmological. The *ballet à cheval*, by taking its musical and choreographic cues from court ballet, brought its enactment of social order to a far vaster stage. As we shall see, it played out the grand ballets' themes of divine harmony with dancers whose physical presence was far more imposing (horses and riders) and with a discipline that was even more remarkable than that governing ballet on foot.

When the knights arrived before the royal pavilion, a Trojan Venus sang three songs written in so-called ancient meters, the first "anapestic," the second "paeonic," and the third "choriambic."[41] Their unremarkable texts express the knights' hunger for battle and laud the queen, who shines like a sun over the French empire; they were penned by Guillaume de Baïf, son of Jean-Antoine de Baïf.[42] Yet no matter how outwardly ordinary, the classical meters cited in Honoré Laugier de Porchères' description refer unmistakably to the work of Baïf and Courville's academy, their search for "Platonic" music in the style of the Greeks, and the *musique mesurée* they produced. The antiquity claimed for the songs implied that their measured quality produced moral discipline in hearers. The music to which the horses danced was also described as *mesurée à l'antique*: Laugier de Porchères says that after the songs, the horses formed a triangle facing the king and queen and began to dance "to the cadence . . . of metric airs composed according to ancient numbers or measures."[43] This remark, too, identifies the ballet as a classical art recovered, one built upon the persuasive forms of classical metrics.

Viewers probably did not liken the simple rhythms of the dance music to those of classical poetry, but we do know that they were impressed by the synchronicity between the choreography and the music, and among the riders. Pluvinel used two basic steps for the ballet: *courbettes* for the knights and *terre à terres* for the squires. The *courbettes* emphasized evenness of cadence and tempo, and François de Rosset wondered at how "the Knights advanced in the same figure, making their horses go half-way into the air with such equilibrium and proportion that all rose up and came down at the same time."[44] He noted how the horses maintained their placement in a triangle even while moving forward, how they all rose up to the same height, and how they rose and fell together in time to the music. Music provided a ruler by which the proportion and equilibrium of the steps could be measured, regulating the chaos of movement, reining it in, disciplining it according to a felicitous set of numbers discovered by ancient musicians.

Rosset tells us that at the end of some figures, the riders all "stopped like statues" when the final cadence of the music sounded, reminding us of the magic significance of immobility, of the sorcerers and enchantresses (Circe, Armide, Ismen, and Caelide) who stopped the action of court ballets with waves of their wands. In the *ballet à cheval*, the music mobilizing the spectacle ends, freezing the horses and in this way drawing attention to its charm. Moreover, this simultaneous halt showed the command that the riders (and the music) exerted over the horses, who had little patience for standing still. In this light it is all the more telling that the engraving of the event captures the horses in a *courbette*, their haunches down and their front legs daintily drawn in as they held themselves aloft. They balance in eternal equilibrium.

The cues the horses received from their riders also suggested a certain magic. For the *haute école* employed oral forms of instruction that persuaded in the much the same way that music was believed to. Singing, tongue clicks, soothing tones, and encouraging cries were the primary tools of contact between horse and rider, and from Grisone to Pluvinel, proponents of the new style of dressage relied on the voice to instruct and command. Grisone lists the voice first in a succession of disciplinary methods, followed by those of increasing invasiveness: the voice, the crop, the bridle, the thighs, stirrups, spurs, and pulling the horse up short (the bit). Likewise, he names the voice as the best encouragement for a horse and, when adopting pleasing and low tones, the best reward.[45] Pluvinel recommends that the voice be used to encourage the horse, or for discipline when the heels, the whip, or the spurs are not enough.[46] And Cesare Fiaschi included in his treatise a series of short tunes corresponding to each of several different steps.[47] In Fiaschi's airs, pitch, rhythm, and vowel sounds interlocked in musical commands keyed to the pace and exertion of the horse's movements. Vocal cues heightened the magic of a beautifully managed horse, for they allowed the rider to avoid extrovert gestures. The same corporeal restraint encouraged in social settings *à pied* could thus be maintained *à cheval*, where it seemed, moreover, to prove the universal value of good grace by smoothing communication between chevalier and his steed. If civility attempted to dictate a code of behavior facilitating social commerce, then good horsemanship trumped even etiquette with its invisible and meta-linguistic discourse based on musical sounds.

Music had the very significant effect of extending these invisible chains of command into a system regulating the actions of all of the dancers. Moreover, this external source of order seemed to emanate from the king and queen, on whose persons the geometry of the ballet was centered. For Pluvinel's figures were geometric, beginning with a triangle for a march, then regrouping into a set of two nested circles for most of the ballet with the knights on the inside and the squires on the outside. The circles broke apart and reformed as the horsemen drew close to one another and made *voltes* (tight circles) before returning to their places; they also exchanged places, turned in place, and made *courbettes* in place. At end of the ballet, the knights formed two lines facing one another, rode through each others' lines, turned, and returned to the center, taking one another's hands and turning, after which the squires formed a chain and passed around one another in succession. These mutable geometric figures— triangles, circles, chains—were borrowed from the choreography of *ballet de cour*, in this way alluding unmistakably to the cosmology of court ballet with its inner and outer orbits of knights and squires and their many *voltes* and pirouettes.

The innumerable turns to right and left showed off the even handling of the horses, while their crossed paths, the way they turned together while the knights held hands, and their weaving between one another showed the horses' willingness to work hard in close proximity to one another. Finally, the relentless *courbettes* and *terre à terres* showed the horses' strength as they arched their necks, tipping their heads down and foaming at the mouth with deep breaths. For while the riders maintained a quiet poise, the horses exerted themselves tremendously during the ten-minute ballet in a denial of the effortlessness projected by court dance, suggesting, instead, the tirelessness of military might. The long skirts of their costumes hid the sheen of sweat on the horses' coats and drew attention downward to what was visible of their legs, but there is no question that their forcefulness must have projected, even if only through the heavy thud of hoofs in time to the music.

Spectators with an eye for military horsemanship would have recognized in the ballet figures based on the *passade à la soldate* and a cavalry maneuver called the caracole, a rotational scheme in which squadrons of pistoleers fired by rank and then rode to the back of the formation to reload. And here we see how the ballet rehearsed a practice with true relevance to battle. Although it often fell apart in the fray of combat, the caracole was the first identifiable drill for large numbers of horsemen, and as such it promoted discipline within the newly emerging cavalry companies that would ultimately replace the lance-bearing heavy horsemen in battle. Practicing the caracole taught riders to find and keep their places in a squadron and not to scatter helter-skelter in retreat, and it habituated their horses to taking directions in the midst of gunfire. After all, many military

horses and riders lacked schooling. When one considers that riding
treatises regularly spent page after page telling how to accustom the
horse to flapping standards, noisy trumpets, flailing drumsticks, the
smell of gunpowder, the sight of fire, scurrying infantry, flashing armor,
wooden bridges, and, of course, the terrors of cannon, musket,
harquebus, pistol, lance, halberd, and pike, it becomes clear that just
getting onto the field and lining up in any sort of formation would
have been, for many horses, quite an accomplishment.[48] The most
rudimentary training for a warhorse required at least a year of concentrated effort, and even then one could not expect to maneuver
much or jump hedges and the like.[49]

As for the riders, Pierre de la Noue observed that as soon as the
lowest page felt his tail in the saddle, he set off in "confusions, turns,
and curves to the right and the left" in an attempt to make *passades à
la soldate* and show off his valiance. Such stunts were "contrary to the
military art, which does everything with beautiful order and good
measure."[50] The caracole proved a wonderful cure-all: as a daily cal-
isthenics, it exercised military horses for concentration, strength, and
precision; it brought greener horses up to snuff by working them
alongside seasoned mounts; it internalized regular formations; and it
challenged the horsemen to adopt the focused mindset required by
the new dressage. Discipline—and this is the importance of both the
caracole and the ballet as well as of dressage more generally—began
with a new mentality for horse and rider.[51] In the words of René de
Menou, "the principal point of our science consists of judgment, to
'make war in the eye' [that is, to note carefully what is happening so
as to profit from the moment], to change an action from moment to
moment as needed, and to work the minds of our horses sooner than
their legs."[52]

Thus the *ballet à cheval* showed off a synchronization associated
both with the spectacles of the court and with the latest techniques of
military discipline. It was at once courtly and military, graceful and
powerful, musical and bellicose, just like the courtiers themselves. At
the end of the ballet, the knights formed up in two lines that
"charged" though one another, an "assault" resolved as the riders
returned to the center, joined hands, turned, and then restored their
perfect circle. In this way, to quote Ronsard's poem about the *ballet
à cheval* from 1581, the riders "imitat[ed] war in the semblance of
peace" (l. 19, "contrefaisant la guerre au semblant d'une paix"); they
established a peace secured with the force of arms.

The chivalric narrative of the carrousel and its jousts told the story
of military virtue in a traditional way associated with the heavy arms

of lance-bearing knights, yet within it, the disciplined ensemble riding of the ballet retold that story in a new way. For a time, the ballet obliged the knights to set aside the lances of the *gendarmerie* and gave them a new vocabulary for heroic acts, one that channeled individual bravura toward a collective effort more typical of cavalry squadrons.[53] The military significance of the fleet squadrons had already been realized, but the social hierarchy that set heavily armored knights above their more lightly armed entourages obstructed acceptance of the cavalry's balletic practices among elites. The exchange of the lance for the pistol implied a relinquishment of individual bravura for more collective strategies that required a new order among *gens d'armes* accustomed to acting on their own. Thus the horse ballet of 1612 rehearsed not only the coordination of cavalry squadrons, but the cooperative mentality it presupposed. The juxtaposition of jousting and equestrian ballet in the carrousel suggests a point of transition from a noble ideal vested in individual action to a more "harmonic" ideal of behavior consonant with civility at court and a new social order in the military.

The *haute école* produced facile horses, it is true, but dressage had a political outcome that went beyond its potential usefulness to battle, for it emphasized the king as the coordinating power of the aristocracy. The age of dueling, private armies, jousting, and individual contest would come to an end, superseded by the external coordination of the nobility. Nobles redefined their culture during this transition to civility through the stylization of equitation, yet this practice bore the imprint of royal supremacy and a loss of autonomy. Just as Pluvinel's academy readied nobles to participate in a monarchy that would become more absolute as the century progressed, the music in Pluvinel's ballet hinted at its value as an instrument of the state.[54] Music regulated a performance of proportion, coordination, and harmony, and as subjects of collective behavior—at least fleetingly—the Knights of the Lily suppressed individual action in favor of stylized and uniform motion. Before they faced off one-on-one in the tourney, the dancers faced the king like a cavalry squadron ready to serve his majesty. Although France would soon enough be plunged back into civil war and Louis would shortly be plagued with worries about the strength of Vendôme's army, the knights' ritual defense of the court was carried out within a musical order that was analogous to the coordinating power of the king.

Politically, carrousels greatly advanced the needs of nobles, lords, and kings to reinforce the visibility of the armed force at their disposal. Throughout the seventeenth century, academies often staged carrousels, and some educators even insisted that nobles learn to perform *ballets à cheval* as a regular part of their schooling.[55] Pierre de la Noue devoted a chapter of *La Cavalerie françoise* to "How to teach horses to dance in order to use them in carrousels," and Claude-François Menestrier presented equestrian ballet as a standard genre of divertissement in his *Traité des tournois, joustes, carrousels et autres spectacles publics* of 1669.[56]

But such art forms were not to remain useful forever. The growing separation between the military career and the noble "profession" meant that while the martial arts continued to register nobility of character, increasingly it was the form of noble display and not the content itself that came to be so important. While even professional courtiers such as Nicolas Faret maintained that "there is no profession more honest, nor more essential to a Gentleman than that of arms," more and more nobles chose careers in jurisprudence and administration with impunity.[57] The Knights of the Lily rode the cusp of an age in which style itself would define the nobleman. Stylized training to warfare became training to stylization, enough to turn the equestrian ballet into a practice for being a gentleman at large, even when one was not engaged in a military career. So while riding continued to be a cultural denominator for aristocrats, ultimately it would be the stylishness of dressage *à la Pluvinel* that expressed nobility, a nobility once vested in the clash of lances in battle and the politically unsustainable chivalry of a warring kingdom.

NOTES

An invaluable component of my research was the opportunity to reconstruct and direct performances of Pluvinel's ballet of 1612 at the Berkeley Festival of Early Music and Exhibition in 2000 and 2002. Thanks truly beyond words goes to CalPerformances and its director Robert Cole, who produced "Le Carrousel du Roi" in collaboration with the Brussels 2000 Festival and the Baroque Spring of Sablon, and our choreographer, Creeky Routson, her assistant, Teresa Trull, our music director, Richard Cheetham, and the costume designers, Thierry Bosquet and Cass Carpenter, all of whom made invaluable contributions not just to the production, but to the process of historical reconstruction. My research in libraries and archives was part of a large project supported by the American Association of University Women, a President's Fellowship from the University of California, the Hellmann Faculty Fund, and the Warburg Institute. It will be published in Kate van Orden, *Music, Discipline, and Arms in Early Modern France* (Chicago: University of Chicago Press, 2005).

1. Antoine de Pluvinel, *L'Instruction du roy en l'exercice de monter à cheval*, ed. René de Menou (Paris: Michel Nivelle, 1625), 200. Pluvinel outlines the program of study, concluding that it aims "de les rendre capables de bien servir leur Prince, soit en paix, soit en guerre." On Pluvinel's academy and subsequent ones modeled on it see Albert Folly, "Les Académies d'armes (XVIe et XVIIe siècles)," *Bulletin de la Société du VIe arrondissement du Paris* 2 (1899): 162–71; Maurice Dumolin, "Les Académies parisiennes d'équitation," *Bulletin de la Société Archéologique, Historique & Artistique* 26 (1925): 417–28; Commandant de la Roche, *Les Académies militaires sous l'Ancien Régime* (Paris, 1929); Ellery Schalk, *From Valor to Pedigree: Ideals of Nobility in France in the Sixteenth and Seventeenth Centuries* (Princeton: Princeton University Press, 1986), ch. 8; and Mark Motley, *Becoming a French Aristocrat: The Education of the Court Nobility, 1580–1715* (Princeton: Princeton University Press, 1990), ch. 3.

2. François de la Noue, *Discours politiques et militaires*, ed. F. E. Sutcliffe (Geneva: Droz, 1967), 147–48. Also see Michel de Montaigne, *Essais*, ed. Pierre Villey and V.-L. Saulnier, 3 vols. (Paris: PUF, 1982), vol. 1, 153; Alexandre de Pontaymery, *L'Academie ou institution de la noblesse françoise*, in *Les Oeuvres* (Paris: Jean Richer, 1599), 3^v–6^r; Salomon de la Broue, *Le Cavalerice françois*, 3 vols. (Paris: Abel l'Angelier, 1602), vol. 1, 2; Thomas Pelletier, *La Nourriture de la noblesse* (Paris: veufve Mamert Patisson, 1604), 96^{r-v}; and Pluvinel, *L'Instruction du roy*, 195.

3. La Noue, *Discours politiques et militaires*, 153. La Noue's advice was seconded with a detailed plan published by Samson de Saint-Germain, Sieur de Juvigny, *Advis de l'établissement de quatre académies en la France* (Rouen, France: Raphaël du Petit Val, 1596).

4. See Pluvinel, *L'Instruction du roy*, 200. This broad curriculum is consistent with that delineated in 1596 by Samson de Saint-Germain, Sieur de Juvigny, *gentilhomme ordinaire de la chambre du Roy*, captain of the king's light horse, and surely a familiar of Pluvinel's academy. Juvigny advised Henry IV to establish four royal academies in the provinces and made explicit recommendations for the faculty and schedule of classes. Each would employ a principal, an *escuyer* (who was also a gentleman), a master of arms, a dancer, a gymnast, a lutenist, a mathematician, a painter, and a preceptor for letters. Saint-Germain, *Advis de l'établissement de quatre académies*, 20–21, 23.

5. Pontaymery, *L'Academie*, 3^r. "Sieur de Pluvinel, qui nous fait voir en gros tous les exercices que l'Italie monstre en detail, ayant basty un Parnasse aux Muses, & dressé un temple à la vertu: car à la verité dire, il n'instruit pas seulement le Gentil-homme en la profession du maniage, mais en la pratique des bonnes moeurs, sans lesquelles toutes sciences ne sont que vanité: aussi qui voit ses escholiers, il voit le maintien des Anges & les vives images des celestes perfections. O heureuse

Noblesse! pour qui le ciel a fait naistre un tant fortable gouverneur: S'est on exercé au maniage? vous avez le voltigement, l'escrime & la danse, le tout sous des personnages que ledict sieur a sçeu heureusement choisir, & qui sont hors de controverse les premiers en leur art. Vous y avez encore les Mathematiques, la peinture & le lut sous les plus excellens maistres que l'on puisse desirer. . . ."

6. Baldessare Castiglione, *The Courtier*, trans. George Bull (London: Penguin Classics, 1976), 94–95. This notion is refuted by Count Lodovico da Canossa.

7. Plato, *The Republic*, trans. Richard Sterling and William Scott (New York and London: W. W. Norton, 1985), 102.

8. See Montaigne, *Essais*, ed. Villey and Saulnier, vol. 2, 642; and La Noue, *Discours politiques et militaires*, 154.

9. Pontus de Tyard, *Solitaire second*, ed. Cathy M. Yandell (Geneva: Droz, 1980), 75.

10. René de Menou, seigneur de Charnizay, *La Pratique du cavalier*, 4th edn. (Paris: Jean Corrozet, 1629), 11.

11. John A. Lynn, *Giant of the* Grand Siècle: *The French Army, 1610–1715* (Cambridge, UK: Cambridge University Press, 1997), 284–87, 601.

12. See Orest Ranum, "Courtesy, Absolutism, and the Rise of the French State, 1630–1660," *Journal of Modern History* 52 (1980): 426–51.

13. Folly, "Les Académies d'armes," 164, and Pelletier, *La Nourriture de la noblesse*, 96[r–v], who tells us that Benjamin's academy was organized according to Pluvinel's model and that others followed in the capital.

14. Menou, *La Pratique du cavalier*, 9–10.

15. On classes of heavy and light cavalry, see Ronald S. Love, "All the King's Horsemen: The Equestrian Army of Henri IV, 1585–1598," *The Sixteenth Century Journal* 22 (1991): 510–33, and Treva Tucker, "Eminence over Efficacy: Social Status and Cavalry Service in Sixteenth-Century France," *The Sixteenth Century Journal* 32 (2001): 1057–95.

16. Thomas Bedingfield, *The Art of Riding*, translation and abridgement of Claudio Corte, *Il cavallarizzo*, bk. 2 (London: M. Denham, 1584), 18.

17. La Broue, *Le Cavalerice françois*, vol. 1, 138, "c'est un grand desplaisir au chevalier armé de toutes pieces, qui est sur un cheval nerveux & naturellement sauteur . . . [parce que] un nombre de sauts . . . seront quelquefois suffisans de le mettre hors d'aleine & de combat."

18. Pluvinel, *L'Instruction du roy*, 86–90; La Broue, *Le Cavalerice françois*, vol. 2, 36–49; Pierre de la Noue, *La Cavalerie françoise et italienne* (Lyon: Cl. Morillon, 1620), 56–75.

19. On horses favoring their right or left sides, see La Broue, *Le Cavalerice françois*, vol. 1, 64–70.

20. Pluvinel, *L'Instruction du roy*, 86, "Votre Majesté à tresbien jugé les passades estre la vraye espreuve de la bonté du cheval, pource qu'en partant on cognoist sa vitesse, en arrestant sa bonne ou mauvaise

bouche, en tournant son adresse & sa grace; & en repartant plusieurs fois, sa force, sa vigueur, & sa loyauté."

21. Pluvinel, *L'Instruction du roy*, 90.

22. La Noue, *La Cavalerie françoise*, 116, "les courbettes sont plus basses du devant à la verité [que les pesades], mais diligemment battuës, prestement avancées & poursuyvies de la crouppe ferme, & bien appuyée sur les jarets qu'il tient fort tendus, portant également les jambes de derriere au ton, & à la vraye mesure d'icelles, sans que l'une ou l'autre retarde, ou avance par quelque inegal mouvement la juste cadance de celles de devant."

23. On the military career see Lynn, *Giant of the* Grand Siècle; and David Parrott, *Richelieu's Army: War, Government and Society in France, 1624–1642* (Cambridge, UK: Cambridge University Press, 2001).

24. Pluvinel, *L'Instruction du roy*, 195, "pour la civilité & pour les moeurs l'escole estrangere n'est pas propre aux esprits François."

25. Pelletier, *La Nourriture de la noblesse*, 96ʳ⁻ᵛ. "La France ne cede maintenant à l'Italie pour bien eslever nostre Noblesse à tous les exercices dont autrefois elle seule se glorifioit par dessus les autres nations de l'Europe. Le premier plan de l'Academie que le Sieur de Pluvinel dressa à Paris pour l'utilité commune de tout ce Royaume, a si bien servy de modelle aux autres qu'à son imitation, ceste eschole y est encores aujourdhuy ouverte par le sieur de Benjamin, au merite, & capacité duquel il ne se peut rien desirer tant il s'aquitte dignement de ceste charge. Ce n'est donc point un Italien qu'on a à nourrir. C'est un Gentilhomme François qu'on desire avoir, les moeurs, la façon, la grace, vrayement à la François & non à l'estrangere. Ce sera donc en la seule France qu'il apprendra à estre à cheval, à courre la bague, à danser, à s'habiller à nostre mode sans estre jugé à son retour plus Italien que François, espargnant en cela le temps & la depense qu'il faudroit faire derechef pour donner de l'eponge sur le tableau & luy rendre l'air de la France."

26. See Gédéon Tallemant, Sieur des Réaux, *Les Historiettes de Tallemant de Réaux*, 3rd edn., ed. Louis Jean Nicolas Monmerqué and Alexis Paulin Paris, 9 vols. (Paris: Techener, 1854–60), on Henry de Montmorency, "il estoit brave, riche, galant, liberal, dansoit bien, estoit bien à cheval, et avoit tousjours des gens d'esprit à ses gages . . ." (vol. 2, 307); on the Comte de Cramail, "Il a tousjours esté galant: il estoit propre, dansoit bien, et estoit bien à cheval" (vol. 1, 507); and, conversely, his criticism of Bassompierre, "il n'a jamais bien dansé: il n'estoit pas mesme trop bien à cheval; il avoit quelque chose de grossier; il n'estoit pas trop bien desnoüé" (vol. 3, 339).

27. Norbert Elias, *The Civilizing Process: Sociogenetic and Psychogenetic Investigations*, trans. Edmund Jephcott, rev. edn., ed. by Eric Dunning, Johan Goudsblom, and Stephen Mennell (Oxford: Blackwell Publishers, 2000).

28. On the repertoire of civility manuals see Roger Chartier, "From Texts to Manners. A Concept and Its Books: *Civilité* between Aristocratic Distinction and Popular Appropriation," in *The Cultural Uses of Print in Early Modern France*, trans. Lydia G. Cochrane (Princeton: Princeton University Press, 1987), 71–109.

29. See the history of manners in Elias, *The Civilizing Process*, 1–182. For a deft overview of civility in early modern Europe see Jacques Revel, "The Uses of Civility," in *Passions of the Renaissance*, ed. Roger Chartier, trans. Arthur Goldhammer, vol. 3 of *A History of Private Life*, general eds. Philippe Ariès and Georges Duby (Cambridge, MA and London: Belknap/Harvard University Press, 1989), 167–205.

30. La Broue, *Le Cavalerice françois*, vol. 1, 4, ". . . il est certain, qu'il n'y a que les plus beaux esprits, qui soient propres pour les plus beaux exercices"; and vol. 1, 3, "Et pour ne point dissimuler, je pense, qu'il n'advient jamais que la perfection d'un tel sçavoir se communique à certains esprits foibles & grossiers . . ."

31. The Letters Patent is reproduced in Frances A. Yates, *The French Academies of the Sixteenth Century*, 2nd edn. (London: Routledge, 1988), 319; I quote her translation, p. 23.

32. The quote comes from Marin Mersenne's extremely important account of the Academy, translated and discussed in Yates, *The French Academies*, 23–25. Although she marshaled the sources to do so, Yates never came to the conclusion that Pluvinel's academy was in some sense a direct continuation of Baïf's.

33. Pierre de Ronsard, "Préface à la musique," in *Oeuvres complètes*, ed. Jean Céard, Daniel Ménager, and Michel Simonin, 2 vols. (Paris: Gallimard, 1993–94), vol. 2, 1171.

34. La Broue, *Le Cavalerice françois*, vol. 1, 3, "Il est aussi nécessaire que le Cavalerice aye beaucoup de jugement naturel, mesmes aux proportions: d'autant que tous les airs & plus beaux maneges sont composez de nombres, de mesures & de plusieurs egalitez qu'il faut soigneusement observer."

35. La Broue, *Le Cavalerice françois*, vol. 1, 3, "je puis asseurer qu'il est fort malaisé que celuy qui ne peut gouster ny comprendre l'harmonie, l'air & la mesure de la musique, & consequemment des instrumens & de la dance, puisse jamais bien entendre les airs & proportions de nos escoles."

36. Pierre de Ronsard, *Cartel pour le combat à cheval en forme de balet*, in *Oeuvres complètes*, vol. 2, 272.

37. Antoine de Pluvinel, *Le Maneige royal où lon peut remarquer le defaut et la perfection du chevalier en tous ses exercices de cet art* (Paris: G. Le Noir, 1623), 63.

38. Descriptions, diagrams, and engravings of the ballet can be found in François de Rosset, *Le Romant des chevaliers de la gloire* (Paris: Veuve Bertault, 1612), fols. 69^r–74^v; Honoré Laugier de Porchères, *Le Camp de la place Royale* (Paris: Jean Micard and Toussaint du Bray,

1612), 116–47; Pluvinel, *Le Maneige royal*, 59–63; and *Histoire generale de tout ce qui s'est passé au Parc Royal sur la resjouïssance du Mariage du Roy avec l'Infante d'Espagne* (Paris: Anthoine du Brueil, 1612), 14–16. For facsimiles of the choreographic and musical sources of the ballet, see *Carrousel 1612*, introduction by Kate van Orden (Geneva and Paris: Éditions Minkoff, forthcoming). On the sixteenth-century origins of the *ballet à cheval*, see van Orden, *Music, Discipline, and Arms.* For an overview of the carrousel see Jacques Vanuxem, "Le Carrousel de 1612 sur la place Royale et ses devises," in *Les Fêtes de la Renaissance*, ed. Jean Jacquot, 3 vols. (Paris: CNRS, 1956), vol. 1, 191–203.

39. Laugier de Porchères, *Le Camp de la place Royale*, 142.
40. Vendôme, La Valette, and Zamet used their own devices; the others were fabricated. See Rosset, *Le Romant des chevaliers de la gloire*, fol. 74^r. The accounts vary in many details. I rely primarily on Rosset with some elements from Laugier de Porchères.
41. Laugier de Porchères, *Le Camp de la place Royale*, 130–31.
42. An attribution made in *Airs de différents auteurs à 4 parties, livre 3* (Paris: Pierre Ballard, 1613), fol. 50^v–51^r.
43. Laugier de Porchères, *Le Camp de la place Royale*, 136, "En cest endroit ils commencerent à la cadence du mouvement des airs Metriques composez selon les nombres ou mesures anciennes." The music for the songs was repeated for the ballet.
44. Rosset, *Le Romant des chevaliers de la gloire*, fol. 72^v, "les Chevaliers s'avancerent en la mesme figure, faisans aller leurs chevaux à mez-air, avec tant d'esgalité, & de proportion, que tous s'eslevoient, & baissoient à mesme temps. La mesme cadance perduë, sonnant à la fin de cest air, les fit tous arrester comme immobiles."
45. Federico Grisone, *Gli ordini di cavalcare* (Naples: G. P. Suganappo, 1550). For a modern edition of sections of Grisone's treatise see Carlo Bascetta (ed.), *Sport e giuochi: Trattati e scritti dal XV al XVIII secolo* (Milan: Il Polifilo, 1978), 205–25, relevant passages at 222–24.
46. Pluvinel, *L'Instruction du roy*, 42, 44, 66.
47. Cesare Fiaschi, *Trattato del modo dell'imbrigliare, maneggiare et ferrare cavalli* (Bologna: A. Giaccarelli, 1556). Selections with plates reprinted in Bascetta, *Sport e giuochi*, 227–40.
48. See, for example, La Broue, *Le Cavalerice françois*, vol. 1, 54–59, and La Noue, *La Cavalerie françoise*, 76–110.
49. La Broue, *Le Cavalerice françois*, vol. 1, 119–20.
50. La Noue, *La Cavalerie françoise*, 71. "Il n'y a si petit compagnon qui ne vueille paroistre bon gend'arme dés qu'il se voit le cul sur la selle, qui faict que dés aussi tost que telles gens sont dessus leurs chevaux, que c'est à eux à trouver leurs jambes, pour passader à la soldate, disent-ils, ne se souciant-pas s'ils vont d'école ou non, ce leur est assez de les faire aller selon qu'ils l'entendent, & qu'ils se persuadent qu'il faut faire pour se monstrer vaillant & courageux: Mais attendu qu'ils

ne considerent-pas que leurs confusions, tours, & détours à droitte &
à gauche, sont contraires à l'art militere [*sic*], qui fait tout par bel
ordre & bon mesure; il faut qu'ils sçachent comme ceste passade,
qu'ils appellent à la soldate, se doit faire pour estre parfaicte."

51. Hans Delbrück stresses this point in *The Dawn of Modern Warfare*,
trans. Walter J. Renfroe, Jr., vol. 4 of *History of the Art of War*
(Lincoln, NE and London: University of Nebraska Press, 1990), 124.

52. Menou, *La Pratique du cavalier*, 105, "le principal poinct de nostre
science consiste au jugement, faire la guerre à l'oeil, changer de
moment en moment d'action, selon le besoin, & travailler plustost la
cervelle de nos chevaux, que les jambes."

53. See Kate van Orden, "Chorégraphies courtoises et militaires," forthcoming in proceedings from the conference "Les Arts de l'équitation
dans l'Europe de la Renaissance," held by the École nationale d'équitation, Saumur, France, October, 2002.

54. For a few of the sources that express the view that absolutism was
"always in the making, but never made"—an interpretation that of
course implicates public spectacles all the more directly in its fabrica-
tion—see Fanny Cosandey and Robert Descimon, *L'Absolutisme en
France* (Paris: Seuil, 2002); Peter Burke, *The Fabrication of Louis
XIV* (New Haven, CT and London: Yale University Press, 1992); and
David Parker, *The Making of French Absolutism* (London: Edward
Arnold, 1983).

55. See Motley, *Becoming a French Aristocrat*, 145–48; and Saint-
Germain, *Advis de l'établissement de quatre académie*, 26.

56. La Noue, *La Cavalerie françoise*, 141–45; Claude-François
Menestrier, *Traité des tournois, joustes, carrousels et autres spectacles
publics* (Lyon: J. Muguet, 1669).

57. Nicolas Faret, *L'Honneste Homme ou l'art de plaire à la court*, ed.
M. Magendie (Paris: PUF, 1925), 12, "Or, comme il n'y a point
d'hommes qui ne choisissent une profession pour s'employer, il me
semble qu'il n'y en a point de plus honeste, ny de plus essentielle à un
Gentil-homme que celle des armes."

PART III

IDENTITY AND SELF-DEFINITION

CHAPTER 8

A HORSE OF A DIFFERENT COLOR: NATION AND RACE IN EARLY MODERN HORSEMANSHIP TREATISES

Karen Raber

In his *New Method and Extraordinary Invention of Dressing Horses* William Cavendish reports that when he was asked by an observer which horses he liked best, he replied "there were Good and Bad of all Nations; but that the Barbes were the Gentlemen of Horse-kind, and Spanish Horses were the Princes."[1] There are nations of horses, as there are of men, and like nations of men horse breeds have their own national character: Barbs, according to Cavendish, are more docile, whereas Spanish horses are unnervingly intelligent; English horses are lumpish and fit only to pull carts, and Turkish horses, although rare and beautiful, are not so physically suited to the high schooling. In this chapter I am going to argue that Cavendish's treatises mobilize a description of horse culture in the interests of a specific human cultural goal: they suggest that only the right kind of Englishman with the right kind of material situation, knowledge, and ideas can secure England's future as a dominant European and global power. If we consider the moment when Cavendish is writing—in exile, during the civil war and Interregnum—then the importance of such a project, and the degree of Cavendish's personal investment in it, are clear. English national identity is under reconstruction in the Puritan

Commonwealth Cavendish has fled. It is equally under construction in the apparently unassuming books he writes about horses.

For Cavendish, the enemies to his project in the *New Method* wear a variety of faces—they appear as notable horsemen of Catholic nations who, while pretending to nobility and authority, perpetuate debilitating error in the art of dressage; or they are the mysterious and ancient desert tribes whose horses and skills in horse handling and horse breeding are at once so desirable and yet so dangerous to the quintessentially pragmatic, rational English horseman. Or equally they may lurk in one's own backyard, fellow Englishmen who insist on importing the worst foreign gobbledygook, or who belong to a class whose Puritan sympathies have already lost England global power through civil unrest and war. All these Cavendish attempts to answer, subvert, or appropriate in his quest to fashion a kingdom of men whose identity is shaped by his methods of horsemanship. In much the same way that Cavendish portrays the steady hand of the aristocratic English rider trained to his "new method and extraordinary invention" better developing the qualities of the animal he rides (whether one of those fiery Spanish or Arabian beasts, or one of the plodding domestic ilk), he implies that England's national future is best trusted to the confident control of an aristocratic horseman like himself.

HORSE AND HOME

Both Cavendish's *New Method* (*NM*) and his additional work in the *General System of Horsemanship* (*GS*) attempt to modify a long tradition of similar works on horses, horse breeding, farriery, and horsemanship. Most early contributions to the genre are redactions, translations, or wholesale borrowings from the famous work of continental and classical writers from Xenophon to Federico Grisone, and most combine practical knowledge about the care and keeping of horses with rudimentary instructions on riding, especially for gentlemen and soldiers.[2] Thomas Blundeville's *Fowre Chiefest Offices Belonging to Horsemanshippe* (1566), reprinted numerous times through the late sixteenth and early seventeenth centuries, is one of the earliest of these, and typical in its reliance on Grisone, the sixteenth-century Italian riding master; John Astley's *The Art of Riding* (1584), Christopher Clifford's *The Schoole of Horsmanship* (1585), and Gervase Markham's *A Discourse of Horsemanshippe* (1593) testify to the ongoing popularity of such treatises with the reading public. Indeed, Markham added *Countrey Contentments* (1615), *Markhams Faithfull Farrier* (1640), *Markhams Maister-peece*, *or What Doth a Horse-man Lacke* (1610), *Cavelarice or the English Horseman* (1607), and a host of other titles to the genre during the seventeenth century, finding horsemanship a profitable topic for his prolific pen. He was not alone: the seventeenth century saw the publication of John Vernon's *The Young Horse-man, or the Honest Plain-Dealing Cavalier* (1644), full of advice for soldiers on horseback. Michael Baret wrote *An Hipponomie or the Vineyard of Horsemanship* (1618) and Nicholas Morgan opined on *The Horse-man's Honour, or the Beautie of Horsemanshippe* (1620).

While the subject of horsemanship inspired many into print, their works do not advance the art itself much over the original treatises by Xenophon and Grisone—and indeed, it may be argued that rather than the enlightened and humane approach of Xenophon, Grisone's arcane and medieval methods won the battle to represent a universally accepted method of training. Nor do most of these treatises stake out a peculiarly English style or technique, although many decry the way England has failed to fully appreciate the value of riding skills. Markham's *Cavelarice*, subtitled with a reference to "the English horseman," is introduced with an epistle to Prince Henry that celebrates the Prince's influence in encouraging a renewal of interest in riding: because of Henry (and Markham's little printed gift to him) "how ever the world shall boast eyther Spaine, France, or Italie, yet it shall then be knowne that they have not brought forth so good Horsemen as have been bred, and are now living in the Empire of great Britaine," suggests Markham.[3] Yet if there is a nationalistic content to the treatise, it is not announced therein, nor does it involve a significant change of method, but rather subsists in English familiarity with the trades and practices of breeding, keeping, and riding that the treatise made possible by its dissemination.

Only Cavendish offers the world a "new method" and announces that he does so in his title. Only Cavendish produces a scientific system, with intensely detailed descriptions of exactly how the horse should place its hooves in each maneuver, accompanied by engravings that illustrate his points (figure 8.1). Other works offer advice on the rider's position and the use of various items of equipment, but Cavendish raises this trend to a whole new level, with many plates showing his own and other masters' perfectly vertical and balanced seat, and others showing proper use of equipment. Cavendish's two treatises must thus be distinguished from the mass of similar publication.

The most obvious explanation for the differences in Cavendish's works emerges out of the circumstances in which their author wrote. His *New Method* was first conceived and created during England's

228

In Terre-à-terre Relevé a Horſe ought to go according to this Figure.

The meaſure of the ground in Terre-à-terre is to allow ſomewhat more than a horſe's length; but you may take more or leſs compaſs, if you pleaſe. The ſame aids muſt be uſed

in Terre-à-terre determiné, and the horſe's poſture the ſame, excepting that Terre-à-terre determiné is lower, being much like the Carriere, only that the Carriere is not upon the volte.

I give you here a univerſal map of horſemanſhip, containing the whole variety of the Manege, *viz.* the Gallop, Changes of all kinds within or without the circle, going upon Quarters to both hands, working the Shoulders or the Croupe either within or without, Demivoltes, Curvettes upon the voltes, or ſtrait forwards ; to Serpentine, or to go in Caprioles, the horſe's head to the wall, going ſideways in an Oval, or in Quarters ; in ſhort, I have omitted nothing.

CHAP.

Figure 8.1. Sample page from William Cavendish, *General System of Horsemanship* (1743), courtesy of the Beinecke Library, Yale University.

civil war, when he was doubly exiled, from his home in England and also from the temporary court of Charles II in Paris, living in Amsterdam and hounded by creditors. Cavendish was a military leader in defense of the Royalist cause, leading the troops that guarded Henrietta Maria as she made her escape, and participating in the disastrous battle of Marston Moor with Prince Rupert. In fact, Cavendish's skills as a cavalryman were sorely tested during the war years, while his faith that advanced horsemanship belonged to the higher, more sophisticated arts suitable for noblemen to display was challenged by the opposition's scathing portrayal of him as effemi nate, impotent, and dissolute. *The Oxford Character of the London Diurnnall Examined* reported that at Marston Moor "danced so quaintly, played his part a while in the North, was soundly beaten, shew'd a paire of heels, and exit Newcastle."[4] His "dancing" in this case refers equally to his riding, perhaps his skill at the "airs above the ground" or the leaping maneuvers involved in Cavendish's cavalry technique.

While abroad, Cavendish like other exiles suffered a radical dislocation of identity attendant on the death of Charles I and the Royalist defeat at the hands of the Parliamentary forces. For Cavendish, war and exile also meant not only a loss of income, but the alienation of those properties that had been the source of his former prestige and power, his estates at Welbeck and Bolsover. Despite his nearly desperate financial condition in exile, however, he purchased expensive horses on which to practice his training methods. This might seem perverse, unless we consider that Cavendish's pastime soothed his sense of loss and displacement, allowing him to exercise the skill he most associated with noble status and service; his riding also attracted the kind of attention designed to mitigate his misery—he was frequently visited and praised by European luminaries and fellow English exiles. As he writes in the *New Method*, "Many French Gentlemen, and Persons of the greatest quality of that Nation, did me the favour to see my Horses; and the Prince of Conde himself, with several Noble-men, and Officers, was pleased to take the pains to goe twice to my Mannage [riding school]" (Preface).[5]

His *New Method* announces on its title page that it will "fit" horses for "the Service of the Field in Time of War, or for the Exercise and Improvement of Gentlemen in the Academy at home." Horsemanship is both a practical art for the defense of a kingdom, and an art that demonstrates an elite class-based mastery that serves its practitioners by allowing the public display of their superior skills in tournaments and pageants. The association of riding skill with the skills of ruling—of good reigning with good reining—was by Cavendish's era well established in art, statuary, and literature.[6] In his early years at court, Cavendish himself instructed the young Charles II in dressage as part of the prince's general training for his future office. In the subtitle to Cavendish's *General System*, the book's publisher, J. Brindley, laments, however, that this art has been "hitherto so much neglected, or discouraged in England, that young Gentlemen have been obliged to have recourse to foreign Nations for this Part of their Education." By developing a native expression of the art, Cavendish's work provides the means to elevate England amongst the Europeans, to situate this "civilizing" art as a specifically English skill.

Cavendish's treatises engage in a dialogue with a number of previous texts and authors, some of whom he names, and some whose names he appears to repress. He observes that "several horsemen have blotted more paper to demonstrate their Natural Philosophy than their art in Horsemanship, endeavoring to discover the constitution and particular disposition of horses by their marks and color." To these horsemen Cavendish responds "there are good and bad of all colours, and of all marks," and the only way to know a horse's temperament is by riding it; as he puts it, "I know no philosophy but trying" (*NM* 28). For Cavendish, who spent evenings in England, Paris, and Amsterdam discussing science and philosophy with the likes of Hobbes and Descartes, scientific method is everything. The failure to apply empirical standards leads to foolishness and error. Correcting previous horsemen's lack of rational method, Cavendish begins with the Italians, represented by the extraordinarily influential Grisone. Although he initially calls Grisone a great horseman, he quickly empties that praise of any meaning with repeated assaults on "Old Grisone," as he calls him, using most often the word "ridiculous" to describe the Italian method of training. "For a Resty Horse," writes Cavendish with contempt, "they Raise a whole Town with Staves to Beat him . . . with Squirts, Fire, Whelps, Hedg-hoggs . . . and the same they do Before a Horse that Runs Away. . . . For a Horse that is Afraid, and Starts, they appoint Whirlegiggs of several Colours, which will make him Ten times Worse" (*NM* 18–19). Italian writers are "tedious," because they write too much of "Marks, Colours, Temperatures, Elements, Moon, Stars, Winds, and Bleedings, than of the Art of Riding; only to make up a Book, though they wanted Horsemanship" (*NM* 4). The Italians, in Cavendish's estimation, have "lost their Latin" (*NM* 83) as horsemen. In his characterizations of Grisone and the Italian tradition, Cavendish borrows from a venerable tradition of Protestant propaganda that associates Italy and

Catholicism with the superstition and ignorance supposedly bred by the Catholic Church. These foreigners who write so much of "Elements, Moon, Stars," and so on trade in foolish belief, rather than science. For the Italians to have "lost their Latin" confirms their degeneration from the standards of both ancient Rome and the early Church, and implies that perhaps others, namely the English, are better preservers of the language of horsemanship.

As we read through the treatises, we quickly discover that for Cavendish nearly all writers before himself are either derivative, usually redacting the error-prone Grisone, or unimaginative and incompetent. The French of course loom large (Paris had become a new center to the exiled Royalist community, and its monarchy was relatively intact, making the French a formidable competitor in the domain of elitist nationalism). Although forced to acknowledge that they have done a little better than the Italians, Cavendish still finds them wanting. The famous work of Antoine de Pluvinel, his 1623 *Le Maneige royal*, Cavendish criticizes for its supposed method, which is "no more than an absolute Routine; and hath spoyld more horses than ever any Thing did" (*NM* 4). There are a lot of similarities between Pluvinel's and Cavendish's texts: Pluvinel's treatise, like Cavendish's, represents horsemanship as an appropriately elite pursuit—his discussion of training methods follows the form of a dialogue between Pluvinel and his pupil the king, recalling Cavendish's education of his own prince. Its form, along with its lush illustrations and expensive binding, may have inspired the similar appearance of Cavendish's book, with the latter's 43 engraved plates (figures 8.2–8.4). Pluvinel includes diagrams to show how to use the stationary post for training, diagrams that show via tiny hoofprints where the horse should place its hooves, and a diagram of an unclothed rider's body on horseback with lines drawn in to indicate the perfect position. A prefatory poem praises Pluvinel for having trained so many well-know cavaliers: "When the others leave behind clever writings / And pupils who are well-schooled / They will never bequeath Masters / As Pluvinel has bequeathed to us."[7] Another notes that "You who wished to possess all the knowledge / Of taming Horses / Do not go beyond the mountains, for you have it in France." Pluvinel's work is thus perhaps more like than unlike Cavendish's.

Cavendish's purpose, however, is to supersede all European writers, including Pluvinel, so Cavendish describes the advantages of his own method: Pluvinel requires that the horse's head be "resolute and steady" in "the old absurd way" (*NM* 39), to which end he ties

Figure 8.2. Sample plate from Antoine de Pluvinel, *Le Maneige royal* (1623). With permission of the Houghton Library, Harvard University.

Figure 8.3. Cavendish performing *balotade* before his castle at Bolsover, from William Cavendish, *General System of Horsemanship* (1743), courtesy of the Beinecke Library, Yale University.

Figure 8.4. In the park at Welbeck, from William Cavendish, *General System of Horsemanship* (1743), courtesy of the Beinecke Library, Yale University.

his mounts to a pillar, while Cavendish seeks to allow the horse a freer forward motion and true flexion through the hindquarters and shoulders: "For this reason I invented the method of working the inward rein, as you may perceive in all my lessons, which is the most excellent invention that can be to make a horse go true, and can't be done by any other method" (NM39).[8] So overall we can say that Cavendish both imitates and tries to supplant Pluvinel's exemplary text, setting a home-grown English version of both the art, and the artful book, in its place. Through Cavendish's efforts, England will thus have an original, practical training manual, based on rational and empirical inquiry about techniques, breeds, and so on; through Cavendish's intervention, England, not Italy or France, will reinvent riding as an elegant, skill-driven noble pursuit. (And if you are wondering what Cavendish has to say about Germans and others, well they are simply disastrous horsemen and not to be counted.)

Catholic Grisone and Catholic Pluvinel: they are rule-bound, superstitious, lacking innovation, and repressive of science and technology. By mobilizing stereotypes, or criticizing actual techniques, Cavendish is able to construct an oppositional identity for the English

Protestant equestrian. His, then, is the superior national product in the marketplace of ideas about horses and riding.

But Cavendish also spends a tremendous amount of time disputing the treatise of another English writer, Blundeville, whose *Fowre Chiefest Offices* was the most reprinted popular text of the sixteenth century. There is nothing unusual about poor Blundeville's text: he too discusses breeds and breeding, riding techniques, and diseases and shoeing in separate sections. Blundeville is no more or less reliant on non-English sources than any other of his day. In fact, I do not believe that Blundeville is really important as a precursor to Cavendish at all. Rather, I believe Blundeville does double duty as a catch-all exemplar for Cavendish: he becomes a figure for the inappropriate import of "foreign goods" (i.e., foreign influences in the art of riding) and also occupies the space Cavendish should otherwise devote to a far more influential source of competition: the many cheap handbooks about horses and horsemanship aimed at the middle and lower classes of rural farmers, especially those by Gervase Markham. When Cavendish criticizes Blundeville for being full of silly notions borrowed from Grisone, he remarks that "Mr Blundeville appears . . . to be a better scholar than a horseman: and was indeed a fine gentleman . . . but tied himself too much to Old Authors, who knew as little as he" (*NM* 31). The *New Method*, on the other hand, "is stolen out of no Book, nor any mans Practice but my own, and is as True as it is New. . . . I am sure it is the Best that hath been Writ yet" (*NM* 42). In fact, Blundeville shares a great deal with Cavendish, especially in his fascination with foreign breeds such as the Turks and the Barbs. The few items of superstition he includes deal with foreign horses—in some countries, Blundeville holds, horses "be made like Unicorns" and Turkish horses "will run forever on a secret word."[9]

But Cavendish insists that Blundeville locks English readers into a kind of dependence, "tied to old authors," that Cavendish deplores. It is important to my argument to note that Cavendish credits Blundeville with being "a gentleman" if no horseman. Unlike Blundeville, many of Cavendish's other precursors in writing English horsemanship manuals were neither gentlemen by Cavendish's standards, nor particularly observant of traditions of authority. The most significant writer of Cavendish's own century is beyond doubt Gervase Markham, whose name appears nowhere in either the *New Method* or the *Methode nouvelle* or the *General System*. About Markham's prolific publication Wendy Wall has observed that, if as I have indicated it is not wholly nationalistic in its content, it constitutes instead a new form of national labor: competing in the market with foreign guides to similar topics, Markham's treatises appealed to a new readership, articulating values of thrift and rural English identity.[10] Middle class in his sentiments as much as his birth, Markham revitalized the genre by passing along country wisdom in readable fashion, selling his cheaper books to a mass audience of country farmers. Markham may have flattered Prince Henry in his *Cavelarice*, but nobles were not his audience, and rarely his true patrons.

It is difficult to believe that Cavendish had not read Markham's many works, especially since he himself claims to have read everything in print on horses: "I have Practised, and Studied Horse-manship ever since I was Ten years old; Have Rid with the Best Masters of all Nations . . . Have Read all their Italian, French, and English Books, and some Latine ones; and in a Word, all that hath been Writ upon that Subject, Good and Bad" (*NM* 41). Markham and his sort thus seem a kind of plural doppelgänger to Blundeville, equestrian advocates of a *new* nationalism, one Cavendish fought against during the early years of the civil war—a nationalism based on liberty from certain kinds of authority, informed by mercantile values and ideologies of egalitarianism. Blundeville the whipping boy steps in when what Cavendish really wants is to erase Markham's breed of national identity, overwriting it with a version of Englishness that is intransigently aristocratic, elite, and attached to the values of the great estates rather than rural smallholdings and subsistence farms. And he is at least successful in erasing Markham's name from the lineage of treatise-writers Cavendish creates. The deepest irony in Cavendish's strategy, if it is one, is that he finds himself borrowing from writers such as Markham the language of the self-made man, liberated from repressive traditions—remember his claim that he has stolen no man's practice, but invented this method all by himself, and has thus liberated England from the dominance of the continental authorities.

ENGLISHING THE EXOTIC

I have argued that Cavendish's horsemanship treatises defend the ideologies of elite Protestant horse culture as a way to preserve the role of the English aristocracy in defining English national identity during a time of turbulence when the future of both his class and his nation seemed in doubt. I now want to consider the way in which Cavendish mobilizes images of race and nation, first in his descriptions of horse breeds and nations of men, and finally in the pictorial additions to his treatises he commissioned from Van Diepenbeck.

Cavendish just loves foreign breeds, especially those from Spain, the Orient, or Africa, which makes him no different from many of his countrymen in the period who sought Andalusian, Turkish, Arabian, and Barb stallions at enormous cost. But he is also fascinated by foreign horse culture in general. He details the curious world of the Arabian this way: "He is Nurst with Camels-milk; there are strange reports in the world of those horses; for I have been told by many Gentlemen of Credit, and by many many merchants, that the price of right Arabians is One thousand, Two thousand, and Three thousand pounds a horse (an Intollerable and an Incredible price)" (*NM* 72). The Barb he notes is "next to the Spanish Horse for wisdom, but not neer so Wise, and that makes him much easier to be dressed." Barbs are "somewhat slender and lady-like" (*NM* 53) and are reputed "never to grow old, because they always retain their natural strength and vigour" (*GS* 21). Turkish horses are "very fine horses, but oddly shaped; their heads were very fine but like a Camels head . . . the croup like a mules . . . and their backs risen somewhat like a Camel. I had a Groom, a Heavy English Clown, whom I set upon them and they made no more of him than if he had been a light as a feather" (*NM* 70). But he approves of the Spanish horse above all: "You must know that of all horses in the world, of what nation soever they be, the Spanish horses are the wisest . . . and strangely wise, beyond man's imagination" (*NM* 49). Unfortunately they are almost too smart to train well.

All this talk of "strangeness" should remind us that, as Gerald MacLean has pointed out, seventeenth-century England constructed "Britishness" via the "global, strange, alien."[11] The Orient, the Ottoman empire, Moorish Spain, and northern Africa represented a particular challenge to travelers, writers, and merchants of the time: England deplored the heathen and barbaric races and nations of these lands, their cruelty, their effeminate surrender to appetite and excess, yet at the same time admired the achievements, the great culture, science, military might, and past dominance. According to Daniel Vitkus, early modern representations of the Oriental and Islamic Other "helped to construct an identity for Protestant England when English identity was developing a proto-imperialist formation."[12] In other words, England found itself simultaneously imitating and denying the other great empire the world had recently known. One of the most desirable products of that empire was equine—strange horses with strange powers and incredible value, these horses that fascinate and also disturb Cavendish with their intolerable expense, their "lady-like" or "camel-like" attributes, and their unimaginable wisdom.

Nor are the horses alone in this. They have their human counter-parts in the treatises. The Turks, Cavendish notes, are the best at keeping their horses—they "cloath them first with a fine linnen cloth and hood next their skin; then with a haircloth and hood . . . and all these are made so fit as to cover their breasts and to come pretty low down to their legs. There cannot be a better way than this for their clothing" (*NM* 82). Spanish grooms are "so diligent . . . and especially are curious about their manes, toppings and tails, making them clean divers ways" (*NM* 82–83). (The French, by the way, are in contrast not good grooms, since they do not rub their horses' legs well.) Strange ways, but admirable.

So what does Cavendish do to tame the implications of cruelty, effeminacy, and alienness of these exotic breeds and their human keepers? He locates these foreigners, these Others both human and equine, right in the middle of the English aristocratic country estate. The many engravings Cavendish commissioned for his treatises include pictures of these breeds and their grooms set against the backdrop of Cavendish's own homes at Welbeck and Bolsover. The aristocratic estate, as any number of critics have pointed out, is more than just a place to live—it is a text in itself, which speaks about power, privilege, and the naturalizing of both.[13] Country estates constituted a discourse that could accommodate and indeed authorize change. Kari McBride summarizes this function: "Rather than denying or impeding the cultural revolutions of early modern England, the (re)articulations of country house discourse served ultimately to mediate change, doing the cultural work that allowed for the transfer of power from one group to another, for the renegotiation of social and economic relationships, and for the emergence of new subjectivities."[14] Race enters the country house via distinctions between whiteness, which comes to mark nobility and Englishness, and the darker skins of servants and others who begin to populate the aristocratic houses and estates by the late seventeenth century. Thus the estate offers an existing discourse into which things difficult and foreign can be inserted, where their implications can be safely assimilated. By *framing* both foreign breeds and foreign practices of grooming and care within the secure containment of the aristocratic Englishman's estate, Cavendish suggests, successful empires can be built, empires that incorporate but are not corrupted by the import of foreign blood or foreign ideas. Both animals and humans are in effect domesticated, controlled, appropriated to the cause of furthering the knowledge and skills of the English when they are inserted into the milieu of Cavendish's own country houses.

If we recall Pluvinel's beautiful engraving, we should immediately recognize that Cavendish omits Pluvinel's style of elaborate artistic frames from his own pictures (figure 8.3). Instead, what frames horse and rider are depictions of Cavendish's estates at Welbeck and Bolsover. In figure 8.4, for example, Cavendish exhibits the airs above the ground in the middle of a park lane at Welbeck, the estate whose woods were plundered by its Parliamentary owner during the war. But in figures 8.5–8.7, we see the framing of the exotic breeds against the images of Cavendish's houses and outbuildings at Welbeck. In the first figure, a groom dressed in Spanish costume leads "The superb horse of Spain" across the grounds outside the castle walls. In the second, a dark-skinned Turkish groom, also attired in the costume of his country, leads "Mackomilia, a Turk," while in the background stands the covered wooden riding arena Cavendish had built at Welbeck. Again, in figure 8.7, an example of a Barb is led by another dark-skinned groom, presumably Arabic or African in origin, while a nice view of Welbeck's turrets and chimneys makes up the backdrop. Finally, in a related plate (figure 8.8), we see Cavendish's self-depiction against a classical background of the "battle won," signaling that Cavendish is the pinnacle of the classical tradition, graced by the gods of antiquity, but bearing fruit in his contemporary world in the field of war (which of course is the opposite of Cavendish's actual personal

Figure 8.5. A Spanish horse, from William Cavendish, *General System of Horsemanship* (1743), courtesy of the Beinecke Library, Yale University.

Figure 8.6. Turkish horse and groom, from William Cavendish, *General System of Horsemanship* (1743), courtesy of the Beinecke Library, Yale University.

Figure 8.7. Barb and groom, from William Cavendish, *General System of Horsemanship* (1743), courtesy of the Beinecke Library, Yale University.

history). This plate repeats one in which Charles II is portrayed in exactly the same position, surrounded by gods but against a background of war being fought, rather than a battle won (figure 8.9). Charles is followed at his bottom right by a cupid-like child complete with a case of arrows who carries the king's helmet. Figure 8.8 transforms this cupid, however, into a Moorish or Arabian boy, taller and considerably more martial in appearance (with a sword at his side), who clearly serves as Cavendish's page and carries his helmet. How are we to read these two images? Is it possible that Cavendish implies that he will win the battle for Charles with his Moorish page in tow? Or is it *because* he has successfully incorporated the strengths of the Moor—equine and human—that Cavendish can conclude the battles Charles might start?

The fantasies illustrated in Cavendish's engravings revolve around the happy homecoming his *New Method* celebrated, a homecoming that seemed to restore his faith in the connections he had drawn in his treatises among aristocratic superiority, scientific, humane, and peculiarly English horsemanship, and the right ordering of a universe disrupted by civil war. Cavendish's horsemanship treatises provide an

Figure 8.8. Cavendish appearing in a scene called "The Battle Won," from William Cavendish, *General System of Horsemanship* (1743), courtesy of the Beinecke Library, Yale University.

Figure 8.9.   The same image as in figure 8.8, but with Charles II as the rider, from William Cavendish, *General System of Horsemanship* (1743), courtesy of the Beinecke Library, Yale University.

imaginative extension of English imperial power at a time when the whole notion of what it means to be "English" is under revision. He invents and disseminates, via his treatises, a version of national identity that preserves aristocratic and elite values against foreign and domestic enemies. In the end, Cavendish's fantasy is that he will emerge as the nation's savior, supported by his equine subjects, Turkish and Arabian, African and Spanish, properly groomed and educated to know their place.

NOTES

1. William Cavendish, Duke of Newcastle's *A New Method and Extraordinary Invention to Dress Horses* (London: Thomas Milbourn, 1667, abbreviated as *NM* in this chapter); the quote is from *NM* 6. Cavendish had also published a treatise in French, *La Methode et invention nouvelle de dresser les chevaux* (Antwerp: Jacques van Meurs, 1657/58; abbreviated as *Methode nouvelle* in this chapter), which marked the beginning of his efforts at writing a complete description of his training techniques. The plates by Abraham van Diepenbeck intended for this first volume were in fact published in a later

translation of Cavendish's 1657/58 French text, entitled *A General System of Horsemanship* (London: J. Brindley, 1743; abbreviated as *GS* in this chapter).

2. Xenophon's classical treatise on horsemanship is the basis for Astley's pamphlet and Blundeville's works; Grisone's *Gli ordini di cavalcare* (Naples: Giovan Paolo Suganappo, 1550) provides the continental equivalent of a masterwork on horse training for many early writers in England.

3. Gervase Markham, *Cavelarice, or, The English Horseman, Contayning all the Arte of Horse-manship, as much as is necessary for any man to vnderstand* . . . (London: Edward White, 1607).

4. Quoted in Leslie Hotson, *The Commonwealth and Restoration Stage* (New York: Russell & Russell, Inc., 1912), 21.

5. Cavendish's passion probably also inspired another visitor to his household in Holland: Thomas Hobbes wrote a pamphlet on *Considerations Touching the Facility or Difficulty of the Motions of a Horse on Straight Lines and Circular* most likely pursuant to the many discussions he and Cavendish had about the nature of the horse. For this and other discussion of Cavendish's horsemanship pursuits see Geoffrey Trease, *Portrait of a Cavalier: William Cavendish, First Duke of Newcastle* (London: Macmillan, 1979), 74ff.

6. See e.g. Walter Liedtke, *The Royal Horse and Rider: Painting, Sculpture, and Horsemanship 1500–1800* (New York: Abaris Books, 1989) or the analysis in Roy Strong, *Van Dyck: Charles I on Horseback* (New York: Viking Press, 1972).

7. Antoine de Pluvinel, *Le Maneige royal où lon peut remarquer le defaut et la perfection du chevalier en tous les exercices de cet art* (Paris: G. Le Noir, 1623).

8. Cavendish's use of the inside rein is indeed a modern invention, one that is followed by La Guérinière's development of the "shoulders-in" in the next century, which takes the horse's suppleness to a higher level and forms the basis for most current dressage training. Riders today may conclude that Cavendish overflexed his horses' heads and necks, but his basic idea shows up in less extreme methods such as those of La Guérinière and even the nineteenth-century French innovator François Baucher, who challenged traditional styles of training with strong suppling through the horse's jaw.

9. Thomas Blundeville, *Fowre Chiefest Offices Belonging to Horsemanshippe* (London, 1566), 5.

10. Wendy Wall, "Renaissance National Husbandry: Gervase Markham and the Publication of England," *Sixteenth Century Journal* 27/3 (1996): 767–85.

11. Gerald MacLean, "Ottomanism before Orientalism? Bishop King Praises Henry Blount, Passenger in the Levant," in *Travel Knowledge: European "Discoveries" in the Early Modern Period*, ed. Ivo Kamps and Jyotsna Singh (New York: Palgrave, 2001), 85–96, p. 86.

12. Daniel Vitkus, "Trafficking with the Turk: English Travelers in the Ottoman Empire During the Early Seventeenth Century," in *Travel Knowledge*, ed. Kamps and Singh, 35–52, p. 39.
13. See e.g. Mark Girouard, *Life in the English Country House* (New Haven, CT: Yale University Press, 1978); Alastair Fowler, *The Country-House Poem: A Cabinet of Seventeenth-Century Estate Poems and Related Items* (Edinburgh: University of Edinburgh Press, 1994); Martin Kelsall, *The Great Good Place: The Country House and English Literature* (New York: Columbia University Press, 1993).
14. Kari McBride, *Country House Discourse in Early Modern England: A Cultural Study of Landscape and Legitimacy* (Burlington, VT: Ashgate, 2001), 9.

CHAPTER 9

"HONEST ENGLISH BREED": THE THOROUGHBRED AS CULTURAL METAPHOR

Richard Nash

Persistent debates in science studies between constructivist and realist accounts of knowledge claims have for some time been seeking a productive alternative to the rhetorical impasse of naive realist and radical relativist articulations.[1] Seeking to negotiate the shifting terrain between these poles, theorists have increasingly been focused on material-discursive models of agency that refuse to privilege one set of commitments over the other, but instead engage equally with both. Engaging with these models of agency, I want to focus attention on the particularly powerful and compelling trope of the Thoroughbred racehorse in early modern cultural formation, and attend to its various significations.

In asking us to reconsider what it means to be "modern," Bruno Latour returns our attention to the end of the seventeenth century to describe a process whereby the "modern" comes into being through the simultaneous and contradictory activities of what he terms "purification" and "translation." Critical to those interrelated activities is an impulse to purify the world into separable categories of Nature and Culture, and simultaneously to mobilize a set of NatureCulture hybrids, on whose denial the modern critical project depends:

> so long as we consider these two practices of translation and purification separately, we are truly modern—that is, we willingly subscribe to

the critical project, even though that project is developed only through the proliferation of hybrids down below. As soon as we direct our attention simultaneously to the work of purification and the work of hybridization, we immediately stop being wholly modern, and our future begins to change.[2]

I am arguing here that one way to read the origins of the Thoroughbred is as a NatureCulture hybrid mobilized on behalf of a particular construction of a modern—and distinctly English—cultural identity. It is important to stress that the figurative work that the Thoroughbred performs in culture does not in any way compromise the reality of the animal—precisely the opposite: because Thoroughbreds are real, living nonhumans, they function all the more powerfully for humans as metaphors.

Thoroughbreds are undeniably real, but are they natural or artificial? The answer is, of course, "both." Culturally created, they operate as "natural" living metaphors for a particular set of cultural values that they thereby reify as innate. Taking seriously the Thoroughbred racehorse as a cultural metaphor in early modern England, certain lines of interpretation suggest themselves fairly readily: the story of the Thoroughbred in terms of "a myth of orgins"; the story of "the Sport of Kings" as a narrative of the anxieties of monarchy in decline; the story of the Thoroughbred as a narrative of Orientalist appropriation. In what follows, I want to sketch the cultural work done by the interwoven readings of this very real, living trope: how the myth of blood purity derived from a foundationalist mythology mobilizes NatureCulture hybrids as natural artifacts; how the mobilization of such NatureCulture hybrids requires the institutionalization of pedigree as an inscription device that writes the Thoroughbred into culture as a technology; and, finally, how the Orientalist appropriation of Arabian bloodstock simultaneously requires and conceals an internal nationalist dynamic of core and periphery, in which a particular model of English nationalism trumps regional interests. Each of these readings is mutually implicated in the other, and together they fashion a powerful braid of early modern English identity.

The General Stud Book (*GSB*), the first volume of which published in 1791, was already a historical document, recording the ancestry of those horses currently comprising the racing stock of England at the time of its publication.[3] Eventually, the *GSB* would come to serve as a registry of blood, with "entry into the canon of the Thoroughbred" restricted to those whose ancestry could be traced to those recorded in its pages.[4] But in the more than a century prior to the publication of the first volume of the *GSB*, no such registry existed. Indeed, even when the first volume of the *GSB* was published, it nowhere included the word "Thoroughbred."[5] The earliest recorded attempt to define the term as it is currently understood was by the Yorkshire farrier William Osmer in 1761: "Let us suppose a case: here are two mares, both originally bred from Arabian horses, and mares, or the descendants of such, which I suppose is all that is to be understood by the term 'thoroughbred'."[6] The *Oxford English Dictionary* (*OED*) cites from 1825 what had become by then customary usage: "The pedigree of Eclipse affords a singular illustration of the descent of our thorough-bred horses from pure Eastern blood." In contrast to this clear-cut usage, the earlier citation in the *OED* (from John Lawrence's *Treatise on Horses*, 1796) may or may not refer to the animals identified in the 1825 usage: "Thorough-bred hacks are the most docile and quiet, and the least liable to shy." For anyone familiar with the reputation of Thoroughbred temperament, it is unlikely that they would be singled out for being "docile and quiet, and the least liable to shy." On the other hand, among those who work with Thoroughbreds (even today) it is also customary to identify problem horses within the breed as "common-bred," and to assert that "well-bred" horses tend to be "well mannered," or frequently act like "a perfect gentleman." Perhaps Lawrence's usage gestures, then, toward not a discrete breed of animal, but a metaphoric extension from human to equine society in which "blood will out" and good behavior denotes good breeding. It is, of course, precisely such metaphoric extension that comes to be definitive of an established English breed: proud, spirited, independent, and well mannered. Such a construction was over a century in the making, for by the time the word "Thoroughbred" was ready to enter both *The General Stud Book* and standard usage, the practice for which the animal was engineered had already been establishing itself as a national sport.

Two brief narratives are deeply entrenched in popular accounts of the origin of horseracing: that Charles II established horseracing on the heath at Newmarket, giving it the reputation it still enjoys today as "the Sport of Kings"; and that

> all [modern Thoroughbreds] traced their descent from three imported stallions of the late seventeenth and early eighteenth centuries, animals who were, though renowned, semi-anonymous, identified only by their English ownership and their somewhat imprecisely supposed country of origin: the Darley Arabian, the Godolphin Barb, and the Byerley Turk.[7]

There is truth in each of these narratives, but as they are mutually exclusive claims, it should come as no surprise that there are also significant difficulties with each. The simple fact is that none of the so-called foundation sires was born until after the death of Charles II, so whatever horseracing he established on Newmarket heath could not have been conducted by their progeny. In 1665, Charles II established a series of "King's Plate" races at Newmarket, to be contested over two to four heats of 4 miles each, under weights of 12 stone (168 lbs.). These races, and the individual matches that were organized to be run at the same meets, mark what is generally accepted as the beginning of the modern racing calendar:

> Charles II converted Newmarket, which had been a mere hunting lodge for the first of the Stuarts, into a genuine centre of the Turf with all the prestige that royal patronage, royal arbitration in racing disputes and the presence of the court for long periods of the year were able to confer.[8]

Undeniably, Charles—who himself rode in some of these races—did much to establish Newmarket as a center of racing, but *The General Stud Book* went further in crediting him with establishing a national breed, based on imported Oriental bloodstock. Significantly, in an appendix listing "Arabians, Barbs, and Turks" imported into England, the *GSB* listed "Royal Mares, King Charles the Second sent abroad the Master of the Horse, to procure a number of foreign horses and mares for breeding, and the mares brought over by him (as also many of their produce) have since been called Royal Mares" (303). Though this line was long accepted without question, it has not held up well under increased historical scrutiny, and it now appears more likely that the so-called Royal Mares may have been the mares salvaged by the Darcy family from the Royal Stud at Tutbury when it was dispersed after the execution of Charles I.[9]

Equine traffic between England and North Africa played a significant role during the seventeenth and early eighteenth centuries, first as a means of diplomatic exchange, and increasingly as a form of commodity exchange on the part of certain English merchant families. Lisa Jardine and Jerry Brotton note the significant equine traffic between Europe and the East, and observe that when Henry VIII founded the Royal Stud at Tutbury, the horses in the stud are likely to have included some of Eastern blood, either directly or mediated through other European imports. Moreover, their reading underlines the ways in which the commodity exchange of fine horses was incorporated into cultural representations of royal power: "We are arguing that representations of power and a vivid shared aesthetic combined in fine breeds of horses, and their circulation and appreciation were integral parts of imperial bids for recognition."[10] The practices by which seventeenth- and eighteenth-century horse owners named their animals are not everything a historian might wish (some had no names, some had several, and many names were given to multiple animals); attempting to trace equine traffic in this period is a daunting and dizzying task. But a few highly visible importations are reasonably well established and attest to both the significance and relative scarcity of such transactions. The *GSB* records that

> King James the first bought an Arabian of Mr. Markham, a merchant, for 500gs, said (but with little probability) to have been the first of that breed ever seen in England. The Duke of Newcastle says, in his Treatise on Horsemanship, that he had seen the above Arabian, and describes him as a small Bay Horse, and not of very excellent shape (303).

In fact, Newcastle goes further and records of the Arabian that "being Trained up for a course, when he came to Run, every Horse beat him." Since Newcastle had traveled throughout Europe, and was rather obsessive in his interests in horsemanship, it may be significant that he writes, "I never saw any but one of These Horses."[11] Most likely, he is referring to what he elsewhere terms "Right Arabians," by which he probably meant an Arabian from Aleppo. The exportation of these was strictly prohibited, and if Markham acquired one, it may have been smuggled out.

In 1637, the Archbishop of Canterbury wrote to Lord Deputy Wentworth, "The greatest news is of the Morocco Ambassador, whose present to his majesty [Charles I] of Barbary horses and saddles of great value attracted much attention."[12] In all likelihood, one of the horses included in that gift was the horse that would ultimately come to be known as Old Morocco, the earliest of the influential progenitors of the breed. The gift was clearly much appreciated. For the first time in history, an English monarch mobilized the English navy in support of an African ally: " 'English gunners' were sent to the old town [Salee] and 'did fearful execution among the crowded defenders of New Sallee, battering the walls beyond repair.' By so doing the gunners help reduce 'Sally to the obedience of the [Moroccan] Emperor.' "[13] Charles, of course, received no corresponding military assistance when confronting his own rebellion a dozen years later. During the ensuing Interregnum, in 1657, Cromwell requested from Turkey's Sultan Mohammed IV a diplomatic gift of an Arabian from Aleppo. He apparently did not realize that Turkish law prohibited

even sultans from such export. Instead, Mohammed sent what was a
not uncommon substitute: a Turcoman–Arabian stallion whose pedigree had one or more Arabian crosses. This stallion is almost certainly
the horse known as Place's White Turk, an animal that (if Alexander
Mackay-Smith is correct) was far more influential than most historical accounts have noted.[14] At the time that Cromwell made the
request, several Turkish merchants who had been captured by
Catholic Spain were petitioning Cromwell for his help in arranging
their safe passage home.[15] Thus, the origin of the Sport of Kings is
implicated in the diplomatic negotiations between England and the
East in the seventeenth century.

Only three Arabian stallions are known to have been successfully
imported from Aleppo. Of these, two—the Oxford Dun Arabian
(1715) and the Oxford Bloody-Shouldered Arabian (1719)—were
imported for the first and second Lords Oxford by the first Lord's
nephew, Nathaniel Harley, a merchant in Turkey. The connection to
the first Lord Oxford, who had been Secretary of the Treasury during the last four years of the reign of Queen Anne, suggests that at
this point the traffic in fine horses was still closely linked to diplomacy
and access beyond the ordinary reach of most individuals. But
Nathaniel Harley's location on the scene as a merchant was obviously
also important, and underlines the fact that mercantile diplomacy was
moving in tandem with state diplomacy. The third Arabian stallion
imported directly from Aleppo was the Darley Arabian (1704)—one
of the three so-called foundation sires, and the one from whom
almost 95 percent of today's Thoroughbreds claim direct patrilineal
(i.e., "tail-male") descent. Thomas Darley acquired the horse on
behalf of his father: "Since my father expects I should send him a stallion, I esteem myself happy in a colt I bought about a year and a half
agoe, with a desygne indeed to send him the first good opportunity."[16] Like most origin stories, the origin of the Thoroughbred is a
tale considerably more complicated than the fable of tripled paternity
most often told. Not only is it a tale implicated in the traffic between
kings, emperors, and sultans of East and West, but it is also inflected
by the emerging traffic between the families of royals, aristocrats, and
merchants as well.

In this context, it is worth noting that the tale of tripled paternity
that emerges during the eighteenth century, and then becomes institutionalized in the pages of the *GSB*, is itself a narrative that blends
anxieties and fantasies of monarchical succession, emergent bourgeois
mercantilism, and Oriental romance. The process by which that tale
becomes institutionalized may itself be instructive. The Jockey Club

was founded at Newmarket in 1752. Eighteen years later, James Weatherby succeeded William Tuting as Keeper of the Match Book; and shortly after that, he added to his duties those previously carried out by Thomas Fawconer as Secretary to the Club. In 1727, well before the founding of the Jockey Club, John Cheney had begun publishing the first *Racing Calendar*. That project had been continued, first by Reginald Heber and William Pond, and then, after the establishment of the Jockey Club, by Fawconer and Tuting. Weatherby took on this project, and it has been carried on by his descendants ever since; although the *Calendar* was purchased from the Weatherby family by the Jockey Club during the last century, Weatherby's continues to publish *The General Stud Book* for the British Horseracing Board. It is unclear whether the idea of *The General Stud Book* originated with the first James Weatherby or with his nephew (also named James) who succeeded him. In either case, the original idea of the *GSB* was descriptive, rather than prescriptive. Drawing on the archival resources of the Jockey Club's library of racing calendars, and supplementing those resources with the cooperation of major Thoroughbred breeders who granted Weatherby access to their private stud books, Weatherby set out to record the breeding history of the animal then racing in England. His method was to list mares in alphabetical order, provide as thorough a pedigree as possible of each mare, and then record in as much detail as possible the produce history of each mare. While the given pedigrees reach back into the seventeenth century, the earliest produce recorded from the 387 mares in the first volume were three fillies out of "Chestnut Thornton, Bred by Mr. Crofts, got by Makeless, out of Old Thornton, by Brimmer–Dicky Pierson–Burton Barb Mare" (145). These fillies were: "[no date given] f[illy] by Commoner; [no date given] ch[estnut] f[illy] Lusty Thornton by Crofts' Bay Barb; 1714 f[illy] Desdemona, by Greyhound" (145). The first two were bred by Mr. Crofts; the last was bred by the Duke of Wharton. The date for Desdemona tells us that the first filly by Commoner must have been foaled no later than 1712.[17]

The original project of a national stud book was manifestly not to document the paternal influence of a particular group of stallions; indeed, for good and logical reasons, that project was properly gynocentric. The resulting stud book is in fact an impressive document of maternity, more than paternity, with page after page of dams listed in large font, centered, and their offspring cataloged beneath them. Weatherby clearly had some criteria for exclusion in mind, for he does not list the dam's produce for every year. Some of these omissions may be due to barren years (though he often remarks such years), or perhaps simply to gaps in the records, but in some instances he specifies "those omitted here were by half-bred stallions." Indeed, however much Weatherby's stud book has come to be thought of as a record of paternity, its original focus on maternity may have had as much to do with beliefs about breeding as with logistical convenience. Writing in 1758, Richard Wall takes issue with what he identifies as the practice of the day:

> Most I have conversed with on the breeding subject seem quite positive that the offspring partakes more in general of the dam, than of the sire; and many arguments they use to support their assertion, of which the following seems most plausible. "Is not, they say, the offspring bred in the womb of the female? And during the time she is with young, is not the foetus nourished entirely by her? As also for the most part after it comes into the world? Therefore by partaking all this time of her nature and properties, it cannot possibly be otherwise."[18]

Wall, it should be noted, finds this doctrine absurd; but we would do well to remember that he is clearly arguing against a widely held view ("Most I have conversed with . . ."). The gendering of the story of origins of the Thoroughbred points to two ways in which Thoroughbreds constituted a particular embodied metaphor for the eighteenth century: on the one hand, they were a site for contesting anxieties about maternal influence; while at the same time, they became a site for reasserting in the face of anxiety patrilineal doctrines of influence and heritability.

If Weatherby was attempting the monumental task of recording the ancestry of all horses racing in England, it is hardly surprising that his work must have fallen short of documenting the entire history of the racehorse, dating back even the little more than a hundred years to when Charles instituted the King's Plates in 1665. Even before Weatherby's first volume was published, however, the myth of tripled paternity was already gathering momentum. In addition to the 387 mares recorded in the *GSB*, Weatherby included an appendix listing 22 imported Arabian, Turk, and Barb stallions. Noticeably, for instance, in the pedigree for that earliest anonymous filly by Commoner out of Chestnut Thornton, none of the so-called foundation sires appears. While Weatherby's book recorded, however incompletely, the diverse origins of the Thoroughbred, it also provided the documentary basis for another kind of analysis. If one read back patrilineally (following the inheritance model of royal succession rather than a model of genetic inheritance), from son to "sire" to "grandsire," and so on, then every horse racing at the end of the eighteenth century could be traced back in this fashion to a small set of foundation sires. This group may have been as large as half a dozen when Weatherby began his project, but soon after the publication of the first volume, it had narrowed to three. And even if it is only a fortuitous turning of history, it seems significant how these three are identified. The earliest, the Byerley Turk, is said to have been taken by Captain Byerley at the siege at Buda, and brought back to England, where he served the captain as a war charger in the Battle of the Boyne.[19] The importation of the Darley Arabian from a merchant in Aleppo was discussed above. The last of the foundation stallions, the Godolphin Arabian or Godolphin Barb, was imported at an unspecified date in the mid- to late 1720s, and was the sire of foals of 1730. He was originally owned in England by the younger brother of the wealthy gentleman Thomas Coke of Norfolk, and on the death of his owner passed to Lord Godolphin.

Two equally romantic (and equally impossible) tales rapidly grew up around this last foundation stallion, and were being recorded by the 1760s. The first tells of his arrival in England; the second of his assertion of dominance as a sire. According to the former tale, the Godolphin was a pure Arabian from Yemen, who was presented as a gift from the Bey of Tunis to the French king. On a visit to Paris Coke saw the horse in the streets of Paris pulling a cart, and at once recognizing his superior form, purchased him on the spot and brought him to England. The second tale maintains that the stallion was employed as a teaser by Lord Godolphin for his Lordship's principal stallion, Hobgoblin.[20] When he was led out to the mare Roxana (recently retired from an extraordinary racing career), he took fire, broke free of his handlers, engaged Hobgoblin in combat, and after driving off his rival, claimed the breeding of Roxana as his rightful prize. From that time forward, according to the tale, he was Lord Godolphin's principal stallion. If such a fanciful tale required rebuttal, it would be easy to supply—Hobgoblin was still racing, and had not entered the stud when the Godolphin Barb was bred to Roxana. The former narrative cannot be refuted quite so conclusively, as we do not know the details of this horse's acquisition, but the story works against itself: if it is remarkable that Coke should recognize such talent in a common carthorse on the streets of Paris, it is no less remarkable that a gift from one head of state to another, of such a valued commodity as horseflesh was, should find itself in the position of the carthorse to begin with.

Taken together, what emerges from these little tales is a mixture of fantasy and anxiety about potency, national identity, and the transgression of class boundaries. The keen eye of the English horseman, Coke, discerns what the French cannot find. The humble carthorse is revealed as "this extraordinary foreign horse" (by the end of the eighteenth century, he was considered the single most significant influence on the breed). If the former story privileges English expertise in recognizing intrinsic merit hidden by class difference, the latter story must undo that narrative to retell it. The remarkable stallion brought to England is again cast in the role of the servant, and this time he must rise up in his own rebellion to claim the prize of love and war. Is it only accident that the object of his desire and motive of his revolt is "Roxana," the stock name given in eighteenth-century England to courtesans in the Turkish seraglio?[21]

Marvelously, these circulating narratives undo themselves. Do they tell the story of usurpation or of a rightful claim to a denied birthright? Are they stories of upward mobility or of natural aristocracy? Do they claim the feminized Orient as conquest or do they drive off the English interloper to assert the Arabian/Barb's rightful claim to an English female only masquerading behind an eroticized Oriental guise? Although the Godolphin Barb emerges most dramatically as the most influential and "prepotent" of the foundation stallions according to eighteenth-century accounts, the narratives surrounding him pose fundamentally indeterminate questions.[22] And those questions, in turn, emphasize the mixture of fantasy and anxiety underwriting the entirety of the tripled paternity narrative. On the one hand, that narrative asserts an unbroken line of patrilineal succession ensuring pure descent. In doing so, it echoes the royalist position articulated after the Interregnum. But as Charles II's long reign gave way to that of James II, the embarrassing usurpation/abdication mess that led to William and Mary, and Anne and Protestant succession versus Jacobite loyalties, and so on, the negotiations over patrilineal succession grow more complicated. When you come right down to it, how reassuring a dynastic narrative can a myth of tripled paternity provide? And consider the metonymic identification of these three progenitors: we are no longer speaking of kings, emperors, and sultans. Instead, we are speaking of captains, merchants, and wealthy gentlemen who will their property to aristocrats: we are, in fact, speaking of upwardly mobile younger siblings, and of alternatives to patrilineal advancement.

One of the early observers of the swirling traffic of class associations attending early horseracing was Daniel Defoe. In his *Tour of the*

Whole Island of Great Britain, Defoe visits all of the major—and several of the minor—sites of horseracing, and he invariably visits those locations when the horses are running.[23] His description of Newmarket blends fascination and horror at the public transgression of class boundaries:

> Being come to Newmarket in the month of October, I had the opportunity to see the horse-races; and a great concourse of the nobility and gentry as well from London as from all parts of England; but they were all so intent, so eager, so busy upon the sharping part of the sport, their wagers and bets, that to me they seem'd just as so many horse-coursers in Smithfield, descending (the greatest of them) from their high dignity and quality, to picking one another's pockets, and biting one another as much as possible, and that with such eagerness, as that it might be said they acted without respect to faith, honor, or good manners (75).

When Defoe goes on to describe the king's trainer, Tregonwell Frampton ("the oldest, and as some say, the cunningest jockey in England"), as winning a thousand guineas one day and losing two thousand the next with equal unconcern, we may imagine that Defoe affects a detachment he did not fully enjoy. Given how prone Defoe was to speculative investment, suffering the frequent financial reverses and bankruptcies for which he is noted, it is hard to imagine that he was not as fascinated as repelled. Repeatedly, however, in his descriptions of race meets, it is the social traffic, the transgressive spirit of carnival and masquerade that draws his eye, just as it drew the eye of the artists John Wootton and Peter Tillemans. If he feigns disgust at seeing the nobility descend to the level of the "horse-coursers in Smithfield," he remains fascinated by their proximity, and the elegance of the assembly is as inviting as the sport itself:

> but, as I say, to leave as little behind me as possible, I was obliged to make a little excursion into the forest, where, in my way, I had the diversion of seeing the annual meeting of the gentry at the horse-races near Nottingham. I could give a long and agreeable account of the sport it self, how it brought into my thoughts the Olympick Games among the Greeks; and the Circus Maximus at Rome [Defoe here seems to forget that precisely these same thoughts occurred to him in vol. i when attending the meet at Newmarket]; where the racers made a great noise, and the victors made great boasts and triumphs: But where they chiefly drove in chariots, not much unlike our chaises, and where nothing of the speed, or of the skill in horsemanship could be shown, as in our races. It is true, in those races the young Roman and Grecian gentlemen rod, or rather drove themselves; whereas in our races the horses, not the

riders, make the show; and they are generally ridden by grooms and boys, chiefly for lightness; sometimes indeed the gentlemen ride themselves, as I have often seen the Duke of Monmouth, natural son to King Charles II ride his own horses at a match, and win it too, though he was a large man, and must weigh heavy. But the illustrious company at Nottingham races was, in my opinion, the glory of the day; for there we saw, besides eleven or twelve noblemen, an infinite throng of gentlemen from all countries round, nay, even out of Scotland it self; the appearance, in my opinion, greater, as it was really more numerous, than ever I saw at Newmarket, except when the king has been there in ceremony; for I cannot but say, that in King Charles II's time, when his majesty used to be frequently at Newmarket, I have known the assembly there have been with far less company than this at Nottingham; and if I might go back to one of these Nottingham meetings, when the Mareschal Duke de Tallard was there, I should say, that no occasions at Newmarket, in my memory, ever came up to it, except the first time that King William was there after the Peace of Ryswick.   (ii. 148)

Defoe's fascination with horseracing as a site of social spectacle of "illustrious company . . . the glory of the day" draws our attention to the circulation between the individually named royals, the precisely enumerated but anonymous "eleven or twelve noblemen," and the undifferentiated mob of "an infinite throng of gentlemen." His description underlines how the social space of horseracing staged the same mix of fantasy and anxiety that structured the breeding practices constructing the breed itself. And Defoe's description also draws our attention to another tension that until now I have been letting pass unremarked. Defoe's description of the Nottingham races explicitly repeats some of the very tropes he had earlier deployed in describing Newmarket (i.e., the Classical reflection, the "concourse of nobility and gentry," and so forth). But he also goes beyond this to compare explicitly the two locations to the advantage of the northern site. Indeed, on more than one occasion, Defoe goes out of his way to sound the praises of northern horses, horsemen, and horsemanship. Such a preference seems at odds with three of the most widely circulated "foundational" claims of the origins of the Thoroughbred: that Charles II established a center for racing at Newmarket; that the Jockey Club has presided continuously over the sport; and that all Thoroughbreds derive from three imported Oriental stallions. But these foundational claims all speak to a process of appropriation ongoing throughout the eighteenth century:

During the second half of the seventeenth century, the Thoroughbred was a small regional, North Yorkshire breed with a narrow foundation of Hobby and Running-Horse strain bloodlines. By moving the center of racing from York to Newmarket following his Restoration in 1660, Charles II inadvertently but fortuitously contributed to enlarging the geographic marketplace for the young Thoroughbred breed.[24]

Reading that relocation as a process of national appropriation of a regional sport enables us to more fully come to terms with how the Thoroughbred functions as cultural metaphor.

Both the Byerley Turk and the Darley Arabian were imported to small breeding farms in Yorkshire, where they serviced a small band of local mares, seldom being bred outside their own stud, and then usually only in the immediate neighborhood. Indeed, the overwhelming majority of racing stock at this time resided within about a 15-mile radius in the north, and most of the imported bloodstock was imported to one of several northern studs, such as Helmsley, Sedbury, Constable Burton, and Marske. When the Godolphin Barb entered Lord Godolphin's stud at Goggmagog in Cambridgeshire, it marked a significant departure from the long-established practice that identified the best horses, horsemen, and horse breeding with Yorkshire. It was, however, in keeping with the growing importance of Newmarket as the site of national sport—and the identification of horseracing with Newmarket was carried out as the triumph of a contest with an older regional sport in the north. Histories of English horseracing typically identify Flying Childers, a son of the Darley Arabian, as the first "great" English racehorse; he raced only in 1721–22, and only at Newmarket, where he defeated the best horses of his day. When the Jockey Club was founded at Newmarket in 1752, it was another step in relocating horseracing from the periphery of the northern counties to the heart of the nation. In his *A Dissertation on Breeding of Horses* (1758), Richard Wall speaks to the relocation of horse breeding from north to south:

Don't imagine, sir, that I am about to revive an old and absurd opinion—that horses could not be bred and reared properly any where in England but in the North; far from it. . . . [I]n process of time, when racing became much in vogue, and when few or no racers were bred but in the North, the price of a tolerable racer became very high:—the gentlemen of the South being then pretty much tired with the great and exorbitant prices asked for every thing of the high-bred kind, determined to set about breeding racers themselves, so that it was then soon brought to a proof, that by contesting the affair upon Newmarket-heath, it was plainly discovered, that horses might be bred to as much perfection in the South of England, as in the North!   (87–88).

William Osmer, who disagrees with Wall on many points, joins with him in identifying the Godolphin Arabian as the most influential single contributor to the breed.[25] By the time the *GSB* appears near the end of the century, the eclipse of northern racing has been effected, and when the phrase "in the north" appears in a description, it carries the connotation that the horse was performing at a lesser level.

One aspect of this relocation is that during the very first decades of the eighteenth century, a nationalist racing scene (centered at Newmarket), in some ways competing with an already established regional racing scene (centered at York), is associated with the fresh importation of Eastern bloodstock. Defoe is again helpful on this topic, clarifying the terms of opposition as they were understood in the 1720s. When he visits Bedale in Yorkshire those horses who, he had earlier noted, "make the show," are manifestly English and not to be confused with any Oriental ancestors. Edward Said's central thesis that in the Orient, Europe found "one of its deepest and most recurring images of the Other"[26] can be illustrated by the moment when Defoe steps forward from his many visits to race meets and deals directly with an assessment of the horses he observes. At Bedale, he offers his summary judgment, one that anticipates the essential paradox of the Jockey Club in the nineteenth century:

> They do indeed breed very fine horses here, and perhaps some of the best in the world, for let foreigners boast what they will of barbs and Turkish horses, and, as we know five hundred pounds has been given for a horse brought out of Turkey, and of the Spanish jennets from Cordova, for which also an extravagant price has been given, I do believe that some of the gallopers of this country, and of the bishoprick of Durham, which joins to it, will outdo for speed and strength the swiftest horse that was ever bred in Turkey, or Barbary, take them all together.
>
> My reason for this opinion is founded upon those words altogether; that is to say, take their strength and their speed together; for example; match the two horses, and bring them to the race post, the barb may beat Yorkshire for a mile course, but Yorkshire shall distance him at the end of four miles; the barb shall beat Yorkshire upon a dry, soft carpet ground, but Yorkshire for a deep country; the reason is plain, the English horses have both the speed and the strength; the barb perhaps shall beat Yorkshire, and carry seven stone and a half; but Yorkshire for a twelve to fourteen stone weight; in a word, Yorkshire shall carry the man, and the barb a feather.
>
> The reason is to be seen in the very make of the horses. The barb, or the jennet, is a fine delicate creature, of a beautiful shape, clean limbs, and a soft coat; but then he is long jointed, weak pasterned, and under

limb'd; whereas Yorkshire has as light a body, and stronger limbs, short joints, and well bon'd. This gives him not speed only, but strength to hold it; and, I believe, I do not boast in their behalf, without good vouchers, when I say, that English horses, take them one with another, will beat all the world.   (ii. 220–21)

Defoe here confronts, for the only time in the *Tour*, a central paradox of the Thoroughbred that continues to be bandied about among breeders today. If his answer is less than fully compelling, it is not notably weaker than any of the alternatives that have followed it. The view that came to dominance in the nineteenth and early twentieth centuries is that the English Thoroughbred paradoxically became the only remaining "pure Arabian" strain. Such a story neatly serves the interests of imperial England, allowing the complete colonization of a breed. Even today, arguably the most influential history of the breed is that written by Lady Wentworth in 1938. In brazenly unapologetic terms Lady Wentworth puts forward the case for "purity of blood," and her text is always as interested in the application to British aristocracy as to Arabian bloodstock, at times in quite colorful ways: "the result of all this is that somebody's pet charger with about as much claim to blue blood as a rat-catcher's dog is imported to England and promoted to the unwarrantable position of a stud horse . . . the Thoroughbred is, as I have said, our finest example of what can be done in England with Oriental blood."[27] Sir Theodore Cook, in his foreword to Lady Wentworth's text, locates her argument about Thoroughbred blood in the context of aristocratic anxiety on the brink of the Second World War:

> To plead for a fundamental aristocracy of blood in anything nowadays is unpopular with the optimists who think that climate and environment can miraculously change black to white, and even more so with the alchemists who imagine that gold can be created from dross that contains nothing but base metal. Yet, to serious breeders, the fact of blood inheritance is a recognized and incontrovertible fact from which there is no escape. "An ounce of blood is worth a pound of bone."   (15)

If, as Wentworth argues in the highest strain of pure-blood argument, Arabian blood, improved by English climate and cultivation, and kept pure from the introduction of impurities from external sources by a vigilant protection of the pedigree register, is the source of the Thoroughbred's manifest superiority, two questions logically arise: first, how can what has come to be identified as "purely English" simultaneously claim to be "purely Arabian" in origin; and second, would a reintroduction of Arabian blood invigorate the breed? Answering the first question is the major undertaking of Lady Wentworth's project, but it is an undertaking that is, in some respects, called into question by the answers available to the second— a question that Lady Wentworth believes is best not asked. She sidesteps the second question by contending that two simultaneous historical changes have rendered such a trial both unnecessary and ill advised. The superiority of English cultivation has been improving the pure Arab strains imported in the seventeenth and eighteenth centuries, at the same time that promiscuous and degenerate breeding practices in Arab countries have allowed that animal to degenerate for racing purposes. She needs some such story, for the simple fact is that on several occasions—in the early nineteenth century, in the late nineteenth century, and near the end of the twentieth century— proposals have been advanced to reintroduce racing Arabian bloodlines. Each time, the proposal has fallen apart because it has been impossible to locate a racing Arabian that can, even while receiving significant weight concessions, compete even with an ordinary Thoroughbred at any distance over a quarter of a mile. How can one reconcile such vast disparity with claims to pure ancestry?[28]

Curiously, Defoe's praise of "Yorkshire" assigns superiority to English stock in precisely that area—strength and endurance (or stoutness)—in which current breeding practice concedes the superior abilities of the Arabian. Ultimately, however, although attempting to sort out the differences between Defoe and Lady Wentworth might lead us to different ideas about what a Thoroughbred is, it would not shed much light on how the Thoroughbred embodies a particular Orientalist encounter of the eighteenth century. In this respect, what Defoe and Lady Wentworth share is a commitment to establishing English identity via Orientalist discourse, in which the encounter of East and West authorizes a contest from which only one identity can emerge as the emblem of purity and superiority. Notably, Defoe's version of this contest not only champions imperial identity ("English horses . . . will beat all the world"), but does so by privileging a specifically sited North Briton identity: "Yorkshire shall carry the man, and the barb a feather." This is, I believe, no accident; throughout the *Tour*, Defoe's preferences in horseracing tilt to the North.

Increasingly, scholars of eighteen-century history have been drawn to considerations of how nationalist and imperialist impulses characterize English discourse in the decades immediately following the Act of Union: "Is Britain a nation? Or is it merely a state composed of the four nations of Wales, England, Scotland, and Ireland? To what extent does it make sense to group the three non-English nations as a 'Celtic periphery' of England?"[29] This last-mentioned alternative is the one popularized by Michael Hechter in *Internal Colonialism*, in which he puts forward, as an alternative to assimilationist theories, a reading of ethnic change that discerns an internal dynamic of core and periphery that reproduces the dynamic of colonial relations.[30] Such a model offers a particularly attractive lens through which to view the historical process by which the Thoroughbred as we know it today can be said to have been invented in the eighteenth century. That is, the question of the origins of the Thoroughbred can be seen as not only a question about Orientalist encounters between East and West, but also a question of internal dissension between South and North. Defoe's northern loyalties, it turns out, are far from isolated. Indeed, by the eighteenth century, Yorkshire was already well established as a breeding center for horses. Defoe writes:

> even all this country is full of jockeys, that is to say, dealers in horses, and breeders of horses. . . . As this part of the country is so much employed in horses, the young fellows are naturally grooms, bred up in the stable, and used to lie among the horses; so that you cannot fail of a good servant here, for looking after horses is their particular delight; and this is the reason why, whatever part of England you go to, though the farthest counties west and south, and whatever inn you come at, 'tis two to one but the hostler is a Yorkshire man.   (ii. 221–22)[31]

A eugenic rhetoric of "improving the breed" has long marked the discourse of Thoroughbred breeding, and its influence continues today. Typically, such doctrines today at least gesture toward notions of evolution and genetics derived from nineteenth-century sources in Darwin and Mendel; but in fact, the rhetoric—and often the practice—is much older and reaches back into the seventeenth and eighteenth centuries to pre-genetic theories of agriculture. For the eighteenth century, the art and science of agriculture was predicated on the notion that the job of man was to improve nature—and to do so by cultivating it. Such a notion, underlying the development of the Thoroughbred, presupposed an ambivalent set of responses to nature and culture. On the one hand, nature was associated with primitive purity, while culture was the location of decadent corruption; at the same time, civilization had the power to cultivate the untapped potential of nature, harnessing to productive ends its otherwise unfocused force. The first set of associations justified a theory of "hybrid vigor" that maintained that breeding "cold" English mares to "hot" imported stallions would improve a breed that had entered decline. This theory, dominant in the seventeenth century, located the virtue of such crosses in the primitive heat of the imported stallion. Moreover, the beneficial effects of such breeding practice were thought to extend only to the next generation, and a newly imported stallion would then be necessary to perpetuate the beneficial influence. It is virtually impossible to ignore the metaphoric applications of such fantasy, and it may be worth noting that this particular form of Orientalism is quite the reverse of what Said noticed in nineteenth-century Orientalism. Instead of gendering a power relationship in which the Oriental is rendered an effeminate Other by the Western Orientalist, the fantasy here is one of hypermasculinity. But the second half of that ambivalent response to nature checks the first. Wild nature requires the management of cultivation. In this framework, cool reason should check and regulate the heat of barbaric passion. It is, of course, this second half that gains ascendancy during the eighteenth century, with respect both to agricultural theories of improvement and to English attitudes toward the East.

The process by which the origins of the Thoroughbred are imagined and then institutionalized during the eighteenth century, even as the breed is being defined, corresponds not only to Orientalist fantasies and anxieties of empire, but also to internal tensions as well. For something like the traffic between East and West can be read in the shifting fortunes of Yorkshire and Newmarket, as well. The ascendancy of Newmarket as the heart of a national sport is brought about at the expense of the original regional sport; racing "in the North" gets marginalized over the course of the eighteenth century. Not surprisingly, the most influential names in the rise of a national racing scene at Newmarket are also the names of an ascendant Whig establishment (Wharton, Godolphin, Newcastle, and so forth); at the same time, the polished urbanity of the successful Whigs is repeatedly contrasted with the caricature of the backwards northern Tory squire, obsessed with his rural sports. In this narrative, the barbaric northern Tory squire, who bred the early racers, becomes the marginalized Other; those rustic origins are disowned in a manner precisely analogous to the impossible double logic of appropriation and purity that is deployed with the Orient: that the Thoroughbred is at once pure English and pure Arabian.

In 1708, William Plaxton, the son of an Anglican clergyman, published "The Yorkshire Racers," a 321-line satire on the recently concluded parliamentary elections.[32] Those elections had been influenced (particularly in Yorkshire) by fears of a Jacobite rebellion, prompted by a recently averted invasion, and by repeated attempts to repeal the Test Act. In Yorkshire, the Whigs associated with the Junto, centered around Lord Wharton, had capitalized on Jacobite fears, while the Tories had rallied support with vigorous appeals to protect the Church of England. A growing division within the Whig party between the court-centered politics of the Junto and a coalition of non-Junto Whigs (whose support in Yorkshire centered around the Duke of Newcastle) created the environment for a tightly contested election, in which much ballot-splitting resulted in considerable power sharing between Whigs and Tories. Although Whigs won a majority of the county elections, their gains were less than could have been expected, and in the five-way parliamentary election itself, one of two seats went to the Junto's candidate, Sir William Strickland, and the other went to the Tory, Viscount Downe, who was the leading vote-getter by a large margin. One recent study of the Whig fortunes in this election concludes that the fact that the Jacobite invasion "did not strengthen their hands in the shire, with the Tory candidates showing no signs of unity, indicates how poor Whig possibilities were in the county. . . . The county electorate did not perceive the Tories as a group of rabid Jacobites. It was they rather than the Whigs who should have felt more content with the result in 1708."[33] This sentiment is corroborated in the opening of the Tory Plaxton's poem:

> Fret not, dear Tom,[34] that thou hast lost the Race,
> You shew'd good Skill, and rid it with a Grace.
> But some must lose; and since it was your Fate,
> Envy not those, whose Luck has won the Plate:
> Your friends and ours their utmost skill did shew;
> And as you jockey'd us, we jockey'd you.   (1–6)

The ensuing poem takes great pleasure in offering a sustained description of the recently concluded election around the now-familiar metaphor that equates a political election with a horserace. Perhaps this metaphor could be traced back to classical antiquity, but it is appealing to consider this an early instance of the metaphoric equating of modern politics and modern horseracing. For the two can be thought of as products of the same cultural moment. When Plaxton wrote his poem, that story of the comic Tory squire obsessed with rural sport was still new; and (perhaps because he was a northern Tory) Plaxton does not see it. Plaxton's poem quite wittily identifies individual politicians with distinctive equine traits, while demonstrating a close familiarity on Plaxton's part with very specific traits of racehorses. More pertinent to this discussion, however, it also draws out several sets of corresponding associations. Whigs, especially those associated with radical dissent, are associated with unsoundness of either limb or wind, with Newmarket, and quite often with imported Oriental origins. Thus, for instance, Conyers Darcy, Lord Holdernesse, a Whig seeking his first election is figured under the name Aulus:

> Aulus came next, a right New-Market Crimp,
> He runs off fast, but has a plaguy Limp;
> A Hinch in's Gate, (as in the North we cry)
> Sometimes he stumbles, oft he treads awry.   (29–32)

William Palmes, a Whig elected from Malton, is derided in similar terms: "All patch'd and paultry, a New-Market Cheat, / Batter'd and Founder'd both in Head and Feet" (184–85). William Lowther is denounced for his Oriental origins: "The tawny Osman, sprung from Turkish sire, / A beast unruly, full of Flame and Fire" (68–69). Similar instances can be found throughout the poem. Perhaps even more telling are the associations surrounding the Tories: they are sound of both limb and wind, responsive, and, above all, "true." This word appears repeatedly, so that the poet tells us Lord Downe "runs true to th' last" (14) and "none can a truer English Horse bestride" (16). In describing Sir Arthur Kaye, narrowly defeated in his first bid for parliament and the son of a longtime Tory M.P., Plaxton repeats himself in all imaginable variations: "Caius . . . prov'd a true-bred Horse. . . . [He] runs true to th' last. . . . His sire was staunch, of honest English breed, / Sure then the colt will have both Truth and Speed" (44, 51, 53–54).

The association of Yorkshire with the "honest English breed" in opposition to the imported cheats from Newmarket anticipates the contrast that Defoe will draw between Yorkshire and the Barb. But, of course, they run directly counter to the myth of origins that will be constructed by the ensuing generations of English horsemen. What may be particularly telling here is the description of Caius as "a true-bred Horse."[35] For certainly, this is an anticipation of the locution "Thoroughbred." Indeed, it is not only a cognate term, but one that is directly linked to the model of patrilineal inheritance that will be the model of "prepotency" used to legitimate the Thoroughbred's claim to special status. The term "prepotency" arises in the eighteenth century to describe a sire's extraordinary influence over a dam in influencing offspring: Thoroughbreds are said to be prepotent over other breeds in that when you breed a Thoroughbred to another breed, the offspring will more resemble the Thoroughbred than the other breed. The term is (and was) also used to distinguish particular individuals; the mythic status of the Godolphin Arabian arises from his reputation for prepotency. One thing, then, that Plaxton's poem reveals to us is the degree to which the familiar myth of the origins of the Thoroughbred appropriates for a different agenda a set of doctrines already in play for an already existing set of regional racers. At the time that Plaxton wrote, the Godolphin Arabian was not yet born, none of the Darley Arabian's offspring was yet of racing age, and the Byerley Turk was still just one little-known sire among many in Yorkshire.

If Defoe is a partisan of the north in the internal dispute sketched a generation later by Wall, we would do well to remind ourselves of the considerable degree of "Whig history" that has shaped the history of the Thoroughbred. Among those narrative strands as "foundational" as the three famous Oriental stallions are the following doctrines: that racing became "the Sport of Kings" under the patronage of Charles II; that Newmarket has been the center of racing since its inception; that the origins of racing can be marked by the establishment of the Jockey Club in 1752; and that soon afterwards, the creation of *The General Stud Book* brought order and gave shape to what has been ever since a clearly defined breed of animal, as well as an industry. None of these statements is false, strictly speaking; but each is open to challenge, as surely as the claim that all Thoroughbreds trace back to one of three sires. While racing certainly flourished and expanded under the patronage of Charles, a thriving sport of racing English hobbies dates from at least the early seventeenth century, and arguably the Oriental stallion with the greatest genetic influence on the Thoroughbred was a horse imported by Oliver Cromwell.[36] Certainly, however, the sport (in its beginnings) was centered in the northern counties. The development of Newmarket at the end of the seventeenth century, first under Charles and then under William, as a southern hub for horseracing, created the opportunity for what had been a rural pastime on the periphery to be claimed as a national sport by those Whig aristocrats who did so much between the reigns of William, Anne, and George for the development not only of horseracing but of a particular brand of Whiggish nationalism. The formation of the Jockey Club in the mid-eighteenth century (a Club founded by these same influential national figures) and the subsequent creation of a national registry by Weatherby under its patronage can be read from this perspective as an appropriating move, in which the assertion of

Oriental influence actually serves to legitimate the claims of what Hechter would term the "core" over the "periphery." Such a reading helps chart the process by which "Arabian" gets appropriated by "English" in opposition to "Yorkshire."

There is a final irony to such a reading of the cultural origins of the Thoroughbred. If we think of Thoroughbreds as NatureCulture hybrids mobilized in the service of cultural formation, it may be useful to think of them in terms of what Actor Network Theory describes as "inscription devices." This phrase is used by students of technology to describe not the engineering design of an instrument but the mechanism by which that technology is inscribed within culture: "all the types of transformations through which an entity becomes materialized into a sign, an archive, a document, a piece of paper, a trace."[37] For the Thoroughbred, this is *The General Stud Book*. It is when the individualized private records of breeding activity are assembled, purged, and inscribed that the Thoroughbred becomes a registered breed. And that particular cultural inscription, with the process of which this chapter has been concerned, is itself predicated on a particular importation from the East. It is not, however, any one stallion or group of stallions or even band of broodmares whose importation is decisive. Rather it is the inscription technology for writing horses into culture—the notion of a pedigree—that is the defining feature that the English appropriate from the Orient. When Thomas Darley wrote home in 1703 that he had acquired a stallion for his father's stud, the merchant made a point of alluding to the recently acquired colt's pedigree: "He is about 15 hands high, of the most esteemed race among the Arabs, both by Syre and Dam, and the name of the said race is called Mannicka."[38] Whereas Lord Godolphin's stallion comes via the streets of Paris from God knows where originally, the Yorkshire merchant makes a shrewd deal for the very best pedigree available. Indeed, it may well be that whatever genetic influence native English racing hobbies once had—and may continue to exert—has been overshadowed by the most profound importation from the Orient—not "blood," but its recording.

The pedigrees of Thoroughbreds are scrupulously recorded back to the mid-eighteenth century via *The General Stud Book*; then there is a period when the record gets sketchier, before dying out altogether. The naming practices of the seventeenth century are notably capricious, which is certainly part of the difficulty, but it is also clear that when England began importing Arabians, Barbs, and Turks, it also imported from those Eastern horsemen the idea of preserving pedigrees. One glaring reason why there is no evidence of the English hobby's genetic contribution to the Thoroughbred is that until the English began importing horses from North Africa and the Middle East, they simply did not keep serious records. When Defoe arrives in Bedale, Yorkshire, he alludes both to the longstanding tradition of horsemanship in that region and to the recently imported practice of preserving pedigrees:

> I met with nothing at or about Bedall, that comes within the compass of my enquiry but this, that not this town only, but even all this country, is full of jockeys, that is to say, dealers in horses, and breeders of horses, and the breeds of their horses in this and the next country are so well known, that tho' they do not preserve the pedigree of their horses for a succession of ages, as they say they do in Arabia and in Barbary, yet they christen their stallions here, and know them, and will advance the price of a horse according to the reputation of the horse he came of. (ii. 220)

The difference alluded to by Defoe in 1724 is considerably elaborated when John Lawrence returns to the same topic at the end of the century:

> The Arabians are, above all nations, attached to their Horses, and the most scrupulous, both with regard to their pedigrees, and their care and precaution in breeding. The names, marks, colours, age and qualifications of all the superior stallions and mares, are generally known among the breeders of that country, as among the breeders of Race-horses in this; but they carry their scrupulosity and precaution far beyond us. On the covering mare, witnesses are called, who give a solemn certificate of the consummation, signed and sealed in the presence of the emir, or some such magistrate. The names and pedigrees of the horse and mare are set forth in this instrument. This ceremony is repeated when the foal is dropped, and a fresh certificate is signed, in which the day of birth is registered and the foal is particularly described. These vouchers like the title-deeds of an estate, pass with the Horse when sold, and in them consists a material part of his value. The prejudices of these people concurring with their leading interest, we need entertain the less suspicion of their fidelity, which is farther confirmed by the testimony of ages in their favour, by the apparent marks of purity and integrity in their breed, and by the unrivalled excellence of those animals in which they deal, and disperse over so many countries.[39]

What Lawrence describes at the end of the eighteenth century as "far beyond us," in fact became almost immediately the official practice still observed today in registering foal certificates. It is no longer possible to imagine a story of success as romantic as the Godolphin Barb's (or his fictionalized twentieth-century counterpart, the Black Stallion), for an obscure carthorse from some unknown country could never gain admission to the exclusive registry of the Blood-horse.

In this chapter, I have sought to present a revisionist account of the origins of the Thoroughbred racehorse, one that attends to this animal's role as cultural metaphor in order to develop a more robust account of its shifting status during a dynamic process of cultural change. Actor Network Theory offers a particularly useful tool for enabling us to elucidate this change by focusing on the various metaphoric roles assigned to the Thoroughbred, as anxieties about patrilineal succession and Orientalist influence work their way through a myth of origins that both seeks to establish a firm "foundation" for a distinctly "English" animal, and at the same time consolidates a national "core" at the expense of a rural "periphery."

NOTES

1. Karen Barad has coined the phrase "agential realism" in describing one such alternative: "The ontology I propose does not posit some fixed notion of being that is prior to signification (as the classical realist assumes), but neither is being completely inaccessible to language (as in Kantian transcendentalism), nor completely of language (as in linguistic monism). That reality within which we intra-act—what I term *agential reality*—is made up of material-discursive phenomena. Agential reality is not a fixed ontology that is independent of human practices, but is continually reconstituted through our material-discursive intra-actions. . . . According to agential realism, reality is sedimented out of the process of making the world intelligible through certain practices and not others. Therefore, we are responsible not only for the knowledge that we seek, but, in part, for what exists. Scientific practices involve complex intra-actions of multiple material-discursive apparatuses. Material-discursive apparatuses are themselves phenomena made up of specific intra-actions of humans and non-humans. . . . Intra-actions are constraining but not determining." Barad's notion of "intra-actions," on which her "agential realism" depends, reconfigures the observer's relationship to nature: we do not observe the nature around us, but rather we observe our own participation within nature. Karen Barad, "Reconceiving Scientific Literacy as Agential Literacy: Or, Learning How to Intra-act Responsibly within the World," in *Doing Science and Culture*, ed. Roddey Reid and Sharon Traweek (New York: Routledge, 2000), 221–58; quote from 235–36.

2. Bruno Latour, *We Have Never Been Modern* (Cambridge, MA: Harvard University Press, 1993), 11.

3. *The General Stud-Book; Containing (with Few Exceptions) the Pedigree of Every Horse, Mare, &c. of Note, That Has Appeared on the Turf, for the Last Fifty Years, with Many of an Earlier Date; together with Some Account of the Foreign Horses and Mares from whence Is Derived the Present Breed of Racers, in Great Britain and Ireland* (London: printed by H. Reynell, for J. Weatherby, junior, 1793).

4. The quoted phrase is from Nicholas Russell, *Like Engend'ring Like: Heredity and Animal Breeding in Early Modern England* (Cambridge, UK: Cambridge University Press, 1986), 95.

5. Instead, "the word 'Thoroughbred' was first mentioned in Volume 2 published in 1821, though the term was not defined. Copenhagen, the Duke of Wellington's charger at the battle of Waterloo, was by Meteor, and the pedigree of his dam Lady Catherine was given as 'got by John Bull, her dam by the Rutland Arabian, out of a hunting mare not thoroughbred' ": Peter Willett, *The Thoroughbred* (New York: G. P. Putnam & Sons, 1970), 102. This definition by negation may be the first use of the term in the official registry of Thoroughbred racing, but its affirmative use quickly entered the lexicon.

6. William Osmer, *A Treatise on the Diseases and Lameness of Horses. In which is Laid Down a Proper Method of Shoeing (in General) and Treating the Different Kinds of Feet* (London: printed for T. Waller, 1761), 247.

7. Harriet Ritvo, *The Platypus and the Mermaid, and Other Figments of the Classifying Imagination* (Cambridge, MA: Harvard University Press, 1997), 76.

8. Willett, *The Thoroughbred*, 22.

9. Alexander Mackay-Smith, *Speed and the Thoroughbred: The Complete History* (Lanham, MD: Derrydale Press and Millwood House, Ltd., 2000), 85–86.

10. Lisa Jardine and Jerry Brotton, *Global Interests: Renaissance Art between East and West* (Ithaca, NY: Cornell University Press, 2000), 151.

11. William Cavendish, Duke of Newcastle, *A New Method and Extraordinary Invention, To Dress Horses, and Work Them According to Nature: As also, To Perfect Nature by the Subtilty of Art; Which Was Never Found out, but by The Thrice Noble, High, and Puissant Prince William Cavendishe* (London: printed by Thomas Milbourn, 1667), 73.

12. C. M. Prior, *Early Records of the Thoroughbred Horse* (London: Sportsman Office, 1924), 74.

13. Nabil Matar, *Turks, Moors, and Englishmen in the Age of Discovery* (New York: Columbia University Press, 1999), 54.

14. "Place's determination to save the White Turk from obscurity at the cost of his own reputation was completely vindicated. During the next 16 years, he overcame formidable obstacles to make it possible for this

stallion to attract the top-class mares whose offspring made him the most influential sire of the seventeenth century" (Mackay-Smith, *Speed and the Thoroughbred*, 125; cf. 5, 7, and passim).

15. Matar, *Turks, Moors, and Englishmen*, 22.

16. John Hislop and David Swannell, *The Faber Book of the Turf* (Boston: Faber and Faber, 1990), 127.

17. Since the gestation period for a broodmare is 11 months, mares are bred once a year. Stud books record their produce sequentially, so the date for Desdemona allows us to infer the latest possible foaling date for the Commoner filly. In breeding parlance, a foal is "got by" its sire and is produced "out of" its dam.

18. Richard Wall, *A Dissertation on Breeding of Horses, upon Philosophical and Experimental Principles; . . . Also Some Material Observations upon Those Sorts of Foreign Horses, Which Are Adapted to Racing; Particularly Those of the Kingdom of Yemine, in . . . South Arabia . . . By Richard Wall* (London: printed for G. Woodfall, W. Cooke, R. Heber, and J. Wilkie, 1758), 14.

19. Prior, *Early Records of the Thoroughbred Horse*, showed, early in the last century, that this story is almost certainly false, although it continues to be widely repeated. There is no record that Byerley was present at the siege of Buda, or indeed in any European action. Some have conjectured (with little evidence) that the Byerley Turk was one of three stallions imported in 1685, following the siege of Vienna (these horses are described in Evelyn's diary).

20. A teaser, as the name suggests, is the stallion sent (like an erotic equine John the Baptist) to prepare the way for the stallion whose service is desired.

21. Defoe's *Roxana* is only the most visible of many appearances of this name in this context.

22. For a definition of the term "prepotent," see below.

23. Daniel Defoe, *A Tour through the Whole Island of Great Britain*, rev. edn. (London: Dent, 1974).

24. Mackay-Smith, *Speed and the Thoroughbred*, 7.

25. William Osmer, *A Dissertation on Horses: Wherein It Is Demonstrated, by Matters of Fact, as well as from the Principles of Philosophy, That Innate Qualities Do Not Exist, . . . By William Osmer* (London: printed for T. Waller, 1756), 50–54.

26. Edward Said, *Orientalism* (New York: Vintage Books, 1979), 1.

27. Lady Wentworth, *Thoroughbred Racing Stock and Its Ancestors; The Authentic Origin of Pure Blood* (London: G. Allen & Unwin Ltd., 1938), 10.

28. Lady Wentworth's answer, which I find thoroughly unpersuasive, is, I should make clear, vigorously set forth. She contends at some length on behalf of racing Arabians (she bred them extensively), arguing that the only ones to be bested in contests with Thoroughbreds were not themselves particularly successful racing Arabians, and she

trots out (the verb is not inappropriate) some scattered examples of successes enjoyed by racing Arabians. There are, however, at this date, many tracks that offer races for racing Arabians, and the evidence is overwhelming that these horses cannot compete with Thoroughbreds.

29. Janet Sorensen, *The Grammar of Empire in Eighteenth-Century British Writing* (Cambridge, UK: Cambridge University Press, 2000), 3.

30. Michael Hechter, *Internal Colonialism: The Celtic Fringe in British National Development* (New Brunswick, NJ: Transaction Publishers, 1999).

31. Defoe's Yorkshireman (or at least his generically "Northern" descendant) survives in the popular (and politically incorrect) comic strip character "Andy Capp." The cartoon began in 1957 to court a north country readership; his name, of course, puns on the racing term "handicap."

32. William Plaxton, *The Yorkshire-racers. A poem. In a Letter from H——S————ton, to his friend T——P————n* (London: printed for the use of all sorts of jockeys, whether north, south, east, or west, 1709).

33. Richard Hall, "Whig Party Fortunes at the Yorkshire County Election of 1708," *Northern History* 32 (1996): 131.

34. Although the poem is ostensibly addressed to a "*T——P————n*," there is a temptation to read the "Tom" of the opening line as a glance at Thomas, Lord Wharton.

35. In a letter of 1710, Lord Bristol refers to his racing stock as "thro'breds," a usage generally accepted as an anticipation of "Thoroughbred," though it seems clearly a contraction of "through-bred." Again, as in the case of Plaxton's use, Lord Bristol's use is too early to refer to the descendants of the so-called foundation sires, and we know that his racing stock was purchased from the Yorkshire studs. In the larger frame of cultural usage, both Bristol's "thro'bred" and Plaxton's "true-bred" bear more than a little affinity to Daniel Defoe's explicitly nationalist usage in the "True-born Englishman." In that satire praising an emergent English identity, Defoe's major point is that a "true-born Englishman" is himself a hybrid medley of diverse influences. The central paradox of true-bred English identity—in humans as well as in horses—lies in their impossible status as simultaneously pure and hybrid.

36. The "hobbies" of the North are the ancestors of Yorkshireman Laurence Sterne's well-known "hobby horses" in *Tristram Shandy* ("away they go galloping like hey-go-mad"). The genetic contribution of the native hobby horse has been eclipsed by the better documented contributions of the imported Arabians. Nonetheless, when Arabians (male or female) were imported to England for breeding purposes, they were presumably bred to something. At one extreme, Lady Wentworth and those who maintain her cause contend that

the only surviving contributors to the Thoroughbred gene pool were the product of the matings between Arabian imports. I do not have the space to pursue this line of discussion thoroughly here, but I will say that I find the position unlikely to the point of incredulity.

37. Bruno Latour, *Pandora's Hope: Essays on the Reality of Science Studies* (Cambridge, MA: Harvard University Press, 1999).

38. Hislop and Swannell, *The Faber Book of the Turf*, 127.

39. John Lawrence, *A Philosophical and Practical Treatise on Horses*, 2 vols. (London: printed for T. Longman, 1796–98), vol. 1, 34.

CHAPTER 10

EARLY MODERN FRENCH NOBLE IDENTITY AND THE EQUESTRIAN "AIRS ABOVE THE GROUND"

Treva J. Tucker

In the late sixteenth and early seventeenth centuries, the traditional French nobility—that is, the long-established hereditary nobility, often referred to as the sword or warrior nobility—experienced a variety of military, political, social, and cultural changes in its circumstances.[1] During this period, many of the elements that previously had defined *noblesse* were being disputed, displaced, or simply rendered obsolete. In order to survive, the nobility was forced—slowly but no less inevitably—to adjust its own belief system regarding the components of noble identity. One of the few commonalties between the old definition of nobility and the new one was the nobility's long-standing relationship with horses.

Many scholars have discussed the shift in the way nobles perceived and defined what constituted true nobility in the late sixteenth and early seventeenth centuries.[2] No one, however, has systematically explored the role played by horsemanship in that shift, and no one has considered manuals of horsemanship as a potential resource for shedding new light on it. Yet these texts provide a wealth of information on noble self-perception and identity during this period and are in fact a valuable resource for accessing the beliefs of contemporary nobles about the qualities of true nobility. For one thing, and in contrast to other sources that reveal those beliefs, these treatises make overwhelmingly clear the central importance of horsemanship to the nobility. Simply by recapturing this overlooked yet crucial element of early modern French noble identity, we gain a new and more complete understanding of this group. Most importantly, however, manuals of horsemanship are a rich resource for better understanding the nobility's response to the various new ideas that threatened its beliefs about the meaning of *noblesse*. These treatises discuss, with exceptional clarity and in great detail, the various qualities—some old, some new—needed by the nobleman in order to be a successful horseman. In doing so, they reveal how the nobility was able to manipulate one longstanding attribute of nobility in order to create for itself a space at once reassuring in its familiarity and yet sufficiently different from what had gone before to allow for change.

Manuals of horsemanship thus expand on what other recent scholarship has revealed: that the nobility's views on what constituted noble identity during this period were a blend of both continuity and change. Nobles were not stubbornly resistant to change, as the old "nobility in decline" school of thought tended to argue; nor were they willing or able suddenly to adopt a radically new sense of identity, as at least one recent scholar has suggested.[3] Instead, nobles adjusted and amended their ideas, a little here, a little there, until—ultimately, gradually, and within the parameters that their belief system allowed—they were able successfully to adapt.[4] Throughout this period of adaptation, horsemanship was far more than a central attribute of nobility. As I will argue in this chapter, horsemanship played a key role in the realm of shifting ideas about noble identity, precisely because it was a source of both continuity and change. Horsemanship was simultaneously a familiar and comforting touchstone during a time when the nobles felt besieged, and a dynamic vehicle for responding effectively to all the changes around them. Horsemanship thus was uniquely useful to the nobles in their quest to adapt but to do so in a way that did not violate their sense of tradition.

To make my argument, I will focus on a specific subset of the type of horsemanship described in the manuals: the dramatic "airs above the ground," also known as the high airs or the *airs relevés*. These movements involved some or all of the horse's legs being off ("above") the ground at some point during the movement: the forelegs during the *pesade* and the *courbette*, and both forelegs and hind legs during the *balotade*, the *croupade*, and the *capriole*. The manuals of horsemanship make repeated reference to certain qualities required by the successful horseman whenever he is mounted but particularly when he is attempting the high airs. Many of these qualities were essential components of traditional noble *vertu*, which long had been viewed by the nobles as a central characteristic of true nobility, but whose meaning and centrality were being threatened from various directions during the later sixteenth century. The manuals also laud the qualities of grace and *sprezzatura* as equally important to the successful mounted performance. These attributes only recently had been added to the noble construct, but by the late sixteenth century they already were becoming increasingly important components of what eventually would be a new definition of nobility. The airs above the ground thus provided nobles with the means simultaneously to display the familiar but threatened qualities of *vertu* and the less familiar but increasingly essential qualities of grace and *sprezzatura*. By doing so, these movements helped ease the nobility's transition from an anachronistic identity that clashed with its political, military, societal, and cultural contexts to an identity that was better suited and more responsive to its actual circumstances.

* * *

In order to address the central thesis, I first must discuss the way in which the nobility was defined going into the sixteenth century and how and why certain elements of that definition were disputed, displaced, or rendered obsolete as the century unfolded. At the beginning of the sixteenth century, members of the traditional French nobility tended to believe that the two qualities most necessary to a true nobleman were military service and virtue.[5] To a nobleman of this period, military service specifically meant heavy cavalry service, which in the early sixteenth century still retained many of its medieval characteristics. A heavy cavalryman wore a full suit of plate armor, rode a powerful horse that also wore plate armor, and fought primarily with lance and sword; when confronting enemy troops, he preferred to use a combination of offensive shock tactics (the charge with lowered lance) and individual hand-to-hand combat. By the dawn of the sixteenth century, this particular type of military service already had a long history as the primary "function" of the French nobility.[6] The continued emphasis on military service as one of the key elements defining nobility may be explained in part by the various perks and privileges that nobles enjoyed, many of which originally had been granted in exchange for the nobles' military service—for the blood that the nobles had spilled or would spill in defense of king and country.[7] The continued correlation between military service and noble status also was facilitated during this period by an increase in opportunities for French noblemen to serve. From 1445 on, a full-time career as a heavy cavalryman in the royal ordinance companies became an option for interested French noblemen, and from 1494 to 1559, the Hapsburg–Valois conflict offered many occasions for nobles to fulfill their military function. This increase in opportunities for nobles to participate in military activity from the late fifteenth century on led to a reemphasis of military service as one of the central elements in the definition of nobility.[8]

As for virtue, to the nobleman of this period the term had little to do with its modern meaning of moral excellence. Instead, it meant something closer to the original Latin *virtus*, or "manliness," from *vir*, or "man." *Vertu* referred to the qualities of the ideal manly man and consisted primarily of things that would be useful to the nobleman while he was fulfilling his military function.[9] Given the centrality of the latter to the nobility's self-perception, it is unsurprising that the contemporary concept of noble virtue had heavily martial overtones. Valor, for example, was considered to be the most important component of *vertu*, and valor included all the traits that would be of obvious use to a warrior—things such as courage, daring, and strength. *Vertu* also included several less specifically martial traits that nonetheless would be equally useful in war—things such as sound judgment, prudence, foresight, wisdom, imagination, resourcefulness, and determination. Of course, any of these qualities, even the most blatantly warlike among them, also could be demonstrated outside of a strictly military context, but it was a common noble belief that they could be demonstrated best in battle.[10] The increase in opportunities from the latter half of the fifteenth century for French nobles to demonstrate their *vertu* in its preferred context only served to reaffirm the continued relevance of their very specific interpretation of virtue as a quality of true nobility. By the beginning of the sixteenth century, the lines separating the concepts of valor, *vertu*, and nobility itself in noble self-perception and definition had become almost hopelessly blurred. To a French nobleman of this period, his identity as a man of *vertu* was inextricably intertwined with his identity as a warrior, both of which in turn were inextricably intertwined with his identity as a true nobleman.[11]

Going into the sixteenth century, France's military circumstances were such that the nobles still were able to justify and define their order largely on the basis of military service and *vertu*. The advent of the Hapsburg–Valois wars in 1494 substantially increased the opportunity for a French nobleman to fulfill his military function if he so desired, and the technological, tactical, and economic changes that eventually would render the medieval heavy cavalryman obsolete still were in their nascent stages. This being the case, for much of the first half of the sixteenth century, the French nobles were able to continue to claim with at least some justification that being truly noble revolved around a certain type of military service and a certain set of personal characteristics, which coincidentally just happened to manifest themselves most gloriously in the pursuit of that particular type of military service.

Unfortunately, in the larger mix of elements that traditionally had defined nobility, the central importance of both heavy cavalry service and its handmaiden, martial *vertu*, was undermined in various ways over the course of the sixteenth century. By the beginning of that century, the military importance of the traditional heavy cavalry already had been declining slowly but steadily for nearly two centuries. Some of the factors that contributed to this slow decline had begun to manifest themselves as far back as the early fourteenth century, when the use of massed infantry formations first began to challenge the efficacy of heavy cavalry. There were, however, several key factors that did not have a major impact until the first half of the sixteenth century. Taken in combination, and more or less coinciding as they did, it was these factors that finally brought about the demise of the heavy cavalryman.

First, gun-bearing infantry was being deployed more effectively against cavalry. By the 1520s, natural or manmade barriers and trenches were being employed on a routine basis in order to protect gunners from cavalry assault while they were reloading.[12] By the 1540s, gunners and pikemen were being deployed in coordinated formations that made both types of infantry more effective against and less vulnerable to mounted attack.[13] Second, from the 1520s on, a new type of fortification began to shift the emphasis in strategy from battle to siege. To capture or defend a fortified emplacement required vast numbers of infantry armed with guns, not a small force of heavy cavalry armed with lance and sword.[14] Third, the development of the pistol in the early sixteenth century led to the appearance, from the 1540s on, of a new form of combat cavalry, the mounted pistoleer. These horsemen were less comprehensively armored than traditional cavalry, so their mounts did not need to be so heavy and were able to move more quickly. As gunpowder weapons became both more prevalent and more effective, the speed and maneuverability of this lighter type of cavalry made it less vulnerable to gunfire.[15] Finally, there was the ongoing issue of costs. Infantry was far less expensive than cavalry of any kind. It cost less to equip, supply, and maintain; it could be paid a lower wage because there were no horses involved; and it was faster—and therefore cheaper—to train because there was no riding involved.[16] If cavalry was needed, mounted pistoleers were a better bargain than traditional heavy cavalry. They required less armor, and their lighter horses were less costly to purchase, easier to obtain, and cheaper to feed.

By the middle of the sixteenth century, it was obvious that the nobility's customary military role was in a state of irreversible decline. The efficacy of the armored heavy cavalryman on his armored warhorse had been undermined by changing strategic demands and by new and more effective technologies, tactics, and troop types, both mounted and foot, and the ever-rising costs associated with heavy cavalry had made both infantry and lighter forms of cavalry far more appealing to military leaders. During the French civil–religious conflict of the second half of the sixteenth century, all these trends continued apace. When that conflict ended in 1598, only a very limited number of infantry and a tiny contingent of cavalry were retained by the Crown on a permanent, paid basis.[17] By the beginning of the seventeenth century, the possibility for most French noblemen of a full-time career as a heavy cavalryman thus had dwindled to somewhere between slim and none. Since cavalry service was the only type of military service considered truly appropriate for those of noble birth, this sharp decline in opportunities for nobles to fulfill their traditional military role made it difficult for them to continue to claim that military service was one of the central elements defining true nobility.

Because so many of the qualities comprising noble *vertu* were so intimately connected to military service, the decline in opportunities for nobles to fulfill their military function also undermined the validity of virtue—at least as it was defined by the traditional nobility—as a required characteristic of the truly noble. To further compound matters, over the course of the sixteenth century, noble *vertu* came under attack from various directions having little or nothing to do with the military changes detailed above.

The biggest challenge to *vertu* as one of the two most important elements defining nobility was a byproduct of the emergence over the course of the sixteenth century of a new subcategory of nobility, based not on military service and martial virtue but on service in royal office. The emergence of this "second" nobility did not undermine virtue itself as a quality of nobility, but it did undermine the way in which the traditional nobility defined virtue. Those who had achieved noble status through office had been elevated into the nobility in recognition of virtues of an entirely different nature from the predominately military *vertu* promulgated by the traditional nobles. The fact that it had become possible to achieve nobility without ever setting foot on a battlefield (or being descended from someone who had) thus undermined the existing definition of virtue, with its heavy emphasis on valor, by demonstrating quite clearly that virtue no longer needed to be martial in order to qualify as a legitimate quality of nobility. The appearance of this "alternative" nobility suggested that there could be a second, equally valid model for *noblesse* that did not involve valor at all and that was based instead on the virtues of acquired knowledge and of demonstrated competence and ability in arenas other than the battlefield.[18]

This expansion of the meaning of virtue to include activities, abilities, and qualities beyond the military sphere supported the arguments of royal officials who claimed that their civil service was just as noble as the (supposed) military service of the traditional nobles, if not in fact superior to it. Clearly, the royal officeholder not only served a viable social function, he also served that function on an ongoing basis. Most of the traditional nobles, on the other hand, fulfilled their supposed military function only intermittently, if at all, and the rest of the time they made no useful contribution to society whatsoever. This being so, the new nobles argued, the civil virtues of royal officials obviously were just as valid and worthy, and therefore just as deserving of recognition as noble, as the martial virtues of the traditional nobles.[19]

The new nobles also argued that a man personally had to demonstrate his virtue (whatever its nature) during his lifetime in order for that virtue to be considered a legitimate quality of nobility. The *vertu* of a nobleman whose only relationship to his military function was through the past service of a distant ancestor or through the potential service of an unknown descendant thus was rendered invalid.[20] Unfortunately, the traditional nobles continued to insist that the only truly noble form of virtue was the one that revolved around qualities that could be demonstrated best on the battlefield. Since their opportunities to participate in the type of conflict necessary to showcase those qualities were becoming increasingly limited, their opportunities to demonstrate their personal virtue, and thus to validate that particular type of virtue as a necessary characteristic of true nobility, were extremely limited as well. The arguments of the new nobility regarding both the nature of virtue as a quality of nobility and the manner in which that virtue was to be demonstrated, coupled with the continuing decline in the nobles' ability to fulfill their traditional military function, undermined the existing emphasis on those two elements within the larger mix of elements that defined nobility.

Paralleling this decline in the validity of military service and martial *vertu* as the central components comprising nobility, several new and entirely non-martial attributes were added to the noble construct during the sixteenth century. One current of thought that had a particular influence on the French nobility, and on the various traits considered quintessential to those of noble status, was the concept of the ideal courtier. This ideal was promulgated first and most successfully by the Italian nobleman Baldessare Castiglione in his book *Il cortegiano*, or *The Book of the Courtier*.[21] Castiglione's book, first published in 1528 and translated into French in 1537, describes in great detail the characteristics of the ideal noble courtier. This individual has all the qualities included in the French concept of *vertu*, but he also has a whole new set of largely social graces that reflect the heightened refinement of the Italian Renaissance.

Among these new characteristics, the two that receive the most attention are *grazia*, or grace, and something called *sprezzatura*. In Castiglione's ideal, grace must pervade every aspect of the courtier's behavior, whether he is dancing, riding, walking, fencing, dining, speaking, or just sitting around doing nothing in particular. As for *sprezzatura*, this is a rather complex concept that may be broadly defined as an attitude of nonchalantly poised self-confidence, the primary purpose of which is to disguise the courtier's efforts so that everything he does or says appears to be natural and spontaneous. *Sprezzatura* allows him to perform any act as if both the skill necessary to the performance and the grace with which the act is performed are totally natural and unaffected—something that the courtier does effortlessly, with no hint of the time and labor he must have invested in learning to do so.[22] Over the course of the sixteenth century, the way in which the French nobles defined true nobility gradually expanded to include these notions of grace and *sprezzatura*.

By the final decades of the sixteenth century, all of these challenges to the existing definition of nobility had combined to make the French nobles extremely uneasy. The fully armored, lance-armed heavy cavalryman was well on his way to becoming obsolete, which negated that aspect of the existing definition of nobility that insisted that true nobility was rooted in that particular type of military service. Virtue as a key element of nobility, and especially that peculiarly martial *vertu* touted by the traditional nobles, had taken knocks from a variety of directions, all of which called into question the viability of this quality as a necessary component of nobility. Finally, both of these central characteristics that had defined nobility for centuries were being supplanted (or at least overshadowed) by the new Italian ideal, which placed more emphasis on grace and *sprezzatura* than it did on military prowess and martial *vertu*.

Mirroring in many ways these shifts in the definition of nobility, noble horsemanship also had experienced a swing away from the military and toward the courtly. Going into the sixteenth century, the types of mounted skills that a French nobleman was taught were those that would contribute to his potential efficacy as a heavy cavalryman. By the end of the century, on the other hand, the types of mounted skills that a nobleman was expected to master had more to do with the display of grace and *sprezzatura* than they did with his military abilities. Much like the new courtly ideal, this new form of horsemanship flourished first in Renaissance Italy. By the second half of the sixteenth century, noblemen from all over Europe were flocking to Italy to learn the new riding style. Many of the French nobles who went to Italy during this period to learn to ride and train horses in the new manner then took their knowledge back to France and opened their own riding academies, where they were able to pass on what they had learned to young noblemen who were eager to master the new riding style and delighted not to have to go all the way to Italy to do so. The first *académie* was founded in Paris in 1594 by Antoine de Pluvinel, and many others, both in the capital and in the provinces, followed not long thereafter. The reputation of the French riding masters quickly surpassed that of the Italians, and by the early decades of the seventeenth century, the Mecca of horsemanship definitively had moved from Italy to France.[23]

A surprising number of these noble horsemen wrote treatises on the art of riding and training in the new style.[24] I chose the five manuals of horsemanship used for this chapter for several reasons. First and most importantly, they all were written during the period when the definition of nobility in France was still in transition, and they all reveal, at varying levels of complexity, shifting ideas about noble self-perception and identity during this period. Second, their authors all were French noblemen who directed or held positions of responsibility at a noble *académie*: they were not mere theoreticians but experienced practitioners of their subject. In addition to the five treatises, I consulted a contemporary dictionary of equestrian terms. In chronological order based on the publication date of each book's first edition, the sources are as follows: La Broue's *Le Cavalerice françois* of 1593–94, Menou's *La Pratique du cavalier* of 1612, La Noue's *La Cavalerie françoise et italienne* of 1620, Pluvinel's *L'Instruction du roy* of 1625, Delcampe's *L'Art de monter à cheval* of 1658, and Guillet's *Les Arts de l'homme d'épée* (the dictionary) of 1680.[25] All six texts focus on the art of riding and training horses in the elaborate movements practiced in the manège, or riding arena, whence the term "manège equitation" used in the rest of the chapter.

The horsemanship of the manège was appealing to French nobles of this period in part because it offered them the opportunity to display many of the cherished and familiar qualities associated with noble *vertu*, albeit in a new and nonmilitary context. This allowed the nobles to reaffirm their connection to at least one imperiled aspect of noble definition during a period when it appeared that so much of what traditionally had defined nobility was under siege. Manège equitation involved complex maneuvers not dissimilar to ballet, and at first glance this type of horsemanship might seem to be a far better vehicle for a nobleman to flaunt his grace and *sprezzatura* than for him to display the qualities comprising *vertu*—qualities such as courage, daring, strength, judgment, prudence, foresight, wisdom, imagination, resourcefulness, and determination. However, while it certainly is true that manège equitation was considered to be an excellent showcase for a nobleman's more courtly qualities, because it was performed on a powerful and often unpredictable beast, it was equally likely to call on the qualities associated with virtue. Although any mounted maneuver had the potential to call on these qualities, the movements that best showcased a nobleman's virtue were the particularly dramatic subset of manège equitation called the "airs above the ground."

Although manège equitation includes a number of movements that could be used to make the same point, in this chapter I will focus on three of the most popular airs of the seventeenth century: the *pesade*, the *courbette*, and the *capriole*. Based on the way the *pesade* and its use are described in the sources, this movement was not considered to be a high air properly speaking.[26] Instead, the *pesade* was viewed as a stepping-stone to the true airs above the ground, and it would appear that most if not all horses trained for the manège were expected to master this movement.[27] All of the sources consulted for this chapter classify the *courbette* as one of the airs above the ground, but it was universally considered to be the easiest of the high airs for horses to perform, and—again—one gets the impression that most if not all horses were expected to master it.[28] The truly high airs, on the other hand—those in which the entire horse was literally "above the ground"—were extremely difficult, and all the authors agree that only certain horses can perform them.[29] Although there were several such airs, they all were variations on the *capriole*.[30] Because these airs were so similar, I will discuss only the *capriole*, which was the most difficult

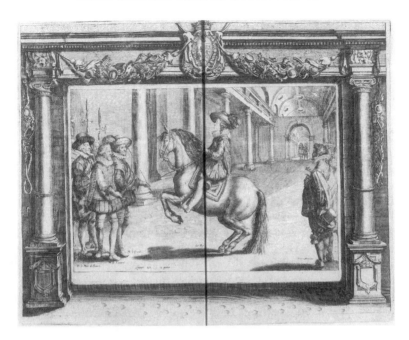

Figure 10.1.   The *pesade*, from Antoine de Pluvinel, *L'Instruction du roy en l'exercice de monter à cheval* (1625). With permission of the Huntington Library.

and dramatic of the *airs relevés*. The *capriole* also best illustrates the argument at hand, yet—as I hope to demonstrate—even riding a horse while it was performing the comparatively sedate *pesade* or *courbette* required far more of the rider than merely grace and *sprezzatura*.

The *pesade* was a highly controlled rear, in which the horse lowered its haunches, lifted its forehand fully off the ground, tucked in its forelegs, and briefly held the pose without moving its hind feet (see figure 10.1). The main purpose of this move was to teach the horse to raise its forehand on command, and the horse was not expected to remain in *pesade* for very long before lowering its front legs back to the ground.[31] Based on that rather prosaic description, one might be tempted to assume that performing this maneuver was not so very difficult. The sources make it abundantly clear, however, that the finished movement could take many weeks of training to achieve. These texts discuss all the problems that can arise during that period of training and all the various techniques that the trainer may have to employ to overcome said problems. To take but two examples from opposite ends of the spectrum of equine temperament, lazy or phlegmatic horses often refuse to come off the ground at all, whereas flighty or hot-tempered horses may rear up too high, sometimes going to such extremes that horse and rider are in danger of going over backward.[32] The latter situation in particular obviously could end in the severe injury or even death of the rider, yet virtually any mounted activity is at least somewhat hazardous. Though the sources rarely refer to anything so ungentlemanly as falling off, they are littered with references to the dangers inherent in riding and training large, strong, and highly temperamental animals that may or may not wish to cooperate.[33]

All this being so, riding a horse while it was learning the *pesade* certainly must have called upon many aspects of a nobleman's virtue. Anyone who was willing to ride a horse while it was being encouraged to do something that normally is a means of unloading its rider had to be at the very least brave, strong, and willing to take risks. The authors of these texts are quick to point out, however, that training a horse to perform the more demanding airs—both low and high—requires far more of the rider than just sturdy muscles and iron nerves. When these authors describe the various types of resistance and evasion a horse might offer, they repeatedly emphasize the intellectual side of riding and training.[34] In a contest of strength, the horse always has the advantage, so the rider must use his superior mental capacities to bend the horse to his will. The successful rider must familiarize himself with all the different types of horses and all the different ways in which they may try to avoid doing his bidding. This fund of knowledge will allow him to assess why a particular horse is responding in a particular way and then to make a wise and prudent choice concerning which correction would be most appropriate for that horse in that situation. In addition, the rider must possess the resolve and determination needed to persist in his endeavor, as most horses will not acquiesce after a single attempt to resist or evade their rider's wishes but will try out an entire repertoire before finally giving in. Perhaps most importantly, the rider must be able to respond to his horse's behavior with lightning speed and under circumstances that may be fraught with peril, in order (ideally) to foresee a potential disobedience and correct it before it actually happens. All the authors, in fact, repeatedly stress the importance of "judgment" in a wide variety of contexts, by which they mean the ability to apply one's knowledge not only accurately but also quickly, since the very fact of being mounted on an unpredictable animal allows the rider no time for studied contemplation of his next move. Finally, because every horse is different and circumstances change constantly, there are no fixed rules that can be counted on to work every time, so the rider must continually adjust to the demands of the moment. In fact, when faced with an unfamiliar resistance, the truly gifted rider will be able to apply his ingenuity and imagination to his knowledge in order to create an entirely new technique to correct it.[35] In short, the successful rider, like the successful warrior, must have many of the qualities associated with virtue: he must be bold, intrepid, and physically powerful; he must have a thorough knowledge of his craft; he must apply that knowledge with wisdom, good judgment, foresight, and prudence; he must be resourceful and imaginative, resolute and determined; and he must be able to function well and respond quickly under perilous conditions.

Clearly, then, the *pesade* was not the casual little trifle that one might have supposed. Yet the *pesade* also was not really an end in itself but was primarily a preliminary to the high airs. Of those airs, the least difficult was the *courbette*, but it still was substantially more difficult than the *pesade*. In the sixteenth and seventeenth centuries, the *courbette* combined the elevation of the *pesade* and the motion of a low air called the *terre à terre*.[36] Understanding the mechanics of the latter is crucial to understanding why the contemporary *courbette* was so demanding. The *terre à terre* was similar to an extremely collected canter, but it differed from the canter in that the front legs left the ground and came back down before the hind legs followed. In a normal canter, one front leg and one hind leg (a diagonal pair) are on the ground at the same time in each stride, resulting in an even three-beat rhythm (1–2–3, 1–2–3). In the *terre à terre*, the front legs and the hind legs move in two distinctly separate pairs of steps, resulting in a broken four-beat rhythm (1–2, 3–4, 1–2, 3–4). According to Guillet's definition of this movement, the forefeet are to be raised only to a relatively low height before coming back down, and the hind feet are to follow with short, quick steps close to the ground. The *terre à terre* can be performed either forward or sideways, in a straight line or on a circle.[37]

Based on contemporary descriptions, the *courbette* was virtually identical to the *terre à terre*, except that the forehand was elevated quite a bit higher in each stride, though not quite so high as in a *pesade*. The forelegs were supposed to remain airborne long enough for the horse to fold them fully, so there would have been a tiny pause—a moment of suspended motion—at the top of each stride. Once the forelegs came back down, the hind legs made the same low hop as in the *terre à terre*, after which the forelegs went back up and then so on in a regular cadenced rhythm for as long as the horse's

Figure 10.2. The *courbette*, performed on a circle to the right, from Antoine de Pluvinel, *L'Instruction du roy en l'exercice de monter à cheval* (1625). With permission of the Huntington Library.

strength and stamina would permit. Like the *terre à terre*, the *courbette* could be performed either forward or sideways, in a straight line or on a circle (see figure 10.2).[38] Clearly, any horse that could perform the *courbette* had to have mastered both the *pesade* and the *terre à terre*, as the *courbette* combined elements of both. Some of the problems that could arise when teaching the *pesade* already have been discussed, but teaching the *terre à terre* had an entirely different set of problems.

The *terre à terre* required a tremendous amount of collection— that is, when the horse raises or "rounds" its back under the weight of the rider, which then allows it to arch its neck and carry its head vertical to the ground and (most importantly) to bring its hind legs further under its body, flexing its hocks and lowering its haunches so that more weight is carried by the hind legs, all of which combines to permit the horse to move with more elevation and suspension in its gaits. Needless to say, correct collection is very physically demanding, so a lazy horse generally is not a very good candidate for highly collected movements, simply because it will be unwilling to make the necessary effort. Collection therefore requires a horse that is at the very least sufficiently active and energetic to meet its physical demands. Horses with naturally active and energetic dispositions do tend, however, to be considerably more lively and spirited than their lazier counterparts. On the upside, a high-spirited or "hot" horse will have more natural brilliance when performing a collected movement; on the downside, it is far more likely to object to some of the other demands of collection, which, in addition to the purely physical effort, also requires the horse to contain itself and to submit to its rider to a degree for which many hot-tempered horses simply will not stand. A really hot horse in fact may react quite violently in an attempt to evade the restriction, both physical and mental, of excessive collection. Since the *terre à terre* required the horse to be enormously collected, training some of the spunkier types to perform this air must have provided numerous opportunities for riders to employ their knowledge, their judgment, and all the other qualities of *vertu* considered essential to conquering the recalcitrant horse.[39]

The *courbette* required just as much collection as the *terre à terre*, yet the *courbette* also was substantially more elevated than the *terre à terre*—almost as elevated, in fact, as the *pesade*. Unlike the *pesade*, however, the *courbette* required the horse to raise its forehand, not just once, but over and over again. To perform this movement correctly, the horse therefore needed even more innate energy and spirit than it did for either the *pesade* or the *terre à terre*. In short, the horse needed precisely the type of temperament that would be least likely to acquiesce to the mental and physical restrictions of extreme collection. Training a horse to *courbette* thus would have been fraught with problems related to balancing the discipline and submission needed for the movement's collected aspects against the inherent exuberance of a horse with a disposition suitable for its elevated aspects. Given the conflicting demands of the *courbette*, one can only presume that getting a horse to the fully trained state must have been littered with instances when the innate spunk required for the repeated lifting of the forehand clashed rather violently with the submissive nature required for extreme collection.

Several of the sources devote page after page to this very issue, covering virtually every resistance that the recalcitrant horse might offer as well as a mind-boggling array of corrections that the rider was expected to have at his disposal.[40] These texts emphasize, for example, that horses with the fiery disposition needed to excel at the more demanding higher airs frequently are unwilling to acquiesce to the discipline and restriction of collection in general and of the *courbette* in particular and that such horses very well may rebel when asked to submit to that degree of constraint. Several authors in fact say that horses with a natural aptitude for the highest airs often will reveal their inclination under precisely these circumstances—in other words, they will leap into the air rather than submit to the excessive collection required for the *courbette*.[41] Obviously, any rider who voluntarily would put himself in such a potentially explosive situation had to be courageous and venturesome; if he hoped to retain his seat, he certainly needed a sturdy set of leg muscles. The language used in these texts to describe the various equine evasions and the skills needed to counter them place even more emphasis, however, on the use of the rider's more cerebral qualities: his judgment, prudence, foresight, wisdom, imagination, resourcefulness, determination, and so forth. Between their descriptions of what the horse might do and their suggestions for how the rider should respond, the sources thus indicate beyond any doubt that training a horse to *courbette* called heavily on a nobleman's *vertu*.

Finally, by far the most dramatic and difficult of the airs above the ground was the *capriole*. In this movement, the horse first lowered its haunches and lifted its forehand off the ground much as in the *pesade*. Its bent hocks then served as a sort of coiled spring to launch the entire horse and all four of its legs into the air. At the highest point of the leap, when the forehand and the hindquarters were at the same height, the horse tucked in its forelegs and simultaneously lashed out with its hind legs (see figure 10.3). The sources are a little contradictory regarding what happened next. Three of them say that the horse always should drop back to the ground in very nearly the same spot from which it began, and three of them say that the move also may be performed going forward, on a circle, or to the side. Either way, what is truly striking is that all these authors make it clear that horses were expected to furnish more than one *capriole* in a row.[42]

All the sources agree that, because this air is so difficult and demanding, very few horses are able to do it. From a purely physical perspective, the *capriole* requires a very powerful horse, one with enough strength to launch itself and its rider fully off the ground. All the authors also emphasize the importance of lightness—both in the sense of light on its feet, or a horse that leaves the ground readily and willingly, and in the sense of light on the forehand, or a horse whose hind legs come naturally under its body and therefore carry more of its weight. A horse's power resides in its haunches, so a horse whose hind legs were not sufficiently engaged would have had a tough time getting airborne. These authors also stress that horses that

Figure 10.3. The *capriole*, from Antoine de Pluvinel, *L'Instruction du roy en l'exercice de monter à cheval* (1625). With permission of the Huntington Library.

are naturally gifted for the *capriole* will be spirited, lively, bold, brave, proud, energetic, vigorous, hot-tempered, fiery, and sensitive.[43] Obviously, such a horse could be a handful, and the experts readily concede that this type of temperament can cause problems. These horses are prone to be anxious, impatient, defensive, malicious, rebellious, and resistant; when pressed to obey, they are likely to react in a reckless, desperate, or even violent fashion. All this makes them difficult to train, and some of them are in fact so hot-tempered that they are suited solely to the very high airs, because their nature simply will not submit to the discipline required for the collected lower airs.[44]

When the explosive motion of the *capriole* is combined with the explosive nature of the horse able to do it, it is easy to see why this movement was regarded as the pinnacle of manège horsemanship. Indeed, the *capriole* had everything a contemporary nobleman could want. It was difficult and dangerous, and therefore was an excellent showcase for his virtue, yet it was also spectacular and dramatic, and therefore was an equally excellent showcase for his grace and *sprezzatura*. All the sources discuss the ways in which manège equitation provided opportunities for noblemen to display both virtue and grace, and several of them explicitly single out the *capriole* for its ability to showcase them simultaneously.

In terms of how the *capriole* called on a nobleman's virtue, some of these authors point out that horses that are temperamentally suited to the *capriole* get even more fiery and excited when they are asked to perform this air. The very nature of the horse thus increases the risk of an accident, while the nature of the movement—its height and its violence—increases the likelihood that any accident will be a nasty one.[45] Clearly, anyone who was willing to attempt the *capriole* had to possess bravery, boldness, and physical strength. Once again, however, the authors are quick to emphasize the more cerebral aspects of horsemanship, which become even more important as the risks increase. They insist, in fact, that the rider must employ more knowledge, judgment, prudence, foresight, wisdom, imagination, and resourcefulness when performing the *capriole* than when performing any other maneuver. Because the *capriole* is so dangerous, it is more important than ever for the rider to foresee his horse's disobedience before it happens, so that he may apply the appropriate remedy and thus prevent an accident. To do this, he must have the knowledge and experience to be able both to recognize a potential disobedience and to correct it quickly and effectively. In this situation more than any other, the rider therefore must be thoroughly familiar with the different types of horses, with the various ways in which they may resist and why, and with all the possible responses to resistance and how and when to apply them. The rider then must employ his judgment, prudence, wisdom, imagination, and resourcefulness in order to decide precisely which method will best preempt the disobedience in question, taking into consideration not merely the vagaries of the particular horse but also those of the particular situation—for example, whether he is schooling in a riding arena, with walls, corners, and pillars to assist him; whether he has ready access to additional equipment and/or dismounted assistance; or whether he is out of the manège and entirely on his own, with only the equipment his horse currently is wearing. Last but certainly not least, the rider must be able to do all of this with lightning speed and without ever losing his cool, so that he can be ready to head off the next potential disaster.[46] Clearly, the *capriole* did indeed call to a high degree on many of the qualities associated with virtue.

On the other hand, because this air was spectacular and dramatic as well as difficult and dangerous, it also was an excellent showcase for the rider's grace and *sprezzatura*. All these authors spend a great deal of time explaining how important it is for the rider performing the *capriole* to maintain his air of graceful nonchalance. There are constant references throughout these texts to the importance of grace and *sprezzatura*, at least in part because manège equitation so often was something one did before an audience. Whenever a seventeenth-century French nobleman was being observed by his peers, his bearing and behavior were being judged against that courtly ideal that insisted that all his actions be performed not just gracefully but *sprezzatamente*—that is, with a level of skill that allowed the performance to appear totally effortless. This being so, the sources tell us, horsemanship will not be esteemed unless it is done with skill, grace, and *sprezzatura*. Grace is in fact so necessary that those who lack it will be mocked rather than admired, and riders are encouraged to develop both the correct position and the correct attitude specifically so that they will be pleasing to watch. All the authors agree that the key to correct position is minimal movement. The less visible the rider's aids are, the less he moves his body, legs, and arms, the more skillful he appears and the more agreeable he is to watch. The perfectly graceful rider in fact sits so still, firm, and straight, and his aids are so subtle, that the audience believes the horse is working of its own volition rather than at its rider's behest. As for the correct attitude, the rider should display an air of casual nonchalance, as if his skilled and graceful performance required no effort at all. Several authors mention that it is important for the rider always to appear as if what he is doing is pleasant and easy. He must never reveal, either by his expression or by his movements, that he feels uneasy or unsure. Instead, he must always appear relaxed and happy, exhibiting the greatest of ease in all his actions, no matter what weird thing his horse may be doing.[47]

All of these maxims are doubly applicable to the *capriole*. Several authors stress that nothing shows off a rider's skill and dexterity so well as the *capriole*, nor does anything generate more contentment and admiration among spectators. First, the violent motion of the *capriole* makes it particularly difficult for the rider to maintain his position, and difficult things done well always are held in higher esteem. Second, the *capriole* is considered to be the most beautiful of the airs, but because of its difficulty, it also is the most rare. Like difficult things done well, the authors point out, things that are rare always are held in higher esteem. In both cases, however, the esteem accorded to such rare and difficult things is predicated on their quality, so a badly performed *capriole* will garner no esteem whatsoever and in fact may garner outright disdain. This being so, it is even more important for the rider to work continually to hide his aids and to maintain his good posture when performing this air than when performing any other.[48]

Because the *capriole* encompassed this unique combination of danger, difficulty, rarity, and beauty, it provided (at least when performed correctly) an unparalleled platform for a nobleman to display both his virtue and his grace. More than anything else, however, the unique nature of this movement offered the ultimate opportunity for him to display his *sprezzatura*. Based on the description of the movement, it seems reasonable to assume that performing a *capriole* simply without falling off would be more than a little challenging, even for a highly skilled rider; performing one with grace would be even more demanding. To go one step beyond grace and to perform this extremely difficult movement with that air of casual nonchalance that indicated to all who watched that this petty little nothing of a maneuver was no more difficult than trotting a circle indeed would be to achieve the height of *sprezzatura*. All contemporary spectators, even those who did not ride, knew precisely how difficult and potentially dangerous it was to perform this movement. This being the case, it is easy to understand why the correct performance of the *capriole* was viewed as the pinnacle of gentlemanly achievements.[49]

*   *   *

In conclusion, it seems clear that riding a high air of any kind did indeed call into play many of the qualities that early seventeenth-century French nobles associated with *vertu*. The sources also make it abundantly clear, however, that manège equitation in general and the airs above the ground in particular were considered to be excellent vehicles for the display of many of the qualities associated with the new courtly ideal, especially grace and *sprezzatura*. Ultimately, the new style of horsemanship and especially the dramatic airs above the ground allowed early modern French nobles to stay in touch with ideas that were comfortingly familiar while simultaneously adopting and adapting to concepts that were new and foreign.

Although little could be done to slow the increasing obsolescence of heavy cavalry service, the simple fact of being mounted allowed the nobles at least temporarily to retain their ties to what had been one of the two most central elements of the definition of nobility for centuries.[50] More importantly, manège equitation in general and the high airs in particular allowed the nobility to recuperate traditional *vertu*, the other longstanding central element of the definition of nobility, from the various threats that menaced its continued viability. First, these new forms of horsemanship provided a substitute, nonmilitary venue for the display of *vertu*, thus freeing it from its ties to a military function that most nobles no longer performed. Second, this transfer of virtue from the battlefield to the manège allowed the nobles to reaffirm and revalidate the way in which they defined virtue and therefore to counter the argument, implicit in the rise of the new bureaucratic nobility, that virtue need not be martial to be noble. The creation of a new, nonmilitary space in which to demonstrate the qualities of nobility asserted that virtue did not necessarily need to be displayed on a battlefield in order to be considered fully noble, but that it still had to consist of the qualities that the traditional nobles continued to insist were the only ones comprising true *vertu*. Third, the relocation of virtue provided the nobles with a new means to manifest its qualities, thus trumping their detractors' insistence that virtue had to be actively demonstrated in order to be valid. Finally, and perhaps most importantly, manège equitation and the airs above the ground allowed noblemen to display many of the new, more courtly qualities that had been added to the definition of nobility over the course of the sixteenth century. By opening up this space for change within a comfortingly familiar context, manège horsemanship helped make it possible for the early modern French nobility to adapt and evolve, and thus to respond to the pressures of their changing environment.

This chapter leaves the French nobility at a point where its sense of identity and self-perception still was in a state of transition. In the face of unavoidable realities, heavy cavalry service as a central attribute of nobility already was being phased out; virtue was being relocated from military to nonmilitary venues; and more courtly qualities such as grace and *sprezzatura* were becoming increasingly important. Eventually, the older elements would be dropped entirely and the newer elements would become the central core of noble identity. By the eighteenth century, the nobility would have moved into a fully "courtierized" identity, in which *vertu* in the sense discussed here had ceased to be a key component. With the demise of virtue, the ability to perform the dramatic airs above the ground also lost its importance, and this aspect of manège equitation gradually faded into obscurity. Yet during the period covered by this chapter, the high airs performed an important function for the traditional French nobility. These airs provided the nobles with an unsurpassed means to display simultaneously both their traditional martial *vertu* and their newfound grace and *sprezzatura*, and they therefore helped ease the nobility's transition from an increasingly obsolete definition to a more relevant and effective one.[51]

NOTES

1. The arguments in this chapter pertain specifically to the traditional French nobles and not to those who had achieved their noble status through service in royal office—the civil, bureaucratic, or robe nobility. The secondary literature that discusses the various challenges faced by the traditional French nobility during the sixteenth and seventeenth centuries (including those posed by the robe nobility) is vast. Some of the more important recent monographs include Jonathan Dewald, *The Formation of a Provincial Nobility: The Magistrates of the* Parlement *of Rouen, 1499–1610* (Princeton: Princeton University Press, 1980); James B. Wood, *The Nobility of the* Election *of Bayeux, 1463–1666: Continuity through Change* (Princeton: Princeton University Press, 1980); William Beik, *Absolutism and Society in Seventeenth-Century France: State Power and Provincial Aristocracy in Languedoc* (Cambridge, UK: Cambridge University Press, 1985); Arlette Jouanna, *Le Devoir de révolte: La Noblesse française et la gestation de l'état moderne (1559–1661)* (Paris: Fayard, 1989); J. Russell Major, *From Renaissance Monarchy to Absolute Monarchy: French Kings, Nobles, and Estates* (Baltimore, MD: Johns Hopkins University Press, 1994); Donna Bohanan, *Old and New Nobility in Aix-en-Provence, 1600–1695: Portrait of an Urban Elite* (Baton Rouge: Louisiana State University Press, 1992); Donna Bohanan, *Crown and Nobility in Early Modern France* (New York: Palgrave, 2001). Many of these books also discuss how nobility was defined and how that definition changed over time (cf. sources in n. 2) and/or how the nobility's ability to adapt to its changing circumstances ultimately allowed it to overcome the challenges it faced during this period (cf. sources in n. 4).

2. In addition to the more general literature on the nobility listed in the previous note, monographs that deal specifically with how the nobles themselves defined nobility in the sixteenth and seventeenth centuries include André Devyver, *Le Sang épuré: Les Préjugés de race chez les gentilshommes français de l'Ancien Régime (1560–1720)* (Brussels: Editions de l'Université de Bruxelles, 1973); Arlette Jouanna, *Ordre social: Mythes et hiérarchies dans la France du XVIe siècle* (Paris: Hachette, 1977); Ellery Schalk, *From Valor to Pedigree: Ideas of Nobility in France in the Sixteenth and Seventeenth Centuries* (Princeton: Princeton University Press, 1986); Jean-Marie Constant, *La Noblesse française aux XVIe et XVIIe siècles* (Paris: Hachette, 1994).

3. The old view of the early modern French nobility as refusing to abandon its outdated belief system and sliding into a state of hopeless decline as a result has been debunked by recent scholarship such as that listed in n. 1; the last major monograph to make that argument was Davis Bitton, *The French Nobility in Crisis, 1560–1640* (Stanford, CA: Stanford University Press, 1969). The other side of that coin—a

nobility that was willing not only to abandon its belief system but to do so with stunning alacrity—has been argued by Ellery Schalk in *From Valor to Pedigree*. Schalk maintains that the French nobility responded to the accumulating pressures of the late sixteenth century by jettisoning traditional noble *vertu* as a defining characteristic and rather abruptly adopting in its place an identity based almost entirely on birth.

4. In addition to the literature on the definition of nobility listed in n. 2, the following are particularly useful on ways in which the nobility adapted to change while simultaneously maintaining its traditions: Roger Mettam, *Power and Faction in Louis XIV's France* (New York: Blackwell, 1988); Kristen Neuschel, *Word of Honor: Interpreting Noble Culture in Sixteenth-Century France* (Ithaca, NY: Cornell University Press, 1989); Jonathan Dewald, *Aristocratic Experience and the Origins of Modern Culture: France, 1570–1715* (Berkeley: University of California Press, 1993); Jay M. Smith, *The Culture of Merit: Nobility, Royal Service, and the Making of the Absolute Monarchy in France, 1600–1789* (Ann Arbor: University of Michigan Press, 1996). The gradual shift in noble identity was a large part of this adaptive process, which ultimately allowed the nobility to retain its position and importance in French society, politics, and culture, rather than collapsing under the combined weight of the various challenges it faced during the late sixteenth and early seventeenth centuries.

5. Other qualities considered quintessentially noble at this time included a certain type of lifestyle, the legal or customary right to various privileges, recognition by the larger social collective, and—most importantly—noble ancestry.

6. How and why military service originally came to be a central attribute of nobility in France, and how and why military service specifically came to mean armored and mounted service, fall outside the parameters of this chapter. For a good overview of those developments, see Constance Brittain Bouchard, *"Strong of Body, Brave and Noble": Chivalry and Society in Medieval France* (Ithaca, NY: Cornell University Press, 1998), especially chs. 1 and 2.

7. By the sixteenth century, French nobles enjoyed a wide range of both legally mandated privileges and purely customary perks; for details, see Schalk, *Valor to Pedigree*, 146–48; Arlette Jouanna, "Des 'gros et gras' aux 'gens d'honneur,' " in *Histoire des élites en France du XVIe au XXe siècle: L'Honneur, le mérite, l'argent*, ed. Guy Chaussinand-Nogaret (Paris: Tallandier, 1991), 43–44; John David Nordhaus, Arma et Litterae: *The Education of the Noblesse de Race in Sixteenth-Century France* (Ph.D. diss., Columbia University, 1974), 19–20, 28–30; Jean-Pierre Labatut, *Les Noblesses européennes de la fin du XVe siècle à la fin du XVIIIe siècle* (Paris: Presses Universitaires de France, 1978), 10; Frederic J. Baumgartner, *France in the Sixteenth*

Century (New York: St. Martin's, 1995), 47; Philippe Contamine, *La Noblesse au royaume de France de Philippe le Bel à Louis XII: Essai de synthèse* (Paris: Presses Universitaires de France, 1997), 332.

8. Regarding the reemphasis of the links between noble status and military service, especially after the establishment of the royal ordinance companies in 1445 and then again with the advent of the Hapsburg–Valois Wars in 1494, see Schalk, *Valor to Pedigree*, 12; Labatut, *Noblesses européennes*, 85; Contamine, *Noblesse au royaume de France*, 329; Philippe Contamine, *Guerre, état et société à la fin du Moyen Age: Etudes sur les armées des rois de France, 1337–1494* (Paris: Mouton, 1972), 470–72, 475–76, 479–80, 550; Jouanna, *Devoir de révolte*, 42–43; Jouanna, *Ordre social*, 61, 140; André Corvisier, "La Noblesse militaire: Aspects militaires de la noblesse française du XVe au XVIIIe siècles; état des questions," *Histoire Sociale/Social History* 11 (1978): 339–42.

9. James Supple, *Arms versus Letters: The Military and Literary Ideals in the "Essais" of Montaigne* (Oxford: Clarendon Press, 1984), 12. Supple defines the Latin *virtus* not just as manliness but more specifically as strength or courage, which merely underlines the relationship between *vertu* and the nobility's military function. Obviously, *vertu* so defined was an ideal that applied specifically to male members of the warrior nobility; see below for alternative views of virtue as seen by (also male) members of the civil–bureaucratic nobility. How these ideas played into the construction of male identity more generally is a topic that (again) falls outside the parameters of this chapter. A number of studies on the construction of masculinity have been carried out for the medieval period and for early modern England, but very little has appeared for early modern France. One recent exception is Kathleen P. Long (ed.), *High Anxiety: Masculinity in Crisis in Early Modern France* (Kirksville, MO: Truman State University Press, 2002). Unfortunately, none of the essays in this collection deals with masculinity specifically in the context of noble identity.

10. Numerous contemporary sources discuss the meaning of this type of *vertu*, the overwhelming centrality of valor therein, and the belief that warfare was its optimal showcase. The work of Arlette Jouanna is particularly useful in this area; see her "Gros et gras," 32–33, 35, 67; *Devoir de révolte*, 41, 44; *Ordre social*, 43–44, 82, 116, 139–41, 146, 203; "Perception et appréciation de l'anoblissement dans la France du XVIe siècle et du début du XVIIe siècle," in *L'Anoblissement en France, XVe–XVIIIe siècles: Théories et réalités*, comp. Centre de Recherches sur les Origines de l'Europe Moderne de l'Université de Bordeaux III (Bordeaux: Maison des Sciences de l'Homme d'Aquitaine, 1985), 8, 18; "La Noblesse française et les valeurs guerrières au XVIe siècle," in *L'Homme de guerre au XVIe siècle*, ed. Gabriel-André Pérouse, André Thierry, and André Tournon (Saint-Etienne, France: Publications de l'Université de Saint-Etienne, 1989), 207–9; "Les

Gentilshommes français et leur rôle politique dans la seconde moitié du XVIe siècle et au début du XVIIe," *Il Pensiero Politico* 10 (1977): 24; "Recherches sur la notion d'honneur au XVIe siècle," *Revue d'Histoire Moderne et Contemporaine* 15 (1968): 605–6. Other sources include Supple, *Arms versus Letters*, 12, 172, 193; Labatut, *Noblesses européennes*, 87–88; Nordhaus, Arma et Litterae, 10–11, 35; Schalk, *Valor to Pedigree*, 21, 29–30; Ellery Schalk, "The Appearance and Reality of Nobility in France during the Wars of Religion: An Example of How Collective Attitudes Can Change," *Journal of Modern History* 48 (1976): 22; Madeleine Lazard, *Pierre de Bourdeille, seigneur de Brantôme* (Paris: Fayard, 1995), 9; Pierre d'Origny, *Le Hérault de la noblesse de France* (Reims, France: Jean de Foigny, 1578; reprint, Paris: J. B. Dumoulin, 1875), 7, 19; François de la Noue, *Discours politiques et militaires* (Basle, Switzerland: François Forest, 1587; reprint, ed. F. E. Sutcliffe, Geneva, Switzerland: Droz, 1967), 231.

11. Throughout the first half of the sixteenth century, texts written about nobility abound with examples that reveal these assumptions. On the roles played in the definition of nobility both by *vertu* and by valor in combat (i.e., by military service, often referred to in contemporary texts as the nobility's "vocation" or "métier"), see Jouanna, "Gros et gras," 17, 21–22, 30; Jouanna, *Devoir de révolte*, 40, 44; Jouanna, *Ordre social*, 22, 60–61, 116, 139–40, 191–92; Jouanna, "Valeurs guerrières," 207; Jouanna, "Notion d'honneur," 603; Schalk, *Valor to Pedigree*, xiv–xv, 3–11, 21, 26–30, 53–55, 202; Schalk, "Appearance and Reality," 20–23; Labatut, *Noblesses européennes*, 85–86; Lazard, *Brantôme*, 9; Supple, *Arms versus Letters*, 186; Origny, *Hérault*, 19, 23, 37; Roger Chartier, "La Noblesse française et les états généraux de 1614: Une Réaction aristocratique?" in *Représentation et vouloir politiques: Autour des Etats généraux de 1614*, ed. Roger Chartier and Denis Richet (Paris: Editions de l'Ecole des Hautes Etudes en Sciences Sociales, 1982), 120–21.

12. La Noue, *Discours*, 363, 370, 375; Treva J. Tucker, "Eminence over Efficacy: Social Status and Cavalry Service in Sixteenth-Century France," *Sixteenth Century Journal* 23 (2001): 1063, 1065; Claude Gaier, "L'Opinion des chefs de guerre français du XVIe siècle sur les progrès de l'art militaire," *Revue Internationale d'Histoire Militaire* 29 (1970): 743; David Eltis, *The Military Revolution in Sixteenth-Century Europe* (London: Tauris, 1995), 23, 46–47, 50; Charles Oman, *A History of the Art of War in the Sixteenth Century* (New York: Dutton, 1937; reprint, New York: AMS, 1979), 33, 44, 224; John Ellis, *Cavalry: The History of Mounted Warfare* (New York: Putnam, 1978), 78–79.

13. Tucker, "Eminence over Efficacy," 1065; Gaier, "Chefs de guerre," 743; Eltis, *Military Revolution*, 23, 44, 49–51; Oman, *War in the Sixteenth Century*, 35; Bert S. Hall, *Weapons and Warfare in Renaissance Europe: Gunpowder, Technology, and Tactics* (Baltimore,

MD: Johns Hopkins University Press, 1997), 186–87; Archer Jones, *The Art of War in the Western World* (Chicago: University of Illinois Press, 1987), 191.

14. On the development of artillery-resistant fortresses and their effect on military strategy in general and on heavy cavalry in particular, see Baumgartner, *France*, 156; Hall, *Weapons and Warfare*, 164–65, 210–11; David Potter, *War and Government in the French Provinces: Picardy 1470–1560* (Cambridge, UK: Cambridge University Press, 1993), 157; Geoffrey Parker, "The Military Revolution, 1560–1660—A Myth?" in *The Military Revolution Debate: Readings on the Military Transformation of Early Modern Europe*, ed. Clifford J. Rogers (Boulder, CO: Westview, 1995), 41–42; Geoffrey Parker, "In Defense of *The Military Revolution*" (referencing his *The Military Revolution: Military Innovation and the Rise of the West, 1500–1800*, Cambridge, UK: Cambridge University Press, 1988), in *Military Revolution Debate*, 337–38, 345–50. Eltis, *Military Revolution*, 29–30, makes the excellent additional point that siege warfare increased during this period not only in response to the development of new types of fortifications but also because any fortress—new or old—could be defended more effectively due to improvements in artillery. This helps to explain why sieges overshadowed battles even in those areas where the new fortresses were uncommon or even entirely absent, a circumstance that admittedly held true for certain parts of France.

15. On the rise of the mounted pistoleer and his arms, armor, mount, and mobility, see Tucker, "Eminence over Efficacy," 1061–62, 1068–69, and sources cited there, especially in nn. 11, 12, 39, and 40.

16. Ellis, *Cavalry*, 61, 65; Parker, "Myth," 44; Parker, "In Defense," 351; James B. Wood, *The King's Army: Warfare, Soldiers, and Society during the Wars of Religion in France, 1562–1576* (Cambridge, UK: Cambridge University Press, 1996), 135–36; Frank Tallett, *War and Society in Early-Modern Europe, 1495–1715* (New York: Routledge, 1992), 29–30.

17. David Parrott, "Richelieu, the *Grands*, and the French Army," in *Richelieu and His Age*, ed. Joseph Bergin and Laurence Brockliss (Oxford: Oxford University Press, 1992), 143.

18. Jouanna, "Gros et gras," 36–37; Jouanna, *Devoir de révolte*, 42; Jouanna, *Ordre social*, 22, 139, 180; Jouanna, "Valeurs guerrières," 214; Jouanna, "Rôle politique," 34; Jouanna, "Notion d'honneur," 605; Supple, *Arms versus Letters*, 77–78; Chartier, "Etats généraux," 121–22; Devyver, *Sang épuré*, 76–77; Dewald, *Aristocratic Experience*, 22; Eugene F. Rice, Jr., "Humanism in France," in *Humanism beyond Italy*, vol. 2 of *Renaissance Humanism: Foundations, Forms, and Legacy*, ed. Albert Rabil, Jr. (Philadelphia: University of Pennsylvania Press, 1988), 119–20; Roger Mettam, "The French Nobility, 1610–1715," in *Western*

Europe, vol. 1 of *The European Nobilities in the Seventeenth and Eighteenth Centuries*, ed. H. M. Scott (New York: Longman, 1995), 115, 118.

19. Jouanna, "Gros et gras," 36–37, 114; Jouanna, *Devoir de révolte*, 42; Jouanna, *Ordre social*, 61, 149, 204; Jouanna, "Perception et appréciation," 16; Jouanna, "Valeurs guerrières," 214; Jouanna, "Notion d'honneur," 606; Schalk, *Valor to Pedigree*, 57; Corvisier, "Noblesse militaire," 344; Lazard, *Brantôme*, 17; Devyver, *Sang épuré*, 77.

20. Schalk, *Valor to Pedigree*, 106, 117–18; Lazard, *Brantôme*, 17; Devyver, *Sang épuré*, 228–29; Rice, "Humanism in France," 120.

21. The material that follows was drawn from a modern English translation of *Il cortegiano*: Baldessare Castiglione, *The Book of the Courtier*, trans. Leonard Eckstein Opdycke, rev. ed. (New York: Horace Liveright, 1929). Other influential examples of early modern courtly literature include Eustache du Refuge, *Traité de la cour, ou instruction des courtisans*, 1616; Nicolas Faret, *L'Honnête Homme, ou l'art de plaire à la cour*, 1630; Baltasar Gracián, *Oráculo manual y arte de prudencia*, 1647. This courtly literature should not be confused with another, preexisting literary tradition, frequently referred to as courtesy books—that is, manuals of civility, manners, and etiquette. These books, many of which were essentially instructional texts, were intended for a wide range of readers (including, but certainly not limited to, the nobility) who aspired to function more smoothly and effectively in the upper echelons of society and in public office in general, and not specifically for that tiny minority who hoped to make a career at court, the vast majority of whom were nobly born. Although this type of literature already had a long history before the sixteenth century, as "civility" became more important in society in general, courtesy books proliferated and enjoyed wide popularity. Some outstanding titles of the period include Desiderius Erasmus, *De civilitate morum puerilium*, 1530; Giovanni della Casa, *Il Galateo*, 1558; Stefano Guazzo, *La civil conversazione*, 1574.

22. For a representative selection of Castiglione's views on grace and *sprezzatura*, see *The Courtier*, 30–31, 34–35, 37.

23. The *académies* were intended exclusively for the education of the hereditary nobility. Although they offered instruction in subjects other than horsemanship, the amount of time devoted to mounted activities outweighed that devoted to all the other topics combined. Sources on these establishments are scarce; a fairly comprehensive selection of the available secondary material in French and English includes Schalk, "Education, the Academies, and the Emergence of the New Image of the Cultured Noble-Aristocrat," ch. 8 in *Valor to Pedigree*; Mark Motley, "The Academy," ch. 3 in *Becoming a French Aristocrat: The Education of the Court Nobility, 1580–1715* (Princeton: Princeton University Press, 1990); Commandant de la Roche [no first name given], "Les Académies militaires sous l'Ancien

Régime, d'après des documents inédits," *Revue des Etudes Historiques* (1929): 409–18; Maurice Dumolin, "Les Académies parisiennes d'équitation," *Bulletin de la Société Archéologique, Historique et Artistique le Vieux Papier* 111 (1925): 417–28, 112 (1925): 485–94, and 113 (1926): 556–72 (issues 111 and 112 are the most relevant); Lucien Hoche, "Pluvinel et les académies," app. 23 in *Contribution à l'histoire de Paris: Paris occidental, XIIe siècle–XIXe siècle* (Paris: Henri Leclerc, 1912); Albert Folly, "Les Académies d'armes (XVIe et XVIIe siècles)," *Bulletin de la Société du VIe Arrondissement de Paris* 2 (1899): 162–71; Albert Babeau, "Les Académies," ch. 4 in *Les Officiers*, vol. 2 of *La Vie militaire sous l'Ancien Régime*, 2nd edn. (Paris: Firmin-Didot, 1890); see also Nordhaus, *Arma et Litterae*, 118–21, 220–26; Hubert de Terrebasse, *Antoine de Pluvinel, dauphinois, 1552–1620* (Lyon: L. Brun, 1911), 5–6, 13–15, 19, 24. These noble *académies* are not to be confused with the literary, artistic, or scientific *académies*, such as the Académie Française, that also were founded in France from the late sixteenth through the eighteenth centuries but for entirely different purposes.

24. To give some idea of the numbers involved, a thorough but by no means all-inclusive search of the bibliographic sources yielded 42 texts dealing with the art of riding and training horses and written in Italian, English, French, and Spanish between 1550 (the date of the first extant early modern treatise on riding) and 1661 (the beginning of the personal reign of Louis XIV, during which the shift from the medieval to the early modern definition of nobility in France was completed); the vast majority of the 42 treatises were written by noblemen. If the cutoff date were extended to 1800, if all European languages and Latin were included, and/or if texts dealing with equestrian matters other than horsemanship (e.g., veterinary care, shoeing, breeding, horse management, or cavalry) were counted, the number would be much higher. Of the available hippobibliographies, the most exhaustive are Frederick H. Huth, *Works on Horses and Equitation: A Bibliographical Record of Hippology* (London: Bernard Quaritch, 1887); Gabriel René Mennessier de la Lance, *Essai de bibliographie hippique*, 2 vols. (Paris: Lucien Dorbon, 1915–17; supplement, 1921); Ellen B. Wells, *Horsemanship: A Bibliography of Printed Materials from the Sixteenth Century through 1974* (New York: Garland Publishing, 1985).

25. In some cases first editions were not available and a later, somewhat revised edition had to be used. The editions actually consulted are as follows: Salomon de la Broue, *Le Cavalerice françois, contenant les preceptes principaux qu'il faut observer exactement pour bien dresser les chevaux...*, 2nd rev. exp. edn. (Paris: Abel l'Angelier, 1602 (bk. 1) and 1608 (bk. 2)); René de Menou de Charnizay, *La Pratique du cavalier, ou l'exercice de monter à cheval...*, rev. exp. edn. (Paris: Guillaume and Jean Baptiste Loyson, 1650); Pierre de la Noue, *La*

Cavalerie françoise et italienne, ou l'art de bien dresser les chevaux, selon les preceptes des bonnes écoles des deux nations . . . (Strasbourg: Jac. de Heyden, 1620); Antoine de Pluvinel, *L'Instruction du roy en l'exercice de monter à cheval* (Paris: Michel Nivelle, 1625); Delcampe [no first name given], *L'Art de monter à cheval: qui monstre la belle & facille methode de se rendre bon homme de cheval*, 2nd rev. exp. edn. (Paris: Jacques le Gras, 1664); Georges Guillet de St. George, *Les Arts de l'homme d'epée, ou le dictionnaire du gentilhomme* (The Hague: Adrian Moetjens, 1680). The first edition of La Broue's treatise appeared under a slightly variant title, *Preceptes principaux que les bons cavalerices doivent exactement observer . . . pour bien dresser les chevaux.* . . .

26. That the *pesade* was not viewed as being in the same category as the truly high airs, at least during the first two-thirds of the seventeenth century, is evidenced by its absence from the lists of commonly practiced *airs relevés* offered by the various authors; see La Broue, *Cavalerice françois*, bk. 1, 140; La Noue, *Cavalerie françoise et italienne*, 112; Pluvinel, *Instruction du roy*, 118; Menou, *Pratique du cavalier*, 112; Delcampe, *Art de monter à cheval*, 190. These lists vary somewhat in their content—some include only the high airs, i.e., the *courbette* and the *capriole* and the latter's various derivative forms (see n. 43), whereas others include both the high airs and the *terre à terre*, a movement that was essentially a less elevated version of and preliminary to the *courbette* (see n. 38 and related text)—but none of the lists includes the *pesade*. La Broue, writing at the very beginning of the seventeenth century, does include something called *pesade saut de mouton* in his list of high airs, but only to say that it no longer is performed; he does not define the move, so it is impossible to know how it differed from a regular *pesade*, although the inclusion of the word "saut" (jump) would imply that it involved some sort of aerial activity, which the standard *pesade* did not.

27. That all horses were expected to master the *pesade* is largely implicit rather than explicit in these texts. La Noue, *Cavalerie françoise et italienne*, 114, 136, and Guillet, *Arts de l'homme d'épée*, 105, are the only authors to flatly state that the *pesade* is the foundation for all the high airs, even the fairly mundane *courbette*. On the other hand, the descriptions of the training progression in all the treatises make it clear that only those horses that have mastered the art of raising their forehands could be expected to perform any of the higher airs, all of which are taught from that basic movement. Several of the authors concede that not all horses are suitable for the lofty activities of the manège, and horses that failed to master the *pesade*, the basic building block for the more complex movements, therefore were unlikely to have enjoyed prolonged careers there. Such hapless clods almost certainly were banished to less exalted pursuits, where the ability to leap prettily about was not a prerequisite for success.

28. That the *courbette* was universally considered to be one of the high airs is evidenced by its presence in all of the lists cited in n. 27. Both La Broue, *Cavalerice françois*, bk. 1, 140, and La Noue, *Cavalerie françoise et italienne*, 112, 116, explicitly identify it as the easiest of the high airs. In Pluvinel, Menou, and Delcampe, this belief is more implicit than explicit, i.e., these authors freely acknowledge that only some horses are able to perform the *capriole* and its related forms, whereas nothing of the sort is said about the *courbette*. It is clear from the texts that most or all manège horses were expected to master this movement, as so many of the other movements could not be performed properly (or at least in their most "perfect" form) without it. Like the *pesade*, the *courbette* was so fundamental to the practice of manège riding that horses that failed to grasp its intricacies almost certainly were shuffled off to less glorious pursuits.

29. La Broue, *Cavalerice françois*, bk. 1, 138; La Noue, *Cavalerie françoise et italienne*, 111; Pluvinel, *Instruction du roy*, 51; Menou, *Pratique du cavalier*, 112–13; Delcampe, *Art de monter à cheval*, 229, 231. Pluvinel, Menou, and Delcampe all agree that the ability to perform the high airs is a gift of nature, thus underscoring the fact that not all horses are so gifted.

30. The *capriole* variations included the *balotade*, the *croupade*, and *un pas et un saut*. For descriptions of these airs, see n. 43.

31. For descriptions of the *pesade* and its purpose, see La Broue, *Cavalerice françois*, bk. 1, 149; La Noue, *Cavalerie françoise et italienne*, 114, 116; Guillet, *Arts de l'homme d'épée*, 105. Pluvinel, Menou, and Delcampe do not use the term *pesade*, but instead refer merely to *lever le devant* or *lever devant*, although Delcampe occasionally does use the term *posade* (according to Guillet, *Arts de l'homme d'épée*, 114, an alternative spelling for *pesade*). Pluvinel also refers to the *courbette en une place* or *courbette ferme à ferme* (in one place) and seems to use this term as an alternative to *lever le devant*—a rather interesting choice, given that the quality of a true *courbette* was judged in part on the proper motion of the hind feet and therefore in theory could not be performed *en une place* or *ferme à ferme* (see sources cited in n. 39). Regardless of the nomenclature, it is clear from the way in which the movement is discussed in the texts of Pluvinel, Menou, and Delcampe, and from the contexts in which it is used, that it is indeed the same as the *pesade*, although none of these authors defines the movement or its purpose as clearly as the other three. For those familiar with the airs above the ground as they are performed today, for example by the Lipizzan stallions of the Spanish Riding School in Vienna, there are several differences between the seventeenth-century *pesade* and its modern counterpart, the *levade*. The first concerns the angle of the horse's body to the ground. In the *pesade*, the horse lifted its forehand to an angle of roughly 45 degrees to the ground; in the *levade*, the angle is only around 30 degrees, which requires far more strength and

balance on the part of the horse. Second, the modern movement is considered to be one of the airs above the ground and thus an end in itself, rather than primarily a training aide for the other high airs. Third, the horse is expected to remain in *levade* for as long as its strength and balance will allow, rather than only long enough to establish the pose before coming back down.

32. On training the horse to *pesade*, the various types of resistance the trainer might expect to encounter, and the relevant remedies, see La Broue, *Cavalerice françois*, bk. 1, 148–49; La Noue, *Cavalerie françoise et italienne*, 114–15; Pluvinel, *Instruction du roy*, 46–50; Menou, *Pratique du cavalier*, 42, 91–92; Delcampe, *Art de monter à cheval*, 35–36. Pluvinel and (especially) La Noue are particularly useful for the more hair-raising forms of resistance.

33. See, for example, La Broue, *Cavalerice françois*, bk. 1, 49, 60, 62, 79, 83; La Noue, *Cavalerie françoise et italienne*, 10–13, 111; Pluvinel, *Instruction du roy*, 3, 15–17, 26, 29, 38–39, 48, 73, 123, 132, 144–45; Menou, *Pratique du cavalier*, 18, 32, 35, 59–61, 64, 72–73, 113, 116, 137–38; Delcampe, *Art de monter à cheval*, 34, 233–34. For additional details on why falling off was viewed as behavior totally unsuited to a gentleman, see n. 49.

34. Part of the reason these horsemen stressed the intellectual qualities needed by the rider was because of the way in which they viewed the nature of the horse. Contemporary science and philosophy portrayed animals as unreasoning forces of nature that had to be forcefully dominated and subdued by rational human intelligence or will. In contrast, the authors of these treatises granted the horse a considerable capacity to think and to feel, even if they did not put equine "reasoning" on a par with human. Horses nonetheless were seen as having at least some capacity to participate in the training process, at least to the extent that riders had to take into consideration their mounts' thoughts and feelings—as well as their innate talents and limitations—if the training process were to succeed. This view of the horse is revealed by the anthropomorphized language used by the authors to describe the training process: the rider clearly retains intellectual superiority, but the equine "mind" with which he is grappling is described as responding and functioning in very human ways. For additional details, see the chapters by Pia Cuneo (5) and (especially) Elisabeth LeGuin (6) in this collection, as well as Karen Raber, "Reasonable Creatures: William Cavendish and the Art of Dressage," in *Renaissance Culture and the Everyday*, ed. Patricia Fumerton and Simon Hunt (Philadelphia: University of Pennsylvania Press, 1999).

35. For a sampling of the more "cerebral" qualities needed by the rider and why they are necessary, see La Broue, *Cavalerice françois*, bk. 1, 3, 49–51, 74, 118, 153, 174; bk. 2, 8, 56–57, 70–71, 125–26, 158, 163, 173–74; La Noue, *Cavalerie françoise et italienne*, 14, 40, 60,

65, 111; Pluvinel, *Instruction du roy*, 2–3, 9–10, 19–20, 31, 36, 40, 48–50, 59, 66–67, 82–83, 85, 89–90, 94, 97, 99–100, 106, 125, 133–34, 144–45; Menou, *Pratique du cavalier*, 25–26, 75–76, 109, 113, 155; Delcampe, *Art de monter à cheval*, 29–30, 40–42, 88–89, 230, 281–82. All these texts are littered with references to the particular importance of using one's judgment when riding and training— for example, to assess a given horse's capabilities and temperament, or to choose which training technique to employ with a given horse in a given situation. Several authors emphasize the concept that there can be no fixed rules in horsemanship. A technique that worked for one horse in a particular situation may not work for another horse in the same situation, while a technique that worked for a particular horse in one situation may not work for that same horse in another situation. (Those who ride will know that this can be taken yet further, i.e., a technique that worked for a particular horse in a particular situation on one day may not work for that same horse in that same situation on the next day, simply due to fluctuations in equine mood.) Precisely because riding follows no rules, the rider constantly must exercise his judgment (not to mention his vast store of knowledge) in order to make the adjustments dictated by the circumstances of the moment.

36. For those familiar with the *courbette* as it is performed today, it should be emphasized that the sixteenth- and seventeenth-century movement of the same name was totally different from its modern counterpart. In the modern *courbette*, the horse rears up fully and then hops forward on its hind legs as many times as its strength and balance will permit; the forelegs never touch the ground. Some of the confusion about the early modern movement may be the result of illustrations in contemporary texts of the *balotade* (see n. 43), which resembles the airborne moment in the modern *courbette*. Under what circumstances and at what point in time the latter was developed, and why it bears the name of a movement that originally differed from it fairly dramatically, unfortunately is not known to me at this time.

37. Guillet, *Arts de l'homme d'épée*, 128–29. Guillet, whose text is a dictionary of equestrian terms rather than a riding and training manual, is the only author who defines the *terre à terre*. The other five authors make repeated references to this movement but never actually describe it, leaving one with the impression that this air was so common at the time these men were writing that they felt no more need to define it than to define the walk, trot, or canter. As was the case with both the *pesade* and the *courbette*, it is clear from these texts that all manège horses were expected to master the *terre à terre*.

38. For descriptions of the *courbette*, see La Broue, *Cavalerice françois*, bk. 1, 149; La Noue, *Cavalerie françoise et italienne*, 114, 116; Delcampe, *Art de monter à cheval*, 191; Guillet, *Arts de l'homme d'épée*, 40–41. Both Pluvinel and Menou make frequent reference to this air but never define it as clearly as the others.

39. Interestingly, none of the texts consulted says anything about the actual training process for the *terre à terre*, although all of them mention it (some more frequently than others) in the context of more complex movements such as *voltes* or *passades*. Pluvinel, *Instruction du roy*, 45–46, claims that he is going to discuss how to train horses to do the *terre à terre*, but in fact he passes straight to training the horse to *lever le devant* (i.e., to *pesade*) as a preparation for teaching it the *courbette*; the *terre à terre* never really is mentioned again in this passage. The premise that at least some horses would have objected to and tried to avoid the demands of the *terre à terre* therefore is extrapolated, in part from descriptions of the training process for other airs, gaits, and movements, and in part from my own experience training various types of horses to collect.

40. See, for example, La Broue, *Cavalerice françois*, bk. 1, 140–44, 149–56; La Noue, *Cavalerie françoise et italienne*, 116–20; Pluvinel, *Instruction du roy*, 50–55. These authors discuss (both in the pages just cited and elsewhere in their respective volumes) the training methods not only for the basic movement but also for its use as part of more complex maneuvers such as *voltes* and *passades*. La Broue provides the most details on the training process and its challenges. He emphasizes that training a horse to *courbette* takes time and that some horses simply cannot (or will not) do it, although it is clear from the text preceding the latter statement that all horses destined for the *manège* are expected to be able to do it. Delcampe defines the *courbette* clearly (see n. 39), but he does not discuss how it is taught; Menou neither defines it nor discusses the training process. In both cases, it almost seems to be assumed that the horse will fall naturally into this *cadence* when the circumstances are right. Neither author appears to address what must have been the far more common instance of a horse that failed to produce the *courbette* spontaneously, without benefit of any formal training.

41. La Broue and La Noue are the most explicit on the lack of congruity between the hot-tempered horse and the subjugation of collection in general and of the *courbette* in particular; see La Broue, *Cavalerice françois*, bk. 1, 98, 147, 158; bk. 2, 29; La Noue, *Cavalerie françoise et italienne*, 113–14, 128. Although these authors do not specify why the *courbette* in particular is so troublesome in this regard, it seems reasonable to surmise that the contradictory demands of the movement contributed to its special status. Specifically on horses that respond to constraint by launching themselves into the air, see La Broue, *Cavalerice françois*, bk. 1, 147; Pluvinel, *Instruction du roy*, 51; Menou, *Pratique du cavalier*, 112.

42. For descriptions of the *capriole*, see La Broue, *Cavalerice françois*, bk. 1, 168; La Noue, *Cavalerie françoise et italienne*, 112, 135; Pluvinel, *Instruction du roy*, 118; Menou, *Pratique du cavalier*, 114; Delcampe, *Art de monter à cheval*, 193–94; Guillet, *Arts de l'homme*

d'épée, 30. La Broue, La Noue, and Guillet stress that the horse must come down as close as possible to the spot whence it took off; Pluvinel, Menou, and Delcampe maintain that this air also may be performed going forward or sideways or on a circle. For those familiar with the modern *capriole*, the early modern movement was virtually identical, except that today the horse always is supposed to come down as close as possible to the place from which it took off and only a single *capriole* ever is performed. Finally, now that the *capriole* has been described, the variations referred to earlier may be defined. The *balotade* is identical to the *capriole*, except that the horse does not lash out with its hind legs at the highest point of the leap but keeps them fully curled under its body. The *croupade* also is identical to the *capriole*, except that at the highest point of the leap the horse again does not lash out with its hind legs but moves them back only far enough to show its hind shoes. *Un pas et un saut* alternates a *courbette* (the *pas*, or step) and a *capriole* (the *saut*, or jump). It was considered less taxing than *caprioles* alone, as the *courbette* phase allowed the horse a brief recovery period before it was asked for another *capriole*. These definitions are from Guillet, *Arts de l'homme d'épée*, 15, 44–45, 100–1; see also La Broue, *Cavalerice françois*, bk. 1, 145–46, 171; La Noue, *Cavalerie françoise et italienne*, 124, 138; Pluvinel, *Instruction du roy*, 139; Menou, *Pratique du cavalier*, 147, 150–51; Delcampe, *Art de monter à cheval*, 192, 196, 266–67, 275, 277–78. Pluvinel does not mention the *balotade* or the *croupade*; La Broue and La Noue clump them together under the same heading (*croupade* in La Broue's case, *balotade* in La Noue's), although La Broue never really defines the movement; and Menou and Delcampe define them exactly as Guillet does. As for *un pas et un saut*, there is a little more disagreement there. La Broue, La Noue, and Menou agree with Guillet's definition but specify that the *courbette* is to be a very low one— almost a stride of *terre à terre* rather than a true *courbette*. Pluvinel and Delcampe differ from Guillet, stating that the *pas* phase actually consists of two "steps," only one of which is a full *courbette*. Pluvinel specifies that the second step is to be a stride of *terre à terre*, while Delcampe leaves the second step's precise contours rather vague; cf. Guillet's definition of *deux pas et un saut* (101).

43. It is difficult to ignore the parallels in the qualities possessed by the ideal equine *caprioleur* and those possessed by the nobleman of true *vertu*. Unfortunately, the only time the authors use these terms to describe a horse is when they are discussing horses suited specifically to the most dramatic of the high airs. Since these animals were far more the exception than the rule, the parallels do not appear to lead anywhere very fruitful. On the other hand, the manuals frequently make reference to the need for the rider not to dominate or suppress but to control and direct his horse's feistier qualities, which presents many interesting and potentially fruitful parallels to the histories of

control, discipline, civility, the body, and so on. For example, just as the rider of this period must shape and monitor the nature, body, and impulses of his horse, so the "civilized" nobleman of this period must shape and monitor his own nature, body, and impulses. This is, however, a complex topic that falls beyond the parameters of this chapter and must await another day; in the meantime, the three chapters in the "Discipline and Control" section of this volume explore various aspects of this topic, as does Raber, "Reasonable Creatures," 54–58.

44. On the ideal qualities and temperament of the *caprioleur*, as well as the character defects that often accompany that temperament, see La Broue, *Cavalerice françois*, bk. 1, 165; La Noue, *Cavalerie françoise et italienne*, 124; Pluvinel, *Instruction du roy*, 119, 122–23, 125, 132; Menou, *Pratique du cavalier*, 116, 118, 137–38; Delcampe, *Art de monter à cheval*, 235–36; see also Guillet, *Arts de l'homme d'épée*, 6, 85, for definitions of terms pertaining to lightness (*allegerir* and *leger*). All five trainers emphasize that very few horses are capable of or suited to this exceptionally difficult and demanding maneuver; even Guillet mentions when defining the *capriole* (30) that it is the most difficult of the high airs. On the temperament (both good and bad) typical of horses with a gift for the high airs in a more general sense (i.e., both the *capriole* and its variations), see La Broue, *Cavalerice françois*, bk. 2, 29; La Noue, *Cavalerie françoise et italienne*, 112–13, 128; Pluvinel, *Instruction du roy*, 123; Menou, *Pratique du cavalier*, 116; Delcampe, *Art de monter à cheval*, 233–34.

45. Pluvinel, *Instruction du roy*, 123; Menou, *Pratique du cavalier*, 116.

46. On the qualities needed by the rider specifically for the successful performance of the *capriole* and the reasons for which he needed them, see Pluvinel, *Instruction du roy*, 123–24, 133; Menou, *Pratique du cavalier*, 116, 138–39, 143; Delcampe, *Art de monter à cheval*, 251–53.

47. On the importance of grace and *sprezzatura* when riding, and especially when riding before an audience, including how those qualities were to be displayed in a mounted context and what would happen to riders who failed to do so, see La Broue, *Cavalerice françois*, bk. 1, 47, 122–23, 139, 173; La Noue, *Cavalerie françoise et italienne*, 32–34; Pluvinel, *Instruction du roy*, 9, 12, 58–59, 72, 75–76, 90, 92–93, 120–21, 140, 142–43; Menou, *Pratique du cavalier*, 25, 105–7, 152; Delcampe, *Art de monter à cheval*, 10–11. Pluvinel's text in particular is filled with references to the importance of grace on the part of both horse and rider.

48. La Broue, *Cavalerice françois*, bk. 1, 171–73; La Noue, *Cavalerie françoise et italienne*, 128; Pluvinel, *Instruction du roy*, 138, 140; Menou, *Pratique du cavalier*, 146; Delcampe, *Art de monter à cheval*, 263, 279–80. Like the concepts of grace and *sprezzatura*, these ideas regarding the relationship between rare or difficult things, correct performance, and the esteem of others come straight out of

Castiglione: "Everyone knows the difficulty of those things that are rare and well done, and therefore facility in them excites the highest admiration; while on the other hand, to strive . . . is extremely ungraceful, and makes us esteem everything slightly, however great it be" (*The Courtier*, 35). It is for this reason that falling off, even when performing a movement as difficult as the *capriole*, was such a disaster for a nobleman. Just as retaining one's position and nonchalant demeanor while one's horse behaved badly was viewed with approval, so parting company with one's horse under the same circumstances was viewed quite harshly. Falling off was seen as a spectacular failure not only of the rider's skill, strength, grace, and *sprezzatura* but also of his good judgment: if he was not ready to perform in the fashion considered appropriate to a gentleman, then he should never have made the attempt in the first place. The rider's peers thus would assume that he fell because he lacked the requisite qualities of true *noblesse*. The possible ramifications of such a judgment fall outside the parameters of this chapter, but they would not have been good and might have been appalling.

49. Although the sections on the *capriole* in all the sources have this premise as a sort of running subtext, some authors are quite explicit. For some particularly flowery accolades on the *capriole* as the *ne plus ultra* of mounted achievements, see Pluvinel, *Instruction du roy*, 138; Menou, *Pratique du cavalier*, 146; Delcampe, *Art de monter à cheval*, 264.

50. The nobility's links to mounted military service were sustained less by manège equitation and the high airs than by various types of mounted pseudomilitary games. These games originated in earlier military and tournament practices, but by the early seventeenth century a successful performance depended on the mastery of skills related far more to the manège than to the battlefield. Such games nonetheless allowed the nobles temporarily to maintain the illusion that they were learning and practicing skills that would be useful to a heavy cavalryman and thus helped to insulate them from the shock of losing military service as a defining attribute.

51. A final note on the issue of belief versus behavior. This chapter argues that manège equitation helped the nobility as a whole to transition from an obsolete definition to a more relevant one by allowing nobles to practice elements of both definitions at the same time. The chapter does *not* claim that, as part of that process, manège equitation became a central attribute of the new definition. On the contrary, the evidence indicates that attending the *académies* in which this riding style was taught was very expensive, so only the upper echelons of the nobility could afford to learn it. However, the belief system that defined the contours of French noble identity always was formed by this small percentage at the top and then trickled down very gradually from there. By the time it reached the petty rural nobility, actual

practice had little or nothing to do with the belief system. Just as the rural noble of ca. 1500 rarely had any real, actual, lived relationship to heavy cavalry service, so the rural noble of ca. 1700 rarely had one to manège equitation. That did not stop him, however, from believing that the qualities embodied by the mounted warrior (ca. 1500) or the mounted courtier (ca. 1700), none of which was limited to the mounted context, were the quintessence of nobleness. Manège equitation and the airs above the ground only had to serve the function for which this chapter argues in the narrow confines of that segment of the nobility that was and always had been the genesis of notions of noble identity. Nobles who fell outside that segment were less impacted by the actual means by which the upper echelons moved from the old definition to the new one than they were by the end product—in this case, the shift away from the highly militarized idea of nobility that prevailed coming out of the Middle Ages, and toward the "courtierized" idea of nobility that prevailed at Louis XIV's Versailles.

CHAPTER 11

"HORSES! GIVE ME MORE HORSES!": WHITE SETTLER IDENTITY, HORSES, AND THE MAKING OF EARLY MODERN SOUTH AFRICA

Sandra Swart

In southern Africa, the smell of leather and horse sweat was the smell of conquest. From 1652, South Africa was colonized by men on horseback, creating a white colonial state and changing the face of the land itself. Although species of the genus *Equus*—such as the zebra and ass—had been present in Africa since earlier times, the horse (*Equus caballus*) is not indigenous, but was introduced into the continent. The histories of horses and white settlers are intimately, indeed inextricably, entangled. Horses were the first domestic stock imported by the settlers upon their arrival at the Cape of Good Hope in 1652. Although the horse had been in regular use in North and West Africa from A.D. 600, there were none in the southern tip.[1] African horse sickness presented a pathogenic barrier to horses reaching the Cape over land.[2]

The human dialogue with the environment is arguably nowhere clearer than in an agro-ecological investigation of history. This chapter seeks to explore a particular facet of horse–human relationships, focusing on the introduction of horses into the Cape and the symbolic and practical ramifications of this introduction. The horse was an integral member of the "portmanteau biota" that accompanied European settlement of the subcontinent from the mid-seventeenth century onward and by the start of the nineteenth century was a ubiquitous presence in the colonial countryside.[3] The early modern settlement that grew, against resistance from the metropole, into a colony in its own right was based largely on the power of the horse in the realms of agriculture, the military, and communications. This chapter asks who lost power and who gained power as modes of production changed, based on the introduction of the horse? It investigates the transformation in human labor and social relations within a settler society that was beginning to define itself as separate from the metropolitan homeland, Holland. It explores how identity roles and social institutions were refracted and reflected through the social ideas surrounding horses. I consider the symbolic and sociohistorical role of the equid in Boer society and chart the historical trajectory of the republican commando system, whose members were invested with an identity predicated, in part, on an organic equestrian skill, to show how the horse was integral to Boer masculine identity. The making ("invention") of the "Cape horse" is discussed as a symbol of settler identity and independence from the metropole. I conclude with a vignette of the transition to the new Union of South Africa in 1910, the freshly minted state that signalled the definitive end of the early modern republics and the entrenchment of the modern bureaucratized state—a state that required mechanization not horses.

SETTLING IN

Although European vessels frequently passed by South Africa on their way to East Africa and India, and sometimes stopped for provisions, no permanent European settlement was made until 1652, when Jan van Riebeeck and about 90 other people set up a provisioning station for the Dutch East India Company at Table Bay on the Cape of Good Hope. The company required a refreshment station for their ships voyaging between Holland and the East Indies to provide food, water, and hospitalization for sick sailors. At the time of Van Riebeeck's landing, the Cape was inhabited by San (Bushmen) and Khoikhoi ("Hottentots") in the southern and central areas, and by black Sintu/Bantu-speakers on the northern and eastern fringes. The company brought Dutch settlers to Cape Town, who farmed and raised livestock and were called Boers (Dutch for "farmers"). Soon after his arrival, Van Riebeeck began to trade with the Khoikhoi, distributed land to the Europeans for farms, and imported Africans (from West and East Africa) and Malays as slaves. By 1662, about 250 Europeans were living near the Cape, and gradually they moved inland, initiating the colonial state. The company ruled the Cape until 1795, except for a brief period of French occupation (1781–84). The British took possession of the Cape during the French revolutionary wars and held it as a colony from 1795, save for a brief return to Dutch rule from 1803 to 1806; a wave of English settlers arrived from 1820 onward.

White settlers moved out from the Cape to hunt, to barter, to appropriate land, and to settle with their livestock. They did this because opportunities in the colony proper were limited, or because they wanted to escape company control, and so they moved into a "frontier" zone already peopled by San hunters, and further north and east by the Sintu/Bantu-speaking pastoralists. With horses and muskets they could shoot the game on which the San depended, and by the 1780s the San settlements had been driven north, after a century of broken conflict. From 1836 to 1838, tensions on the frontier led to a second, more deliberate emigration from the Cape colony, by Boer groups escaping British frontier policy and the liberal aspects of British rule to set up republics of their own. In 1800, southern Africa was a region without any easy routes for wheeled traffic; communications were slow and effected at the speed of horses. By 1900, however, much of this had changed, with the early modern state replaced by the modern. The main reason was the discovery of diamonds in 1867, and of gold in 1886, which started rapid industrialization and awoke Britain's imperial interest. After a devastating war between the Boer republics and Britain in 1899–1902, Britain began to devolve power back to South Africa from 1906 to 1907. Conciliation did not hold—there was conflict between those who embraced modernization, often accompanied by anglicization, and those who retained a nostalgia for the early state forms. Previous attempts to consolidate Afrikanerdom found a focus in a reaction against the imperial connection, and in opposition to war against the Germans in 1914, which brought several ex-commando leaders out at the head of a rebellion. The rebellion was easily suppressed and the new state was able to consolidate.

As Necessary as Bread?

The Dutch East India Company had selected Jan van Riebeeck as founder and first commander of the settlement. He had to bring every piece of equipment, vegetable seed, and necessary stores for his 125-person community. A biblical profusion of plagues, storms, wild beasts, and food shortages afflicted the early years of the settlement. Yet above all this, the commander argued that his biggest problem was the perpetual shortage of horses. He wrote in his journal, "soo nodigh als broot in den mont zÿn" ([Horses] are as necessary to us as bread in our mouths).[4] He recorded in November 1654 that "it is to be wished that we had a few more horses than the 2 we have at present, both of which are being used for brick-making. We should then be able to get from the forest everything we need, both timber and firewood, as the roads are quite suitable for wagons" and, in April 1655, "we are therefore still urgently in need of another 6 or 8 horses."[5] Van Riebeeck judged horses to be his "greatest and principal need," imploring, "Horses! Give me more horses!"[6]

Van Riebeeck's requests became petitions, and then pleas, but were ignored by Amsterdam.[7] The settlement was faced with managing construction initially with no draft animals of any sort. It was not part of the Dutch tradition to use oxen for draft. Moreover, while oxen were occasionally ridden by some indigenous groups, controlled by a stick thrust through their nostrils, they were untrained in drawing wheeled vehicles.[8] The company suggested Van Riebeeck avail himself of the "indigenous horses." Three wild members of the horse family were local to the area—the mountain zebra (*Equus zebra*), Burchell's zebra (*Equus burchelli*), and the quagga (*Equus quagga*), now extinct.[9] With their apparent immunity to horse sickness, zebras were an inviting proposition and Van Riebeeck initially planned to tame them, but he found that he could not even catch them. The Swedish explorer Andrew Sparrman noted in the late eighteenth century that it was, in fact, possible to tame zebras, and that as they showed little fear they could be turned out with horses at night to protect them against predators.[10] A span of zebras was even briefly utilized to run stagecoaches to Pietersburg at the end of the nineteenth century.[11] But a Cape Town burgher unwisely harnessed some half-tamed zebras to his chaise, with the result "that they directly ran back into the stable, with the carriage and their master in it, with such prodigious fury, as to deprive him and everyone else of all desire to make any further trials of this kind."[12] A Cape Town guidebook noted resignedly in 1819, "the zebra is said to be wholly beyond the government of man." Whatever degree of tameness is possible in zebras, then, it did not fit them for use as part of Van Riebeeck's task.

Van Riebeeck wished not merely to build a town, but to reshape the landscape, to change the native ecosystem. The first white settlers in 1652 attempted what is common to most settlers—to make themselves "at home" on the land by making it like "home." This would be achieved particularly well by the introduction of horses, which were not only an alien species but had the potential to transform the physical environment with their draft power.[13] Van Riebeeck planned in part to reshape the landscape with horses, to remove the bushes, plow the soil, and cut down shrubs and trees with that arboreal animosity common to settler societies, and to encircle his settlement with a hedge of wild almonds.[14] He argued that horses would prove invaluable in transporting lumber, and sand, clay, and firewood to make bricks for construction, and in revolutionizing agriculture at the settlement by plowing and threshing.[15] Horses and free burghers were inextricably intertwined in his evolving vision for the development of the country; with enough horses he believed he could provide provisions for the eastern settlements—and fashion a colony rather than merely a provisioning station.[16] Van Riebeeck attempted further to persuade the company by arguing that only horses would allow for the exploration of the hinterland. In May 1653, he observed, "I wish we had a dozen [horses], when we could ride armed to some distance in the interior, to see whether anything for the advantage of the Company is to be found there. . . ."[17] He argued that it would accelerate the settling period, saving both time and human labor,[18] and contended that horses would make the settlers independent of the Khoikhoi, enabling them to acquire construction materials and wood without native help, thus freeing them from an unavoidable policy of conciliation.[19] The company, however, acceded only to requests that delivered immediate material results, and his letters were ignored by his superiors in Amsterdam.[20] Moreover, creating a colony was not the original plan; rather, the company envisioned merely a refreshment station at which to refuel ships en route from Holland to the East.

Despite Van Riebeeck's grand vision, the process of bringing horses to the Cape was a hit-and-miss affair, influenced by both social and ecological factors. Horses and white settlers had set out for the Cape in the same year, 1652; the horses, however, were driven onto the island of St. Helena by a storm.[21] In 1659, 16 more horses were imported from Java. These horses—together with a pack of hunting dogs—were imported in part to instill fear into the Khoikhoi, who were beginning to initiate raids upon the settlement. The awe, indeed the veneration and consternation, inspired by equids and the usefulness of these emotions in instilling a sense of settler superiority is a common theme in colonial literature. In June 1660 the settler authorities used horses to demonstrate settler superiority to the Khoikhoi, who were cattle-raiding: "the Commander, galloping along the near bank . . . soon disappeared from their view. His purpose was also to demonstrate the speed of the horses, which caused great awe among them."[22] Van Riebeeck noted with satisfaction that the local population was astonished and impressed by horses because of the "miracles" he performed with them. There were concomitantly several attacks on horses: for example, two horses were killed by Khoi in July 1672 to undermine the white power base. It is not certain whether these attacks were motivated by the intention to wipe out all horse stock, or whether a horse acted as a proxy for the white settlement as a whole, being perhaps one of its most visible and vulnerable manifestations.

Mounted men were also able to decimate the indigenous population. Robin Law has shown that in West Africa, horse-borne warriors facilitated territorial expansion and that armies utilizing the mobility afforded by horses could dominate other groups.[23] Horses played a crucial role in expanding the feasible scale of political organization. The domination and control over indigenous groups was rendered practicable by horse-power in the south as in the east. A useful comparative illustration is provided by the Spanish conquistadors, who came to the Americas in the early 1500s, bringing with them domesticated horses. These travelers noted that the natives, who had never seen horses before, believed that horse and rider were all one animal. The conquistadors, like the Cape settler community, had only a small stock of horses, yet the Indians' astonishment at these "horse–men" contributed to their submission to the conquistadors.

The Spanish colonizers had recognized the tactical and symbolic value of the animal, and consequently prohibited Indians from owning or even riding horses without the specific permission of their masters. Their efforts, of course, eventually failed, and the horse became a part of native culture. Similarly, in the Cape, despite desperate efforts, horses were not contained by white society. From the time that the Sotho, for example, overcame sociopolitical and economic hurdles and acquired their first horse, the "ox without horns" as they called it, in 1825, they reinvented themselves as an equine society.[24]

Ultimately, however, for the early settlers sponsored by the Dutch East India Company, the long journey between Holland and the Cape militated against sending Dutch horses to Cape Town. Only once in the settlement's first 125 years were equids imported from Europe, when two horses and four mules arrived safely in 1676. The company resorted instead to sending stock from its base in Java. In 1653 four Javanese ponies were imported, but the stallion of the herd was eaten by a lion a few days after its arrival. In 1673, two more

Javanese ponies were introduced. The Javanese imports were small, hardy creatures, thirteen-and-a-half hands (54 inches) high. They were also known as "South East Asia Ponies," an amalgam of Arab and Mongolian breeds, their ancestors having been acquired from Arab traders in the East Indies.[25] Another useful source of horses was Persia. In 1683, 4 horses were imported from Persia via Mauritius, and in 1689, 11 more came from Persia directly.

Several factors beyond the sheer distance of South Africa from trade centers militated against the successful introduction of horses. Conditions during transport were difficult—in 1673 all but two of a cargo of horses drowned, and in 1690 all of the horses in another cargo died on the arduous sea voyage. On land, conditions were equally dangerous. African horse sickness was a perennial problem:[26] an acute, febrile, and infectious disease, believed by the settlers to be carried by evening miasmas, it was the scourge of the wet season.[27] There was no natural fodder—hay or grain—available in the region, and forage was often of low quality. Predation by lions and other wildlife played a minor role, killing some of the prime stock and necessitating unrelieved vigilance, as exemplified by the first Javanese pony's fate. In June 1656, when his own best stallion was eaten by lions, Van Riebeeck anguished, "This has greatly inconvenienced us, when one considers all the work done by horses—one alone does more than ten men in pulling the plough, in carrying clay, stone, and timber from the forest."[28] Horses occasionally died from misuse by settlers, and legislation was introduced to prohibit the premature working of colts and fillies.[29] Once the indigenous population realized the extent to which horses formed the white power base, there were attacks on horses. Finally, stock theft increasingly became a factor as local communities realized the utility of the horse. But despite these limiting factors, there was a steadily growing horse industry in South Africa. Although overworked and preyed upon by wild lions, the Javanese ponies bred successfully, until by 1662 they formed a herd of 40. They were now integral to the defense of the settlement, allowing 18 mounted men to patrol the border against cattle-raiding Khoisan. By 1667 there were 50 horsemen on watch duty. The importance of these animals can be indicated anecdotally: when one of these guards and his mount drowned while drunkenly fording a river, for instance, the mare was mourned more than the soldier.[30]

By 1665, horses had become more widely available and were no longer tightly controlled by the burgeoning state, which is indicated by the fact that a public horse auction was held that year, and free burghers were granted the right to breed horses. However, horses continued to be a public asset, and were considered vital to the functioning of the settlement, leading to the imposition of social and legal controls on their use or abuse. In May 1674, for example, a man was prosecuted for shooting his own (rogue) horse.[31] Inbreeding was affecting the herds, and certain birth defects—such as a hindquarter droop—were becoming obvious, so measures were taken to help prevent the deterioration of stock. In 1688, the governor also tried to prevent overwork of animals, imposing a fine of 40 rixdollars if colts under the age of three years were used. Measures were also taken in 1689 to import new stud stallions.

In 1700, there were 633 horses in the Cape settlement. By 1715 the Dutch East India Company owned 396 horses and the white settlers had 2,325. In 1719, when the first crippling epidemic of horse sickness hit, the horse industry survived despite the loss of 1,700 horses. By 1744 the colonists had 5,749 horses.

THE "CAPE HORSE"

Horse breeding thus continued at a steady rate, slowly resulting in a "breed" of horse that came to be known as the "Cape horse," a fusion of Javanese pony (itself of Arab–Persian stock), imported Persians (1683 and 1689), South American stock (1778),[32] North American stock (1782), English Thoroughbreds (1810), and Spanish Barbs (1807).[33] The breed thus had a particularly significant Arab and Persian genetic influence. In 1769, the Cape-based horses were divided into two groups—one "breed" to meet the needs of riding, transport, and the cavalry (the breed that eventually became the Boerperd) and one to meet the desires of the racing fraternity, which used Thoroughbreds (usually a Thoroughbred sire and a colonial dam). This latter breed was variously known by English-speaking settlers as the "Colonial," the "South African," and the "Boer horse," and by Dutch-speakers (who were to become the "Boer" or "Afrikaner" nation) as the "Hamtam" (an area in which horse breeding was carried out), "Melck," or "Kotzehorse" (surnames of famous breeders), even "Bossiekoppe" (bushyheads) if the speaker was unimpressed by the breed's qualities.

Horses, like other African livestock breeds, developed in response to a wide range of climates, environmental stresses, and, perhaps particularly, anthropogenic demands. The Cape horse was phenotypically very different from English Thoroughbreds and American Saddlers. It was a small, hardy horse.[34] In 1845 the first "scientific" description was offered: 14.3 hands, "brown," compact, short legged, calm, well mannered, constitutionally strong, disease resistant. As previously

noted, for the first hundred years, the breeding stock was largely
Arabian and Persian, with an injection of English Thoroughbred
blood from the nineteenth century. This globalized process of breed
amalgamation was increasingly stamped on an indigenous process,
generating a peculiar type of animal belonging to the Cape.
Moreover, Boer settler riding styles replaced those of the European
founders. The trot, for example, which was considered "unnatural"
by the Boers, was replaced by an ambling jog called a triple, or slow
gallop, that was easy to ride while carrying a whip or gun.[35] The combination of a hardy indigenous breed and new ways of using the
breed's gaits led to a sense of national pride in the Cape horse (occasionally rueful, given the breed's rough qualities). George Thompson,
for example, noted, "I had travelled this day about 56 miles, the
last 30 at full gallop on a hardy African pony, saddled for me fresh
from the pasture. This would have killed almost any English horse,
but the country breed of Cape horses is far more hardy than
ours. . . ."[36] Lady Anne Barnard recorded her favorable impression of
the Cape horse: "A little more size in the breed would render the
Cape horse very good; they already have a cross of the Arabian fire
and are hardy in the greatest degree."[37] Heinrich Lichtenstein noted
that these horses were "so fine, that they [were] very much sought for
at the Cape as riding-horses" and that "The Africans [horses],
besides, owing to their being accustomed from their youth to seek
their nourishment upon dry mountains are easily satisfied, and grow
so hard in the hoofs."[38] Lady Duff Gordon observed,

> Cape horses . . . [s]uch valiant little beasts, and so composed in temper,
> I never saw. They are nearly all bays. . . . They are not cobs, and look
> "very little of them," and have no beauty; but one of these little brutes,
> ungroomed, half-fed, seldom stabled, will carry a six-and-a-half-foot
> Dutchman sixty miles a day, day after day, at a shuffling easy canter,
> six miles an hour. You "off saddle" every three hours, and let him roll;
> you also let him drink all he can get; his coat shines and his eye is
> bright, and unsoundness is very rare. They are never properly broke,
> and the soft-mouthed colts are sometimes made vicious by the cruel
> bits and heavy hands; but by nature their temper is perfect.[39]

More has been written about the deterioration and disappearance
of the Cape horse than about any other aspect of its history. From
1860, careless breeding with inferior stallions was widespread in order
to feed the export trade. There was popular demand to breed from
English Thoroughbreds, and as a result, pedigree became paramount

to the exclusion of merit.[40] "Blood weeds," as they became known, polluted the gene pool, precipitating a general decline in stamina, size, hardiness, and sound conformation. The state attempted breed improvement through the importation of Hackneys in 1888 and 1891. Nevertheless, Australia gradually came to dominance over South Africa in remounts destined for India. Moreover, since 1854 periodic revisitations of horse sickness had inflicted crippling losses on the Cape horse herds. In 1854, 65,000 horses and mules out of 169,583 were lost; in 1870, a further 70,000 died, and in 1891 3,100,000 horses died from the disease, almost 20 percent of the total stock.[41] To further compound the effect, in 1869 the Suez Canal was opened up and the Cape lost its position on the trade route between Europe and the East. Mineral discoveries and subsequent rapid industrialization from 1870 onward drew attention away from horse breeding, which gave way to accelerated mechanization of the work horses had once done. Railways were built from the seaports to the mining centers, superseding the ox-wagon and horse-drawn transport. By 1904, an equine enthusiast, Captain Hayes, could pronounce the Cape horse of fifty years earlier to be as "extinct as the quagga."[42]

HORSES, THE LAND, AND NATIONALISM

South African horses and South African identity became increasingly wrapped up in each other, particularly in terms of Boer (and later Afrikaner) masculine identity. There is a great tradition linking Afrikaners to the land as farmers.[43] Theirs is a discourse familiar from other European countries and their colonies; it is a discourse about rootedness in the land, one that invokes the traditions of agrarian labor.[44] This agrarian nationalism in Boer society depended in large part on horses and horsemanship.

Unlike the horse in the American West, horses did not represent freedom or wildness to the white settlers; rather horses spoke of civilization.[45] This was arguably because the settlers found no indigenous feral horses to tame, and instead had to resort to the extremely difficult import of horses. The existence of these imports was, as we have seen, a precarious thing, threatened by disease and predators, both human and animal. They were not wild creatures to be tamed but extensions of Western civilization to be nurtured and protected in order that they might serve the white expansionist project.

In any society, the land and its creatures are seldom simply material resources, but rather are invested with social meaning. Sidney Plotkin notes, for example, that "nothing is more intimate in the life of a community, or more reflective of its most sacred commitments and prerogatives, than its treatment of land."[46] Social constructions of nature and the land afford us windows onto national identity. Anthony Smith has shown how brokers of culture engaged in vernacular mobilization transform the physical terrain into "ethnoscapes," expressing and indeed insisting upon a sense of connectedness to the nation's ethnic past and its "character."[47] The Boers, as agrarian nationalists, imagined the environment as an agrarian ethnoscape: a cultivated landscape of agricultural labor and a reservoir of national history and identity.

THE COMMANDO SYSTEM

As previously noted, the original desire of the Dutch East India Company was simply to maintain its Cape settlement as a refueling station, but communities cannot be controlled and this one escaped beyond its hedge of wild almonds. Moreover, the Dutch East India Company conceded eventually that a colony would buttress the Cape against incursions by other seafaring nations and would be useful as a self-supporting community. Immigration to the Cape from Holland and Germany was encouraged, and many Huguenot refugees seized the opportunity to repatriate. By the end of the eighteenth century the settlers had spread out north and eastwards beyond the station's original borders. Wherever these Boers went, horses went with them.

The first armed militia controlled by whites in southern Africa was established by the Dutch East India Company. At first the company had no large garrison and therefore relied on a few soldiers supplemented with local farmers and the indigenous people who volunteered or were compelled to join a commando. A commando system is a method of military organization in which an army is divided into units by drawing soldiers from a particular place and then using them primarily in that area. These units are thus a brotherhood of local warriors—in the case of South Africa, warriors who owned horses and guns. Commando refers to the general ideologically charged nature of the commando system, with its sociopolitical implications. The first commando was established in 1670. By the nineteenth century, in trekboer communities the commando system had become the dominant military mode. Members of the commando were expected to provide their own mount and saddlery, a rifle, and 30 rounds of ammunition. Within this regulated system, discipline was based on the normally acceptable mores of the family, and leaders developed idiosyncratic forms of control: one Boer general, for example, used *sjambokking* (whipping with a rawhide whip) and beatings with horse whips to keep his troops in order.

Boer and Afrikaner masculinity became institutionalized in the republic's commando system, which functioned as a practical and symbolic mode of South African national masculine identity. The horse-based commando system extended into politics, culture, and social mythology.[48] Cavalry has always had an important influence on both political structure and social institutions: as far back as Aristotle, who contended that cavalry states tended to be oligarchies because ownership of horses was necessarily restricted to a wealthy minority, a reliance on mounted forces created elite social groups who could control a nation's political future by offering or withholding their support in war.[49] Horse culture in South Africa reinforced the complex interconnection of military, economic, and political power, coupled to social institutions.

Boer commandos were usually committed to a republican form of statehood, which they saw as integral to their "nature" as Boers. Commando was also clearly part of the social machinery that constructed Boer/Afrikaner manhood: to be a "man" in Boer culture meant to aspire to commando status, participation in that brotherhood, and defense of one's region and country, extending to defense of its national ideology.

Ethnographic studies of commando life are rare, but it would appear that enrolling in the commando was a rite of passage, meaning that commando provided a system for assigning status that was important in the early socialization of young Boer men. The manner in which a man acquitted himself in the commando would affect his status as a man in the community at large, and his status in the social realm would in turn decide his authority in the commando.[50] Horsemanship was an important demonstration of manhood, showing strength and the ability to control a powerful animal with skill. Interestingly, stallions received special treatment among the horses of the Boers, reflecting a more widely applied gender distinction. The traveler Charles Thunberg noted in the late eighteenth century that while mares and colts were expected to forage for themselves, stallions were fed specially cultivated barley. Moreover, mares were perceived as having little importance and, as it was considered undignified to ride one, fillies were seldom broken or handled.[51]

The myths about commando described a specifically Boer past and present, and eventually helped justify the Boer Rebellion. The anthropologist Malinowski has argued that myths are pragmatic charters of extant institutions, corresponding to social arrangements. A myth is "not merely a story told, but a reality lived. . . . It expresses, enhances, and codifies belief; it safeguards and enforces morality; it . . . enforces practical rules for the guidance of man."[52] Myths about masculinity and horsemanship were used by South African Boers to mobilize support, maintain law and order, maintain social stability, and ensure social solidarity in the early state. If the commando simultaneously represented defense of freedom and a structure of authority, it also played into Boer self-definition in terms of the replacement of the early republic with the modern state. And if the end of the early republic meant an end to a true Boer identity, it also meant the replacement of the horse with machines, and the erasure of masculine identity and prerogative.

In this version of the world, horses operate metonymically as a way of remembering or preserving the (idealized) past. When the horse-based commando system was removed by the 1912 Defence Act, that moment signaled the end of the early modern republic and the beginning of the modern bureaucratic state, and it sparked a consequent rebellion. General De Wet, a rebel leader, famously maintained that a "Boer without a horse is only half a man." But the modernizing state triumphed, compelling Boers and Afrikaners to abandon life in the countryside at the cost of their traditional lifestyle. Urbanization was a part of the poor white's new life: in 1899, 2.6 percent of people who could be crudely classified as Afrikaners lived in urban areas; by 1911, the figure had reached 24 percent.[53] The trek to the cities was a journey to the mines, railways, and factories.[54] Probably many who took part in the government schemes or moved to the city planted their "sole hopes for the future in the possibility of returning to the past."[55] This nostalgic *ubi sunt* motif was a powerful element of populist rhetoric.[56] Many poor whites increasingly believed that a return to the republican lifestyle could be achieved if smaller farmers and poor whites were reinstated on the land. It was believed that this should be accompanied by traditional means of relief: doles of horses, cash, and livestock. O'Connor, writing immediately after the rebellion, noted that the majority of rebels were men who had not "an acre of ground or a decent flock of sheep to their names," to whom "On commando" means "a happy time of riding around on horseback from town to town, living on the country as they proceed."[57]

The modernizing state presented a political, economic, and social threat to the Boer way of life, both real and mythic. In part, the rebellion was a movement built by men on nostalgia for a past only recently faded and yet already reimagined by them, a past nostalgically represented as a "Golden Age."[58] Nostalgia for a republic that had never really been and the desire to be once more the men that ran it proved strong. In the buildup to the First World War, Afrikaans-speaking males living on the periphery of the new locus of central state power in Pretoria began to turn to alternative authorities to express their grievances and to gain support. In the southwestern Transvaal and the northern Free State particularly, farmers and *bywoners* (share-croppers) who were alienated by the state's failure to alleviate the economic recession turned not to the state, but to their old commando leaders.

The new military of the modernizing state also threatened to extinguish republican masculinity. The 1912 Defence Act imposed colonial training methods, uniforms, a ranking system, a very hierarchical bureaucracy, disciplinary codes, and promotional norms.[59] Military professionalization entailed overt social differentiation and hierarchy, which the commando system had formerly served to mask.[60] Commando had been socially and politically pivotal to the development of an Afrikaans culture, so when it was hijacked by the modernizing state, this too alienated republicans. Cultural images of commando may have corresponded little to the reality of warfare, but seductive imagery propagated by rebel leaders helped fuel the republican nostalgia that centered on a particular understanding of mounted manhood.

The inexorable machine of the capitalizing, modernizing state meant the end of the central symbolic and practical role of the horse. One moment may epitomize the end of a particular kind of leadership invested in the old horse-based commando system and embedded in a lifestyle that was rapidly disappearing. Near the end of the rebellion, with the rebels in disarray and the leadership on the run, General De Wet decided that his only hope lay in joining the other remaining free rebel leader across the Kalahari, in German territory. At Maquassi, however, heavy rains turned sand into mud, into which the horses' hooves sank.[61] On the trail of his mounted commando was a petrol-driven fleet, a caravan of cars, brought up from Kimberley by train. At a little oasis in the veld, the cars converged, and defeat was complete. De Wet's comment is, perhaps, the best metaphor for the end of a social identity predicated on mounted manhood and the commando, brought about by the modernizing state and all it entailed. He said wearily, "It was the motor-cars that beat me."[62]

NOTES

1. For the horse, and particularly for descriptions of how it played a role in major shifts in the balance of power in West Africa, see Robin Law, *The Horse in West African History* (Oxford: Oxford University Press, 1980).
2. African horse sickness is a serious insect-borne disease of horses, mules, and donkeys that is spread by a virus. It is endemic to the African continent, and is characterized by respiratory and circulatory damage, accompanied by fever and loss of appetite.
3. A. W. Crosby, *Ecological Imperialism: The Biological Expansion of Europe, 900 to 1900* (Cambridge, UK: Cambridge University Press, 1986). On more general horse history, see Harold Barclay, *The Role of the Horse in Man's Culture* (London: J. A. Allen & Co., 1980); Charles Chenevix-Trench, *A History of Horsemanship* (New York: Doubleday, 1980); Juliet Clutton-Brock, *Horse Power: A History of the Horse and Donkey in Human Societies* (Cambridge, MA: Harvard University Press, 1992).
4. H. C. V. Leibrandt, *Précis of the Cape Archives: Letters Despatched 1652–1662*, 2 vols. (Cape Town: Richards, 1900), vol. I, 407.
5. J. van Riebeeck, *Journal of Jan Van Riebeeck, vol. I, 1651–1655*, ed. H. B. Thom (Pretoria: AA Balkema, 1952), 272, 307.
6. Leibrandt, *Letters Despatched*, vol. I, 407.
7. H. C. V. Leibrandt, *Précis of the Cape Archives: Letters Received 1649–1662* (Cape Town: Richards, 1898 (vol. I) and 1900 (vol. II)), vol. II, 253.
8. Traveling by ox was a deeply unsatisfying mode of transport—as David Livingstone observed two centuries later, riding his ox "Sinbad" through Angola, with the ox trying to decapitate him on every overhanging bough. David Livingstone, *Missionary Travels and Researches in South Africa* (London: Murray, 1857), ch. 18.
9. Colin P. Groves, *Horses, Asses and Zebras in the Wild* (Hollywood, FL: Ralph Curtis Books, 1974).
10. Andrew Sparrman, *A Voyage to the Cape of Good Hope, towards the Antarctic Polar Circle, and around the World, but Chiefly into the Country of the Hottentots and Caffres, from the Year 1772 to 1776* (London: Robinson, 1785).
11. A "span" refers to those animals "spanned in" to a cart or wagon.
12. D. Child, *Saga of the South African Horse* (Cape Town: Howard Timmins, n.d.), 6.
13. For a discussion, see Thomas Dunlap, *Nature and the English Diaspora: Environment and History in the United States, Canada, Australia and New Zealand* (Cambridge, UK: Cambridge University Press, 1999).
14. *Uitgaande briewe*, no. 493, 670.
15. It was a rudimentary system: horses turned the ground over with a massive plow requiring eight or ten horses, and the harvested

grain was trodden out by horses on circular threshing floors in the open air.

16. *Uitgaande briewe*, no. 493, 143.
17. *Uitgaande briewe*, no. 493, 143
18. S. F. du Plessis, *Die verhaal van die dagverhaal van Jan van Riebeeck* (D.Litt. diss., University of Pretoria, 1934); J. van Riebeeck, *Dagverhaal van Jan van Riebeeck, Commandeur aan de Kaap de Goede Hoop* (The Hague: Nijhoff, 1892–93), 434; *Uitgaande briewe*, no. 493, 143.
19. Van Riebeeck, *Dagverhaal van Jan van Riebeeck*, 446.
20. A. J. H. van der Walt, *Die Ausdehnung der Kolonie am Kap der Guten Hoffnung (1700–1779) eine historisch-okonomische Untersuchung uber das Werden und Wesen des Pionierlebens im 18. Jahrhunder* (Berlin: Ebering, 1928), 2.
21. Later (1655 and 1656) a handful of these were recaptured and brought to the Cape.
22. Leibrandt, *Letters Despatched*, vol. II, 311; *Uitgaande Briwe*, no. 493, 1098–99.
23. Law, *The Horse in West African History*, 182.
24. This chapter focuses on white society, however. For a discussion of the equine revolution in Sotho society, for example, see Sandra Swart, "The 'Ox without Horns': The Basotho Pony and the Transformation of Sotho Society, c.1825–2001," paper presented at the International Conference on Forest and Environmental History of the British Empire and Commonwealth, University of Sussex, UK, March 19–21, 2003.
25. From this Javanese stock the South African horse eventually developed, winning renown as a cavalry mount of the British army in India, and forming the nucleus for the horse breeding industry in Australia. See Jose Burman, *To Horse and Away* (Cape Town: Human and Rousseau, 1993); P. J. Schreuder, *The Cape Horse: Its Origin, Breeding and Development in the Union of South Africa* (Ph.D. diss., Cornell University, 1915).
26. See the *Cape of Good Hope Government Gazette*, September 17, 1830; no. 1288.
27. It does not spread directly from one horse to another, but is transmitted by midges, which become infected when feeding on infected horses. It occurs mostly in the warm, rainy season, when midges are plentiful, and disappears after the frost, when the midges die. Most animals become infected in the period from sunset to sunrise, when the midges are most active.
28. See Sandra Swart, "Riding High—Horses, Power, and Settler Society, c.1654–1840," *Kronos* 40 (2003): 58.
29. *Origineel Plakkaat Boek*, 1735, 1753, 82.
30. Child, *The Saga of the South African Horse*, 13.
31. Child, *The Saga of the South African Horse*, 22.

32. John Barrow, *Travels in the Interior of South Africa, in the Years 1797 and 1798* (New York: N. Y. Johnson Reprint, 1968).
33. The horses of Spanish origin were taken from two French ships boarded during the Napoleonic wars.
34. F. J. Van der Merwe, *Ken Ons Perderasse* (Cape Town: Human and Rousseau, 1981).
35. M. H. Hayes, *Among Horses in South Africa* (London: Everett, 1900).
36. George Thompson, *Travels and Adventures in Southern Africa* (London: Henry Colburn, 1827).
37. Lady Anne Barnard, *Letters of Lady Anne Barnard . . ., 1793–1803 . . .* (Cape Town: AA Balkema, 1973), Sept. 1798.
38. H. Lichtenstein, *Travels in Southern Africa in the Years 1803, 1804, 1805 and 1806* (reprint, Cape Town: Van Riebeeck Society, 1965). See also Anon., *Sketches of India, or, Observations Descriptive of the Scenery, etc. in Bengal . . . together with Notes on the Cape of Good-Hope and St. Helen* (London: Black, Parbury and Allen, 1816), 74.
39. Lady Duff Gordon, *Letters from the Cape, 1861–62* (Cape Town: Maskew Miller, 1925), 86–87.
40. Schreuder, *The Cape Horse*, 39.
41. Schreuder, *The Cape Horse*, 47.
42. Hayes, *Among Horses in South Africa*, 72.
43. This may be in contrast to the reality of agricultural economics; the poet Roy Campbell, for example, sarcastically noted that "Beards are the only crop the Boers have ever grown without a government subsidy"; quoted in J. Crwys-Williams (ed.), *Penguin Dictionary of South African Quotations* (London: Penguin, 1999), 57.
44. Katrina Schwartz, "Contesting the Ethnoscape: Globalization, Nature and National Identity in Post-Soviet Latvia," paper presented at the Annual Meeting of the American Political Science Association, San Francisco, August 30–September 2, 2001; Katrina Schwartz, *Wild Horses and Great Trees: National Identity and the Global Politics of Nature in Latvia* (Ph.D. diss., University of Wisconsin–Madison, 2001).
45. See, for example, Elizabeth Lawrence, "Rodeo Horses: The Wild and the Tame," in R. Willis (ed.), *Signifying Animals: Human Meaning in the Natural World* (London: Routledge, 1990).
46. Sidney Plotkin, *Keep Out: The Struggle for Land Use Control* (Berkeley: University of California Press, 1987), 2. See also William Cronon (ed.), *Uncommon Ground: Rethinking the Human Place in Nature* (New York: W. W. Norton and Co., 1996), 25–26.
47. Anthony D. Smith, *Myths and Memories of the Nation* (Oxford: Oxford University Press, 1999).
48. P. H. Frankel, *Pretoria's Praetorians, Civil–Military Relations in South Africa* (Cambridge, UK: Cambridge University Press, 1984).
49. Aristotle, *Politics*, trans. C. D. C. Reeve (Indianapolis, IN: Hacket, 1998), 1321a.

SANDRA SWART

50. Frankel, *Pretoria's Praetorians*, 24.

51. Charles Thunberg, *Travels in Europe, Africa and Asia, Performed in the Years 1770 and 79*, vol. II (London, 1793). Law, *The Horse in West African History*, 45, notes a similar phenomenon in West Africa, where mares had to feed themselves by grazing and were unpopular for riding.

52. Bronislaw Malinowski, *Magic, Science and Religion and Other Essays* (Glencoe, IL: Free Press, 1948), 79.

53. John Bottomley, *Public Policy and White Rural Poverty* (Ph.D. diss., Kingston, Queens University, 1990), 248.

54. Bottomley, *Public Policy and White Rural Poverty*, 250.

55. L. Salomon, *Socio-economic Aspects of South African History, 1870–1962* (Ph.D. diss., Boston University, 1962), 116.

56. A "where are?" formula for lamenting the vanished past.

57. J. K. O'Connor, *The Africander Rebellion* (London: Allen and Unwin, 1915), 12. Many discouraged men must have remembered the old republican days when they could have received a free rifle on receipt of a certificate of poverty. While on campaign, burghers had been fed and clothed by the state, and their families had received support.

58. See Sandra Swart "Desperate Men: Rebellion and the Politics of Poverty in the 1914 Rebellion," *South African Journal of History* 42 (2001): 161–75; Sandra Swart, " 'You Were Men in War Time': The Manipulation of Gender Identity in War and Peace," *Scientia Militaria* 28/2 (1998): 187–99; Sandra Swart, "A Boer and His Gun and His Wife Are Three Things Always Together," *Journal of Southern African Studies* 24/4 (1998): 737–52.

59. *Staatskoerant*, G.K. no. 1, 31.5.1910; 871, 22.7.1912.

60. Bengt Abrahamsson, *Military Professionalization and Political Power* (Beverly Hills, CA: Sage, 1972).

61. Today called Makwassie, near Wolmaransstad.

62. Eric Rosenthal, *General De Wet* (Cape Town: Dassie, ca. 1950), 153.

Chapter 12

Learning to Ride in Early Modern Britain, or, The Making of the English Hunting Seat

Donna Landry

During the eighteenth century, Britons developed a distinctive way of riding on horseback that gave them a patriotically charged experience of so-called native freedoms.[1] What came to be known as the "English hunting seat," whether its practitioners were English or Irish, Scots, or Welsh, emerged during the early modern forging of the nation as an imperial metropole.[2] Both this new disposition of the body on horseback and the rhetoric of native freedoms as guarantors of cultural superiority and imperial prerogative were manifestations of Britain's "gentlemanly capitalist" version of mercantilism, of Britain's participation and rise to dominance within the capitalist world system between the late sixteenth century and the mid-nineteenth century.[3] Indeed, the very question of an English seat may have been most hotly debated precisely during moments of national crisis and identity formation or reformation, though the evidence for this is not conclusive.

What the evidence does substantiate, I think, is that the style of riding developed in the British Isles in order to follow hounds, particularly when pursuing foxes over enclosed land, was developed with a sense of cultural superiority allied with imperial destiny. When eighteenth-century Britons started jumping obstacles at flat-out racing pace on Thoroughbreds while hunting, turning the tops of their boots down, and taking their stirrups up a notch or two in order to negotiate at a gallop the new enclosures of what Robert C. Allen has identified as the second or landlords' Agricultural Revolution,[4] they departed from continental equestrian practice at least partly, but crucially, in the name of national superiority and imperial sovereignty. This tradition of supposed superiority in cross-country riding continues to this day. And that is why the British public who follow equestrian sports grow indignant when British teams fail to win at international Combined Training or Three-Day Event competitions, particularly if they have not at least distinguished themselves in the cross-country phase (the three phases consisting of dressage, the cross-country, and stadium or show jumping). As one long-time competitor has observed, "Britain used to dominate the world, and sadly we seem to have lost our edge."[5] The rise and decline of the English hunting seat might stand as a metonym for the fate of the British empire.

A NATIONALIST HISTORY

Investigating the history of riding over fences requires recovery work to get beyond received commonplaces. The only histories of early modern British horsemanship available are popular histories. These vary in their adherence to the conventions of academic scholarship. However, a book such as Charles Chenevix Trench's *A History of Horsemanship* (1970) is highly regarded among the more literate in the professional horse-coping community in Britain. His version of horsemanship's history deserves some attention since from the ethnographic point of view, what people in a field of endeavor regard as their history counts as valuable evidence. (As it happens, I have found Chenevix Trench's extensive use of primary sources to be judicious and fundamentally accurate, even in the case of quotations, despite the absence of footnotes in his book.)

Like other popular historians, Chenevix Trench delivers a progress narrative, in which modern riding practices emerge as the rational products of a series of innovations and the extinction of older practices. This whiggish tendency is now historically suspect. Developments in any social practice are likely to be uneven; horsemanship may not have been the beneficiary of uninterrupted enlightenment and improvement. Supposedly outmoded practices, if anything general can be said about them, tend to hang around, especially in country districts. And what the elite do is as likely to be scorned as imitated by the lower ranks in the British Isles.

If, however, one were to grant the provisional usefulness of a grand narrative for the making of the English hunting seat, as earlier historians of horsemanship have done, the story would be one of the continual shortening of the stirrup leathers so that riders could ride ever faster horses ever more quickly over fences. Shortening the stirrup leathers to a length that made standing in them easy encouraged free forward movement of the horse—an instance of enacted liberty—while increasing the security and comfort of the rider over rough terrain—preserving the precious body of the enlightened Briton.

This shorter-is-better sense of national superiority appears to have held from some time in the later seventeenth century until very late in the nineteenth, when from 1897 onward the Italian cavalry officer Capt. Federico Caprilli (1868–1907) and the American jockey Tod Sloan put their stirrups up even higher, thus causing the English to look askance at the practice.[6] Caprilli's was a scientific, logically consistent *sistema* for covering all types of terrain, based upon close observation of equine and human anatomy in action. Sloan's seat was designed solely for flat racing, and was perhaps not invented by him so much as copied "from diminutive Negro stable-boys," as Chenevix Trench speculates.[7] Whether Caprilli was influenced by what he had read or heard of Sloan, who was after 1897 "engaged in making himself painfully conspicuous in the most expensive London restaurants," strikes Chenevix Trench as "extremely doubtful."[8] After Sloan's and Caprilli's seats became fashionable, the traditional English hunting seat looked like riding long and sitting down and back, comparatively speaking—almost like dressage, except that the lower legs and feet were carried more forward than was desirable in the dressage seat. It appeared as a sort of middle way, a splendid British compromise.[9]

The consensus among British historians of horsemanship as to the state of riding styles before Caprilli could be summarized as follows. By the end of the eighteenth century there remained "the two ancient styles of horsemanship," the Eastern and the Western, but a third was emerging:

> The natural style developed by the horsemen of Eurasia who rode short, on a snaffle-bridle, with no thought of collection but allowing their horse free forward movement: and the style of western Europe, where educated, scientific horsemen rode long and concentrated above all on collection induced by spurs and a curb-bit. But there was also a third school of horsemanship, if anything so thoughtless and unscientific can be so pretentiously termed; that of the English (and American) hunting-man, who rode fairly long like his ancestors, but

whose riding was based, like the Cossack's, on extension rather than collection.[10]

During the next 170 years, in the opinion of Chenevix Trench and others, the history of horsemanship is one "of the interaction, and, in certain cases, coalescence of these three rival schools."[11]

When the splendid British compromise is combined with the notion that horses show initiative in foxhunting because they enjoy it, we have a potent recipe for free forward movement of horse and rider as the quintessential experience of Englishness or Britishness. Lt.-Col. S. G. Goldschmidt put this idea particularly forcefully in 1927: "One often hears it said that a polo pony has a fondness for the game. This is not true. The only work that a horse is put to in this country from which it derives any enjoyment is hunting."[12] Knowing how to ride across country without hindering an English or Irish Thoroughbred hunter that enjoys its work is the essence of the hunting seat, and thus the essence of being British.

UNACKNOWLEDGED ORIENTALISM AND THE "ENGLISH" HUNTING SEAT

Looking to the East for the cultural origins and forms we associate with the Renaissance—whether in the arts, architecture, or horsemanship—has only recently begun to figure on Western research agendas.[13] The early modern sources themselves are not very forthcoming regarding European opinion of the Eastern seat. This is rather surprising given the military might of the Ottoman empire for several centuries before its first significant defeats at the hands of European armies in the late seventeenth and early eighteenth centuries. As Captain Lewis Edward Nolan observed in 1853, "For ages, the finest cavalry seen in Europe was indisputably that of the Turks."[14]

The superiority of the Turkish cavalry had both technological and technical origins. Miklós Jankovich has argued that the first people in the Arab world to use the stirrup "were persons of Turkish origin."[15] Lynn White, Jr., suggests that the iron foot stirrup was most likely a Chinese invention, inspired by the Indic cultures to the south which had developed a toe stirrup for the unshod foot, a simple loop attached to the saddle girth.[16] Impractical for colder climates, the toe stirrup gave rise to the foot stirrup no later than the early fifth century A.D. in China—very likely in the Altaic mountains, among the Turkic-speaking nomads who lived by horse keeping.[17] The stirrup was beginning to be adopted by Muslim horsemen—first the

Persians, then the Arabs—by A.D. 694, and was widely diffused through the Islamic world by the ninth century A.D.[18] Although the precise timing of the arrival of the stirrup in the West is still a source of debate, most scholars agree that its adoption by European horsemen had begun to have a profound effect on military tactics by the tenth century.[19]

If Turkic–Chinese stirrups were an Eastern piece of technology that revolutionized military culture in the West, Eastern techniques for training horses and horsemen may also have been influential. A visit to Constantinople may have been as important for European horsemanship as was the rediscovery of Xenophon's work on horsemanship (*The Art of Horsemanship*, ca. 365 B.C.E.). In Naples in 1550, Federico Grisone published his famous treatise *Gli ordini di cavalcare*, which initiated a humanist discourse on horsemanship partly inspired by Xenophon. As John Astley commented in his "breefe treatise" *The Art of Riding*, with its "due interpretation of certeine places alledged out of Xenophon, and Gryson," in 1584, Xenophon "setteth downe that shape and forme that Art should imitate."[20] Grisone's treatise appeared in new editions almost every year during the 1550s and by 1568 had been translated and published in France, Germany, and Spain.[21] Thomas Blundeville's *A Newe Booke Containing the Arte of Ryding, and Breakinge Greate Horses*,[22] which brought England into the picture in 1560, was largely a translation of Grisone (more than one British Library copy has "by Gryson" inked in on the title page). Other English translations of Italian works subsequently appeared.[23] Grisone was riding master at what may have been the earliest known European riding school, if the school indeed was opened in Naples in 1532 as most sources maintain. According to Walter Liedtke, Grisone's academy was established by the nobleman Giovanni Battista Pignatelli, perhaps inspired by a visit to Constantinople.[24]

Pignatelli's and Grisone's—and thus, via translation, Blundeville's—Ottoman connection, if it existed, suggests two possible kinds of influence. Liedtke speculates that, like the Crusaders before him, Pignatelli "must have been impressed by the small but fast and agile Arabian horses" he would have seen in the Ottoman capital, which, "imported to the West, were used to develop new breeds, especially in Italy and Spain."[25] The influence of Arabian blood on European breeds was well known in the early modern period. As Nathaniel Harley, an English merchant at Aleppo, observed in 1705, the Arabian was "probably the Root of the best Breeds in the World, The Barbary & Spanish Horses are descended

from 'em, and the Naples from the last."[26] The relationship between
the importation of Eastern bloodstock into Europe and changes in
equitation should not be underestimated. The appeal of horses from
the Near East in contrast with the weight-carrying medieval
European warhorses was profound. The Eastern bloodstock was small
but fast, agile, and highly sensitive to human demands through centuries
of intimate domestication. Different modes of dealing with such
different equine physical and mental capabilities were required.

Ottoman influence, therefore, might well have extended beyond
the favorable impression made by Turkish horses of Arabian and
Turkmene or Akhal-Teke breeding.[27] Liedtke does not speculate
about the possible impression made by Ottoman horsemen on
Western European visitors. And yet it seems likely that, if Pignatelli
was inspired to open a riding school after a visit to Constantinople,
then that inspiration might have owed as much to what he saw there
of horsemanship and cavalry training as to the horses themselves.

Between the time of Xenophon and the Renaissance revival of
Greek equestrian ideas, there existed from the eighth century onward
in the Islamic world an elaborate discourse on horsemanship or
furusiyya—the theory and practice of hippology, veterinary care,
farriery, and equitation. This discourse combined Islamic with pre-
Islamic, especially Sasanian, ideas[28] and was transmitted orally as well
as by means of treatises in Arabic, Persian, and Ottoman Turkish, displaying a mixture of Arab, Iranian, Turkish, and Greek influences.[29]
As Rhoads Murphey has observed, the horse and horse culture were
"formative" as a "central element in state institutions in the steppe,"
as in the desert, so that horses were both materially and symbolically
important for the Ottomans and Mongols; however, the question "as
to whether the horse played a more significant role in the mythology
or the reality of rule" remains, according to him, "still open."[30]
Robert Irwin finds Qipchak Turkish and Mongol Mamelukes, long
after their conversion to Islam, continuing to consume horsemeat
and mares' milk ceremonially in Egypt, a practice that he concludes
was not so much a challenge to Islam as a reflection of "an innocu-
ous nostalgia for the ways and tastes of nomadic life that they had
known as children on the steppes."[31] As J. M. Rogers concludes in
the best study of Ottoman *furusiyya* to date, despite Ottoman historians' "pride in their nomadic past," the traditions they recorded "do
not go back earlier than the origins of the Ottoman state in the early
fourteenth century," and thus show strong Mameluke influences.[32]
Mameluke treatises have traditionally been beset by problems of

sources, dating, authorship, translation, and other bibliographical difficulties, so the scholarly treatment of *furusiyya* remains underdevel-
oped.[33] What does seem clear is that *furusiyya*, as the complete
training of horse and rider in both courtly and military modes, was
often exhibited in the hippodrome or *maydan*, the outdoor enclosure
where schooling was conducted, of which there were particularly
famous examples in Cairo and Baghdad.[34] In Constantinople, displays
of horsemanship in open squares—including perhaps the *at meydani*,
or "horse *maydan*," built on the site of the classical hippodrome—
may have impressed European visitors such as Pignatelli.

What might have been the effect of seeing up close the forward
style of riding common, by this time, to the Turkic horsemen of the
Central Asian steppes and the Arab horsemen of the desert? How
influential might this example of a fundamentally different seat—with
very short stirrup leathers, riding forward—have proved to be? The
evidence here is patchy and contradictory. Blundeville, writing in
1560, appears to be the first to mention the Turks in relation to
riding short. After William Cavendish, the Duke of Newcastle, slights
this reference to Ottoman example a hundred years later, not much
more is said about it in English sources until the nineteenth century.
The exception is Richard Berenger, George III's Gentleman of the
Horse, who wrote dismissively in 1771, "The Turks ride with their
stirrups so short, that their knees are almost as much bent, as when
they sit upon their hams upon a sofa."[35] Berenger implies, without
explicitly stating, that the Turks, like the Arab horsemen he has
previously criticized for using harsh bits and "working upon false
rules, or perhaps without any," consequently "never attain that grace,
exactness, and certainty, which the principles of the *Art*, if known,
would insure to them."[36] The Arabs receive the full brunt of what,
after Edward Said, we cannot fail to recognize as budding Orientalist
prejudice, whereas the Turks are represented more ambivalently.
Berenger adds, "The Turks seldom use *Spurs*, or carry a whip or
switch, nevertheless they have an absolute command over their
horses, and make them do whatever they please."[37] Such grudging
acknowledgment of equestrian effectiveness is hardly evidence of
influence, especially since Berenger's evidence regarding the Turks
and the Arabs is purely citational—from Dumont and Hasselquist,
respectively.[38] Yet the British themselves were departing from continental practice during the seventeenth and eighteenth centuries, no
doubt in accordance with ancient native British or Celtic custom, but
also with suggestive similarity to the Eastern or "Turkish" seat.

Two hundred years earlier, more respect had been paid to Ottoman example. Blundeville "more than once refers to 'riding short after the Turkey fashion,'" as Chenevix Trench notes.[39] In the twenty-eighth chapter of the second book of *The Arte of Ryding*, Blundeville describes *corvetti* [*courbettes*] and the *capriole*, two of the *haute école* "airs above the ground," and recommends that *corvetti*, "a certaine continuall prauncynge and dauncynge uppe and downe stil in one place, and sometimes sydelynge to and fro," only be undertaken if the rider and horse have sufficient aptitude and have accustomed themselves to this new seat:

> [I]f your horse be very light, and you have accustomed to ryde shorte upon hym, after the Turkey fashion: you may teache him also the *Coruetti*, but if he be great of stature and that you ride longe upon him, after oure fashion, then the *Capriole* is most meete for him.[40]

Blundeville also observes that the Spaniards practice the *corvetti* "moste uppon their Jennettes, and specyallye when they ryde shorte after the Turkey fashion."[41] A hundred years later, William Cavendish, Duke of Newcastle, would chastise Blundeville for his use of "Turkey fashion" here:

> To Ride short, he calls after the *Turkish* Fashion, wherein he is Deceived; for it is *A La Genette*, which is the *Spanish* Fashion too; and to Ride Short in *Corvets* is his Mistake, for I would Ride Longer in *Corvets* than any other *Ayre*.[42]

Newcastle insists rather too quickly that the Spaniards (who might be said to be closer kin to the English in belonging to Christian Europe) are as good exponents of riding short as the Turks. He evades the question of a different tradition—"A La Genette"—which came to Spain from the Barbary States of North Africa, where Islamic Arab horsemanship was practiced, displaying Mameluke and Ottoman influences. Islamic Arab–Turkish horse culture was being pushed further to the margins of the English discourse than it had been in the sixteenth century. Elsewhere in his book the Duke confesses that he had never traveled to Constantinople, but had "Spoken with many Gentlemen that have been There, as Likewise with diverse Merchants that came from Thence," and that all who had seen the horses of the Ottoman capital agreed, "That there are *There*, the most *Beautifull-Horses* in the World . . . And certainly they are Brave *Horses!*"[43] Might this acknowledgment of the horses' bravery be a covert hint of appreciation for the virtues of the ferociously effective Ottoman cavalry?

Ironically, by the nineteenth century, the Ottoman empire had begun attending ever more keenly to Western example, even in military matters. According to a source well known to Ottoman historians, Charles MacFarlane's *Constantinople in 1828* (1829), Sultan Mahmut II had been so impressed by the ability of an Italian Cavalry Officer, Signor Calosso, to master an unruly horse that he employed Calosso as his personal riding master and as cavalry instructor to his favorite troops, the lancers.[44] Mahmut insisted on learning a European cavalry seat in the traditional fashion, beginning by riding bareback, and, as a result, impressed MacFarlane as "the best horseman, *à l'Européene*, in his regular army," who sat "firm and erect, and might really pass muster among a regiment of our fine horse-guards, and that with credit."[45] The troops, however, were having difficulty adjusting to the European saddle, which they found easier to fall out of than their Turkish "cradles" had been, quipped MacFarlane, and they were constantly taking up their stirrups " 'a point or so' to make themselves comfortable."[46] Not until the Turks ceased to sit cross-legged "like tailors" and grew accustomed to chairs and stools of "christian-like elevation," MacFarlane opined, would they take naturally to the flatter European saddle and long-legged seat.[47] MacFarlane himself had felt "in purgatory" when riding extremely short on a bulky Turkish saddle, and thought it natural that the Turks should feel the same about the European seat.[48]

Not until its glory days had passed, in the mid-nineteenth century, did enthusiastic admiration of the Ottoman cavalry appear in print in English. A proponent of a more forward seat than was practiced in any European army, and an advocate of free forward movement of the horse, the Irishman Captain Nolan went so far as to opine that Pignatelli's and Grisone's "Neapolitan school" was "of Eastern origin" and therefore "doubtlessly good," but that "[w]hatever ease" the school may have possessed had been "stiffened out of it in France and Germany, as also in every part of Italy."[49] By the time of the appearance of Nolan's book in 1853, one consequence of the Tanzimat reforms of Sultan Mahmut II and his son and successor, Sultan Abdulmejid I, was that, as Nolan himself reported, the Turkish cavalry was now so contemptible in its inept imitation of the French manner of riding long and wearing tight pantaloons that "it may now safely be said that the Turkish cavalry is the very worst in the world."[50]

We have seen, quite in our own day, this effective and really brilliant cavalry reduced, by the spirit of imitation and ill-understood reform, to a condition beneath contempt. . . . The men, always accustomed to sit cross-legged, and to keep their knees near the abdomen, cannot be taught to ride with the long stirrup, *à la Française*. They are always rolling off, and are frequently ruptured; they . . . have seldom any other weapon except an ill-made, blunt, awkward sabre. Their horses are now wretched *rosses*. The good breeds have died out. . . .[51]

"Mounted as they are, armed as they are, and riding as they do," Nolan concluded, they could be dispatched by "any English - hussar . . . armed only with a stout walking-stick."[52]

The term "hussar" is a clue to what had been suppressed from British military history. By the late eighteenth century, the influence of Turkish and Turkish-influenced Hungarian cavalry methods on British military thinking was profound. Captain Nolan himself, a pupil of Colonel Haas, instructor of the Austrian cavalry, had also served for some time in the Hungarian Hussars.[53] Impressed by their performance during the Seven Years' War, British commanders attempted to imitate the mobility and firepower of Hungarian light dragoons, using Hungarian-type saddles and a better class of troop-horse.[54] The Napoleonic campaigns resulted in a near-reversion to "the original Danubian type," as Anthony Dent puts it, even to the adoption of the name Hussar, so that by the time "the Light Brigade of Balaclava fame" charged the Russian guns they "had the clothing, the saddlery, and the accoutrements partly of Polish Ulani (in the Lancer regiments) and partly of Hungarian light horsemen."[55] These borrowings have become so completely normalized that at a state reception at Windsor Castle, for instance, the Household Cavalry will most likely be led by a drum-horse "accoutred in the Turkish manner and bearing brass kettle-drums ultimately of Turkish or Tartar origin," while the King's Troop of the Royal Horse Artillery will parade "in their full-dress uniform of Hussar (that is, Hungarian) pattern."[56]

Why should the legacy of Eastern influence on British horseman-ship, and on European horsemanship in general, have gone so relatively unacknowledged? In Edward Said's terms, the ideological mechanism at work would appear to be the West's tendency to imagine itself as superior to, and thus entitled to appropriate, the so-called Orient. By the late eighteenth century, Orientalism circulated as both a scholarly discourse and an imperial administrative tool, saturating popular culture and manifesting itself as "a battery of desires, repressions, investments, and projections."[57] Orientalist assumptions so commonplace in Western culture as to go unremarked include the failure to recognize Oriental knowledges as knowledge, as having any scientific or systematic value. A related function of Orientalist thinking has been to regard the Orient as a source of raw materials but never of cultural practices or end-products. Thus whatever was imported into Britain became British by dint of use and habitual consumption.

Eastern techniques and technologies, like exotic luxury goods, were highly prized, but they became immediately naturalized on European soil. With regard to horses and horsemanship, this mindset became commonplace during the seventeenth century. One telling example is that of Eastern equine bloodstock, the foundation of the modern English (and Euro-American) Thoroughbred horse.[58] Upon importation, these stallions and mares became the naturalized property of their English owners, though they might bear a name signifying Oriental origin—the Byerley Turk, the Darley Arabian, Lord Harley's Dun Arabian. Within a generation, however, their progeny were regarded as distinctively "English" and could even be reexported as such.[59]

One of the ironies of history is that in the twentieth century Turkish cavalry officers attended the Italian Cavalry Schools of Pinerolo (Turin) and Tor di Quinto (Rome): Lt. Anni Effendi (1925–26), Capt. Vehli Bey (1928–29) (Pinerolo); Lt. Anni Effendi (1927), Capt. Wekki Omar (1929) (Tor di Quinto).[60] After the—singularly unsuccessful, according to Nolan—reeducation of the Turkish cavalry to something like a European seat during the Ottoman empire's moment of modernizing by Europeanizing itself, the modern Turkish republic sent its officers to Italy to relearn riding forward, with shorter stirrups, a reinvention of the Turkish seat, now packaged as the modern Italian—but also international—forward seat!

AN ALLEGORY OF ENGLISH FREEDOM

Until 1800, the entry "To Ride" in *The Sportsman's Dictionary* meant "riding the Great Horse" or "learning the manage" (1735, 1778, 1785, 1792)—what we would today call dressage.[61] By the end of the eighteenth century, the spirit of expedition had won the day. The Duke of Newcastle's efforts at disseminating classical horsemanship by means of his own empirically tested system had failed to convert the equestrian public to "managed riding." Native British and Celtic preference for snaffle bridles and free forward movement had never been thoroughly suppressed, and had received new stimulus with the coming of the Orientally derived Thoroughbred.[62] Exiled during the Interregnum that followed the English Civil War, the Royalist Newcastle studied with, and distinguished himself among, French and Dutch riding masters. He first published a treatise in French (1658),[63] then in 1667 *A New Method and Extraordinary Invention, to Dress Horses*. Newcastle's attitude toward his countrymen, like his attitude toward riding short in the Turkish fashion, gives us some insight into the state of horsemanship in seventeenth-century England.

Since the Duke was aiming at nothing less than an empirically unfalsifiable system, he argued defensively—"Many say, that all things in the *Mannage* is nothing but Tricks, and Dancing, and Gamballs, and of no Use"[64]—but he was utterly confident of his superior wisdom: "I wonder how men are so Presumptious, to think they can Ride as *Horse-men*, because they can Ride forward from *Barnet* to *London*, which every body can do; and I have seen VVomen to *Ride* Astride as well as they."[65] The proving ground was the manège, and it should be the proper study of all who called themselves gentlemen:

> Another, because he hath *Ridd a Hundred Miles* in a *Day*, (which a *Post-Boy* can do) thinks Himself a *Horse-man*; or, Because he can Run a *Match* with his *Groom*, or Leap a Ditch, or a Hedg, in *Hunting*, and Hold by the *Main*, he thinks he is a *Horse-man*; but his *Hunts-Boy* doth as much. . . . And I have seen many Wenches Ride *Astride*, and Gallop, and Run their *Horses*, that could, I think, hardly Ride a *Horse* Well in the *Mannage*.[66]

The untutored Briton, outridden by a mere groom, or worse, a wench, is no gentleman. And wenches were apparently to be seen riding astride and even racing in Newcastle's day. Free forward movement across country was the desideratum, whether for business or sport, not the elegant discipline of the manège. As John Lawrence remarked in 1798, "The decline of Riding-house forms in this country, and the universal preference given to expedition, fully confirm the superior use and propriety of a jockey-seat."[67] John Adams confirmed that the manège was out of fashion in 1805, while defending it:

> For, certain it is, masters of old taught only one style of riding, which was the *manege*; and this being the truth and foundation of all good riding (which I must acknowledge it is, and shall make it so appear) they neither practise nor taught any other. The obvious consequence is, that gentlemen are as emulous of riding fast, as of riding well; and finding persons who had learned to ride in a style so ill calculated to

travel far, or fast, or endure its fatigue; they ridiculed the idea of learning to ride at a school, but preferred, or sought to copy, a hunting-groom, or racing-jockey.[68]

The British liked nothing more than expediting matters (the efficient use of time in a commercial sense) and making expeditions (the positive seeking out of adventure and even danger). The sports of the aristocracy and gentry no less than business and commerce partook of this spirit of enterprise. The result of the preference for riding from Barnet to London as expeditiously as possible was that, as Adams commented in 1805, "reciprocal contempt has subsisted between the *manege* riding and *jockey* riding ever since."[69] Adams made it his business to "reconcile both, and make them friends with each other," which he hoped to do by playing to both sides, "making each party appear to be in the right; which is certainly the case here, since both styles of riding will be found proper for their respective purposes."[70] That Adams succeeded in this admirably modern appeal to reason and utility is borne out by his emergence in the twentieth century as an early hero of the modern forward seat so important in eventing competitions.[71]

Adams's hymn to the English seat outside the manège, whether road-riding, hunting, or racing, is couched in a rhetoric powerfully evocative of national superiority; it is a little allegory of British freedom:

> The rider participates the like ease or unrestrained liberty . . . laying aside all unnecessary restraint when we can perform to our satisfaction without it. . . . This freedom and ease, so desirable and universally admired, is affected by every person who is in the habit of riding, but with this difference; some unite system with negligence and ease, and others negligence and ease without system.[72]

The spirit of expedition may have contributed most crucially to what appears to have been a truly British invention: rising to the trot (in American English, "posting"). This method of riding has been popularly attributed to eighteenth-century postilions or post-boys, who had to bestride coach horses going full tilt at a "spanking trot." Not only the British historians but also Jankovich claim that easing the body by rising in the stirrups was invented in the British Isles. Jankovich suggests that a horse's natural gaits are the walk and the gallop, and the trot only occurs when passing from one to the other, usually when "changing down" from the gallop to the walk.[73] Hence Eastern horsemen rode at the walk and gallop, not rising to the trot but leaning forward from the waist to sit out the occasional trotting stride. However should commerce have been conducted, we have to wonder, if Britons had not been able to travel freely on horseback by road, covering the miles as expeditiously as possible without excessively tiring themselves or their horses? And for this, trotting was essential. "Since the rider's ease and convenience is the principal consideration in riding on the road, it is admissible when the trot is extended to an unpleasant roughness, to ease the jolting by rising in the stirrups," John Adams advised in 1805.[74] Arab and Akhal-Teke horses may travel easily at a canter or gallop, but other breeds last longer at the trot. It was known in the late eighteenth century that this easing of human and horse had been going on for much longer in Britain than the previous few decades.[75]

Michael Baret had recommended rising to the trot as early as 1618, and neither John Lawrence, who knew of Baret in the 1790s, nor anybody else seems to have found any earlier mention in print:

> if he would help his horse in his trot, pace or any other assault, for delight, then let him clap both his knees close to the points of the saddle, and onely keepe time with his seate, to moue the better spirit to the horse: and not to sit as some doe, (which are not esteemed the worst horsemen) without any motion, (like logges) on their horse backes, with their legges stretched out in their stirrups, (as if they were on the racke) but as their horse causeth them, (they forcing him by extremities,) hauing no agility to helpe him.[76]

Free forward movement at all gaits—a little allegory of the liberties of the freeborn British subject—necessitated rising to the trot.

Returning to the early modern sources reveals even more clearly than does the received history a strain of national identity articulated through the English seat. But that notion of Englishness at the core of imperial Britishness may be as oddly bound up with Easternness as with native predilections.

Is there a trace memory of this history in John Buchan's *Greenmantle* (1916)? No book codes nationality more blatantly in equestrian terms than Buchan's First World War thriller. The narrator Richard Hannay—English-identified, of Scottish extraction, brought up in South Africa: a perfect colonial cocktail—delights in distinguishing the nationalities of his fellow secret agents by their seats. Approaching the novel's denouement, as the British and their allies strive to outwit the Germans and join forces with the Russians, our heroes are forced to gallop "furiously" in the dark on small

Turkish horses.[77] John S. Blenkiron, the fat American, whose "thighs were too round to fit a saddle leather," and who preferred "a gentle amble and a short gallop" to this "mad helter-skelter," loses both his stirrups and finds himself sitting on his horse's neck.[78] Americans had better have brains and guts, in other words, because economic prosperity has physically softened them. The Scotsman Sandy Arbuthnot, on the other hand, who possesses a remarkable ability to get "inside the skin of remote peoples,"[79] is a "wonderful fine horseman, with his firm English hunting seat."[80] Even the Scots ride like the English, then, when they ride well, and to ride well is to have been formed in the cut and thrust of the hunting field. What is most ironic is that Sandy, riding into Erzurum with "his firm English hunting seat," is wearing not "proper clothes,"[81] but the "green mantle" of the prophet of Islam he had been sent to find and had ended up pretending to be.

> He was turbaned and rode like one possessed, and against the snow I caught the dark sheen of emerald. As he rode it seemed that the fleeing Turks were stricken still, and sank by the roadside with eyes strained after his unheeding figure. . . .
>   Then I knew that the prophecy had been true, and that their prophet had not failed them. The long-looked for revelation had come. Greenmantle had appeared at last to an awaiting people.[82]

Beneath the turban and flying robes of the forward-going Islamic horseman lurks a Scotsman—himself a product of English cultural imperialism. The exquisiteness of this Orientalist fantasy lies in its reversal of a history in which the hunting field could be said to be haunted by the specters of Eastern horsemen, as if inside every top hat or hunt cap and pink coat there lurked an Arab or a Turk. Hark to Sandy Arbuthnot.[83]

NOTES

1. There is no space in this chapter for a comparative analysis of what Americans call "English" versus "Western" (cowboy) styles of riding. In this chapter, "Western" riding refers to the styles of riding employed in Western Europe, as opposed to "Eastern" styles invented in Asia. The American Western style derived historically from a Spanish combination of Arabic and European styles. For a good technical discussion of American Western riding, see Charles Chenevix Trench, *A History of Horsemanship* (London: Longman, 1970), 145–47, 224–47.
2. See Benedict Anderson, *Imagined Communities: Reflections on the Origin and Spread of Nationalism* (London and New York: Verso,

1983); Linda Colley, *Britons: Forging the Nation 1701–1837* (New Haven, CT and London: Yale University Press, 1992); Paul Langford, *A Polite and Commercial People: England, 1727–1783* (Oxford and New York: Oxford University Press, 1992); and Gerald Newman, *The Rise of English Nationalism: A Cultural History, 1740–1830* (New York: St. Martin's Press, 1987).

3. P. J. Cain and A. G. Hopkins, *British Imperialism: Innovation and Expansion, 1688–1914* (London: Longman, 1993), 12.

4. Robert C. Allen, *Enclosure and the Yeoman* (Oxford: Clarendon Press, 1992), 21.

5. Lizzie Purbrick, quoted in Adella Lithman, "Hell-Raiser with a Heart of Gold," *Horse and Hound* (June 17, 1993): 18.

6. Everyone agrees about 1897 as the year of Sloan's international impact, as that was the year in which he first came to Europe from the United States and raced at Saint-Cloud; see Chenevix Trench, *A History of Horsemanship*, 186. Piero Santini, a pupil of Caprilli, gives 1897 as the starting date for his master's work on his new system of horsemanship, to which he devoted the last ten years of his short life; Santini, *Riding Reflections* (1933; rev. edn., London: Country Life, 1950), 1.

7. Chenevix Trench, *A History of Horsemanship*, 239. See also Edward Hotaling, *The Great Black Jockeys: The Lives and Times of the Men Who Dominated America's First National Sport* (Rocklin, CA: Forum, 1999).

8. Chenevix Trench, *A History of Horsemanship*, 250.

9. There are important differences between Caprilli's extremely practical forward seat for riding across country, which many British (and American) riders quickly adopted as their own, or blended with the traditional hunting seat, or even combined with some aspects of classical practice, and the relatively insecure, though aerodynamic, "monkey up the neck" flat-racing jockey's seat adopted by Sloan; see Captain F. C. Hitchcock, "*To Horse!*" (New York: Charles Scribner's Sons, 1938), 244. In fact, one could see Caprilli's *sistema* as the logical extension, influenced by Eastern precedents, of taking those stirrups up a notch or two in order to jump fences at speed, while the Sloan jockey's seat is only good for flat racing on racecourses, where balance will be comparatively undisturbed, with most of the strain of the perilous crouching position being taken by the thighs, and the knees clearing the saddle, limiting grip to the barest essentials.

10. Chenevix Trench, *A History of Horsemanship*, 152–53.

11. Chenevix Trench, *A History of Horsemanship*, 153. See also Elwyn Hartley Edwards, *Horses and Their Role in the History of Man* (London: Willow Books–Collins, 1987), 145–46.

12. S. G. Goldschmidt, *Bridle Wise: A Key to Better Hunters—Better Ponies* (London: Country Life, Ltd. and New York: Charles Scribner's Sons, 1927), 9.

13. See Miklós Jankovich, *They Rode into Europe: The Fruitful Exchange in the Arts of Horsemanship between East and West*, trans. Anthony Dent (London: George G. Harrup, 1971). The best Western scholarly study of horses in East–West relations to have appeared to date is Lisa Jardine and Jerry Brotton's chapter, "Managing the Infidel: Equestrian Art on Its Mettle," in *Global Interests: Renaissance Art between East and West* (London: Reaktion and Ithaca, NY: Cornell University Press, 2000), 132–85, which is indebted to Jankovich.
14. Lewis Edward Nolan, *Cavalry: Its History and Tactics* (London: Thomas Brown, 1853), 24.
15. Jankovich, *They Rode into Europe*, 83.
16. Lynn White, Jr., *Medieval Technology and Social Change* (London, Oxford, and New York: Oxford University Press, 1962), 14–15. See also Hugh Kennedy, *The Armies of the Caliphs: Military and Society in the Early Islamic State* (London and New York: Routledge, 2001), 171–73.
17. White, *Medieval Technology and Social Change*, 15.
18. White, *Medieval Technology and Social Change*, 18–19; Kennedy, *Armies of the Caliphs*, 172–73; Rachel Ward, "Stirrups from the Islamic World," in *Furusiyya*, ed. David Alexander, 2 vols. (Riyadh: King Abdulaziz Public Library, 1996), vol. 1, 84–91.
19. See, for example, Bernard S. Bachrach, "*Caballus et Caballarius* in Medieval Warfare," in *The Study of Chivalry: Resources and Approaches*, ed. Howell Chickering and Thomas H. Seiler (Kalamazoo: Medieval Institute Publications [at] Western Michigan University, 1988), 194–197; Bernard S. Bachrach, "Animals and Warfare in Early Medieval Europe," in *L'uomo di fronte al mondo animale nell'alto Medioevo* (Spoleto: Centro italiano di studi sull'alto Medioevo, 1985), 733, 737–749; Matthew Bennett, "The Medieval Warhorse Reconsidered," in *Medieval Knighthood V: Papers from the Sixth Strawberry Hill Conference*, ed. Stephen Church and Ruth Harvey (Rochester: Boydell, 1995), 34; Carroll M. Gillmor, "Cavalry, European," in *Dictionary of the Middle Ages*, ed. Joseph R. Strayer, 13 vols. (New York: Scribner, 1982–1989), vol. 3, 201–202. White, *Medieval Technology and Social Change*, 27, dated the impact of the stirrup on Western military tactics to the time of Charles Martel, in the early eighth century, but the more recent scholarship dates the stirrup's role in military change to a much later period—the very late ninth or even early tenth century.
20. John Astley, Master of the Queen's Jewell-house, and first in a long line of Astleys to profess horsemanship in England, *The Art of Riding, Set Foorth in a Breefe Treatise, with a Due Interpretation of Certeine Places Alledged out of Xenophon, and Gryson, Verie Expert and Excellent Horssemen* (London: Henrie Denham, 1584), 15.
21. Walter Liedtke, *The Royal Horse and Rider: Painting, Sculpture, and Horsemanship 1500–1800* (New York: Abaris Books and the Metropolitan Museum of Art, 1989), 23.

22. [Thomas Blundeville], *A Newe Booke Containing the Arte of Ryding, and Breakinge Greate Horses, together with the Shapes and Figures, of Many and Diuers Kyndes of Byttes, Mete to Serue Diuers Mouthes. Very Necessary for All Gentlemen, Souldyours, Seruingmen, and for Any Man that Delighteth in a Horse* (London: Willyam Seres, n.d. [1560]).

23. In addition to Astley's *The Art of Riding*, see Thomas Bedingfield's translation of Claudio Corte's *Il cavallarizzo* (Venice: Giordano Ziletti, 1562), also published as *The Art of Riding* (London: Henrie Denham, 1584).

24. Liedtke, *Royal Horse*, 21. Liedtke's source both for Pignatelli as the founder of this early academy and for his visit to Constantinople is another popular history, this one Italian: Luigi Gianoli's *Horses and Horsemanship through the Ages*, trans. Iris Brooks (New York: Crown Publishers, 1969), 103, which makes no mention of the available documentation. To complicate matters further, in an appendix to Liedtke's book, Alexander Mackay-Smith claims, on the basis of no named evidence, that the riding school at Naples was opened in 1532 by Grisone (p. 90) and that Pignatelli, who had been a pupil of Cesare Fiaschi of Ferrara, merely joined Grisone's academy, becoming a celebrated instructor to Salomon de la Broue, Antoine de Pluvinel, and the Chevalier de St. Antoine, Charles I's riding master and equerry (p. 89). Since I have been unable to do any primary research in Italian archives, I am offering Gianoli's version of events as at least grounds for speculation. Finally, although Naples was acknowledged as the leading city for riding schools in the sixteenth century, Mantua is now credited with the earliest known *cavallarizzo* still standing, built in 1538–39.

25. Liedtke, *Royal Horse*, 21.

26. Nathaniel Harley, Letter to Mr. "Auditor" Edward Harley, Esq., Aleppo, December 29, 1705, BL Add. MSS. 70143 (Nathaniel Harley's letters 1682–1720), 179^v–180^r.

27. See Jankovich, *They Rode into Europe*, 80–7, for discussion of the interpenetration of Bactrian or Turanian horses and horse culture from the Central Asian steppes—the "Turkish" heritage—with Arab horse breeding and horse keeping practices.

28. Shihab al-Sarraf, "Furusiyya Literature of the Mamluk Period," in *Furusiyya*, ed. Alexander, vol. 1, 118–35; this passage on p. 118.

29. G. Douillet and D. Ayalon, "*Furusiyya*," in *The Encyclopedia of Islam, New Edition*, ed. H. A. R. Gibb, B. Lewis, C. E. Bosworth et al., 11 vols. (Leiden: E. J. Brill, 1960–2000), vol. 2, 952–55.

30. Rhoads Murphey, "Horsebreeding in Eurasia: Key Element in Material Life or Foundation of Imperial Culture?" *Central & Inner Asian Studies* 4 (1990): 1–13; these passages on pp. 1, 10.

31. Robert Irwin, "Eating Horses and Drinking Mare's Milk," in *Furusiyya*, ed. Alexander, vol. 1, 148–51; this passage on p. 151.

32. J. M. Rogers, "Ottoman Furusiyya," in *Furusiyya*, ed. Alexander, vol. 1, 176–83; this passage on p. 176.

33. al-Sarraf, "Furusiyya Literature of the Mamluk Period," vol. 1, 118.

34. F. Vir, "*Maydan,*" in *The Encyclopedia of Islam, New Edition*, vol. 6, 912–13.

35. Richard Berenger, *The History and Art of Horsemanship*, 2 vols. (London: Printed for T. Davies and T. Cadell, 1771), vol. 1, 130.

36. Berenger, *History and Art of Horsemanship*, vol. 1, 113.

37. Berenger, *History and Art of Horsemanship*, vol. 1, 130.

38. See Jean Dumont [Baron de Carlscroon], *A New Voyage to the Levant: Containing an Account of the Most Remarkable Curiosities in Germany, France, Italy, Malta, and Turkey; with Historical Observations Relating to the Present and Ancient State of those Countries*, 2nd edn. (London: Printed by T. H. for M. Gillyflower et al., 1696), 263–65, and Frederick Hasselquist, M.D., *Voyages and Travels in the Levant; in the Years 1749, 50, 51, 52. Containing Observations in Natural History, Physick, Agriculture, and Commerce: Particularly on the Holy Land, and the Natural History of the Scriptures*, trans. Charles Linnaeus (London: Printed for L. Davis and C. Reymers, 1766), 72.

39. Chenevix Trench, *A History of Horsemanship*, 151.

40. [Blundeville,] *The Arte of Ryding*, bk. 2, ch. 28, 2nd page; 5th page.

41. [Blundeville,] *The Arte of Ryding*, bk. 2, ch. 28, 2nd page.

42. William Cavendish, Duke of Newcastle, *A New Method and Extraordinary Invention, to Dress Horses, and Work Them According to Nature: As Also, to Perfect Nature by the Subtilty of Art; Which Was Never Found out, but by The Thrice Noble, High, and Puissant Prince William Cavendishe* (London: Printed by Thomas Milbourn, 1667), 20.

43. Cavendish, *A New Method*, 70–71.

44. Charles MacFarlane, Esq., *Constantinople in 1828. A Residence of Sixteen Months in the Turkish Capital and Provinces: With an Account of the Present State of the Naval and Military Power, and of the Resources of the Ottoman Empire*, 2nd edn., 2 vols. (London: Saunders and Otley, 1829), vol. 1, 504; vol. 2, 174–80.

45. MacFarlane, *Constantinople in 1828*, vol. 2, 179, 180; vol. 1, 504.

46. MacFarlane, *Constantinople in 1828*, vol. 1, 504; vol. 2, 179, 187.

47. MacFarlane, *Constantinople in 1828*, vol. 2, 188.

48. MacFarlane, *Constantinople in 1828*, vol. 2, 187.

49. Nolan, *Cavalry*, 141.

50. Nolan, *Cavalry*, 26.

51. Nolan, *Cavalry*, 25–26.

52. Nolan, *Cavalry*, 27.

53. *The Training of Cavalry Remount Horses, by the Late Captain Nolan, a New Edn.* (London: Parker Son and Bourn, 1861), 1 n.

54. See Anthony Dent, "Translator's Preface," in Jankovich, *They Rode into Europe*, 6–8; this passage on p. 7.

55. Dent, "Translator's Preface," 7–8.
56. Dent, "Translator's Preface," 8.
57. Edward W. Said, *Orientalism* (1978; reprint edn., London and New York: Penguin, 1995), 8.
58. For more on this phenomenon, see Donna Landry, "The Bloody Shouldered Arabian and Early Modern English Culture," *Criticism* 46/1 (2004): 41–69.
59. Some 200 horses designated as "Oriental" were imported into England between 1660 and 1750 alone; "The Thoroughbred" (Lexington, KY: International Museum of the Horse website, http://www.imh.org/imh/bw/tbred.html, accessed June 30, 2004). "English horses in fact were being recognised as among the best all-purpose breeds as the seventeenth century progressed," a sentiment echoed "by the numerous foreigners who bought English horses"; Peter Edwards, *The Horse Trade of Tudor and Stuart England* (Cambridge, UK: Cambridge University Press, 1988), 51. The records of the Duke of Newcastle's stud at Welbeck Abbey demonstrate "how entirely of Eastern origin was the racehorse of the hundred years immediately after the Restoration, the Stud being virtually composed of pure-bred Arabians, Turks, or Barbs, it being impossible to differentiate between these various breeds"; C. M. Prior, *Early Records of the Thoroughbred Horse Containing Reproductions of Some Original Stud-books, and Other Papers, of the Eighteenth Century* (London: The Sportsman Office, 1924), 102.
60. Piero Santini, *The Forward Impulse* (London: Country Life, 1937), 113–17.
61. *The Sportsman's Dictionary: Or, The Country Gentleman's Companion, In All Rural Recreations: With Full and Particular Instructions for Hawking, Hunting, Fowling, Setting, Fishing, Racing, Riding, Cocking*, 2 vols. (London: Printed for C. Hitch, C. Davis, S. Austen, 1735); *The Sportsman's Dictionary . . .*, rev. exp. edn. (London: Printed for Fielding and Walker, 1778); *The Sportsman's Dictionary . . .*, 3rd edn. (London: Printed for G. G. J. and J. Robinson, 1785); *The Sportsman's Dictionary . . .*, 4th edn. (London: Printed for G. G. J. and J. Robinson, 1792).
62. Berenger reports that, three years into his reign, Charles I had decreed that curb bits replace snaffles in the army, and in riding generally, and that snaffles be used only in "Disport"—hunting and racing; *History and Art of Horsemanship*, vol. 1, 194–95.
63. William Cavendish, Duke of Newcastle, *Methode et invention novvelle de dresser les chevavx par le tres-noble, havt, et tres-pvissant Prince Gvillavme Marquis et Comte de Newcastle . . .* (Antwerp: Jacques Van Mevrs, 1658).
64. Cavendish, *A New Method*, 5.
65. Cavendish, *A New Method*, 11.
66. Cavendish, *A New Method*, 46–47.

67. John Lawrence, *A Philosophical and Practical Treatise on Horses, and on the Moral Duties of Man towards the Brute Creation*, 2 vols. (London: Printed for T. Longman, 1796–98), vol. 2, 251.

68. John Adams, *An Analysis of Horsemanship; Teaching the Whole Art of Riding, in the Manege, Military, Hunting, Racing, and Travelling System. Together with the Method of Breaking Horses, for Every Purpose to Which Those Noble Animals Are Adapted, By John Adams, Ridingmaster*, 3 vols. (London: Printed by Albion Press, Published by James Cundee, and Sold by C. Chapple, 1805), vol. 1, pp. xvi–xvii.

69. Adams, *An Analysis of Horsemanship*, vol. 1, p. xvii.

70. Adams, *An Analysis of Horsemanship*, vol. 1, pp. xvii–xviii.

71. V. S. Littauer, *More about the Forward Seat: Modern Methods of Schooling and Cross-Country Riding* (London: Hurst & Blackett, 1939), 30–2.

72. Adams, *An Analysis of Horsemanship*, vol. 2, 6, 8.

73. Jankovich, *They Rode into Europe*, 99.

74. Adams, *An Analysis of Horsemanship*, vol. 2, 8.

75. Lawrence observed in 1798 that "It is somewhat remarkable, that the seat on horseback, recommended by Baret in the reign of James I, is precisely the same as that practised by our jockies and sporting men of the present day"; *A Philosophical and Practical Treatise*, vol. 2, 20. In the entry on "Horsemanship" in the *Sportsman's Dictionary* of 1800, Lawrence again comments, "We cannot speak to the antiquity of the English fashion of rising in the stirrups during a trot, and of preserving time with the motions of the body, in unison with those of the horse; but the knowledge of it is discoverable in BARET, and in no author before him"; *The Sportsman's Dictionary . . .*, 4th rev. exp. edn. (London: Printed for G. G. J. and J. Robinson, 1800).

76. Michael Baret, *An Hipponomie or The Vineyard of Horsemanship: Deuided into Three Bookes, By Michaell Baret, Practitioner and Professor of the Same Art* (London: Printed by George Eld, 1618), 54.

77. John Buchan, *Greenmantle* (1916; reprint edn., Harmondsworth, UK: Penguin, 1958), 248.

78. Buchan, *Greenmantle*, 248.

79. Buchan, *Greenmantle*, 29.

80. Buchan, *Greenmantle*, 248.

81. "Sandy, of course, had no European ulster, for it was months since he had worn proper clothes"; Buchan, *Greenmantle*, 248.

82. Buchan, *Greenmantle*, 271.

83. It would be inappropriate to read Sandy Arbuthnot as exemplary of early modern British imperial agency, as Buchan's is clearly a later formation. See Daniel Goffman's *Britons in the Ottoman Empire 1642–1660* (Seattle and London: University of Washington Press, 1998), 3–6, on the need for historical particularity. Buchan's characters may not belong to the early modern period, but they are, like the twentieth-century English hunting seat itself, products of a process initiated then.

INDEX

Bolded page references indicate illustration or figure